29.95

INSURGENCY AND COUNTER-INSURGENCY IN IRAQ

Crises in World Politics

(Centre of International Studies
University of Cambridge)

TARAK BARKAWI
JAMES MAYALL
BRENDAN SIMMS
editors

GÉRARD PRUNIER
Darfur—the Ambiguous Genocide

FAISAL DEVJI
Landscapes of the Jihad

MARK ETHERINGTON
Revolt on the Tigris

AHMED S. HASHIM

Insurgency and Counter-Insurgency in Iraq

Cornell University Press
Ithaca, New York

Originally published in the United Kingdom by
C. Hurst & Co. (Publishers) Ltd, London.

First published 2006 by Cornell University Press

ISBN-13: 978-0-8014-4452-4 (cloth: alk. paper)
ISBN-10: 0-8014-4452-7 (cloth: alk. paper)

Printed in the United States of America

Librarians: Library of Congress Cataloging-in-Publication data are available.

Cornell University Press strives to use environmentally responsible suppliers and
materials to the fullest extent possible in the publishing of its books. Such
materials include vegetable-based, low-VOC inks and acid-free papers that are
recycled, totally chlorine-free, or partly composed of nonwood fibers. For further
information, visit our website at www.cornellpress.cornell.edu.

Cloth printing 10 9 8 7 6 5 4 3 2 1

Dedicated to my family.
Also to the men and women of the US armed forces who
have served with honor, courage, professionalism
and rectitude in Iraq

CONTENTS

ACKNOWLEDGEMENTS

Baghdad, 3 November 2003. The time was 1530, or 3.30 p.m. in civilian parlance. After a three-hour trip in a C-130 Hercules from Qatar, my Iraqi-American colleague (who was 'delivering' his package—me—to Central Command forward) and I braced ourselves for the stomach-churning defensive descent into Baghdad International Airport, which the US military with its pronounced fetish for abbreviation referred to as BIAP. It was, in more authoritarian times, known as Saddam International. Because it was November, it was not oppressively hot, but as I lumbered off the plane in my desert camouflage uniform, and wearing a flak jacket with ceramic armored plates and several other accoutrements, I began to sweat profusely. No matter; soon I would be in an SUV on the road into Baghdad.

Imagine my lack of surprise as I discovered that Murphy's Law was fully operational. Our escort from the unit I was assigned to was not there to drive us on the 6-mile dash on one of the most dangerous roads in the world: from the airport to the Green Zone highway. A phone call to the palace would fix the problem. I went into a nondescript shabby building where harried US military staff were dealing with troops that were either embarking on planes leaving Iraq or disembarking from arriving transports. You could tell the difference between those leaving and those arriving simply by looking at the expressions on their faces and their body language. I could not get through by landline telephone to the Republican Palace. My colleague's tri-band telephone did not work either. So we decided to wait until someone or something showed up and took us to our destination. We hung around the makeshift military terminal, our nostrils permanently assaulted by a line of smelly portable toilets that were strategically placed next to a small commissary where personnel could buy drinks and snacks. As it transpired, we could have waited until hell froze over, because the message to the Central Command (CENTCOM) folks at the Palace had never arrived. It had entered the black hole of misdirected messages, never to emerge.

By 1730 my colleague began suggesting that we take a cab into town; I was not about to get into a local cab dressed as I was. Even if I had changed, I still had four military kit bags and a backpack that would have given me away as definitely not being a local. Around 1800 an ancient Daihatsu minibus wheezed into the parking lot and stopped by a sign that read 'CPA Bus Stop'. From it emerged a beefy American driver: contractor, I thought, driven to Iraq by the prospect of easy tax-free money but certainly not by the lure of danger. The Coalition Provisional Authority was in the Republican Palace and since we were going there, it did not require an abundance of Cartesian logic to conclude that this was our best chance to get to the presumed safety of our destination before nightfall.

We clambered into the bus with a small group of other arrivals. It took us into a parking lot in the palace grounds but far from the main entrance to the palace itself. Almost immediately my colleague and I were faced with an almost insurmountable problem. I had five bags and he had one. Mine were extremely heavy. There was simply no way I could lug all this stuff to the main gate. As luck would have it, I found lying in a ditch an airport cart that someone must have brought with his luggage from the airport. I pulled it upright, but it promptly leaned over and almost tumbled on its side again. It was missing two wheels. We piled the gear on to it. My colleague held it upright on the wheelless side and I began pushing it forward. It required tremendous effort and constant coordination. People walked by looking at us strangely, except for one loud American civilian—presumably an employee of the CPA—who exclaimed rather boisterously to his colleagues as they walked by, 'Hey, this cart is missing wheels!'

It took an eternity to reach the main gate. There we stopped by a table full of paperwork and manned by well-armed US soldiers who looked as if they meant business. Concertina wire, bright klieg lights and concrete blocks were everywhere, but especially around the entrance. I realized for the first time since arriving that this was a war zone. I had my assignment papers and a whole slew of identifications. There was one snag: I did not have a CPA-issued ID card. That was simply not a problem for the sergeant with whom I spoke: I could not enter until I procured an ID, but I could not procure an ID until I entered!

By this time sweat was dripping in well-etched rivulets down my face, and I was in a fury. We were at an impasse until the sergeant suggested that someone from the inside could come out and escort us in. Brilliant idea, I thought.

'May I use your phone?' I asked.

'I don't have one,' he replied, but there was one inside the ID office, which was mere meters away.

I didn't suggest that I go in and call, but rather that one of the soldiers go call CENTCOM forward. The connection was finally made; and an impressive US Marine Corps lieutenant colonel, a man who became a great friend and colleague but whose life was tragically cut short in 2004, emerged to escort us in.

The chow hall was about to close and I was ravenous. I dumped everything in my office and double-timed to the main hall where a

US company contracted to provide food for the hundreds of civilian and military employees working and living in the palace was serving its bland offerings. I was told that after eating I should immediately make my way to the ID office to get my identification card. I thought that I should repair to the office and pick up my flak jacket and helmet.

'You don't need to do that,' someone said. 'Getting an ID won't take long.'

As soon as I stepped into the ID office, the Green Zone was mortared. Chaos ensued. Civilians and military personnel dove under desks; others ran out and dashed back to the main building. I found myself under a metal desk, and next to me lay a flak jacket without body armor and a helmet. Better than nothing, I thought. I also knew that the insurgent mortars were inaccurate and that they did not have much time to stay in place and zero them in. I did not think that the ID office was high on their list of targets, but an errant mortar round landing on us would not have been a good start to my deployment in Iraq. A young woman—a Hungarian, as I later found out—sat beside me; she started searching frantically for something.

'Are you looking for these?' I asked, pointing to the tight flak jacket and helmet that I was wearing.

'Yes, they are mine,' she said rather tremulously.

I took them off; it was not her fault that I did not have mine. I resolved that from that day forward I would not go anywhere without my protective gear. As if reading my mind, the US Marine colonel strode into the ID office with my helmet and flak jacket. This is how my first day of work at CENTCOM forward ended.

Why was I there? I was in Iraq first and foremost to work on formulating an understanding of the Iraqi insurgency, and ultimately to help end it. This book is an account of the violence that occurred in Iraq after Operation Iraqi Freedom, from April 2003 to the summer of 2005. I spent time in Iraq between November 2003 and late March 2004 working in an official military capacity on the insurgency and counterinsurgency for CENTCOM. I regret, however, that the study cannot be undertaken primarily as a personal account of my sojourn in that hapless country due to the sensitivity of the issue, nor does it make use of any official sources of any kind. Nonetheless, my tour in Iraq during that time has helped me enormously in writing this book.

Many individuals, in the United States and in Iraq, have helped me immensely with this study. I want to thank the countless US military personnel for their time spent with me and to the US military for its sacrifice and dedication during a difficult endeavor. I want to thank in particular my colleagues at the Naval War College, Newport, Rhode Island, especially the college's senior faculty and administration for supporting my deployment to Iraq, and my colleagues in the United States Army, particularly in CENTCOM, for facilitating my deployment with the Commander's Advisory Group, which is General John Abizaid's think-tank of 'intellectual officers'. Most have chosen to remain anonymous. I want to thank my Iraqi-American colleague—who must also remain anonymous—for all his help and for escorting me around Baghdad when it was still relatively safe to do so.

There is one individual, however, who deserves an enormous amount of thanks, and this is Colonel H.R. McMaster, commander of 3rd Armored Cavalry Regiment, with whom I served in western Iraq in fall 2005. Without his support, and that of his dedicated and able staff, this endeavor would not have been possible. I wish to thank Iraq experts Charles Tripp, Toby Dodge and Gareth Stansfield for their time and constructive substantive comments. The manuscript would not have seen the light of day if not for the indefatigable endeavors of Michael Dwyer of Hurst & Co. (Publishers), who patiently awaited my ever-expanding study after I missed numerous deadlines, and of David Barrett, who made it a read-able product. I wish to thank Brendan Simms and Tarak Barkawi of Cambridge University for their support and comments on how to improve the manuscript. Any errors of interpretation or analysis rest with me alone.

Finally, the views expressed in this study are solely mine, and do not represent those of any US government institution with whom I am affiliated. Any criticism, explicit and implicit, of the US effort stems from love of country and from a desire to see it 'get it right' for its own national security, and to highlight the siren song of parochial and ideologically minded approaches.

Writing a book is a labor of love, but it takes time from family. Time lost is difficult to regain, but I hope that my family, for whom this book is written and to whom it is dedicated, will understand and forgive me the time lost.

Tal Afar, Nineveh Province, Iraq   AHMED S. HASHIM
September 2005

PREFACE

Background and purpose of the study

Three weeks after the fall of Baghdad on 9 April 2003 and the collapse of Saddam Hussein's regime, an ebullient President George W. Bush landed on the aircraft carrier USS *Lincoln*, the crew of which displayed on the bridge an enormous banner that read 'Mission Accomplished'. A few weeks later, in front of US troops deployed in Qatar, President Bush said: 'America sent you on a mission to remove a grave threat and to liberate an oppressed people, and that mission has been accomplished.'[1] In the light of the US military victory in Operation Iraqi Freedom (as the war was dubbed), over an enfeebled and poorly led Iraqi army, it certainly looked that way. Notwithstanding the fierce debate over the levels of force required for the conventional war, the United States conducted a brilliant military campaign in March-April 2003 to overthrow the regime of Saddam Hussein. But from the very beginning the plans for the postwar period went off the rails. The achievements of the United States in Operation Iraqi Freedom highlighted once again that country's unchallenged prowess on the conventional battlefield. Yet the three-year engagement in Iraq, from the end of conventional military operations in April 2003 to the fall of 2005, reveals a remarkable ineptitude in securing peace and stability. This has been most evident in the failure of the United States to find a solution to a virulent and deadly insurgency that has claimed thousands of lives. The failures are all the more embarrassing in the light of the ambitious postwar goals the United States had in mind for Iraq.

Over the course of the few weeks following the fall of Saddam's regime it became abundantly clear that the military victory was soured by the resulting lawlessness in the country, by the manifest inability of the United States to implement the promised postwar reconstruction, and above all by the outbreak of a seemingly unexpected insurgency on the part of the disgruntled Sunni Arab population in the center of the country. The Iraqi army lasted barely three weeks, but two and half years later the United States was being held at bay by a shadowy insurgency that was still going strong in fall 2005. It has derailed US political goals in Iraq, destabilized the new quasi-sovereign Iraqi political entity that emerged after 30 June 2004, and had a serious impact on Iraq's political progress towards elections. There was, therefore, considerable relief when a significant percentage of the population managed to vote on 30 January 2005 without the disruption and mayhem promised by insurgent groups. Much of this success was due to stringent US security measures and the determination of Iraqis to vote in the face of relentless violence. But within weeks the violence surged again, and April to October 2005 were dismal months with serious casualties inflicted on innocent Iraqi civilians, the Iraqi security forces and the weary but dedicated US military personnel. Without a doubt the tenuous security situation in the country since May 2003 has contributed enormously to the slow pace of reconstruction, rebuilding and reconciliation, and the establishment of political stability. In short, even if it is ultimately defeated this insurgency has been costly. It did not have to be this way. The Iraqi insurgency has become the paramount national security concern of the United States. This book is the story of this insurgency and of the US responses to it. It analyzes the insurgency's origins, motivations and evolution, and the US policy and strategic and operational responses to it.

Definitions and conceptual methodology

Like the conflict between Hezbollah and Israel in southern Lebanon, the Iraqi insurgency defies easy categorization.[2] I do not intend to get bogged down in definitional quagmires or extensive analyses of the characteristics of the type of conflict now occurring in Iraq. For the sake of brevity, I have forsaken extensive analysis of theory or case studies of other insurgency and counter-insurgency campaigns.[3] The study is, however, implicitly influenced by the vast theoretical literature on insurgency and counter-insurgency and by the myriad comparative and historical case studies of past and ongoing insurgencies.[4]

But the problematic issues of what we mean by insurgency, terrorism and counter-insurgency need to be addressed however briefly. I argue that the violence in Iraq is an example of a 'small war', insurgency or guerrilla warfare.[5] Although I use the term insurgency throughout the study for the sake of consistency, I view all three terms as interchangeable.[6] The new draft US Army Field Manual Interim (FMI 3-07.22) *Counterinsurgency Operations* defines insurgency as 'an organized movement aimed at the overthrow of a constituted government through the use of subversion and armed conflict'.[7] This is fine, but the Iraqi insurgency broke out during foreign occupation and before the constitution of a legitimate government. In this context, an insurgency can be waged by a people against a foreign occupation of their country. The noted long-time student of insurgency Bard O'Neill, in his well-known book *Insurgency and Terrorism*, defines insurgency as 'a struggle between a nonruling group and the ruling authorities in which the nonruling

group consciously uses *political resources* (e.g. organizational expertise, propaganda, and demonstrations) and *violence* to destroy, re-
formulate, or sustain the basis of legitimacy of one or more aspects
of politics'.[8] Among the most often cited definitions of insurgency
is one developed by the US Central Intelligence Agency (CIA). It
is not very elegant but it is useful in that it mentions some of the
key characteristics of insurgency such as 'protractedness' and political warfare:

Insurgency is a protracted political-military activity directed toward
completely or partially controlling the resources of a country through
the use of irregular military forces and illegal political organizations.
Insurgent activity—including guerilla warfare, terrorism, and political
mobilization, for example, propaganda, recruitment, front and covert
party organization, and international activity—is designed to weaken
government control and legitimacy while increasing insurgent control
and legitimacy.[9]

The violence in Iraq is also an example of terrorism. This is another term that has caused considerable definitional problems. Terrorism has been a pressing concern for many countries, and over
the years academics, policy-makers and state officials throughout
the world have provided a wide range of definitions of the phenomenon. Many are self-serving political definitions while others are
very legalistic. The definition provided by the United States State
Department declares that terrorism is 'premeditated, politically
motivated violence perpetrated against noncombatant targets by
subnational groups or clandestine agents, usually intended to influence an audience'.[10] This is not an elegant definition; moreover, the
last part of the sentence—'usually intended to influence an audience'—is a weak formulation. I contend that terrorism *definitely* is
intended to influence an audience. Others would argue that it self-
servingly leaves out violence by the state. I do not wish to get into
this debate here; but the above definition suffices in that it declares

that it is premeditated, politically motivated, and is undertaken against noncombatants or unarmed people. In this context, Bard O'Neill's definition may be more value-free as he states that it is 'violence which is directed primarily against noncombatants (usually unarmed civilians), rather than operational military and police forces or economic assets (public or private).'[11]

The relationship between insurgency and terror is complicated and I will not be able to solve it here, either on definitional or moral grounds. Insurgents throughout history have used terror against innocent civilians or government forces in the course of their struggles. Does this make them terrorist organizations? From the standpoint of their enemy, the state and its forces insurgents are terrorists. This approach serves to delegitimize both their means and ends. But there has often existed a perception, even among dispassionate observers of an insurgency, that those engaged in it may have legitimate grievances and goals. But what about their means, which may include what can be described as terrorism? Some insurgents, mindful of the negative consequences for their cause of mass killing of civilians have practiced—for want of a better phrase—'discriminate' terrorism. That is to say, they limit their attacks to civilians who are part of the state infrastructure, to perceived 'collaborators', and to security forces in barracks or at home and out of uniform. But these perceived enemies do encompass a large group of people, many of whom are noncombatants.

The Iraqi insurgency has witnessed the unquestionably pervasive ideological sanctioning and use of terrorism. The so-called nationalist and Ba'thist insurgents have actively killed Iraqi civilians who 'collaborate' with the occupation and the perceived subservient Iraqi government. These individuals or groups are seen as a legitimate target. And moreover, neither of these insurgent groups has any qualms about eliminating members of the security forces even after they have been kidnapped or captured.[12] But it is unclear whether all Iraqi insurgent groups have condoned mass killings of civilians, particularly of those of a different religious and sectarian hue. This is not because these particular insurgents are morally scrupulous; rather it is because some of them are simply not interested in promoting ethno-sectarian strife as part of their strategy.

Other violent groups in Iraq practice indiscriminate terrorism and have no qualms about mass killing of civilians. It is here that we begin to enter the dark and foreboding characteristic of insurgent warfare.[13] While such indiscriminate use of violence against innocent civilians may be motivated by sheer hatred based on ethnic or religious differences—in other words, an expression of existing antipathies—it is also *instrumental* in that it has a rational operational goal or set of goals, whereby the insurgents hope that it elicits an equally nasty or horrific response by the government or the specific group that is targeted. This indiscriminate or blind terrorism and the counter-response accelerate the unraveling of the government's legitimacy. It can also be designed to create or highlight a wide ethno-sectarian chasm between 'Us' and the 'Other,' (the latter being the evil enemy), such that there can be no compromise or a return to the status quo ante.[14] For groups such as the notorious Abu Mus'ab al-Zarqawi's Al Qaeda affiliate in Iraq, the indiscriminate killing of innocent civilians is part of their strategy. That strategy includes the ignition of sectarian strife between Sunni and Shi'a. His bloody actions in Iraq have undeniably succeeded in creating and deepening ethno-sectarian divisions and caused a significant legitimacy issue for the wider insurgency and its public image.

Counter-insurgency constitutes the set of policies taken by the state to combat an insurgency. What constitutes effective counter-insurgency strategies and whether states are able to implement them depends on a host of factors including the political goals of the counter-insurgent, the resources available, and the organizational culture of the counter-insurgent's military forces. Counter-insurgents are almost never ready to confront an insurgency at the beginning. It takes time and effort and considerable trial and error before the counter-insurgent mobilizes the right set of instruments for an effective strategy. Some may not succeed; and in their frustration they view the use of brute force at the operational level as a way out or a panacea for all their problems. And finally, just as insurgency has its 'dark side' in the presence and use of terrorism, so does counter-insurgency with the possibility of descent into unlawful measures including wholesale detentions that round up the innocent and the guilty, the use of death squads, the sanctioning of abuse and torture. Even counter-insurgency campaigns that have succeeded have not always been clean. The British successes in Malaya against the Malayan Communist Party and in Kenya against the Mau Mau had their 'dark sides'. In the latter case the brutality of the British counter-insurgency campaign against the Kikuyu tribe that led the insurgency has been brought to light.[15]

Outline of the study

The study starts with a chronological narrative of the conventional war during Operation Iraqi Freedom and of the insurgency from its outbreak in late April 2003 to the end of October 2005. It then seeks answers to the following questions.

First, I address three interrelated questions. Who are the insurgents? The United States initially refused to believe that members of the Sunni Arab community would rise up and that an even larger element would lend passive or active support to insurgents. Unsurprisingly, the insurgents were referred to as 'regime dead-enders', 'former regime elements', 'Ba'thist thugs and killers'. And finally, there is my favorite and most Orwellian of all the terms, 'Anti-Iraqi Forces'.[16] The reluctance to view the violent reaction by the Sunnis as an insurgency encompassing a larger set of people than mere former regime remnants was also matched by a desire to promote the idea of an extensive foreign hand in the violence. What are the origins, motivations and causes of the insurgency? In other words, why has a significant element of the Iraqi population engaged in armed rebellion? There has been a manifest failure among policy-makers in the United States and among observers to understand the origins of this insurgency. There was a deep reluctance on the part of the United States to admit that the Sunni Arab community had grievances that needed to be addressed after the collapse of their world in 2003. However much the Iraqi government and the coalition deny it, the Sunni inhabitants of Iraq may have legitimate grievances, as I endeavor to show below. Anger at the collapse of their privileged position is not objectively a legitimate grievance, and a return to the situation as it existed prior to the downfall of the Ba'thist regime when they exercised a monopoly of power is not legitimate goal. What do the insurgents want? And do they all want the same thing? The articulation of negative ('what we do not want') and positive ('what we do want') goals has often been the domain of the leaders and of the ideological-propaganda unit of an insurgency. Because of the myriad insurgent groups with dif-ferent ideologies or worldviews, the articulation of negative goals in the Iraqi insurgency ('we want the foreign occupation and its collaborators out') has been much easier than the articulation of positive goals ('our vision of an Iraq liberated from foreign occupa-tion is...'). This said, however, there is increasing evidence that the various insurgent groups have begun to articulate 'positive goals,' that is to say, their vision of what they want to see for the future of the country. But because the insurgency remains fractured and fractious, the various groups have different positive goals.

Second, the study addresses the issue of how 'men rebel'. This refers to the organizational and institutional infrastructure of rebellion. Insurgencies cannot occur without some form of organization. The outside world has been baffled by the opacity of how the insurgency functions as well as by the prevalence of dozens of groups with different, and at times conflicting, political agendas. Despite the fact that the organizational structure of this insurgency is not very transparent to us, enough exists to build a picture of its leadership and structures and of its cadres, however incomplete.

Third, with what means do men rebel? What are the operational goals and tactical concepts associated with this specific insurgency? Most of the means used by the Iraqi insurgents are not particularly original to them and can be recognized among insurgents the world over, past and present. The Iraqi insurgents know that they cannot meet the US forces head-on in a combat situation due to the imbalance in firepower, training and equipment. 'Abu Ali'a, a member of a notorious insurgent group, Ansar al-Sunnah, told the Spanish newspaper *El Mundo*: 'The only way to defend ourselves is by guerilla warfare, which as we all know was a Spanish invention. The Americans outdo us in terms of equipment and numbers, but we know the terrain, we choose the appropriate circumstances and weapons and we can inflict a lot of damage on them.'[17] 'Abu Ali's history is inaccurate (the Spanish did not invent guerrilla warfare, they merely provided it with a modern term), but he is not saying or doing anything that would be alien to an insurgent or guerrilla fighting anywhere, or for that matter in the past.

Fourth, it has been argued *ad nauseam* that insurgencies need popular support. To gain such support the insurgents must articulate a *cause* and the people need to view that cause as legitimate, in the sense that it embodies their grievances and promises them redress. As the noted French theorist of counter-insurgency warfare, David Galula, said in the 1960s the ideal cause is the one that 'can attract the largest number of supporters and repel the minimum of opponents.'[18] But what do we mean by popular support for an insurgency that may take place in a country that is divided by deep class, regional, or ethno-sectarian fissures? Many insurgencies have occurred in such divided societies, and these divisions do have an impact on an insurgency. This, in effect, means that an insurgency's 'popular support' may be limited to one class, region, or ethno-sectarian group. Iraq is a deeply divided country and we need to explore the impact of ethno-sectarian divisions in Iraq on the insurgency. One of the critical weaknesses of this insurgency is that its base of support is limited. This is an issue that needs its own chapter, and in this context I address the respective positions and roles of the Kurds and the Shi'a—two communities that do not support the Sunni insurgency—in post-Saddam Iraq in detail.

Fifth, how has the United States dealt with the insurgency over the past two years? It is trite but accurate to state that the best strategy for a government—whether it is local or a foreign occupier—is to prevent an insurgency from breaking out. But the United States went into Iraq with goals and assumptions that ultimately contributed to the deterioration of the situation. Moreover, the US military establishment—the most powerful in the world and one of the most successful in waging conventional warfare—has proven yet again, only thirty years after the Vietnam debacle, that despite its talent and enormous material resources it has neither the organizational nor the cultural flexibility to deal with insurgencies. The United States made several policy blunders in the aftermath of the overthrow of Saddam Hussein's regime. It compounded these strategic mistakes by operational and tactical ones and failures once the insurgency had broken out. It has been hampered in devising a successful counter-insurgency by its pre-invasion goals/assumptions and post-conventional war mistakes and *ad hoc* operational and tactical solutions that have plagued the US effort in Iraq.

Sixth, how do insurgencies end? Analysts often tend to ignore the vital issue of the termination of insurgency war. From the vantage point of fall 2005 when this study was completed there was considerable debate on the future course of the insurgency in Iraq. Some believed that it was on the verge of defeat or of waning because of war-weariness on the part of the Iraqi population and of the signal failure of the insurgency to prevent the January 2005 elections for a national assembly or the adoption of the draft constitution on 15 October 2005 after a nationwide referendum. Others have argued that there are fractures within the insurgency and that so-called 'mainstream' nationalist insurgents who are in contact with organized Sunni political forces in Baghdad are seeking a negotiated end to the insurgency. It has also been argued that the lull in the insurgency in the immediate aftermath of the successful elections of 30 January 2005 was merely a time during which the insurgents were lying low and regrouping.

In a book of this nature, which deals with an ongoing event of critical national security importance, several major caveats are in order. The Iraq conflict continues at the time of writing, and hard data are difficult to come by because this is not an ordinary research setting. Access into Iraq is not easy and it is extremely difficult to conduct 'field research' on a dangerous issue such as the insurgency. It will be years before the United States allows access to hard operational data on the insurgency and on its countermeasures. There are no dusty records or official memoirs available. Not surprisingly, there have been few analytical studies of the Iraqi insurgency and fewer still that rely on 'field data' derived from close-up observation on the ground and discussions with individuals, soldiers and officials present in Iraq. In this context, there will not be a definitive study of the Iraqi insurgency and of the US response to it for years to come.[19] In the course of my tour in Iraq I managed to do open source field research and I have incorporated some of the data in this study which relies on a wide variety of open sources, insurgent statements and websites on the Internet and on observations and open interviews with diverse Iraqis in Iraq between early November 2003 and mid-March 2004, and then between July and end of September 2005. While I intend to build up as complete a picture as possible given the existing constraints, in no way do I claim that this preliminary full-length study is either the definitive or complete study of the Iraqi insurgency.

Moreover, I have focused my attention primarily on the insurgency itself rather than on the counter-insurgency campaign, largely because I wish to correct the considerable number of erroneous assumptions that have been and continue to be made about this insurgency and its nature. Similarly, the dynamics of Iraqi political and socioeconomic developments over the course of the past two years are addressed only in so far as they are of relevance to the evolution of the insurgency and the violence in Iraq. To do otherwise at this juncture would make this study an unwieldy endeavor.

Finally, this analysis of the insurgency and of the US response to it ends in October 2005. I realize that by the time the book appears in print in early 2006, much will have occurred on the ground in Iraq. It suffices to argue here that the study is beset by a tension between the author's hope that Iraq succeeds as a stable entity progressing towards the rule of law and good governance on the one hand and the fear on the other hand that the political dynamics in the country portend greater violence not only by insurgents but among its various ethnic groups.

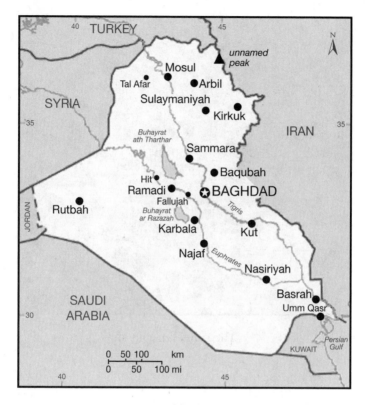

Iraq

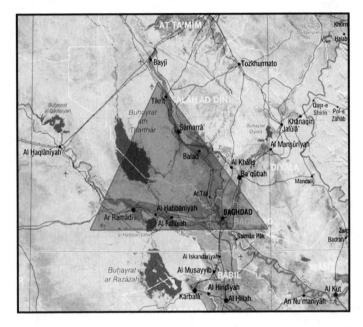

The Sunni Triangle

EVOLUTION OF THE IRAQI INSURGENCY

FROM CONVENTIONAL TO PARTISAN WARFARE
DURING OPERATION IRAQI FREEDOM

Iraqi officials vowed before the war—when it seemed inevitable—
and during it that they would use any method to fight the Coalition. Indeed, prior to the outbreak of hostilities Tariq Aziz, Iraqi
Deputy Prime Minister and the most cosmopolitan member of the
ruling elite, indicated on several occasions that Iraq would fight
very differently from 1991, when vastly superior Coalition forces
outclassed its conventional military. Observers claimed that the
regime had absorbed lessons of Vietnam and other 'asymmetric'
conflicts that had pitted a powerful conventional force against a
weaker one. The regime may have tried to gain insights from past
conflicts in which the stronger side had been defeated. As a retired
Iraqi general said in an interview with an Arab journalist:

The considerable difference in power between Iraqi forces and the US-led
alliance would naturally result in Iraqi forces resorting to guerilla warfare
tactics in a hit-and-run sort of confrontation, aimed at slowing down the
invasion and inflicting as many casualties as possible on enemy troops.
America's high-tech weapons and air superiority would not be quite as effective in a guerilla war by well-prepared and armed regular and irregular
forces in urban areas.[1]

Indeed, the United States feared that it would face some nasty
urban warfare against the Iraqis. Urban warfare is regarded as the
great equalizer for those who are weaker or who are defending

against an attacker. US Army and Marine Corps training was designed to minimize that equalizing effect. Hence the US military
undertook intensive training for units in urban mock-ups at Fort
Polk, Louisiana.[2] Iraqi dissidents stated that Qusay—Saddam Hussein's trusted younger son—had been appointed to implement a
new national security plan with the twin purpose of defending the
urban centers by turning them into 'Saddamgrads' and of suppressing domestic dissent.[3]

   As the Coalition war machine bore down on Baghdad, Tariq Aziz
analyzed the war in the only way he could, arguing that morally and
in terms of morale Iraq had the upper hand over the Coalition forces
despite the latter's technological superiority. He cited examples of
stiff Iraqi resistance in Basra, Nasiriyah, Najaf and Karbala, saying:
'They are now in the desert, they raid civil [sic] Iraqi places and the
Iraqi forces fight them and inflict losses on them; so when we speak
about victory, we are confident of victory. Victory is when you defeat aggression. Victory is when you prevent aggression from ful-
filling its objectives.' Asked what kind of a conflict the coming one
would be, Aziz answered: 'It should not become a religious one. It
is a conflict between independence and neo-colonialism.'[4] He said
that its aims were to secure oil, protect the state of Israel and target
Iraq's longstanding attempts to construct a 'modern, nationalist,
advanced state.'[5] This has been a constant refrain from Iraqi leaders
including Saddam and propagandists since the 1970s. If that was
the case, and for many Iraqi nationalists it was, why did the Iraqi
military not organize a more robust defense of the homeland?

*The structural, organizational and societal weaknesses of the Iraqi
armed forces*

When Operation Iraqi Freedom started on 19 March 2003 very few
people expected the Iraqi armed forces to put up much of a fight

against the vastly better-trained and equipped Coalition forces. In fact the prewar Coalition claims that Iraq represented a dire military threat were unsupportable. By 2003 Saddam's military was in dire straits.[6] The weaknesses of the giant force of 1990–1 were magnified manifold in the smaller and depleted force structure of 2003. A leading US defense analyst, William Arkin, who had studied the two wars between Iraq and the United States extensively, said in October 2002, 'They were a paper tiger in 1991, and they're a tissue paper tiger today.'[7] The only forces that were seen as relatively effective were the better-trained and better-equipped Republican Guard and Special Republican Guard divisions, which made up only 20 percent of the total ground forces.[8] Moreover, despite the massive amounts of resources expended on them before the imposition of sanctions, they had never been good—for a wide variety of structural and societal reasons. Indeed, the weaknesses of the Iraqi army were legendary despite the huge build-up and the improvements during the Iran-Iraq war (1980–8). Most of the shortcomings go back a long time, and have been explored in considerable detail elsewhere.[9] The following is a brief summary of those shortcomings; it is important to address them because they have had an impact on Coalition efforts to build a new Iraqi security sector between 2003 and 2005.

One of the greatest weaknesses of the Iraqi army was that Saddam feared it.[10] Despite the Iraqi leader's determination from the earliest days of the Ba'th seizure of power to build armed forces with powerful combat capabilities, the evidence clearly shows that their war-fighting prowess was not considered as important as achieving political control over them. This was clearly reflected in the purges of professional officers and their replacement by politicized flunkies and the implementation of rigid controls over command, control and communications. Not surprisingly, Iraqi forces fared poorly against Kurdish guerrillas in the 1970s because of the shortage of competent professional officers and the tight control exercised by the regime over operations. This was repeated during the Arab-Israeli war of 1973, when the Iraqi expeditionary forces sent to help Syria shore up its defenses performed poorly.

The bloody eight-year Iran-Iraq war revealed many material and organizational weaknesses in the Iraqi military. The rigid controls that Saddam exercised over operational matters during the Iran-Iraq and Gulf wars angered the officer corps, and this anger exploded after the dual debacles of the battles of Faw in January 1986 and Mehran in July of that same year, in both of which better-led Iranian forces defeated well-entrenched Iraqi troops. Saddam neither trusted the officer corps nor wished to have middle-ranking and senior officers formulate operational plans unsupervised. Moreover, as the armed forces expanded dramatically from the mid-1970s onwards, ensuring political loyalty preoccupied Saddam and his subordinates more than professional capability.

Saddam may also have felt that too much operational independence on the part of the officer corps would inflate the egos of successful commanders and would also conflict with the political goals and directives issued by the civilian leadership. Officers who are too successful begin to seek a more enlarged role for themselves and may thus express opinions that are political rather than operational. Thus, even too much military success could impinge in a negative manner on civil-military relations. Staff General Nizar al-Khazraji, chief of staff of the Iraqi army at the time of the Kuwait crisis, has talked at length on the policies instituted by Saddam, which, while they helped prevent coups by the army, ultimately worked to make it a militarily ineffectual force. With respect to the Iraqi army's dismal performance in 1991 he says, 'Let me say here that the main point of weakness in 1991 was pushing the army to a war they did not want to fight ... The army did not want to fight and the issue was clear because of its injustice ...'[11] On the other hand, Khazraji argues, the Iraqi army fought well during the Iran-Iraq war despite Saddam's interference, because 'there was strong nationalistic sentiment during the war. There was a feeling that Iraq was defending itself and its land ...'[12] The regime was effective at thwarting attempted coups and Khazraji said many factors played a role in the regime's ability to survive these threats: 'a system of security monitoring of military units' was in place because the 'Iraqi regime gives priority to its security and is diligent in this regard ... A second factor is the enthusiasm of Iraqi officers and the ignorance among them of the need to be completely secretive during preparations. A third factor is that the regime not only strikes suspects, but takes the initiative to strike elements that are considered unfriendly, which prevents the meeting of forces.'[13] What Khazraji means in this last convoluted sentence is that the ever-paranoid Saddam was effective in striking first and in disrupting potential or suspected enemies before they even had a chance to conspire against the regime.

One of the major factors in the weakening of the cohesion, morale and professionalism of the Iraqi army stemmed from the Ba'thist regime's policy of putting civilian overseers in charge of the military and of giving military rank to civilian relatives of Saddam and then positioning them in important commands or posts. In the words of Khazraji:

There is a civilian from the special security forces of Qusay Saddam Husayn involved in every matter. This civilian's job is to follow up matters and monitor those who issue orders, officers and soldiers, which is why the officers call him the teacher. The officers feel bothered and annoyed and ridicule civilians who were assigned tasks they have no knowledge of except in terms of writing reports. They are annoyed by people who joined the army at low ranks with no education or intellect but were promoted to the rank of general, such as Ali Hasan al-Majid, the president's cousin, who was a soldier and became a staff general and assumed the

Defense Ministry. Another example is Husayn Kamil, who was an ordinary soldier and became a staff general and was given the defense portfolio, and Izzat Ibrahim who is now deputy commander in chief; he was a civilian who sold ice and was then given the rank of staff general. It is a blatant farce to give an ignorant or semi-ignorant soldier a military rank that usually takes a lot of experience in courses, war colleges, and theoretical and field experience to reach.

The elements I have mentioned are hated very much. Support in the army comes from military success, strict discipline, shouldering responsibility, caring for those under your command, and being a role model. These elements are hated because they treat military personnel in an arrogant and patronizing manner that offends them.

The problem is not just that these elements do not understand the nature of the work, its context, and its requirements; rather, they also insist on imposing their opinion and on using force as a mode of treatment with a tendency to use violence. This resulted in arbitrary orders unprecedented in the history of armies, which only caused obstruction and offense. It is a tragedy for absolute blind loyalty to be the only criteria [*sic*] at the expense of qualifications, experiences, and the rules of working in an organization.[14]

Material and organizational shortcomings are much easier to see and ostensibly to deal with than those that stem from 'social' factors; the latter are deep-seated and often reflect profound political and social fissures. Saddam also exercised tight control over the officers for societal reasons. Iraqi military power has traditionally rested on fragile social foundations. Saddam's infamous statement, made during the Gulf crisis of 1991, that the United States was a society that could not withstand 10,000 casualties in a battle, whereas Iraq could, was bravado. Saddam could not afford excessive casualties among Iraqi forces during the Iran-Iraq war. Such attrition would have affected each of Iraq's three major ethnic groups in different ways, and damaged the stability of the state and the security of the regime.

The regime could not afford heavy casualties among the Kurds, who were the least nationalistic element within the country and often inclined to desert to guerrilla forces in the north. During the Iran-Iraq war, the regime found it necessary to promise the Kurds that they would serve primarily in the north against Iranian infiltration rather than in the bloody stalemate on the southern front. Nonetheless, Kurdish soldiers deserted by the thousands to join the Kurdish guerrillas, who took advantage of Iraq's preoccupation with the war against Iran to launch yet another insurgency against Saddam's regime.

The Shi'a Arabs made up the bulk of the infantry, the forces that suffer the highest casualty rate in any war. Iraqi infantry casualties in the offensives against the Kurds in the 1970s were extremely heavy, particularly among the Shi'a rank and file and among the Maghawir special warfare units that were used in the mountainous and rugged terrain of the north. This caused disturbances within the Shi'a community in 1974. In this context, during the war with Iran, it was to be expected that heavy casualties in the infantry units would hit the Shi'a hardest. Not surprisingly, Iraq exhibited considerable reluctance to rely on regular infantry during operations.

Finally, most of the officer corps and enlistees in elite units came from the Sunni Arab middle class and the tribes of the center. Heavy casualties among this group could have threatened the ethnic base of the regime. Heavy casualties in the battles of Faw and Mehran in 1986 among the Sunni Arab personnel may have contributed to grumbling and dissension among the elite and the officer corps, which forced Saddam to give officers something that he was congenitally loath to do: more operational freedom on the battlefield. Not surprisingly, the Iraqi army did better in the field from late 1987 to the end of the war in mid-1988. But Saddam was not about to let the officer corps forget who was the 'real' military 'genius' in the Iraqi military. After the war he tightened political control over the military and purged hundreds of officers. Saddam, however, could not abide the enhanced prestige of the armed forces and, said Khazraji, started a policy of liquidations and purges as soon as the war ended because army officers had apparently developed a high opinion of themselves: 'Liquidation operations started then [after the Iran-Iraq war]. The Iraqi Army emerged victorious from the war and the officers returned with their heads raised high, for they had participated in tough battles. This feeling among senior officers worried the authorities, which started carrying out executions and liquidation and exile operations.'[15] Such instability is not conducive to professionalism.[16]

The Iraqi defeats in operations Desert Storm and Iraqi Freedom may have been unavoidable because of the vast technological disparity between Iraqi and Coalition forces. But it was not just technological disparity that doomed the Iraqi armed forces. In the view of many military observers, and former Iraqi officers and regime officials, the Iraqi defeat was made easier as a result of the nature of Saddam's controls over the armed forces and the deep societal fissures he had created and promoted over the years.[17]

Indeed, during Operation Iraqi Freedom neither the regular army, which was a poorly trained and demoralized force, nor the RG and the SRG divisions—the regime's best-equipped forces—fought effectively. Attempts by the RG to make a stand outside Baghdad unraveled rather quickly due to lack of coordination and cohesion among the units, and the leadership's poor strategic management of its forces. For the most part, the Iraqi forces simply melted away. The conduct of the war by the Iraqis during the conventional war was inept. There was no initiative to do anything out of the ordinary to stop or delay the Coalition advance; the Iraqi forces also proved incapable of preparations for urban warfare.[18] Documents captured from the abandoned headquarters of the Iraqi army's 51st Mechanized Division highlighted serious morale

problems among the troops. One document referred to the desertion problem and attributed it to the lack of water and ice, and
concern for family. Another document, intended to raise morale,
instructed officers to tell their men that they were fighting a *jihad*
(holy war): 'Muslim armies in the early days of Islam beat the Ro-
man and Persian armies with the power of faith and *jihad*,' it ran.
Also some of the Iraqi military's planning was taken up with the
worrisome prospect of restive local inhabitants hindering the *national* war effort; the 51st Mechanized Infantry Division expected
anti-regime outbreaks in Basra and Az Zubayr, close to its area of
operations, and had contingency plans for 'terminat[ing] enemy
agents and mobs'.[19] The Iraqis had little or no situation awareness
of their own forces or those of the enemy.[20]

An Iraqi major in the 2nd Infantry Division, Saleh Abdullah
Mahdi al-Jiburi, knew that the conflict was between two very un-
equal forces but thought the Iraqis could do better in trying to sty-
mie the United States: 'We knew we could not match the American air power, but we thought we could increase their losses to a
point the Americans would say the Iraqis are an equal match for us
and they would stop the war.' He clearly did not expect his brigade,
which fought in Baghdad, to suffer serious desertion as it did, nor
to succumb to the severe battlefield attrition that had occurred by
the end of the war: the brigade lost one-fourth of its 4,000 soldiers, including 200 men from his battalion.[21]

Iraqi officers claimed that Saddam Hussein and his sons crippled
the army by issuing a multitude of erratic and contradictory orders.
Moreover, units barely communicated with one another and were
often paralyzed by lack of imagination and initiative. An Iraqi officer, Colonel Raaed Faik, complained about irrational and erratic
orders from the regime's top decision-makers, particularly Qusay,
who commanded the Republican Guard: 'These were the orders
of an imbecile. Qusai [*sic*] was like a teenager playing a video war

game.'[22] Command incompetence, poor preparation, craven leadership and the wholesale desertion of troops compounded these problems. Command structure was confused and confusing, and Saddam created rival military forces to keep an eye on each other so that they did not have time to threaten his regime.

The elite units were well-armed and well-paid; the regular units and regular army officers schemed to undermine elite units, hoarding information and avoiding contact with Coalition forces. In the words of one Ba'th Party militiaman: 'We were like 10 different armies fighting their own private wars.'[23] Morale was low in many units, particularly those of the regular army.[24] Even before the war broke out, the regime had a serious problem with the level of desertion within the armed forces. Imprisoned deserters were amnestied and sent back to their units; numerous documents captured by Coalition forces show that Ba'th Party cadres were instructed to increase ideological instruction in the forces in order to improve morale and readiness. Most of it was to no avail. Desertions soared as Coalition units moved nearer to Baghdad; units listed as full strength were less than half that, and some ceased to exist in the space of twenty-four hours. Major Jafar Sadiq, a special forces commander, 'woke up on the morning of April 5 and an entire battalion had gone. They had become vapors.'[25] Desertions had depleted his company from 131 men to ten in the space of two days. Many soldiers simply quit and went home after changing into civilian clothing.

The few commanders who knew how bad the situation had become did not dare to relay such information up the chain of command. As one general said, 'It was well known that President Hussein did not care to receive bad news.'[26] Because of the way Iraq's forces were organized—many rival units/organizations that responded only to commands from the regime leadership—commanders were paralyzed by an inability to make cohesive and integrated moves. 'Initiative was discouraged. No one dared make a decision.' As Colonel Faik said, 'Professional soldiers can't fight without orders and inspiration from their leaders. But we had clowns for leaders. This is our tragedy.'[27] The defeat was traumatic for Iraqi officers. A Colonel 'Asad' blamed Saddam and his cronies, particularly his two inept sons: 'We are already used to his mistakes from the Iran-Iraq war and Kuwait. Every plan of Saddam was a disaster.' The colonel also conceded that the Iraqi army of 2003 was simply incapable of fighting a modern war because it had not recovered from the pounding of 1991 and had not replenished its equipment: 'You can't fight with what was left ... and this war was not just about what you learn at the military academy—it is technological, and we recognized that. The Army believed that from the first bullet fired by the British in the south, it would lose.' Major Saleh Abdullah Mahdi al-Juburi stated that 'the way we fought this war was to try to damage American troops as much as possible so that the US and British people would put pressure on their leaders to stop the war'. Instead, the pressure mounted on the Iraqi army, many units of which were either decimated or collapsed and then melted away.[28]

If we look at Iraqi society as a whole, and not merely the armed forces, it becomes clear that this was a people at the end of its tether. Iraqi national morale was low to begin with; the people had been beaten down by two previous wars and a devastating sanctions regime that impoverished every sector of the Iraqi population; in the run-up to the war a traditionally fearful people who would never approach foreigners in the streets and talk to them had started to throw caution to the winds. A Western reporter in Baghdad was treated to the spectacle of Iraqis offering their views of the regime. One Iraqi stated: 'We had eight years of war with Iran in the 1980s, and all we got was death. Then we had the war over Kuwait, and more death. Nobody here wants another war.

We want jobs. We want peace, not death.'[29] Towards the end the evidence mounted that the regime had lost its way.[30]

Nor was the Hussein regime able to implement an effective partisan-warfare campaign during the war itself, despite the fact that the war's highlight was an unpleasant but short-lived episode of violent *irregular* combat initiated by the Iraqis. Traditionally, partisan warfare has been defined as a kind of insurgency or irregular warfare that takes place in conjunction with the regular forces of a state primarily against a foreign enemy who has invaded its country.[31] An Iraqi general, Ahmed Rahal, said the regime did not even prepare for guerilla warfare adequately: 'We should have mined the roads and bridges. We should have planned a guerilla war. We were crippled by a lack of imagination.'[32] Several commanders were led to believe that the casualties inflicted on US forces in Mogadishu would ensure that the United States would have no stomach for a fight in an urban environment. Even that belief did not matter because Iraq made few if any preparations for urban combat.

Regime supporters, military personnel out of uniform or fighting in small tactical formations, irregular forces such as the Fedayeen Saddam ('Saddam's Martyrs') and non-Iraqi Arab volunteers conducted a brief but intense harassing form of partisan warfare in the third week of March 2003 against Coalition forces advancing towards Baghdad.[33] The Fedayeen base pay per month was 40,000 dinars—double the typical state-employee salary—and 100,000 dinars for experienced fighters. Salary was not the key perk: they had access to cheap plots of land, good schools and scarce consumer goods.[34] Four thousand guerillas from other Arab countries joined them. The initial influx of foreign fighters into Iraq to fight the advancing Coalition forces was motivated by a resurfaced Arab nationalism, outrage born of the pictures of devastation seen on television, the utter impotence of the Arab world, and a new-found Islamic fervor. A Jordanian Islamist stated that many people in the region viewed the US attack on Iraq as a 'campaign against the Arab nation ... The Americans are insulting everybody, not just Saddam Hussein or the Iraqis.'[35] An Egyptian volunteer added that if Arabs did not fight the United States in Iraq, other Arab countries would be next on the list: 'Look, Saddam is not an angel from Allah, we know that. But if they take Tikrit, then is Cairo next? That is why I urge all Muslims to come and fight in the streets of Iraq.'[36] This is eerily reminiscent of the Bush administration cliché that if the terrorists are not fought in Iraq, then we would have to fight them in the continental United States. A Lebanese volunteer in Beirut who was asked what he was doing standing in line at the Iraqi Embassy at the height of the war stated with chilling finality: 'I want to be in a martyrdom operation. I want to blow myself up and kill as many Americans as I can. I cannot stand by and watch Muslim children being murdered by Americans.'[37] Some of the foreign fighters detained and threatened to execute deserting Republican Guards, according to Iraqis interviewed.

In many cases the Iraqis and foreign volunteers fought tenaciously and courageously, and used guerilla tactics, often fighting out of uniform, mingling among civilians, and attacking 'soft targets' such as logistics convoys.[38] For many Coalition troops the harassing attacks of the Fedayeen and of the Arab volunteers were an unpleasant surprise and resulted in vicious firefights, particularly in the vicinity of the towns of Muhaydi as-Salih and 'Aziziyah. The Bush administration and US forces also seemed to have underestimated the lure of nationalism; many Iraqis who took up arms against the Coalition during Operation Iraqi Freedom did so because they wanted to fight not for Saddam Hussein but for their country. An Iraqi engineer returning from Amman to Baghdad at the height of the war, ostensibly to take part in the fight, claimed that his decision was 'not about defending Hussein. It's about defending Iraq. The war has made me a nationalist.'[39] Another Iraqi insurgent stated: 'It's the principle of the matter. I'm furious about foreigners invading our country. I'll stop in Baghdad and volunteer to fight in the city.'[40] Many of the claims made by Iraqis about fighting the advancing Coalition forces turned out to be bravado but the nationalist sentiment that motivated the statements *was not*, and those who did not fulfill their wish to fight the Coalition during Operation Iraqi Freedom were to get their chance in the coming months when they joined the insurgency that was to bedevil the Coalition from late April 2003.

The last few days of March 2003 were a 'low point in the war' for US forces. Sandstorms, overextended logistics lines, and ferocious attacks by Iraqi irregulars cast doubt on the progress of the war. The ferocity of the Fedayeen surprised US commanders, particularly in the southern city of Nasiriyah, where they had planned on a short battle against presumably weakened and demoralized Iraqi forces. Instead, US marines found themselves in five days of almost nonstop vicious combat against irregular forces that did not respect the laws of war. 'Nasiriyah was more difficult than we envisioned. I thought there would be a few of these knuckleheads out there and we would blow past them. It turned out there were more of them and they were more fanatic,' said US Marine Colonel Larry Brown.[41] It was the same in many other locations. Colonel Ben Hodges, commander of 1st Brigade, 101st Air Assault Division, which faced some stiff resistance, said: 'The enemy always gets a vote. You fight the enemy and not the plan. I personally underestimated the willingness of the Fedayeen to fight, or maybe overestimated the willingness of the Shiites to rise up.'[42] Indeed, the ferocity of the Iraqi resistance during Operation Iraqi Freedom and the generally lukewarm reception was a bitter disappointment to US soldiers, who had been told to expect little of the former and a lot of the latter. A staff sergeant of 1st Battalion, 30th Infantry Regiment, out of Fort Benning, Georgia, said: 'The amount of resistance, I don't understand. We're there to help them get them out of the regime.' A lance corporal with the 2nd Battalion, 8th USMC, added: 'We were very surprised. We were told when we were going through Nasiriyah that we would see little to no resistance. We were more prepared for what happened in the Gulf War [of 1991] when they turned over and surrendered most of the time. They weren't rolling over like we thought they would.'[43] But no statement reflected the surprise of the United States more than one by Lieutenant General William Wallace, commander of V Corps, who, on 27 March said, 'The enemy we're fighting is different from the one we'd war-gamed against.' He added, 'I'm appalled by the inhumanity of it all.'[44] This is disingenuous. He must have known that one of the key characteristics of irregular warfare is its barbarity. Moreover, historically neither side of an irregular conflict has been immune from a descent into barbarity. Even some senior members of the Bush administration—an administration that is reluctant to question the pillars of its sacrosanct policy in Iraq—admitted that they had acted on mistaken assumptions. As one said: 'We underestimated their capacity to put up resistance. We underestimated the role of nationalism. And we overestimated the appeal of liberation.'[45] The policy-maker in question, however, seemed unable or unwilling to comprehend that for many Iraqis this was not a liberation but an occupation, pure and simple.

Suddenly we were bombarded with analyses trying to account for the Iraqi regime's success in asymmetric warfare, and the Fedayeen Saddam were transformed into a renowned albeit irregular enemy, much as the Republican Guard had been built into a vaunted and feared enemy on the eve of Operation Desert Storm in 1991. But ultimately the Fedayeen and other irregulars made little difference. Courage, tenacity and poor planning were not enough against some of the best-trained and best-motivated troops in the world. Often the Iraqis did not fight effectively or with much tactical sense.[46] Fedayeen fighters would often charge US troops in large groups with no understanding of fire and maneuver. As one marine officer described it, 'They will charge as a human wave, a dozen of them coming right at a position, and they'll get mowed down. Then another 12 will jump up and charge and they'll be killed.'[47] David Zucchino, a foreign correspondent for the *Los Angeles Times*, was embedded with a unit of the US Army's 3rd Infantry Division (Mechanized) during Operation Iraqi Freedom. He witnessed at first hand the poor tactics of the Iraqi forces, which did not stand a chance against the force that was bearing down on them. Of some firefights described in his book *Thunder Run*, he writes:

The Iraqis seem to have no training, no discipline, no coordinated tactics. It was all point and shoot. A few soldiers would pop up and fire, then stand out in the open ground to gauge the effects of their shots. The big coax rounds from the tanks and the Bradleys sent chunks of their bodies splattering into the roadside ...

The enemy kept coming. Soldiers and civilian gunmen were arriving now in every available mode of transportation—hatchbacks, orange-and-white taxis, police cars, ambulances, pickups, big Chevys, motorcycles with sidecars. Major Nusio, the battalion executive officer, opened fire on a huge garbage truck with a soldier at the wheel. He was thinking to himself as the soldier keeled over and the truck crash-landed: *A garbage truck? These people are so stupid—stupid but determined.*[48]

Another analyst writing on the episodes of irregular war concluded that the irregular Iraqi forces had shown much tenacity and put extra pressure on the invading forces, especially in the earlier stages of the war, but added 'they succeeded in inflicting only minimal casualties on the Coalition troops and ultimately failed to halt, or even seriously delay, the US advance on Baghdad.'[49] Indeed, expectations of a quagmire vanished with the swift and stunning progress of US forces in the last week of March and first week of April. Saddam believed his officers had betrayed him. His youngest daughter, Raghida, repeated this charge in exile in Jordan on 1 August 2003. This may well be true, but even if the officer corps did betray Saddam, they had their reasons for doing so. The Iraqi leader's megalomania and paranoia, which had resulted in executions, purges and forced retirements of officers, were among the main factors behind the weaknesses of the armed forces. As for the worrisome but short-lived irregular campaign during the course of the conventional war, it fell short because it was poorly planned and did not have the support of the populace. Baghdad fell on 9 April 2003 and with the symbolic toppling of Saddam's kitschy statute in Firdos Square in the center of the city, a brutal regime—despised by most of its people—came tumbling down.

The evolution of the Sunni insurgency, April 2003 to April 2005

Political developments and the evolution of the insurgency in 2003. Chaos and violence erupted in Iraq following the ignominious collapse of the Ba'th regime.[50] Compounding the problem of the collapse of law and order and of essential services was the concern that Iraqis expressed over the future direction of their country. This was reflected by the plaintive plea of a former policeman at a demonstration in late June 2003: 'What is our fate? Where is our government?'[51] Coalition efforts to re-establish law and order, basic services and some form of governance were chaotic and comic. As the United States moved towards war with Saddam's regime, the Bush administration set up an organization called the Office of Reconstruction and Humanitarian Assistance (ORHA) under the aegis of retired General Jay Garner. Its task was to ensure the recovery of Iraq and the provision of basic services pending the transfer of power to an interim authority composed of Iraqi opponents of Saddam as was expected by those political opponents and their supporters in the US Defense Department. ORHA, as I will detail later, proved to be out of its depth in Iraq. In late April 2003 the Bush administration pulled the plug on Jay Garner. He was replaced on 1 May by Ambassador L. Paul Bremer III, who was to head the newly created Coalition Provisional Authority (CPA). Its task was to exercise executive, legislative, and judicial powers while rebuilding the state's infrastructure and beginning the job of reconstruction.[52] To mollify Iraqi anger, particularly that of the political leaders who thought that power was theirs, Bremer entered into intense negotiations to set up the Interim Governing Council (IGC) to consult and advise him on all matters relating to the temporary governance of Iraq. The IGC came into existence on 13 July 2003 just as the security situation in the country worsened.

My focus here is the reaction of the Sunni Arab community to the collapse of the regime and of their paramount position in the political configuration of Iraq. That minority group's grievances, including the threat to their identity in the new post-Sunni Iraq, our mistaken assumption that they would accept their loss of status and privileges 'lying down', and certain 'muscular' aspects of the US response to their discontent fanned the flames of violence.[53]

Sunni Arab opposition to and dislike for the occupation was evident from the very beginning. This is not surprising, because they saw themselves as the target of the invasion. Some were bound to have taken up arms anyway because of the manifest threat that the invasion represented to their identity and material interests, which were tied to the former regime. However, what made a significant element of the community turn to open violence was, to a great extent, the dynamics of the situation in the aftermath of the regime's collapse, including the inherent weaknesses in the Sunni community's ability to represent itself effectively, and the mindset and policies of the Bush administration and occupation officials towards that community. It did not take long for Iraq's Sunni Arabs to overcome their initial shock at the collapse of the Ba'thist regime and begin to show their displeasure. On 19 April 2003, even before the outbreak of the insurgency, thousands of members of this community staged a major demonstration and marched through the streets of the heavily Sunni Baghdad suburb of Adhamiya demanding an end to the US occupation and the emergence of an Islamic state without any distinction between Sunni and Shi'a.

Many who ultimately became insurgents did not immediately join the insurgency to combat the foreign occupation. Instead, they adopted a wait and see attitude; that is to say, they wanted to see whether the Americans were going to be liberators or occupiers. A Western journalist interviewed an articulate insurgent by the name of 'Abu Mujahid', a former member of the Ba'th Party. While it would be accurate to say that the insurgent in question—a man who may have killed US soldiers—was trying to show himself in the best light possible, it is worth summarizing the entire interview in order to give the lie to the cliché that the insurgents were either regime dead-enders or terrorists. The insurgent begins with a statement that turns out to be incongruous with the image of moderation he was trying to present but which, no doubt, accurately reflected his sentiment:

Saddam. I liked him. He was a strong leader. But I was in the Ba'th Party and I knew that his men, mostly even Saddam's sons, were corrupt. They stole and stole from the Iraqi people. So I waited to see whether the Americans would liberate or occupy our lands … I had always looked at the American government as respectable until now. I had met Americans before and always respected them. I still do. They are educated, they know how to build things, how to think and how to work hard. They promised to liberate us from occupation, they promised us rights and liberty and my colleagues and I waited to make our decision on whether to fight until we saw how they would act.[54]

The insurgent told the Western reporter that he was disappointed in the US behavior towards Iraqis and by the collapse of law and order. He claimed to have seen both commendable and ex-ecrable behavior by US soldiers in the course of their interactions with Iraqis:

There have been some that say 'hello' or 'peace unto you' in Arabic to me. They give our children sweets and do their jobs with respect ... but others treat us like dogs. I saw one put his boot on the head of an old man lying on the ground [during a raid]. Even Saddam would not have done such a thing. It was then I realized that they had come as occupiers and not as liberators. And my colleagues and I then voted to fight. So we began to meet and plan. We met with others and have tried to buy weapons. None of us are afraid to die, but it is hard. We are just men, workers, not sol-diers ... But my colleagues and I don't hate the American people or even most of the soldiers. We just want them out of our land ...[55]

Denunciation of the United States and its occupation of Iraq emanated from the Sunni mosques almost immediately. At Friday prayers in a major Baghdad mosque—the Abu Hanifa—in early June 2003 Imam Mu'ayad al-Ubaidi launched into a vitriolic dia-tribe against the United States and its supposedly overweening ar-rogance: 'There are only two powers now in the world. One is America, which is tyrannical and oppressive. The other is a warrior who has not yet awakened from his slumber, and that warrior is Islam. May God help reverse the evil, so that the evil ones slaughter themselves with their own hand. How can you blame a person who is being strangled if he hurts the person who is strangling him?'[56] Sunni Arabs in attendance concurred with the *imam*. Majid Hamid al-Bayati said: 'They have destroyed our institutions, our people and our security. They have totally erased us.'[57] The Sunni Arabs were articulating their fears of material and identity deprivation.

Unlike the Shi'a or the Kurds, who had well-organized political parties and ideologies, the Sunni Arabs found themselves politi-cally and organizationally adrift from the earliest days of the post-Saddam era. This is unsurprising. The Sunni community had been under closer supervision and control by the regime than the other two precisely because many of its members were at the center of political power and patronage. Contrary to the perception encouraged by the Bush administration and the occupation authorities, the Sunni community was not uniformly pro-Saddam; most attempts to overthrow him were made by the Sunnis. Thus any manifestation of independent political activity by Sunnis was swiftly crushed. However, the community clearly benefited from being at the center of power and identifying themselves with a state that they had helped set up eighty-three years ago and had dominated since. For many Sunni Arabs the collapse of that paramount position constituted a massive psychological blow and required a political response. Hence there was a scramble to create political organizations or re-establish older ones that had gone underground.

The Iraqi Islamic Party (IIP)—modeled after the Middle East's oldest Islamic mass party, the Muslim Brotherhood, which was founded in Egypt in the 1930s—functioned clandestinely for decades, and re-emerged from the shadows after the downfall of Saddam Hussein's regime. The party had been established in 1960 but banned by Iraq's military rulers almost immediately; many of its members fled but others stayed and worked underground. For many years Saddam's regime tried to crush manifestations of Islamism in and around Mosul, the party's main area of strength. The party dismissed Saddam's attempt to bolster his legitimacy through religion in the 1990s. The IIP emerged openly in Mosul very soon after the downfall of the regime and pursued charity work in the city, opening free health clinics, mounting patrols in neighborhoods to discourage looting, and distributing donations to the needy and to hospitals. It quickly gained adherents among the city's professional class, doctors, lawyers and engineers. It also opened hundreds of branch offices in various locations. The IIP claimed that it had a clear plan that called for reorganizing 'Iraqi society and state in accordance with the teachings of the Islamic religion'. Its leadership argued that because of the catastrophe inflicted on the country and its people by the defunct regime, the IIP would seek to work actively with all parties and tendencies within the country; and that it would not shy away from engaging in the political discussion concerning the future of the country.[58]

The IIP is not very fond of the United States. As one party member observed to a US journalist: 'They are occupiers. The Americans are occupying us now. This is a fact.'[59] But it did not take up arms against the Coalition and it participated in the IGC. Headed by Muhsin Abd al-Hamid, a party member of Kurdish origin, the party sought to play a constructive political role. It even entered the political process and sought to mobilize the Sunni population. It has not been very successful to date. Curiously its participation in the political process under the occupation has detracted from its struggle to build legitimacy and a base of support among the Sunni Arab and Turkmen elements of the population. On the other hand, while it has shown some efficiency in its various offices in the larger cities it has not had the resources or ability to reach the vast majority of the Sunni population. Moreover, the unstable situation in the large cities and the suspicion with which it has been viewed by the Coalition authorities and other Iraqi parties have not made its task any easier. Some of its party members have wondered why its offices have been raided and its senior leaders temporarily detained.[60] In short, it has no traction with the young and the disgruntled elements of the Sunni Arab or Turkmen population, many of whom have gravitated towards religious extremism, the insurgency or criminal activities.

Sunni clerics play an important role in articulating the grievances and disgruntlement of the Sunni Arab population. Traditionally, as I will show in greater detail below, the clerical establishment in Sunni Islam has not been as politically powerful or, more importantly, as independent of the state as the Shi'a clerics. In one of the first major anti-occupation messages issued by a cleric, barely two weeks following Saddam's ouster, Sheikh Ahmed Kubeisi preached at the Abu Hanifa Mosque, 'You are masters today. But I warn you against thinking of staying. Get out before we force you out.'[61] His message to the Iraqis was to avoid sectarian divisions: 'We fear that sectarianism will be exploited by our enemies. Both Sunnis and Shiites should work for unity.'[62] But many Sunni clerics went beyond warning the occupation of troubles to come. Some called for active opposition to the occupation. 'The future is jihad,' said Sheikh Muhammad Ali Abbas, a cleric in Ramadi, in early June 2003, just as the insurgency was starting. This was one of the earliest overt statements of violent political opposition by a Sunni cleric. 'Do you know of anyone who can accept this humiliation? Do you just let them occupy your land while you sit and do nothing?'[63]

On 14 April 2003 a large number of Sunni clerics under the leadership of noted scholar Dr Harith al-Dhari formed the Association of Muslim Scholars (AMS). The AMS billed itself as a political, social, cultural and economic organization dedicated to the articulation of Sunni goals in the confusing post-Saddam period, and to furthering Sunni interests. As I will detail later, the AMS was destined to play a voluble role in the politics of the country.

For many others among the Sunni population the onus for the onset of the insurgency lay with the presence and/or policies of the US military and the Coalition occupation authorities. For them the insurgency began in late April 2003 with the outbreak of violence by the Sunni Arab population in what has come to be known as the 'Sunni Triangle', an area bounded by the cities of Baghdad, Ramadi and Fallujah. On 28 April 2003 US soldiers shot and killed fifteen people at an anti-US rally close to the Al Qaid school in Fallujah; sixty-five were wounded. Sentiment against the United States in the city—which admittedly was not particularly friendly to begin with—'jumped several notches'.[64] A city resident whose son was shot in the stomach said ominously: 'We won't remain quiet over this. Either they leave Falluja or we will make them leave.'[65]

The explanation for the violence that plagued Fallujah from the beginning of the occupation until its destruction in November 2004 needs to await detailed political and sociological analysis following the end of the war or greater access to primary data. But the idea that Fallujah was an intractable pro-Saddam and pro-Ba'thist bastion that was determined to fight in support of the former leader is belied by the reality on the ground. Indeed, in the early days of the occupation many leading residents of Fallujah rejected the clandestine call of the deposed Iraqi leader to 'escalate jihad against the occupation forces', proving that the city was not primarily up in arms in support of their former president. A statement issued by the city's leading intellectuals, clerics and officials stated, 'We are as innocent of you, Saddam Husayn, as was the wolf of Joseph's blood'.[66] The statement castigated the United States for failing to implement its promises to restore basic services, move its troops out of the city center and set Iraq on the road to sovereignty and stability. A few sociological vignettes, however, are available to put the Fallujah insurgency into context.

Like most midsized cities in Iraq, Fallujah is not particularly remarkable or appealing. It was founded as a garrison town by the Ottoman Empire in the latter parts of the nineteenth century. The city is dominated by the large and powerful Sunni Arab Dulaim tribe, large numbers of whose men joined the armed forces and security services. It is known as *medinat al-masajid* (city of mosques) for its abundance of mosques. Indeed, the joke that people tell goes: 'What lies between two mosques in Fallujah? Yet another mosque.' While it had prided itself on being a conservative Muslim city, where mainstream Islamic beliefs and Sufism permeated local life; US behavior and attitudes did not mix well with these beliefs. Fallujah had witnessed the rise of Salafist tendencies among its youth in the 1990s. The Arabic word *salaf* means predecessor or early generation, and refers to the Companions of the Prophet (the Sahaba) and the two succeeding generations of early Muslims, under whom Islam was practiced in a pure and pious manner. Muslims who view themselves as Salafis want to see the restoration of pure and pious religious practice, without the syncretism and impurities of later centuries. In short, they believe that Muslims have deviated from true Islam and that they need to be shown the errors of their current ways and to change for the 'better'. Every year, Fallujah's three religious colleges produced dozens of graduates who went to study in Baghdad and returned, often with radical thoughts much to the chagrin of the regime. During Saddam's rule, Islamic militants bombed music stores and the city cinema, and some publicly destroyed television sets in a major thoroughfare in 1999.[67] Many of these individuals viewed the United States in simple black-and-white terms as the enemy of Islam.

During the period of UN sanctions on Iraq after its disastrous Kuwait venture in 1990–1, Fallujah became a focal point of the smuggling trade and of the barely legal import-export commerce across the borders with Syria and Jordan, especially in consumer goods and construction materials and equipment. The trade involved an alliance between the tribes and members of the Ba'thist regime's security services who lived in the area and more often than not were related to the tribes. The security services facilitated the process of smuggling, while the tribes provided access to their kin in Syria and Jordan. As the sanctions regime began to bite, government control over cities like Fallujah and the provision of services to the population began to decline due to the atrophy of administrative structures, which in turn was because of the dramatic loss of revenue. The regime in Baghdad protected—indeed, promoted—these smuggling operations because they provided revenue and income (regime officials sought their own cut and participated in these activities because their salaries had been eroded considerably). As a result certain sectors of the community, particularly tribal sheikhs and nouveau riche entrepreneurs, prospered, as did Fallujah. The United States put an end to the practice, irritating a large element of the population. All the propaganda about reconstruction notwithstanding, the United States was unable to provide an alternative source of gainful employment or income.

Of course, Saddam's return-to-faith campaign in the mid-1990s merely highlighted and consolidated the conservative Islamic image of the city. He used state funds to renovate old mosques and build new ones. Another unintended consequence of the erosion of state surveillance over conservative Sunni Muslim cities like Fallujah and the state's promotion of religion was the emergence of extremist Sunni tendencies. In the late 1990s the city witnessed a steady increase in the number of Salafists. The regime wanted to revitalize religion; it did not wish to revitalize a religious extremism that would come to haunt it as an ideological threat. But the regime's ferocious coercive apparatus of the 1970s and 1980s had deteriorated. Moreover, the re-emergence of strong kinship ties and religious indoctrination had replaced loyalty to the regime. Hazem al-Amin, a well-known Arab journalist with the London-based Arabic daily *Al-Hayat*, quotes a Fallujah native: 'My oldest brother is a member of these groups, and he was discharged from the army for his affiliation to these people and he became unemployed, and he started to spend most of his time in the mosque. The Baathists were closely following him, and whenever they could they would arrest some of the members of this group ... My oldest brother was never imprisoned because my youngest brother was a member of the Baathist party, and he always protected him.'[68]

Finally, neither the occupation authorities in Baghdad nor the Bush administration acknowledged that Iraqi distaste for the international community—particularly the United Nations, the United States and Great Britain—had become ingrained in the psyche of many Iraqis, excepting the Kurds. People have forgotten or conveniently ignore the fact that during the first Gulf war between the Iraqis and a previous US- and British-led Coalition in 1991 a British Tornado airplane dropped a bomb intended for a key river bridge in Fallujah on a market in the city. The fact that the death toll of 130 civilians—a number verified by human rights organizations—may account for some of the suspicion and visceral hatred for foreign occupiers is also conveniently forgotten or ignored as observers focus on Fallujah's supposedly fanatical devotion to the former regime. The omens for a positive interaction between the local residents and the occupation forces were not good, but the slide into confrontation was the distinct product of policies on the part of the occupiers.

The dissolution of the Iraqi armed forces by the occupation authorities in the summer of 2003—discussed in detail below—was devastating to a city that had many men in the armed forces. The anger among the former military men of the city was evident at the height of summer. A Western journalist refers to Ahmed Ismael, an Iraqi army officer from Fallujah who found himself out of work and with a grim future after Bremer dissolved the Iraqi army. Ismael has nine children and, like many other military personnel whose world collapsed in May 2003, he spends much of his time in coffee shops. Another officer expressed his frustration and anger thus: 'I used to have more than a thousand men under my command. Now, I sit here with nothing to do. Of course, I'm angry at the Americans who took away everything I had.'[69] The dissolution of the Iraqi army threw those members of the former military from the area around Fallujah on the mercies of their richer relatives who had grown prosperous under the era of smuggling. Abu Basel complained bitterly: 'I am retired army officer, I was imprisoned for ten years in Iran during the battle of Qadissiah, and I was released three years ago. Now I am unemployed after the dismantling of the army, and I have not been paid 100 dollars during the past six months. I am a father of nine children and I have a wife.'[70] Farhan al-Muhammadi, a Fallujah native and key figure in the former Ba'th Party who became a major insurgent leader, found disgruntled officers such as Abu Basel to be fertile soil for recruitment into the insurgency.[71]

Attacks on US troops were common from May 2003 onwards and the US military began to see the entire city as enemy territory. This is a normal and understandable reaction; unfortunately, it perpetuated the cycle of violence. The propaganda or mutual perceptions acted to raise the level of hostility and contempt. In the words of a Fallujah farmer: 'They are occupiers. They have no morals, absolutely none. We've gone from Saddam Hussein to George Bush.' Fallujah's clerics did not work to lower tempers but actually helped to raise them. The cleric of the Khaleed ibn Walid Mosque praised the first serious attack on US troops by insurgents in Fallujah on 27 May, in which two soldiers were killed and nine wounded. The cleric was reported to have said: 'We're all with the resistance against the occupation. The Americans are occupiers. Occupiers cannot come and provide people with happiness and freedom.'[72] In October 2003 US forces arrested a leading cleric, Sheikh Jamal Shaker, for inflammatory statements calling for *jihad* against the United States.

Insurgent fighters in Fallujah echoed such anti-Coalition sentiments. A *mujahid* named 'Mohammed', a former student of foreign languages at Baghdad University, told a Western journalist that he had welcomed the downfall of Saddam at the hands of the Americans, but that the latter 'should have left Iraq immediately [after the war]'. He proceeded to rhetorically question the journalist: 'How would you feel if French soldiers or Arab soldiers invaded your city, and killed your friends, your family? We won't stop fighting until the occupation ends.'[73] The tribes around Fallujah had begun to turn against the Americans because of the daily affronts to tribal honor and pride, things that, if fixed, would have helped lessen the hatred. As Sheikh Hamad Mutlaq of the Jumali tribe said, 'The hatred toward the Americans was heightened when they started to arrest the sheiks and insult them in front of their people—even in front of women.'[74]

For a large number of Sunni Arabs in areas other than Fallujah, particularly those who were associated with the former regime and also for Islamists, the logic of the situation—that is, a foreign occupation—demanded a nationalist and religious response. Thus violence escalated over the course of the summer of 2003. Initially, confusion reigned concerning the nature and identity of the attackers.[75] US casualties in May 2003 were five killed and twenty-two wounded; twenty were killed and thirty-nine wounded in June. The military responded by massive raids or search and cordon operations such as Operation Peninsula north of Baghdad, Operation Scorpion west of Baghdad, and Operation Sidewinder in western and central Iraq. US troops arrested hundreds of suspects and proclaimed optimistically that they were gaining ground. These operations netted many suspects, including many mid-level Ba'th Party operatives who had been providing command and control and funds for the insurgents. However, a senior US Central Command (CENTCOM) officer spoke too soon when he reported at the end of July, 'I think we're at the hump now. I think we could be over the hump fairly quickly.' A combat officer out in the field with the 4th Infantry Division echoed that sentiment: 'I think we are fixing to turn the corner. I think the operations over the next couple of weeks will get us there.'[76]

Despite the optimism, top Bush administration officials acknowledged in late summer 2003 that their plans for postwar Iraq had been flawed on the security front. They admitted that little thought was given to the possibility of resistance. 'Every briefing on postwar Iraq I attended never mentioned any of this,' said a civilian policy advisor.[77] A chastened Paul Wolfowitz, then Deputy Secretary of State, said: '… it was difficult to imagine before the war that the criminal gang of sadists and gangsters who have run Iraq for 35 years would continue fighting, fighting what has been called a guerilla war.'[78] General Richard Myers, chairman of the Joint Chiefs of Staff, defended the country's lack of preparation for this kind of war, arguing: 'This enemy is not like any enemy we've fought before. They are still very shrewd, and they are still evil.'[79] It is not clear that this is accurate; the United States has fought shrewder and better-organized irregular enemies than the Iraqi insurgents. The Bush administration was simply not expecting a wily and determined enemy in Iraq.

It was inevitable that people would begin to make reference to a Vietnam-like quagmire. Although no two insurgencies are alike, it is a fruitful academic, policy and operational exercise to compare and contrast. It was simply incorrect, however, to suggest that the situation on the ground in Iraq approximated that in Vietnam three decades ago. The misrepresentations and policy mistakes and failures of the Iraq war may rival those of the policy-makers who gave us the Vietnam War; we do not, as of now, have the full picture. But one day the full extent of the policy formulations for the war with Iraq will come to light just as they did for the Vietnam War.[80]

However, there are significant differences between these two cases of insurgency.[81] First, there is the disparity in the levels of violence between the two situations. While no one should cast doubt on the horrific violence in Iraq it does not even begin to approximate the levels of the Vietnam War. Second, the Communist side received massive outside support from North Vietnam itself and from the two giants of the Communist world, the Soviet Union and the People's Republic of China. The level of foreign support for the Iraqi insurgency is questionable. Third, the Iraqi insurgents are certainly not on the same level as the Viet Cong in terms of organization and combat effectiveness. Fourth, the impact of the Iraq war on domestic politics in the United States has not, as of yet, become the problem for the Bush administration that the Vietnam War was for the presidencies of Lyndon Johnson and Richard Nixon. Statements by senior officers like General John Abizaid that the violence in Iraq approached 'classic guerilla warfare' were closer to the mark than the facile comparisons made with Vietnam and indicated a clear understanding of the ominous trend in the security situation in Iraq.

As the security situation in the country deteriorated Bush administration officials latched onto every positive event as a sign that better times were ahead. The formation in July 2003 of the IGC, which was to share power with the CPA and which consisted of handpicked key political figures was expected to assuage Iraqi anger and humiliation at occupation. Instead, many viewed the IGC with disdain: it was composed largely of exiles, it had a sectarian tinge, and moreover, it did nothing to restore law and order and stability. The insurgency continued to grow. The deaths of Saddam Hussein's two violent sons, Uday and Qusay, in a firefight in Mosul in July 2003 was seen as having dealt a decisive blow to the burgeoning insurgency of the former regime elements because the two were alleged to be key players. Their deaths had no appreciable negative impact on the insurgency; indeed, it spiked.

By late summer 2003 the security situation in the country had deteriorated markedly as the insurgents branched out into targeting high-value and high-visibility foreign targets and critical economic installations. Among the most important targets were the Jordanian embassy, bombed on 7 August, and the UN headquarters at the Canal Hotel, during the destruction of which on 19 August the UN chief in Iraq was killed. It was unclear who carried out the devastating attack on the UN headquarters, but there was no shortage of culprits:

Iraqis who watched their once-comfortable living standards collapse over the past 12 years under the impact of U.N. sanctions have a rather different perspective on that organization than the rest of the world. Saddam's regime brought those sanctions upon itself by its invasion of Kuwait in 1990, but since Iraqis never chose Saddam in any meaningful sense they feel no blame for that crime—and they certainly bore the punishment. The Iraqi resistance does not discredit itself at home by attacking the UN.[82]

However, a shadowy group called the Army of Muhammad (see p. 156 for more details) claimed responsibility for the attack on the UN headquarters in an audiotape it sent to the Lebanese Broadcasting Corporation, stating that a unit from the Abdallah Bin Iyad Brigade was directly responsible for the operational aspects of the assault. The tape included a warning to the Coalition, read by a masked man:

We warn you to withdraw from our beloved homeland and let our people decide their fate and rebuild what was destroyed by your sinfull [sic] hands. You are wrong and evil. These are your actions. You have taught this people how to hate and steal ... You have tried once again to drive a wedge between the Sunni and Shiites. You have failed ... We swear by God, prophet Muhammad, and Islam, that we will teach you one lesson after the other. You will experience bitter defeat, God willing.[83]

The insurgents also began targeting oil pipelines and water mains, and personnel who worked in any area of the reconstruction process. By late August 2003 many foreign contractors and aid workers had left Iraq. The more dangerous and decrepit their country became in the postwar period the more the Iraqis blamed the Americans. Many wondered how it was that Saddam had managed to get the country up and running relatively efficiently so quickly after the devastation caused by the bombing in the first US-Iraqi war, in 1991.[84]

If sabotage hindered reconstruction then the United States would be discredited and the frustration of the Iraqi populace would increase further. In mid-August 2003, Paul Bremer said: 'We could and did anticipate we would have criminality, we knew we would have some resistance from the old regime, we knew we would have some terrorism—but I am a little uncomfortable with the amount of terrorism we have seen and the number of terrorists we are seeing coming in.'[85] By fall and winter 2003 matters had become worse. The violence in Iraq naturally set back reconstruction.

Some of the insurgent attacks in early summer 2003 were undertaken by professional groups.[86] However, the majority were perpetrated by amateurs and cash-strapped individuals hired by former regime loyalists to carry out hit-and-run attacks. First, the insurgents got more proficient. US forces had killed most of the 'dumb' ones; the tactics, techniques and procedures (TTPs) of the surviving insurgents became more lethal as a result of experience.[87] Second, their proficiency had also increased as a result of the role of former professional military personnel who increasingly opted for the path of violence out of nationalistic and religious reasons. By fall these disgruntled military personnel—with no profound sympathy for the defunct regime but outraged over the loss of status, privilege and jobs as a result of the disbanding of the armed forces in May 2003—were increasingly active in the ranks of the insurgency. Given the professionalism of some of the ambushes and attacks carried out by insurgents in and around cities like Tikrit and Ramadi—recruiting grounds for many of the better soldiers in the former Iraqi armed forces—it was clear that military personnel had either trained the attackers or participated in the attacks. Senior or mid-ranking officers would often act as mentors or advisers for cells of novice but enthusiastic insurgents.

By fall 2003 the violence had captured the attention of the Bush administration, the military and of the media as a result of spectacular and bloody attacks on US/Coalition forces, nongovernmental organizations (NGOs) and Iraqis working with the Coalition. In October 2003, administration officials began admitting that they were surprised by the intensity and resilience of the insurgency.[88] In early November 2003 dire prognostications began to appear, especially from US intelligence agencies such as the Central Intelligence Agency (CIA), which argued that the insurgency was gaining support among the populace.[89] November 2003 was a terrible month in terms of casualties for the United States.[90] The response of US forces was to go after the former regime insurgents with greater vigor. By the end of November 2003 understanding the insurgency and dealing with it had risen to the top of the US agenda. The capture of Saddam Hussein himself in early December 2003 was regarded as a significant victory against the insurgents because of the important role the former leader was alleged to have played. Instead, the Coalition discovered that the former Iraqi leader had played more of a symbolic role for the former regime insurgents than an active role in directing it. The hope that his capture would usher in 2004 on a positive note for the country was to be dashed. Another, opposite belief suggested that the former dictator's capture would actually release the insurgency from his brooding shadow and transform it into a nationalist one. Neither theory was borne out in reality. Violence escalated, but the insurgency did not become nationalist. The end of the road for Saddam did not mean an end to the Ba'thist element of the insurgency. Moreover, many of the Islamic-nationalist insurgents blamed the party and the former regime for the disasters that have befallen the country. Pessimism was at an all-time high by early fall 2004; a leading policy analyst, Anthony Cordesman, termed the US occupation a 'dismal failure'.

The evolution of the insurgency in 2004. Iraq was roiled by political turmoil and a significant upsurge in the insurgency in 2004. By the end of 2003 the CPA was beset by growing demands on the part of the Iraqi population for more meaningful progress towards a restoration of Iraqi sovereignty. These demands accelerated in early 2004 and an agreement was reached to return the country to the Iraqis at the end of June 2004. On 28 June the CPA was dissolved and an interim government under US ally Iyad Allawi as Prime Minister took over. These steps are explored in detail in Chapter 5, but suffice it to say that these negotiations and political agreements and the restoration of sovereignty had no visible impact on diminishing the insurgency.

Indeed, 2004 was a particularly bloody year in Iraq, with a spike in terrorism and in the insurgency. It was characterized by a surge in the kidnapping of civilians, the assassination of Iraqis working with the Coalition, the steady drumbeat of deaths among the hapless Iraqi security forces who were targeted again and again, and the gruesome executions of Iraqi and foreign hostages. However, the focal point of the insurgency was the city of Fallujah, which was to become the hub of two major battles, the first in April 2004 and the second in November of that year.

In early April 2004 four Americans working for a major private security company were murdered in Fallujah. The execution of these four US contractors and their grisly mutilation made the city a byword for barbarity. One resident said: 'This is a bad advertisement for everything we stand for. We may hate Americans. We may hate them with all our hearts. But all men are creatures of God.'[91] An Iraqi policeman in Fallujah gave the usual excuses of the illtrained and timid Iraqi police force as to why they refused to get involved: 'What happened was between Americans and insurgents. If we got involved, we would have been killed.'[92] The local Iraqi Civil Defense Corps was headquartered close to where the incident took place, yet they made no effort to come to the rescue of the trapped contractors. Even if we were to grant them the excuse that they could not have done much to prevent the ambush, they could have prevented the barbarity that was inflicted upon the corpses.

The United States was determined to teach the city's inhabitants a lesson and prepared to move into the city. The bloody battle in Fallujah in April 2004 is, perhaps, a microcosm of the evolutionary cycle of an insurgent group: that is, to maneuver your conventional opponent into a position in which whatever option it takes represents a political defeat, even if the insurgents are beaten *militarily*. Hundreds of insurgents congregated in the town, particularly in the Jolan neighborhood. They were well-armed and motivated, and many were well-trained. They dug in and decided to make a stand in this city of 300,000 inhabitants. The United States had four options in dealing with the city: to lay siege to it and bombard it till it surrendered; to take it in a potentially bloody urban assault; to walk away; or to negotiate a deal with the defenders. None of these was palatable to the United States because whichever option it decided upon would ultimately represent a defeat.

Laying siege to the city and bombarding it till it surrendered would have had a negative effect inside Iraq and overseas. Indeed, the relatively constrained application of US military force during the battle was a public relations disaster (the Americans were heavily criticised by their Iraqi allies), a portent of what would have occurred if the United States had gone for an all-out siege. To cite just one possible outcome, the Governing Council would probably have totally unravelled.

The United States could have launched an urban assault, which would have been costly in terms of casualties to the Marines, the insurgents and the civilian population. It would have destroyed the city—and totally destroyed US credibility—but also would have resulted in the elimination of a considerable number of the insurgents.[93] Walking away was not an option for the United States because that would have represented both a political and a military defeat. Ultimately the United States negotiated with the insurgents via intermediaries to bring about a cessation of hostilities. This end result was viewed as a major political and military victory by the insurgents and the inhabitants of Fallujah, who were their staunch supporters. It was a political victory because the United States had backed down and more importantly it had negotiated with the enemy. One of the key things that all insurgent movements crave in the course of their conflict with their adversary is *recognition*. The insurgents believed that they had also won militarily because they had fought the United States to a standstill. It matters little that both sides knew that the razing or taking of the city was within the capabilities of the US military. The fact remains that the cost would have been too high, and a US military victory under those circumstances would have been no win. By contrast, the insurgents won because they were undefeated and emerged intact to fight another day.

That year also witnessed a Shi'a insurgency when the cleric Moqtada al-Sadr launched two abortive uprisings, in April and August. The situation in Iraq in early spring 2004 was certainly grim. Sunni insurgents from the Baghdad suburb of Adhamiya joined with Shi'a insurgents of the heavily Shi'a suburb of Khadimiya across the Tigris to launch attacks on the US presence.[94] The Americans faced one of their most violent days in Iraq to date on 6 April 2004, when twelve troops were killed in Ramadi, ten of them from one Marine unit, Echo Company. Meanwhile, in the south Moqtada al-Sadr urged his fighters on against the US and Coalition forces: 'America has shown its evil intentions and the proud Iraqi people cannot accept it. They must defend their rights by any means they see fit.'[95] The Mahdi Army (or Jaish al-Mahdi) had easily rolled over Iraqi security forces in Kufa, Najaf, Nasiriyah, Basra and Sadr City and taken over government offices in many places. In Kufa, Moqtada's militia completely replaced the police and security forces.[96]

The tough US tactics in Fallujah and Shi'a holy cities in the fighting of spring 2004 threatened to drive a major wedge between the United States and the twenty-five-member IGC. Adnan Pachachi, a well-respected Sunni Arab politician, criticized US actions and called them 'illegal and totally unacceptable'.[97] The violence of spring 2004 and the Coalition response elicited concern and pessimism among a wide range of observers. 'We need a fast turnaround and we need it right away. We are on the brink of failure,' said retired General Joseph Hoar before the US Senate. Anthony Cordesman, one of the best-known strategic commentators on the Middle East, argued that there was the threat of 'a serious strategic defeat'.[98] The lofty goals of the conflict—assuming that they were really held by the architects of the war—were fading fast from the agenda by mid-2004. As Noah Feldman, a fluent Arabic-speaker, New York University professor and one-time advisor to the hapless occupation authorities, said: 'At this point the most optimistic definition of success—the warmest, fuzziest dreams of Paul Wolfowitz—I think are thoroughly dashed. The creation of a liberal, secular democracy was never realistic and it's understood that it's not going to happen.'[99] Abdul Jalil Mohsen, a former Iraqi general and member of the Iraqi National Accord, a prominent group represented on the IGC, reflected on the collapse of the security situation in the country in spring 2004: 'We could not imagine the deterioration leading to such a point. It's getting worse day after day, and no one has been able to put an end to it. Who is going to protect the next government, no matter what kind it is?'[100] Among officials inside the Green Zone (the main base for Coalition officials, in central Baghdad) the mood was grim: 'It will take a lot of doing for this not to end in a debacle. There is no confidence in the coalition. Why should there be?'[101]

The CPA was dissolved on 28 June 2004 and L. Paul Bremer, the proconsul who had come to rule Iraq with high hopes almost fourteen months before but had been outmaneuvered by an unassuming senior Shi'a cleric time and time again, quietly left a country that was in a shambles, wracked by rampant violence, and had an appointed interim government headed by the pro-US former Ba'thist Iyad Allawi. Although Iraqis admired Allawi for his toughness—he had survived a vicious assassination attempt by agents of the former regime—his government was to have little or no traction with the majority of the Iraqi people.[102]

Between the handover of power to the transitional government in mid-2004 and the end of that year, insurgents devoted considerable effort to killing those whom they saw as collaborators. One of the most gruesome incidents came in mid-September 2004, when a car bomb killed forty-seven people and injured 114 others outside the Al-Karkh police station. Most of the victims were policemen or police recruits. This kind of carnage may ultimately backfire on its perpetrators. One Iraqi witness to this incident told a Western journalist: 'What happened here has really nothing to do with Islam. Why are these people targeting Iraqi police recruits? They just want to get a salary because they are unemployed. The people who did this are terrorists.'[103]

But fortunately the nightmare scenario that caused senior US officials and officers so many sleepless nights, namely a 'coordinated Shiite and Sunni uprising', did not happen.[104] The ugly word 'quagmire', first used when the insurgency emerged full-scale in fall 2003, began reappearing with depressing frequency.[105] In late summer and early fall 2004 observers of the Iraqi scene concluded that the insurgency was not letting up, and that indeed it was more lethal than before the handover of sovereignty to the interim government of Iyad Allawi. The guile and skill of the insurgents seemed to have increased as well, leading one senior US Marine officer to state: 'No one is underestimating our opponents. These guys are adaptive. They learn. They are creative.'[106] Some officials and officers, though, professed to see a silver lining even then. Their optimism was built on the historically based belief that it takes time and patience to subdue insurgents. However, the optimistic claims of the Allawi government and the Bush administration that things were proceeding smoothly in Iraq were belied by data that showed considerable insecurity throughout much of the country.[107]

In fall 2004 a city more important than Fallujah, Ramadi (capital of the unstable Anbar Province), was consumed by severe violence. Insurgent attacks had eliminated Iraqi government control over the city and slowly but surely eroded its administrative infrastructure. The provincial governor's three sons had been kidnapped, and were released only after he had resigned. The deputy governor of the province was kidnapped and killed. The president of the regional university and other key officials were kidnapped. Ten contractors working for the United States were killed. Posters directed at members of the National Guard and police appeared on the walls of mosques, simply stating: 'Quit or we'll kill you.'[108]

Another city that caused concern was Samarra. In early October 2004 US forces, in conjunction with Iraqi security forces, launched a strike on the city. This was meant as a dress rehearsal for the coming assault on the key insurgent and terrorist stronghold of Fallujah.[109] Indeed, despite the violence in the Sunni cities of Ramadi and Samarra, Fallujah continued to be the focus of attention of both the Coalition and the interim Iraqi government.

In November 2004 the United States decided to retake Fallujah from the insurgents. It was hoped that the recapture of this key insugent sanctuary and the elimination of hundreds of fighters would break the back of the insurgency. The first battle of Fallujah had ended unsatisfactorily from viewpoint of the Bush administration and US Army, both of which increasingly felt the city should have been assaulted in April.

Foreign insurgents and their Iraqi supporters continued to conduct operations against the Coalition in defiance of the desires of Fallujah's elders. Colonel Fadil al-Janabi, the city's chief of police, complained to a senior cleric that his men were being intimidated by the jihadists, many of whom were Saudis. The local *mujahideen* or *muqawamah* (resistance) had also had enough of the Salafi-jihadists. The foreign insurgents who established a base of operations in Fallujah could not have done so without the support of or acceptance by local Iraqis who shared a similar worldview or beliefs. One of the leading insurgent leaders in Fallujah was Omar Hussein Hadid, an electrician around thirty years of age whose Salafist tendencies had drawn the attention of the Ba'thist security services long before the overthrow of the regime. Hadid's mentor in the 1990s, Muhammad al-Issawi, had fought on the side of the Chechens in the first insurgency in the early 1990s. When he returned to Iraq he took Hadid under his wing and together they launched a campaign against sinful behavior in Fallujah, threatening owners of beauty parlors and music stores. They blew up the only movie theater in the city. The Ba'th regime killed Issawi but Hadid escaped, though not before allegedly murdering a senior Ba'th official from Fallujah in revenge. Little is known about his whereabouts between the mid-1990s and the downfall of the Hussein regime, when he returned to Fallujah to open an electrical store. He did not remain in business long; when the insurgency erupted Hadid gathered together a small informal 'army' of like-minded insurgents.

Nonetheless, this nexus between foreign extremists and some Iraqis did not necessarily succeed in gaining the sympathy or support of those local self-professed nationalist insurgents. There were reports that the *mujahideen* themselves were trying to form a political wing. Talib Saha, a member of the local insurgents, seemed to be enamored of the Irish Republican Army: 'We like the way the IRA was able to enter in politics and have ministers in charge of government, like Martin McGuinness.'[110] Australian journalist Michael Ware, who did some brilliant reporting from Iraq, met with a number of Iraqi insurgent groups, including, it seems with one of the more sophisticated and better-organized ones. Its members told him that they do not trust the foreign fighters and that many are neither trained nor skilled enough to be insurgents.[111]

Nonetheless, to the consternation of its inhabitants and local fighters, Fallujah had come under the sway of militant and extremist groups that imposed a theocratic reign of terror. Leaflets that were distributed from Salafist-dominated mosques contained exhortations such as: 'In the name of God, kill them wherever they are and never take them as friends or allies. For those who have no honor and who prefer Jews to Muslims, it is just to spill their blood. You will suffer mighty and punishing blows. Now, go!' Such leaflets always included the names of Fallujan natives who had allegedly collaborated with the 'infidel' occupier, and included individuals from a wide range of the city's population. Having one's name appear on leaflets distributed by insurgents did little for one's longevity, and many people either disappeared or were killed. The local Iraqi Salafists whose mosques and activities were financed by funds received from 'charities' in the Gulf and local sympathetic merchants were stiffened by a group of Jordanian, Saudi and Yemeni Salafists. Their center seemed to be the al-Falahat quarter in the city. There was little love lost between some of the insurgents who had been part of the former regime—and Fallujah had provided the regime with many security and military personnel—and the Salafist opposition to the 'infidel' occupation. As one Salafist *imam* in the city, Sheikh Ahmed Abbas al-Issawi, indignantly framed it: 'Us, unite our forces with those of Saddam? A man who tried to support Milosevic against our Muslim brothers in the former

Yugoslavia!'[112] The sheikh proceeded to disclose why he believed the Salafists were the most powerful opponents of the US presence by stating that they had no fear of martyrdom as they fought to chase the invaders and unbelievers out of Muslim lands.[113]

By June 2004 Fallujah took on the trappings of an Islamic mini-republic that lived largely according to its own rules, namely those of the extremist Islamist elements of the insurgency supported by foreign jihadist fighters and radical preachers. They imposed draconian religious edicts governing daily life, edged out the more moderate insurgent groups and drowned the voices of the tribal sheikhs, who as a group tend more towards bargaining and conciliatory behavior. That very month insurgents, most likely Islamist extremists, attacked and wounded a dozen members of the Fallujah Brigade, which was made up of former insurgents.[114] In June 2004 a jihadist website claimed that the *mujahideen* in Fallujah had pledged loyalty to Zarqawi in a ceremony allegedly attended by the master terrorist himself; the Al-Fallujah principality, which had been divided among the insurgent factions, 'pledged to al-Zarqawi to continue their forward march until death to create the Islamic caliphate in Al-Fallujah, followed by the rest of Iraq and the neighboring Arab and Muslim countries'.[115]

In late summer and early fall 2004 it became very clear that the United States and the interim Iraqi government were going to act decisively in Fallujah. Indeed, Lieutenant General John Sattler of the US Marine Corps was quoted as saying 'the status quo in Fallujah cannot stand'.[116] First, the local Iraqi forces that were supposed to take over security and stability were either intimidated by or had joined the insurgents. Thus the city was not even under nominal government control. Second, by late summer this rebellious city had been fully transformed into an insurgent sanctuary. One of the principles of insurgency warfare is the requirement for sanctuaries, which can be either internal (within the country in question) or external (in neighboring states). The Iraqi insurgency has no external sanctuaries, so the insurgents realize that their only safeholds are in the urban jungle of Iraq's cities. Sanctuaries allow the consolidation of power from which to strike out at other parts of the country. Indeed, Fallujah became an indoctrination and training center, an arms depot, and a 'processing' station for foreign fighters. Third, Fallujah was perceived to be the sanctuary not only for local insurgents, but also for the extremist terrorist groups whose kidnapping of foreigners and Iraqis was capped by gruesome beheadings that came to dominate the media in late summer and fall 2004. The internal and international revulsion at these acts made it seemingly easier to take the final decision to root out a burgeoning 'nest of terrorism'. Finally, Fallujah had to be secured as a prelude to ensuring stability and security in the Sunni-dominated center of the country in readiness for the general elections of 30 January 2005, which it was hoped would begin the process of creating a new and independent stable and secure post-Saddam Iraq.

In this context, something drastic had to be done to reduce the violence, and because its 'epicenter' was Fallujah an example had to be made of it. Senior officials of the Bush administration, for whom the idea of reducing the political power and importance of the Sunni Arabs was part of their unstated ideological vision for post-Saddam Iraq, were not averse to the liberal use of force to teach this intractable Sunni outpost a lesson.

The insurgents varied in their tactical abilities and proficiency during the November 2004 fight. In some places the insurgents seemed disciplined and cohesive, in others they would expose themselves needlessly and suffer the consequences. Insurgent mortar fire was much more accurate in November 2004 than it had been in April. The myriad insurgent groups in Fallujah seemed to have divided the city into four distinct defensive zones, each of which represented different groups. The northern zone was

defended by former members of the Iraqi military, including former Special Forces and Republican Guard members, organized
into a group known as the *maghawir al-fatah* (victorious commandos). These units were divided into the following kinds of combat
units, each having a specific task. The first type was an anti-infantry
unit to engage advancing Coalition infantry forces, and which was
armed with a medium machine-gun, a sniper and a heavy machine-
gun. The number of men was not specified but was probably three.
The second type was an anti-mechanized unit to engage Coalition
armor, and which had two RPG-7 triggermen, two medium ma-
chine-gunners, and two men each armed with a 40-millimetre grenade launcher. All in all, superior US firepower and training paid
off against the insurgents, who were by no means lightly armed
when it came to face-to-face firefights. The insurgents were, however, unable to match the full panoply of firepower that US troops
could call upon. When insurgent units proved difficult to dislodge,
US forces called upon air, tank and artillery strikes to facilitate the
process. After two days of fighting, US forces managed to wrest
control of a third of the city of Fallujah from insurgents.[117]

Many insurgents and their leaders fled Fallujah before the start
of the US-led offensive in early November 2004. This seemed to
be confirmed by a mid-ranking insurgent leader—a major in the
former Iraqi army—with the *nom de guerre* Abu Khalid, who in an
interview with a journalist said: 'From a military point of view, if
a city is surrounded and bombarded, then the result of the battle
is preordained. It is not a balanced battle. So we told half of our
fighters to leave the city and the other half to stay and defend it.'
Abu Khalid claimed that a debate had taken place among the insurgent leaders about how many fighters should leave the city and how
many should be evacuated to fight elsewhere: 'There were different
views about that. They discussed percentages like 20 percent inside
the city and 80 percent outside, to save as many fighters as possible

for future operations. In the end, they settled on a 50-50 split.'[118] After the US takeover of Fallujah, many insurgents dispersed into the various towns and villages that dot the Euphrates River. The town of Haditha, about 140 miles northwest of Baghdad, remains a way station for foreign jihadists coming into Iraq across the desert from Syria. It is barely functioning, because the police and municipal workers have either gone into hiding or turned their backs on their jobs due to insurgent threats.[119] Key leaders like Abdallah al-Janabi and Omar Hadid initially were reported to have been killed; subsequent reports indicated that they had escaped to reorganize their groups. Al-Janabi was said to have fled back to his ancestral town of Yusufiyah, just south of Baghdad. The whereabouts of Omar Hadid are unknown; he could have disappeared into the deeply entrenched insurgent network in Mosul or may have sought sanctuary among the insurgent network in Syria.

The Bush administration, the US military and outside observers thought that the collapse of Fallujah as a sanctuary would constitute a crushing blow for the insurgency. In fact the assault on Fallujah enraged and further alienated the Sunni community,[120] while the glee with which the Kurds and Shi'a greeted the city's downfall drove another wedge between them and the Sunnis.

In November and December 2004 the violence, far from being reduced by the assault on Fallujah, actually spread far beyond the city to other relatively quiet areas and cities.[121] The insurgents who had escaped continued to launch attacks elsewhere from their refuges in centers along the Euphrates. Outside Fallujah the insurgents struck back at different towns, killing scores of Iraqis and six American soldiers in Baghdad and Samarra, among other places.[122] Mosul, Iraq's third-largest city, witnessed a horrific descent into chaos and barbarity—with vicious attacks on officials, security forces and election workers—before US forces managed to restore some semblance of order by mid-January 2005.[123]

In 2004 there were also devastating attacks on the Shi'a Arab community by extremist Sunni Islamists whose goal was to foment intersectarian violence between Sunnis and Shi'a. For Sunni extremists such as Abu Musab al-Zarqawi, the much sought-after Jordanian terrorist who heads the Iraqi branch of Al Qaeda, the promotion of sectarian violence was justified on several grounds and served a number of purposes. The Shi'a were attacked on religious grounds, for allegedly having strayed from true Islam. But the attacks on the Shi'a were not motivated solely by religious differences. Some groups within the insurgency excoriated the Shi'a for their alleged support of the occupation and for participating in attacks against the resistance. The hatred for the Shi'a among the extremist religious elements of the insurgent and terror groups was more openly displayed after the assault on Fallujah, where the Shi'a community was castigated either for staying on the sidelines or for participating in the assault through membership of the Iraqi security forces, which had a minor role in the urban battle. Abu Musab al-Zarqawi stated: 'The battle of Fallujah removed the ugly mask of the damned Rafidha [a derogatory term for Shi'a among Sunni extremists], whose hatred [for Sunnis] was manifested in this battle.'[124] Mainstream Sunni Arab insurgent and politically active groups did not use such inflammatory language but they made it clear that they viewed the Shi'a participation in the attack on Fallujah in a very poor light. Finally, the attacks on the Shi'a were designed to goad them into a counterresponse, one that would increase the level of violence immeasurably, render the US presence untenable and thwart the elections planned for January 2005.[125]

Political developments and the insurgency from January to August 2005. As the landmark elections of 30 January 2005 drew close the insurgents and terrorist groups such as that of Abu Musab al-Zarqawi increased the tempo of their attacks against Iraqi security forces and polling stations. This was part of their declared strategy to disrupt the elections. In the two weeks prior to the elections, insurgents vastly stepped up their warnings to Iraqis about voting. One insurgent group, the so-called Higher Command for Jihad—Iraq, which seemed to be an umbrella organization for a dizzying mix of nationalist and Islamist insurgent subgroups, issued a warning on the Internet to the Iraqi population:

This is an urgent call to the people of Iraq about the so-called election operations in Iraq. A warning not to approach the polling centers, from the north to the south of Iraq. All polling stations will be targeted for up to one thousand meters by the Iraqi Army fighters, the Republican Guards Forces, the heroic Special Guards Forces, the courageous National Security Forces, Hussein's Fedayeen fighters, the Iraqi National and Islamic Resistance, and the noble Arab volunteers. These areas will be attacked with all kinds of weapons and bombs in specific operations.[126]

To back up their warnings many of the groups across the country launched attacks, including assaults in the southern Shi'a-dominated towns such as Numaniyah, Kut and Basra.[127] Zarqawi's group claimed more than 100 attacks in January 2005 alone. Fortunately the insurgents did not manage to disrupt the voting on 30 January. While there was a significant number of suicide attacks, the stringent security measures in effect may have stymied the ability of the insurgents to operate freely.[128] Determined to brave threats issued by insurgents, Shi'a Arabs, Sunni Kurds and other minorities turned out in high numbers to vote.[129] But the relatively low Sunni Arab turnout was a reflection of Sunni fears of marginalization in the post-Saddam era and of intimidation by insurgents and terrorist groups.[130] It was also symptomatic of their cynicism about and contempt for the entire process, which they saw as selling out Iraq to US and Iranian interests. Large numbers of Iraqi Arabs, Sunni and Shi'a, viewed the two main parties of the Shi'a slate, Dawa and the Supreme Council for the Islamic Revolution in Iraq (SCIRI), which won the majority of seats in the new national assembly, as fronts for Iran. Many Shi'a, especially those who followed Moqtada, regarded the United Iraqi Coalition (UIA) as 'an Iranian list'. US officials hope that the Kurds, who received the second-largest vote in the election, will check the rising power of the Shi'a.

Although the election was accorded the great significance it deserved, few predicted that the immediate post-election environment would see a diminution of the insurgency.[131] Nonetheless, there was a fervent hope among both the Iraqis and US officials that the post-election period would witness a decisive turn against the insurgency. In the immediate wake of the elections there was a pervasive optimism among the people and there were reports that citizens were providing the police and National Guard with more information and tips about suspected insurgent activities in their respective neighborhoods.[132]

For two full days after the elections Iraq was relatively peaceful until the insurgents struck back with a vengeance on 2 and 6 February 2005, when they resumed their deadly suicide bombings and assaults on the hapless Iraqi security forces. Unfortunately violence continued unabated. The Shi'a celebration of Ashura in late February 2005 was marked by the deaths of dozens of people in a wave of bombings and suicide attacks. Shi'a leaders called upon their people to continue to show restraint in the face of these provocations by groups seeking to cause sectarian strife between Sunnis and Shi'a. Adel Abdel-Mahdi, a senior SCIRI official, was defiant: 'We are not going to raise our arms because we are attacked, or because Zarqawi and others want to push us into civil war.'[133] The number of security personnel killed in May was unprecedented in scale: 151 police were killed that month in contrast with 86 in April; 325 were wounded in May in contrast with 131 in April; while 434 civilians were killed in terrorist attacks in May, up from 299 in April, according to a Health Ministry official.

With successful elections, many Iraqis began looking at the US presence with a critical eye. US intelligence circles predicted that the Iraqis would press for withdrawal of foreign forces following the elections. US intelligence, however, is remarkable for the consistency with which it has been wrong. The situation in Iraq was more complicated and required a more nuanced approach. Indeed, while many Iraqis ideally would like to see the Coalition leave, most did not think the United States was going to withdraw any time soon after the elections. They pointed to the continued US presence in Germany and Japan. The United States is in Iraq, goes the deeply ingrained refrain, to take control of Iraq's oil, help Israel, establish bases close to Iran, and create opportunities for US businesses. 'We wish they would go. But we know the Americans. We know their history: wherever the Americans go, they never leave easily. They establish bases and stay.' What is curious, though, is the remarkably schizophrenic Iraqi attitude towards the US presence, because many Iraqis, including those who routinely castigate and complain about it, believe that it is only the United States that prevents the country slipping further and further into chaos. Said one Iraqi: 'Let's be frank. When they go in the streets, blocking traffic and waving their guns, the people don't like them here. People look at them as imperialists. But, right now, the Americans are a must. If they leave, we will end up with a second Taliban in Iraq.'

The Sunni Arab nonparticipation was, of course, bound to have political implications.[134] Abdel Salam al-Kubaisi, a member of the AMS, believes that for the Sunni minority 'the crux of the problem is the occupation'.[135] He continues: 'If there is a timetable for withdrawal backed by international guarantees, we can appeal to the majority of the resistance fighters and most of them would heed the call to stop. We could spare the blood of our sons and people. If there is no timetable the occupation will be permanent. We all know that under occupation, there is no chance for any legitimate

Iraqi government.'[136] That may be so, but once again for the Sunni Arabs the situation is complicated by the exquisite dilemma that they face in reality. On the one hand, the US presence targets them because the insurgency stems from that community and because there is a deliberate anti-Sunni Arab bias in the US policy on Iraq. Logically, then, the solution would be to force the United States to withdraw. On the other hand, the US presence protects the Sunni Arabs, as it does the Sunni Kurds, from the tyranny of the majority. Many Shi'a are delighted that the United States is weakening the Sunnis for them, so that they do not have to engage in a massive and brutal counter-insurgency effort in the coming years as they restructure Iraqi identity to reflect their vision. But to some extent this approach is self-defeating. There exists the strong possibility that the Shi'a will be faced with a long-running Sunni Arab insurgency and terror; like the Kurds in the past, the Sunnis will be the spoilers.

Many Sunni Arabs acknowledge that it was a failure of historic proportions that they did not vote. Had they done so they would have diluted the power of the Kurds, who are not really interested in Iraq *per se*, and the Shi'a, who are split over the role of religion in the state. One crestfallen sheikh remarked after the elections: 'We made a big mistake when we didn't vote. Our votes were very important.'[137] To rectify this glaring error the Sunnis began to demand significant positions in the new government and a leading role in the drafting of the proposed constitution.[138]

Many politically active Sunni groups rejected the legitimacy of the elections of 30 January 2005. Logically this means that they could have denied the legitimacy of any government that was to arise as a result of the elections. But instead of focusing on this, as the insurgents did, the politically active Sunni Arab groups sought to mobilize themselves and the population in order to participate in the political arena. More often than not these Sunni groups and the insurgents are proceeding along separate paths. Salah Umar al-Ali, a former official in the Iraqi Ba'th Party, told the Saudi newspaper *Al-Watan*:

The relentless insistence on the importance of Sunni participation in the future authority, and on the inappropriateness of their dismissal, marginalization or other terms to the same effect, is but an attempt to portray the deep crisis in Iraq as being due primarily to the participation or lack of it of one entity or another in the incumbent authority. *Those in power avoid speaking of the core reasons for the current Iraqi crisis and the impossibility of reaching any national solution which grants our people security, stability, and complete sovereignty unless a timeline for the withdrawal of the occupation forces is set.*[139]

Ali points to one of the key weaknesses of the Sunni Arabs, disunity, which is reflected in the wide gap between those who are willing to deal with the United States and those engaging in violent conflict: 'Following the war, the Sunni fighters, who crushed many of Bush's dreams for Iraq, failed to create a cohesive public leadership which could be involved in political affairs or negotiations with the new government. The militants are yet to demonstrate noteworthy willingness to engage in talks, and have constantly attacked US-led forces, the newly born Iraqi security forces, and any Iraqis they deem as collaborators.'[140]

The anxieties of the Sunni Arab community were reflected in the views of important tribal political players such as Mashaan al-Juburi and Abdel Rahman Asi al-Ubaidi. Juburi made it clear that he intended to participate in the elections despite the threats and intimidatory tactics to prevent him from doing so. Convinced that the Shiites would emerge winners, Juburi argued for participation on the grounds that he needed to be in the political process in order to oppose their policies by peaceful means: 'It is better to show people that they can say no and still be a part of the political organization. Otherwise, people will see they have no one in the political system. They will lose hope, and when they lose hope they turn to violence.'[141] Asi, a politician from Kirkuk, was hoping on the other hand for a postponement of the elections so that the Sunnis could organize themselves better, and was adamant that the army should be reconstituted and the Ba'th Party be allowed to participate. Only the traditional pillars of power can offset the Shiite bloc: 'If these political parties, which have their base in Iran, win the election, there will be very dangerous consequences for Iraq.'[142]

Muhsin Abd al-Hamid argued that his party would not have withdrawn had it thought its decision to boycott was incorrect:

Our expectations were vindicated. The elections were incomplete and the figures published by the electoral commission proved this to be true. At least one third of the people in the governorates of Mosul, Salah-al-din, al-Anbar, Diyala, and areas in Kirkuk and Baghdad did not participate. Therefore, we consider these elections flawed in terms of voters' turnout and legitimacy because the council that will emerge as a result of these elections will not represent all of the Iraqis.

Bashar al-Faydi, a spokesman for the AMS, argued:

... we continue to consider the elections illegitimate because they were held under occupation, that they were not fair or just, that not all the Iraqi people's sections participated, and that the elections were supervised by those with vested interests. This opens the door wide for suspicions. Moreover, there are no international observers. What is new is that we were confronted with a handicapped baby. The next government will neither be formed solely by the occupation forces, like the present government, nor will it be the outcome of a free and fair election process under normal criteria ... All the media and experts said that the elections represented a success for Bush. They did not say they were a success for the Iraqi people...[143]

Despite the boycott of the elections, the AMS issued a conciliatory statement that indicated a desire to be included in the formation of a new government.[144] But of course there was still an

adamant insistence on a timetable for the withdrawal of the occupation forces from the country, for reasons summed up by Umar
Raghib, a senior spokesman for the AMS: 'I do not think that the
occupation forces would allow any government to be formed unless this government follows its dictates. The continued presence
of the occupation means that Iraqi blood will continue to be shed
and the Iraqis will continue to lead a sorrowful existence. This is
what we see. Let the occupation leave and then we will be ready
for everything.'[145]

In an interview, Muhsin Abd al-Hamid of the IIP revealed the
depth of the discontent among the Sunnis over the elections. Abd
al-Hamid reiterated the position that the election results represent
only 60 percent of the Iraqi people. The rest, mainly Sunnis who
did not get to vote, had their seats distributed to the winners. The
IIP seems to agree with many Shi'a that because the country is
97 percent Muslim this majority has the 'right to draft the constitution based on the laws of the Islamic nation'. The divine law is
flexible and capable of meeting the demands of the modern world.
Hence, 'the new constitution, which the Iraqi people will daft [sic],
must include a clear role of Islam in life because the popular support for Islam is strong and the vast majority are Muslims. However, we completely agree that other religions and denominations
must have rights in the constitution. The Islamic *sharia* does not
prevent this. No compulsion in matters of religion.'[146] This position is going to place the Sunni Islamists in direct opposition to the
Sunni Kurds. However, in contrast with most of the Shi'a position
on federalism, the IIP supports the Kurdish call for federalism:

We in the Iraqi Islamic Party consider that the Kurds should be involved
in a federation because of their circumstances, their history, and the
atrocities committed against them and the nature of their borders. We
believe that an autonomy or federation for the Kurds will strengthen national unity … They always said that they wanted to be united with us in

a country whose capital will be in Baghdad ... They do not demand secession. They say: our capital is Baghdad, our flag is the Iraqi flag; the army
is one, the treasury, the currency, and the Foreign Affairs Ministry will be
the same and so on.[147]

Muhsin Abd al-Hamid was being over-optimistic. This does not
mean that all Sunni groups are, but the IIP is a big political group
and it remains to be seen whether this stance is dominant even in
this party, which contains a large group of Sunni Arab nationalists
who believe in a strong centralized state.

The leaders of the new government have tried to reach out to
mainstream nationalist insurgent groups to persuade them to give
up violence and engage in the political process. Hajim al-Hassani,
the Speaker of the National Assembly and a Sunni Arab, said that
'many of the insurgents have kept fighting because they look at
Iraq as an occupied country.' With the new government in place,
there is a chance to convince them that Iraq was sovereign. Humam
Hammudi, the chairman of the commission named by the National
Assembly to draw up Iraq's constitution, said that the government
was in contact with Iraqi insurgents, trying to persuade them to
lay down arms and join the political process. Hammudi, a cleric
in SCIRI, stated, 'The contacts are becoming more promising and
they give us reason to continue them.'[148] Shi'a and Kurdish groups
alike have been engaged in talks with representatives of insurgent groups. But many influential Sunnis have argued that no real
dialogue concerning conciliation can be reached until the Coalition
leaves and the perceived deliberate marginalization of the Sunni
community is reversed. 'The Muslim Scholars Association considers those who target the occupiers, and whoever assists the occupiers, as honest and respectable,' says Sheikh Omar Raghib.[149] Moreover, the fragmented nature of the insurgency ensures that it cannot speak with one voice; insurgents have also voiced contempt for
or even targeted Sunni politicians and groups. Mashaan al-Juburi,

who turned against Saddam and is now a lawmaker, meets frequently with a wide variety of Sunni groups, including those with ties to the shadowy insurgency. Nevertheless, he narrowly escaped an assassination attempt in early spring 2005 in Tikrit.

The most public overture the new government has made so far was the call for amnesty for insurgents by the Kurdish president, Jalal Talabani, who issued a statement saying, 'Those who believe that what they have done is a manifestation of resisting the [US-led] occupation, I call upon them to come and join the democratic process.' Talabani's offer did not sit well with other members of the government. 'The government does not have the right to conduct negotiations with terrorists,' retorted Sheikh Jala Aldin al-Saghir, a National Assembly member and top aide to Ayatollah Sistani, and a virulent opponent of the insurgency.[150]

Another sore point of contention is the Shi'a desire to continue with and deepen the process of de-Ba'thification. Under Iyad Allawi, many Ba'thists were brought back into key security posts, particularly in counterterrorism and special commando battalions. Journalist Trudy Rubin interviewed some of these Ba'thists in January 2005. They had turned against Saddam in the 1990s, and stress that they are loyal to the post-Saddam system. US officials and military personnel view them as among the most efficient commanders in the evolving Iraqi security sector. But the Shi'a want to clean them out. Abdul Aziz Hakim, who lost twenty-four close relatives to the former regime, is adamant about de-Ba'thification: 'We have principles. One is de-Ba'thification, and according to these rules improper persons should not be given positions.'[151] This uncompromising position is hardly likely to assuage Sunni fears. Nor is Abdel Aziz al-Hakim sticking to this line purely out of principle. He and his Iranian supporters want to make sure that the Ba'th Party, historically noted for its ability to seize the state, can never again act as a vehicle for the seizure of power by the Sunni Arabs.

The new Shi'a-dominated government intends to adopt a tougher counter-insurgency approach than the outgoing Allawi government. This alarms the Sunni Arabs, because all indications are that the Shi'a intend to focus on military means rather than on implementing a basket of effective counter-insurgency measures. 'Our policy will be to develop the security forces and uproot the terrorist cells ... we will not let this grow,' said Jawad al-Maliki,[152] a member of the political bureau of the Da'wa party, the Islamist party of incoming Prime Minister Ibrahim al-Jaafari. The Shi'a made every effort to take control of the key Interior Ministry, which controls tens of thousands of paramilitary troops, police and special commando battalions. They plan to increase deployment of the special commandos, known as Maghawir (Fearless Warriors).

The emergence of a new government under the leadership of Ibrahim al-Jaafari in late April 2005 led the Bush administration to repeat its optimism about the way things were proceeding in Iraq. 'We're making major progress. Iraq is in the last throes, if you will, of the insurgency,' said Vice-President Dick Cheney.[153] The commander of US and Coalition ground troops in Iraq, Lieutenant General John Vines, echoed that sentiment: 'Less than one year ago, there was no government in Iraq—there was no Ministry of Interior, there was no Ministry of Defense—and Iraq was not a sovereign country. Since that time, they have held an election, selected their own transitional government, and they are writing their own constitution at the same time we are building their security forces. So we have made enormous progress, and my assessment is we are on track.'[154] But as these senior officials were expressing such optimistic sentiments the insurgency was refusing to go away. Iraq witnessed horrific violence during the spring and summer of 2005 and serious political deadlock. The Jaafari government has proven itself to be indecisive in the eyes of many Iraqis. Finally, the committee that was set up with so much fanfare to draft the permanent constitution was deadlocked over critical and fundamental issues by late July 2005 and well into mid-August. A chronological narrative of the insurgency and concurrent political developments in Iraq between April 2003 and October 2005 is not sufficient to understand the deeper origins and motivations of the insurgency. Why did it break out and was it inevitable? What accounts for its resilience? What are its weaknesses? The following chapters will address these deeper issues.

2

ORIGINS AND MOTIVES OF THE INSURGENCY

Few observers of the post-Saddam Iraqi scene expected an insurgency to break out in Iraq after conventional combat operations were officially declared to be over. On the contrary, there was a deep-seated optimism among the architects of the conflict that the war would be over quickly and that Iraq would return to normality in fairly short order, the ensuing chaos and disorder notwithstanding. When the insurgency did break out in early May 2003 there was little concern on the part of the senior US officials, military officers and the CPA, which had been set up to run post-Saddam Iraq on a temporary basis. In the early days the insurgents, often amateurish and clumsy, were described as former regime 'dead-enders' who would be soundly defeated. On 27 June 2003 Paul Wolfowitz, the Deputy Secretary of Defense and one of the key architects of the war, stated 'The direction is pretty clear. It is toward a more secure Iraq.'[1] On the insurgents he added: 'They lack the sympathy of the population, and they lack any serious external support. Basically, they are on their own.'[2] He made this statement in a month when the insurgency was beginning to take off—the first attack on the civilian aspect of the occupation occurred that month, as did the first attacks on and threats against Iraqis said to be collaborating with the occupation. Wolfowitz's statement is clear evidence that US knowledge or understanding of the political and socioeconomic situation on the ground in Iraq both before and in the aftermath of the collapse of the regime was almost nonexistent.

The Bush Administration's characterization of the insurgents as regime dead-enders was simply not accurate. To the question of who is involved in the insurgency, the answer is that its support base is the Sunni Arab community (with some significant Sunni Turkmen 'input'), which makes up anywhere between 18 and 20 percent of the total population and lives in the center of the country. The popular base and sociopolitical make-up of the insurgency is addressed in detail in Chapter 3. 'Who' having been identified, the issue becomes why they are rebelling and what they want.

Protection of Sunni Arab identity and fears of marginalization

In 1921 the British institutionalized the ascendancy of the Sunni Arab minority over the new state of Iraq. In April 2003 the United States overthrew the Sunni Arab-dominated regime of Saddam Hussein and with that act it ended Sunni Arab ascendancy over the country. A total of eighty-three years separated these two seminal events in Iraqi political history. The past, present and future of that country cannot be understood without reference to the key events that have occurred in between these two key dates.

How do we understand the origins and nature of Sunni Arab domination of Iraq? What contributed to its maintenance over the decades? Why did a large element of the Sunni Arab community react with violence to the attempt to restore balance to the internal constellation of forces within Iraq and thus begin an insurgency in spring 2003 that was still going strong in the winter of 2005?

First, the emergence of the Sunni Arabs should not be seen as primarily being due to the rise of an *internal* balance of power among ethnic and sectarian communities, which ultimately favored them as a community. It is not clear that by themselves Iraq's Sunni

Arabs would have been able to rise to dominate the country.[3] The outside world had a considerable role in giving birth to the ascendancy of this community, in institutionalizing its domination, and ultimately in overthrowing it.

Second, in retrospect it is easy to see that the overwhelming power of the Sunni Arabs, who were a minority of the population even then, was unwarranted and has been responsible for many of the trials and tribulations of modern Iraq. This domination by a minority with a strong but narrowly circumscribed identity and ideology has meant that Iraq has suffered serious legitimacy problems over the course of its political history since 1921, when the state was formed. While the Sunni Arab community proved over the course of eighty-three years of rule that it was strong enough to maintain power, it never succeeded in establishing an ideological hegemony that the entire country regarded as legitimate. The end result has been the accumulation of deep-seated grievances and a quest for vengeance on the part of the 'losers'. This partly accounts for the utter lack of sympathy with which Shi'a and Kurds view the current plight of the once-dominant Sunni community. This lack of sympathy or empathy translates into politics and policies that marginalize the Sunnis and drive them further into the arms of the insurgency, thus perpetuating the kind of legitimacy deficit that Iraq exhibited under Sunni rule. A brief foray into Iraqi history and state-building strategies is necessary in order to understand the underlying motivations of the insurgency as a sociopolitical and economic phenomenon.[4]

The Ottoman Empire established control over Mesopotamia in the early sixteenth century, mainly in an effort to forestall their Safavid rivals in Iran from incorporating the region into their empire. Mesopotamia was hardly a worthwhile gain. The Ottomans inherited a region that had declined precipitously from its glory days during the Abbasid dynasty. Instead, it was a semi-anarchical and poorly developed land with numerous mutually suspicious ethnic and sectarian groups. The Ottomans interacted little with the Kurds, who had the mountainous terrain of northern Mesopotamia as a buffer against encroachments by Ottoman troops. The Ottoman Turks and the Sunni Arabs shared a common religious heritage (Sunni Islam) but the racial gap between them in the early days of Ottoman control was huge. As British historian and colonial official Stephen Longrigg put it: 'The very appearance, manner and language of the Turkish Aghas was strange and foreign to Arab eyes and ears.'[5] The Ottomans looked with considerable suspicion upon the Shi'a of southern Mesopotamia, whom they viewed as a fifth column for Shi'a Iran.[6] The Shi'a, in turn, elected to have nothing to do with the Sunni Ottomans. The former 'scorned the pretensions of the new Khalif [in Istanbul]. From the Holy Cities [Najaf and Karbala] radiated influence strong in its appeal, hostile to the Sultan and by reaction friendly to the Shah [in Iran].'[7] Shi'a suspicion of the Ottoman government never ceased, and as Hanna Batatu pointed out in his magisterial work on Iraq, 'To the strict Shi'is, the government of the day—the government of the Ottoman Sultan that led Sunni Islam—was, in its essence, an usurpation … They were, therefore, estranged from it, few caring to serve it or to attend its schools.'[8]

In any case, early Ottoman suzerainty over Mesopotamia was characterized by inefficiency, corruption and decentralized control from Istanbul. Furthermore, not only were the Kurds and Shi'a excluded, but also it seems that they voluntarily opted out of the Ottoman system. They neither demanded much of it nor expected onerous demands or benefits in return. Matters in this somnambulant province changed in the late nineteenth century, when Istanbul attempted to implement widespread reforms and modernization throughout the empire. Mesopotamia was lucky to have an energetic official, the governor Midhat Pasha, in charge of

the series of reforms known as the Tanzimat. Arriving in Mesopotamia in April 1869 Midhat Pasha overhauled the administration
and bureaucracy, set up a modern education system, improved
the transportation system and enforced conscription. While it is
easy to exaggerate Midhat Pasha's lasting influence and success,
he relied on locally recruited officials to implement his reforms.
This meant that the Ottomans began to rely on the Sunni Arabs,
the only large ethno-sectarian group that they could trust in that
province, and more importantly the only one willing to play such
a role among the province's expanded administrative elite. Most
important of all was that the Ottomans began increasingly to recruit Sunni Arabs from Mesopotamia and to a lesser extent Sunni
Kurds into the ranks of the Ottoman army as officer cadets and not
just as enlisted men. But while the Ottoman path to modernization
ultimately failed, the empire's attempts set the stage for the genesis
of Sunni Arab domination of the administrative and coercive apparatus of the future Iraqi state.[9]

Indeed, the Ottoman path to modernization was disrupted in
the center, where a litany of military defeats, political and bureaucratic ossification, and above all the rise of the reactionary and au-
tocratic Sultan Abd al-Hamid II (1878–1909), who turned his back
on the Tanzimat, led to strong nationalist sentiment among the enlightened intelligentsia and officer corps. Arabs from those provinces who had joined the administration and the military forces
of the empire witnessed first-hand the slow but steady and seemingly irreversible decline of the Ottoman Empire. Those who had
come into contact with Europe, through travel there, education in
modern European institutes and universities, or, for the officers,
instruction in advanced European military schools, could not help
but compare the lot of their empire with the power and strength
of Europe.[10] Moreover, the incorporation of this backwater province into the global economic system and the rise in literacy and

greater political consciousness among certain sectors of the population led to the emergence of social groups with a nascent sense of nationalism and an awareness of the distinct differences between them and their Turkish overlords. The evident decay of the Ottoman Empire and the rise in Pan-Turanianism (Turkish nationalism) occasioned a response from the various other subject races of the Ottoman Empire, including the Arabs of Bilad ash-Sham (Syria) and Mesopotamia. Arab officers in the Ottoman army became susceptible to the siren song of Arab nationalist ideals expounded by Arab intellectuals.[11]

Towards the end of World War I the British, then embroiled in a fierce fight with the Ottoman Empire in the Middle East sideshow of that war, managed to seize three *vilayets* (provinces), Basra, Baghdad and Mosul. Together these regions constituted poverty-stricken and backward Mesopotamia—home to a wide range of ethno-sectarian groups. 'Our armies do not come into your cities and lands as conquerors or enemies but as liberators,' said General Stanley Maude, commander of the British forces, as he entered Baghdad in 1917.[12] The British flooded the country with earnest and adventurous young military officers and middle-aged administrators who spent a great deal of time trying to build up their knowledge of yet another acquisition. But London was in a quandary over the future disposition of the territory. The Acting Civil Commissioner, Arnold Wilson, an intense man with a fondness for quoting from the Bible, found himself in constant conflict with London and with many of his colleagues, including Gertrude Bell, a woman who was his equal, if not superior, in determination and desire to get what she wanted. The key issue of contention was whether Iraq would be under direct control of the British or would be allowed a measure of self-government under British supervision. The prevarications of the British ultimately irritated and alarmed many of the region's inhabitants, who increasingly resented the 'infidel' presence and grew suspicious of the occupiers' designs. The awarding of Iraq to Britain as a mandate further inflamed the passions of the populace. Another problem was the growth in and institutionalization of efficient state administration, to include 'oppressive' taxation. For the tribes, unaccustomed as they were to efficient governance, this was a pretext for revolt.[13]

A violent rebellion erupted in the summer of 1920. Curiously, the first incidence of violence took place near a small backwater town by the name of Tal Afar; in June 1920 a British patrol was ambushed and suffered deaths. The British retaliated by sending a column of troops, which ravaged the harvests in the area, destroyed the homes of suspected troublemakers and 'chased the entire population of Tal Afar, innocent and guilty alike, into the desert'.[14] Tal Afar then slipped back into a well-deserved obscurity, from which it was roused in fall 2005 when some observers stridently accused the US Army of doing 'similar' things in its earnest attempts to restore stability and security in the town. The 1920 revolt's center of gravity was further south, where the British were alarmed by mass meetings and demonstrations of Sunni and Shi'a seemingly united in a nascent nationalism in cities such as Baghdad. Deadly attacks were conducted against the British presence and forces, including the army and local Arab police in the central Euphrates region, which the insurgents controlled by July 1920. Slowly but surely the thinly stretched British forces recovered the initiative and beat the revolt, often using methods that would be deemed 'unsavory'. It had been expensive in human and financial terms.[15]

This expensive victory led the British to seek a resolution to Iraq's uncertain status. They concluded that the best way to maintain control was through the co-option of local elites, and hence chose elements from among the Sunni Arabs.[16] By 1921 the British had institutionalized the predominance of the politically active Sunni minority (about 20 percent of the total population) over the new state of Iraq. The British imposed an alien Sunni Arab prince, their wartime ally Faisal, a Hashemite and the son of the Sharif Husayn of Mecca, as king. His coronation took place on 23 August 1921 in a strange ceremony held at six o'clock in the morning. It had, said John Keay, in his delightful and witty book on the history of the West's modern interactions with the Middle East, all the 'dignity of a school concert'.[17] Faisal recognized that the new state of Iraq was built upon weak foundations. Indeed, he lamented that fact in a famous memorandum that has been quoted ad nauseam.[18] He was dependent on the British and on hundreds of Arab officers who had deserted the Ottoman army and joined him. They became the ruling elite. Sunni Arab civilian administrators and bureaucrats took over the state and imposed an educational and cultural system that promoted pan-Arab nationalism and sought to tie Iraq closely to the Arab world to the west.[19] The Ottoman administration in Mesopotamia set the stage for the emergence of Sunni Arab domination; the British built upon it and institutionalized it.[20]

The pro-Western monarchy was overthrown in 1958, with the so-called Iraqi Revolution, and there was a fleeting moment when it seemed that Iraq's non-Sunni majority would be integrated into the political process. However, from 1958 to 1968 a coterie of nationalist military regimes dominated by conservative and often religious Sunni Arabs ruled an unstable and isolated Iraq that had little backing or support from the outside world. From 1968 to 2003 a peculiar Iraqi totalitarianism under Saddam Hussein, one heavily dominated by a minority from within the Sunni minority, ran the country. Now, three years after the collapse of the regime, we are just beginning to understand the key to its ability to perpetuate its horrendous rule for more than three decades. It did rely to some extent on outside support for its continued perpetuation, particularly during the Iran-Iraq war of 1980–8. But it largely managed on its own through the use of three critical internal

devices: oil income, which allowed the state to provide basic services and build modern infrastructure; a massive coercive establishment to keep the inhabitants in line; and neo-patrimonialism
or patronage to pay off groups to support the regime. The Ba'thist
state, which ran a state capitalist system, created a large public-
sector middle class that transcended ethno-sectarian boundaries in
that it included Shi'a and some Kurds and Turkmen, but which was
largely dominated by Sunni Arabs.[21] But while it portrayed itself as
nonsectarian and progressive, the Ba'th regime relied extensively
on the Sunni Arabs to control the coercive apparatus of the state,
namely the armed forces, the intelligence and security services.[22]
Iraq's national identity was described in exclusively Arab nationalist terms, and the regime's internal and external policies reflected
that orientation. In short, the primary beneficiaries of the Ba'thist
system were Sunni Arabs, but they also suffered politically and so-
cioeconomically as the regime's legitimacy eroded over the course
of the past decade. Saddam was, of course, forced to rely on an
increasingly narrow circle of Sunni Arabs to maintain his power.[23]

The political struggles until the downfall of Saddam, over ideological orientations and resources, were between and among the
Sunnis, the group at the center of power and that defined the state.
These struggles were over minor ideological orientations and resources. Since Saddam's ouster in 2003, politics in Iraq has been
driven not only by ideology and resources, but also by identity. The
Sunni Arabs no longer define Iraq, and that, coupled with what
they perceive as their deliberate marginalization, has presented
them with a deep identity crisis. It is true that people often fight
fiercely to protect privileges and positions of dominance as much
they fight to gain more of these resources. It is equally true that
people also fight not only to maintain or advance things they value
materially, but also for a set of *nonmaterial* values that are subsumed
under the rubric of identity. In short, as Erik Ringmar points out

in his study of Sweden's involvement in the disastrous Thirty Years War in the early seventeenth century, sometimes people fight not to maintain or restore their material benefits or what they believe they are entitled to. They also fight to defend or promote their sense of self or identity against dire threats, real or perceived.[24] For the Sunni Arabs the downfall of the regime in April 2003 was not only or even primarily the collapse of power and privileges—indeed, many of them had little power and few, if any, privileges—but of the entire nationalist edifice that has been in existence for more than eight decades and that had *identified* Iraq with them. This was cataclysmic. It constituted a grievance. For a while after the collapse of the Ba'thist regime the Sunni community was not only in shock, but also confused and aimless. Ultimately the shock and resultant anger, as well as Coalition policies that struck at the Sunni Arabs' identity and self-worth, have contributed to the emergence and perpetuation of the insurgency.

Identity crisis stems from a disruption of one's world and milieu and the quest to make sense of the changes by posing the interrelated questions of how you fit in that new world and whether and how you can remake your identity to fit the new circumstances.[25] To repair this will take much more than simply providing the Sunnis with material resources and political power in accordance with their percentage of the population. For them the Coalition invasion and occupation of the country that they had dominated and built in their own image for eighty-three years constituted a massive blow. The Sunnis are questioning their future and role in the new Iraq. Some have voted with their feet and left the country *en masse*. Others are trying their hand at politics. Many more have chosen to fight. Indeed, many are not fighting to restore their privileges but to survive.

The blow to their identity is manifested in the dire and gloomy comments of numerous Sunni Arabs in the aftermath of April 2003.

For example, a former member of the Iraqi security/intelligence service from Duluiyah was on top of the world when Saddam was in power, but lost his livelihood and was forced to sell diesel fuel illegally to survive in post-Saddam Iraq. He told a journalist: 'We were on top of the system. We had dreams. Now we are the losers. We lost our positions, our status, the security of our families, stability. Curse the Americans. Curse them.'[26] Another resident of Duluiyah expressed his view of the status of the Sunnis now: 'We are now a *shaab bidun* [people without].'[27] The sentiment is widespread in the so-called Sunni triangle. In Tikrit a shop owner laments: 'We were the heads of the Arabs, and the people were happy. But by God, time has turned its face on us, and we've now been placed at the mercy of the villains.'[28] It is clear that there is not only socioeconomic disenfranchisement, but also deep identity disenfranchisement.

For many Sunni Arabs Saddam's capture was a disgrace that was very much tied to the issue of identity and honor. 'He's supposed to fight with honor, he's supposed to defend his honor. We believed in him, that he would always resist. We can't believe that he would be reduced to his level, as a coward,' said a former officer from Duluiyah.[29] In this context, it is not surprising that Sunni Arabs have taken pride in the feistiness of Saddam during his trial hearings in October 2005. For them he is fighting back and they approve of his challenging the legitimacy of the court that was set up to try him.

We cannot wish away the role of identity crisis as a grievance and as a prime cause of the insurgency. But we do because identity is such an intangible commodity (not readily transparent to observers) that it is not easy to point it out as a cause and say 'so and so is fighting because his sense of worth or values have been threatened'. It is much easier to say that 'so and so is fighting to retain his privileges and position of power'. We in the United States love to quantify things, and material things such as resources are more readily identifiable than 'fuzzy' matters like identity or culture. What makes the role of identity difficult to assess is that it is often intricately tied to privilege or position. Often a person sees his or her sense of worth or value as being tied to a particular position or level of achievement in society. And when that position is destroyed so is the sense of worth or value.

The crisis in Sunni Arab identity has also exacerbated a latent prejudice against the 'unwashed' Shi'a hordes and alien Shi'a forces. The officer from Duluiyah whom I have quoted above was virulently hostile in his views of the Shi'a, whom he was well aware stood to benefit from this collapse of Sunni Arab paramountcy. Of the Shi'a he said: 'These people with turbans are going to run the country. What do they know? Iraq needs people like us.'[30] The intrepid journalist Nir Rosen received a good taste of the bitterness of the Sunni Arabs in the aftermath of the dramatic changes in Iraq. He interviewed a wealthy Sunni Arab businessman from the middle-class Baghdad suburb of Adhamiya. Like the whites of South Africa, who continue to fret over the fate of the country whose identity they had shaped for centuries, the businessman feels disenfranchised. He had not lost anything materially—at least at that time—but had lost his identity: 'The Americans made a big mistake when they came to Iraq. Sunnis ruled Iraq for 400 years. Sunnis always worked in the security and administration of Iraq.'[31] His laments did not automatically make him a supporter of Saddam. The businessman claimed that the former regime had expropriated a successful food-processing plant that he had owned: '[Saddam] took it like a piece of cake.'[32] As a nationalist Sunni Arab he suffers from that intense dislike for and fear of the Shi'a, whom the Sunnis view as a fifth column for the Islamic Republic of Iran and its *ajam* (non-Arab) Persian denizens. Of course, added to that was the ineluctable class gap between the (former) haves and have-nots, whose roles were slowly being reversed. 'Most Shiites are simple-minded,' said Nir Rosen's host. 'I will kill myself if they rule.'[33] His immediate neighbors in the suburb live on the one street that has Shi'a in it. The anonymous middle-class Sunni Arab said of them: 'They hate us and we hate them.'[34]

For many of Iraq's Sunni Arabs, and even for those Sunni Turkmen who have imbibed the Arab nationalist ideology, there is something ineluctably non-Arab or anti-Arab—indeed, even anti-Iraqi—about the Shi'a of their country.[35] This sentiment is directed primarily at the exiles returning from Iran but has spread to encompass 'native' Shi'a Arabs. There is an undercurrent of contempt among a wide range of Sunnis for the Shi'a, whether from the south, particularly the rural types, or those who are returning from decades of exile in Iran or elsewhere. 'We can control "our" Shi'a,' one Sunni former general told me.[36] The returning exiles were viewed as sinister, wanting to implement an Iranian-style religious theocracy and to subordinate Iraq to the Iranians. Throughout the Sunni Arab community there was, from the beginning, a palpable element of fear over the erosion of identity as Iraq slipped under the control of the emergent Shi'a majority. Clerics joined the chorus of Sunni voices expressing fear of the Shi'a. Sheikh Bilal Ahmed Ismail, an Islamic scholar from Fallujah, said: 'Even many Sunnis suffered under Saddam. Some of the resistance is fighting in his name, but the eager voices among Sunnis is (*sic*) fighting against his name. So the *mujahideen* of the resistance, Saddam has nothing to do with them. Instead, they fight for two reasons: We will never accept colonization; we see a national task to drive the Americans from our country. And just as important, we fear Shiite power.'[37] Similar views were expressed by Sheikh Abdallah Dakhil al-Farraj al-Jibouri, a leader from one of the largest Arab tribes. He has little time for the Shi'a, whom he views with contempt: 'They cannot rule Iraq properly. They cannot take charge of Iraq in the same manner as the Sunnis. The Shiites are backwards. They are barbarian savages, they do not know true religion, theirs is twisted, it is not the true religion of Muhammad.'[38]

Many Iraqi and US officials, as well as many academic observers of the post-Saddam Iraqi scene, have glossed over the growth of ethno-sectarian hatreds in Iraq. The refusal to recognize this fact is driven by the desire to continue to promote the idea of Iraqi progress towards democratic governance. The notion of ethno-sectarian harmony in Iraq is essential to the maintenance of the fiction that there is progress towards a higher level of political values, as represented by democracy. But ethno-sectarian harmony is unfortunately a fiction in Iraq. I had a taste of this visceral ethno-sectarian divide when I was in Iraq between November 2003 and March 2004, and then again between July 2005 and September 2005. During my first deployment I could sense this, and individuals from the various communities were not averse to making jokes about each other. On the other hand, they often expressed a desire not to see the situation disintegrate into civil war. In the summer and fall of 2005 the situation was vastly different. People still hoped that the country would not succumb to civil war, but they were not optimistic. Unfortunately they no longer made jokes about each other. Instead, they expressed sentiments of virulent hatred. In the summer and fall of 2005 many Sunni Turkmen and even Kurds expressed sentiments similar to those quoted above, in a series of long and fascinating discussions in the old Ottoman castle, the Qala'a, in Tal Afar, during interminable meetings with sheikhs, and out in the field, during the offensive to clear the city of insurgents. All sorts of calumnies were directed at the Shi'a. A common refrain was that they had simplistic political views. Another was that they were so primitive and childlike that they needed to turn to their clerics to tell them what to do, including how to vote. The Kurds proved as contemptuous of the Shi'a as of the Sunnis. Neither did the Shi'a soldiers from the south hold back. They viewed the Sunnis as oppressors and the Kurds as arrogant backstabbers.

The identity crisis suffered by the Sunni Arabs as a result of the collapse of 'their' state has been exacerbated by their apparent inability to establish themselves politically with parties or organizations that can articulate Sunni grievances and draw people away from the insurgency, by the overt sectarianism of the post-Saddam era, and by Coalition policies.

The first victims of Saddam's Ba'th regime were the Sunni Arab nationalist military officers, civilians and Ba'th party intellectuals. Indeed, Saddam never depended on a wide base of Sunnis from Baghdad or Mosul. He increasingly came to depend on the ruder and simpler Sunnis from small towns or rural areas, and over time even that circle grew narrower. But Saddam kept a close watch on the Sunni Arabs because of the simple fact that it was members of this community who could overthrow him. Political parties or organizations that did not meet or subordinate themselves to the ideals of the Ba'th party were proscribed. Sunni Arabs who fled into exile were never able to create powerful, broad-based opposition groups. This stands in stark contrast to the Shi'a and the Kurds. An Arab journalist said that unlike the Sunnis, 'the Shiites and Kurds are represented by individuals and parties that have wide bases, influence, and a rich political experience'.[39] The Shi'a have benefited from Iranian support that continued for many years. The Kurdish parties had a decade to build up an administrative structure and effective political parties free of Saddam Hussein. Unsurprisingly, 'What unites the Iraqis in the Sunni areas is their frustration and sense of being wronged because there is no one who represents them, speaks on their behalf, or expresses their aspirations. They were politically unprepared for the post-Saddam period, compared to the Shiites and the Kurds.'[40] Sunni Arab leaders were aware of this bitter reality.

Well into the occupation and the emergence of the new Iraq, the Sunni Arabs continue to lack any strong unifying leader or leadership. In this, once again, they contrast remarkably with the Shi'a and the Kurds. No Sunni political group or personality working legitimately in the political arena has been able to mobilize the Sunni populace, nor has such a group or person been able to reach out to the insurgents and to pull them into the process. Why? They lack the constituency, the strength of personality and a positive program to offer the people or the insurgents. Salah Mutlak, the head of a legitimate Sunni political group, the National Dialogue Council, says: 'We should be the ones who stop [the insurgents]. But we are not talking to people in that way because we have no solution to offer them. We have nothing to offer them. We have to give them hope. There is no hope now.'[41] Moreover, in an interview in July 2005, he stated: 'When part of the country has had a big role for centuries and suddenly you take all the power away from them, of course they will defend themselves.'[42] In short, one can argue that the insurgency has been the Sunni Arab means of political participation.

The problems of the Sunnis working legitimately within the political arena have been exacerbated by their wishful thinking on a key issue. Many, including almost all of those with whom I talked, deny they are part of a minority and endorse a goal of returning to dominance. This is, of course, a pipe dream. Adnan al-Dulaimi, the head of the Sunni *awqaf* (endowments)—the same man who has urged Sunni Arabs to participate vigorously in the political process—seems to believe that his community is not a minority: 'There are some voices who say that the Sunni Arabs are a minority. We want to prove to them that we are not a minority. We are the sons of the country. We are responsible for the history of Iraq.'[43] There is a difference, however, between believing that your community is not a demographic minority and believing that it is entitled to dominance. Some Sunnis have acknowledged that they may not be a majority in demographic terms but are entitled to their position of dominance by virtue of their history—that they were responsible for the emergence and development of the Iraqi state.

The Sunnis were shocked by the overtly sectarian basis of the IGC, and Sunni representation on the council was very weak. In July 2003 the newly formed Association of Muslim Scholars (AMS) issued a statement that the IGC was not only illegitimate but also formed with a sectarian bias: '[The IGC] divided the Iraqi people along sectarian lines and gave a certain sect an absolute majority over all components and groups of the Iraqi people without relying on accurate surveys or statistics.'[44] The AMS has waded into the issue of sectarianism in politics, but more than that has categorically rejected the idea that the Shi'a constituted the majority of the Iraqi population: 'The [sect] that was given the majority—with our respect for it [*sic*]—does not in fact represent the absolute majority over all components and groups of the Iraqi people ... Indeed, this sect does not represent the majority among Iraqi Muslims.'[45] The AMS also castigated the IGC for making the day on which Baghdad fell (9 April) a national holiday, arguing that this 'decision kills the national pride and patriotic spirit within the Iraqis'.[46]

Their detractors would argue that the Sunnis cannot complain about this because they had previously dominated the country. The response of Sunni intellectuals, former officials, officers and even ordinary people is that they were never trying to impose sectarian politics on the country. They then proceed to argue that Shi'a political control in Iraq means religious governance because the Shi'a seek to impose the notion of *velayat-e-faqih*, or rule by the jurisconsult (i.e. rule by the most politically and theologically qualified Shi'a cleric) and domination by the Iranians.[47] Indeed, for many years (particularly since the early 1980s, with the rise of Shi'a political activism and the Iranian Revolution) Saddam himself argued ad nauseam that the introduction of religion into politics was a recipe for disaster in Iraq. According to many Sunnis, the fact that Iraq has gone the way of sectarianism over the past three years has forced them to turn to their religion in response.

By early 2004 leaders in the Sunni Arab community knew that they had to act in the political arena in order to reverse the precipitous decline of their people. In December 2003 key leaders set up the Majlis Shura ahl al-Sunna to promote the political interests of the community, by peaceful means of course.[48] The hapless IIP struggled to mobilize a constituency that has viewed the party as complicit in the occupation. Sunni politician Abdul Salam al-Kubeisi says the IIP has done little more than 'market the occupation'.[49] For many Sunni Arabs the Sunni sheikhs whom the United States began to court assiduously in order to curb the insurgency are compromised, and their standing is low because they are seen as willing to deal with anyone in return for patronage and money.

The Sunni parties and groups opposed the decision to hold elections for a transitional government in January 2005 (see Chapter 5). They believed that Iraq could not hold legitimate elections while the country was still occupied. The AMS was at the forefront in urging the Sunnis to boycott the elections. This stance was no less strident than that of those Sunnis actively engaged in violence. But soon after the election results showed that the Shi'a and Kurds had won convincingly and were the key political forces in the country, Sunni political groups began to reconsider their previous stance, recognising that they had made a mistake. In the aftermath of the elections, however, the Sunnis were faced with several political problems that impeded their effective political participation.

If the politically active Sunni groups were now going to involve themselves in the post-electoral political process to gain as much as they could for a community that was now further disenfranchised, what was going to be the relationship between the politically active parties and the insurgency? Were the former going to constitute themselves as the political arm of the insurgency? In short, was the AMS going to be the Iraqi equivalent of Sinn Fein (the political arm) to the Iraqi counterpart of the Irish Republican Army (the military arm). After all, the AMS was on record as expressing strong support for the *muqawamah* (a term meaning 'resistance' that the Iraqi insurgents use to refer to themselves). One of its spokesmen, Dr Muthana Harith al-Dari, the son of the AMS leader Dr Harith al-Dari, told a Baghdad television station in spring 2005: 'We believe that the Iraqi people are entitled to resist the occupation. Resistance is a legitimate right and duty guaranteed by heavenly charters and worldly laws ... relations with the Iraqi resistance factions are based on the fact that we share a common goal, that is, the liberation of Iraq. We still insist on achieving this goal.'[50] However, an effective parallel political arm of the insurgency has not yet emerged. Muthanna al-Dari had an explanation for the failure to have a political wing when he was queried on the issue:

As I said we are a group of national forces opposed to occupation. All these forces are close to the feelings of resistance because they believe in the liberation of Iraq. Let me ask you if the Iraqi situation allows for the emergence of political forces that embrace the language of resistance. The Iraqi situation does not allow this to happen because the political and religious forces working in the arena like the Association of Muslim Scholars are fought against even for simple political reasons.[51]

Al-Dari is quite correct in his analysis. But it is not the complete picture. The Sunnis' failure to create an effective political wing of the insurgency stems from other, equally insidious problems. It is a function of the myriad insurgent groups with different personalities and agendas on the one hand, and on the other the existence of equally diverse and relatively weak Sunni political groups on the political stage. The divisiveness and weaknesses of the Sunnis was exhibited starkly during much of 2005. In the long haggling over ministries that led to the formation of the Jaafari government in late April 2005, the Sunni Arabs lost out again. It was partly a function of their political weaknesses. During the intense negotiations over the Defense Ministry, instead of banding together as one the various Sunni groups put forward separate lists of nominees. The fact that the Sunnis were stymied in their attempts to play a political role was also perceived as a function of discrimination by the Shi'a. Fakhri al-Qaisi is a Sunni Arab dentist, hard-line Islamist and prominent member of the National Dialogue Council, a political group that includes sheikhs, professionals, clerics and even former Ba'thists. He and his fellow council members gave up hope trying to influence the Shi'a-led government to be more inclusive. 'They offered us joke ministries,' he complained.[52] Politically he and his fellow Sunnis in the National Dialogue Council are regarded as closet insurgents, and for their pains their political offices were raided in early May by security forces of the Shi'a-controlled Interior Ministry. Qaisi sees himself as an Iraqi, as do many Sunni Arabs, and his three wives are apparently Shi'a. But as a measure of how communally and ethnically divided the country has become, he seems to have been transformed into a virulent Sunni Arab nationalist. He is apoplectic that when US troops raided his house last year—an occurrence depressingly familiar to many prominent Sunnis in the new Iraq—they brought Shi'a militia with them: 'If the US troops came alone, we would shake their hand. But they brought our enemies with them.'[53] Behind the rise of the Shi'a he sees Iran, and has taken to referring to the Shi'a religious parties as 'Safawis', an allusion to the Turkic dynasty that once ruled Iran and transformed it into a Shi'a entity.

At least in the beginning, Coalition policies such as the dissolution of the Iraqi army and the Ba'th Party and indifferent treatment of the Sunnis seemed deliberately designed to ensure their marginalization. Among the policy-makers in Washington, DC, there was also a mindset that was profoundly hostile to the Sunni Arabs, as I will discuss in the final chapter. Sunni Arabs picked up on this very early on in the occupation. 'The problem with the Americans is that they have no respect for us,' says 'Abid' an educated, English-speaking Sunni Iraqi who was originally favorably disposed towards the United States.[54] A Sunni Arab businessman told his interlocutor, well-known journalist and academic Mark Danner, who has traveled extensively in the country, that: 'You Americans, you have created your own enemies here.'[55] Dr Abdullah Hasan al-Hadithy, a Sunni cleric and professor at the University of Islamic Sciences in Baghdad, stated: 'The Americans don't treat the Sunnis well at all, and there are a lot of us in the population: thinkers, experts, scientists, military leaders. They sidelined the Sunnis, and we don't appreciate this because we want to rebuild the country, too.'[56] Adnan al-Janabi was Minister of State in the interim government of Iyad Allawi. One day he was arrested and roughly handled by US soldiers manning a checkpoint leading to the heavily guarded Green Zone, where he worked. After the event, Janabi, a Sunni, told a British journalist: '[The Americans] made every single mistake they could have thought of to alienate the Sunnis. The US is behaving as if every Sunni is a terrorist.'[57]

These sentiments were similar to those expressed to me by a number of Sunni Arabs (and Sunni Turkmen) whom I met during the past three years in Iraq. These Sunnis told me that many within the community had been ready—indeed, more than willing—to work with the Coalition to move the country forward towards a better future. While these individuals had reluctantly accepted the fact that their community had been toppled from dominance (who accepts 'status collapse' willingly?), they did not accept the perceived 'minoritarization' of the community. This must be explained in some detail, because we are not necessarily talking here about demographic weight, although as I have mentioned throughout the study I continue to be baffled by the strident claim by Sunnis that they are the numerical majority. Based on my extensive discussions with the Sunni Arabs and Turkmen, I hit upon the awkward term 'minoritarization' to describe the Sunni view that there was a deliberate process of political marginalization of a community that has been central to the political evolution of the country, and a sustained assault on its identity with the intent of humiliating and dishonoring it, and rendering it impotent. In short, the Sunni community's status was to be reduced to what the Coalition and ultimately the majority chose to give them, not what they themselves could attain by playing a key and central role. The Sunni Arabs contrast their position with that of the Kurds, who were seen as favored by the Coalition, the officials of which did their utmost to give that community a 'leg up' in post-Saddam Iraq.

In concluding this section one could argue that the British were wrong on practical and moral grounds to guarantee their control over Iraq through the medium of institutionalizing the dominance of a minority of the population. They gave the Sunni Arabs a head start at independence. I am not, however, a believer in the corrosive and nonsensical view prevalent in the region that all of the ills of the Middle East can be laid at the feet of colonialism and the machinations of the foreigner. The region's indigenous peoples and particularly their rulers need to take their share of the blame. The Sunnis of Iraq are reaping what they sowed by their atrocious treatment for eight decades of almost 80 percent of their population. Nonetheless, the circle is incomplete unless one looks at the manifest hypocrisy, impracticality and immorality of the manner in which the Coalition of the Willing decided to implement its democratic design for the future of Iraq. While the idea of bringing democracy to Iraq is laudable and noble, it cannot be achieved by the blatantly politicized notion that as long as we have the majority of the population on 'our' side (the 76 percent that is Kurd and Shi'a, and that says it is with us), we can safely ignore the grievances, aspirations, identity issues and material needs of that 22 percent (Sunni Arab and Sunni Turkmen) that has proved to be 'obstreperous'. One journalist declared that the United States has done little to address Sunni concerns. It has often dismissed the grievances of the Sunnis, raided their organizations and even detained respected figures. [58]

In the early days of the occupation, a common response of some US officials in Washington, DC, and among the Coalition authorities at the Republican Palace in Baghdad was, 'Why should we address these concerns?' or 'The Sunnis don't deserve anything'. Thus the conclusion was, 'We do not need to engage them'. In the summer of 2003 a US officer based outside one of the unsettled Sunni cities asked the CPA for money to buy some generators for the populace. He was told by a 'CPAer' that he could not have the money or the generators because we could not afford to show the Sunnis 'favoritism' or that we were 'rewarding them' for their violence. Unsurprisingly, given the option of going down in ignominy or fighting, the Sunnis chose to fight. One of the more moderate Shi'a, the secular Ghassan al-'Attiyah, director of the Iraqi Foundation for Development and Democracy, put it well: 'The Sunnis will not give in. If you fight them, you turn them into national heroes. You must find the moderates and deal with them.'[59] Once the Sunnis took up arms, the reaction in Washington, DC, within the Bush administration and its neoconservative supporters was that they would have to be cowed into submission. After all, among some circles in the United States it is believed that the 'only thing they understand is force'. Yet with the passage of time and the obvious intractability of the insurgency many officials say Sunni inclusion and participation in the political process is key to defusing the insurgency. I address the ideological underpinnings of this 'Sunniphobia' in Chapter 5, as part of the discussion of the structural problems of the US counter-insurgency campaign.

Motives of former regime elements

The US characterization of the insurgency as regime dead-enders led by the deposed Ba'th Party and senior leaders of the former regime reveals considerable ignorance about the nature of the party, its entrenchment in society and its ability to act effectively as a clandestine entity. Contrary to the belief that the Ba'th Party faded away and played little or no role in the insurgency, there is compelling evidence that it did not simply evaporate and that, indeed, its members did play significant political and operational roles. It also issued statements that outlined its operational goals—regarding how to fight the occupiers—and political goals for a 'liberated' Iraq. The fact is that this party functions well in clandestine mode because it has experienced working 'underground' when it was out of power and hunted by its enemies, and had prepared for the possibility of overthrow once in power. Indeed, the specter of overthrow stalked the Ba'th regime from the very moment it seized power in Iraq in 1968. There is some evidence that the regime started to think about the unthinkable—a US-led invasion to unseat it—as early as 1998. Only three years after the Ba'th came to power the United States orchestrated a *coup d'etat* by the Chilean military against the radical regime of Salvador Allende. Years later, Saddam declared that the Ba'th would never permit such a thing to occur in Iraq. Popular rebellions in Eastern Europe—particularly that in Romania, which overthrew Saddam's friend and amateur totalitarian brother-in-arms, Nicolae Ceausescu—worried the Ba'th regime. After 1991 it was neither popular uprisings nor the manipulation of internal forces by outside forces that preoccupied the Ba'th regime. Indeed, its remarkable ability to deal with and defeat two ethno-sectarian uprisings by the Kurds and Shi'a in the north and south, respectively, increased its confidence that it could handle 'internal traitors'. Its confidence must have been further enhanced when it defeated other foreign-supported internal efforts to unseat it in 1995–6. On the contrary, its problem became one of how to deal with the threat of a direct foreign invasion to unseat it. When the Ba'th regime was deposed and Saddam went into hiding until his capture in mid-December 2003, he apparently continued to exhort the party to pursue the struggle against the foreign presence in the country. This 'sinister' presence naturally needs to be fought and the fight needs an ideological justification to underpin it.

Shorn of the onerous duties of running a complex state and society, the conditions characterized by clandestine operations allow the party not only to plot secretly but also to devote considerable time and effort to ideologically turgid output. It has done so in the past when it was not in power and is doing so again now that it has gone into hiding. The Ba'thist insurgents have given themselves a wide variety of names and created a Political Information and Publication Service to disseminate their views on the war. In the mindset of the Ba'thist insurgents the 'resistance' has moved from being merely a reaction to the presence and actions of the occupier to becoming an integrated strategic vision. This means that the phase of initial resistance was *ad hoc* and, indeed, somewhat disorganized. It is now better organized, they say, with solid ideological justifications for opposing the occupation, a formulation of operational goals stating how to oppose it, and a political vision for the 'post-occupation' phase. The Ba'th party issued a statement in celebration of Saddam's birthday on 28 April 2005. It reasserted the party's commitment to the deposed leader to 'continue the armed resistance and destroy the occupation, liberate and protect Iraq, and destroy the agent government'.[60]

In setting up their ideological justifications for opposing the foreign presence, the Ba'thists begin by pointing out that two distinct poles are engaged in a dynamic conflict with one another in Iraq: 'The occupation has produced its own facts, effects, and implications, which stem from and are linked to the program that it seeks to impose and implement in occupied Iraq and in the rest of the region.'[61] The US program, they say, is to achieve political and economic hegemony of the region, beginning with Iraq: 'Consequently the armed Iraqi resistance and its political leadership are waging this confrontation to produce a counter balance to the facts, effects, and local implications that occupation has produced.'[62] This nationalist rhetoric has been part and parcel of the Ba'thist ideological discourse since the 1970s. The strong Sunni Arab nationalist element and fears concerning dastardly foreign forces conspiring against Iraq are evident in the following insurgent leader's statement, which is typical of Sunni and Ba'thist nationalist discourse:

What the Arab brothers do not clearly realize is that Iraq is living under two occupations. One is an obvious occupation, namely, the one carried out by the US forces and their allies. The second is a secret occupation carried out by the Iranian intelligence services, which have sent more than 12,000 operatives to Iraq. These persons are given political cover by some Iraqi circles. They are carrying out very serious actions in Iraq, particularly among the sons of the Shiite sect. They are assassinating Ba'thists and enlightened, progressive Shiites. They are helping the US forces to pursue members of the resistance, and are providing them with name lists of Ba'thists, many of whom are in the occupation forces' jails now.[63]

The statement concludes by reiterating that the primary goal of the US invasion of Iraq was to 'protect the Zionist entity's security'.[64] This last point is one that many Iraqi Arabs, Sunni and Shi'a, fervently believe was a motivation for the invasion of Iraq.

But the Ba'thists have also discovered that it is to their advantage to stir up Iraqis on the basis of religious sentiment, which is a powerful tool for mobilizing people in favor of a cause. Moreover, the Ba'thists face a stark reality in Iraq: the rise of religious feeling among the population and the increase in piety among ostensible Ba'th Party members. They had to join that bandwagon in order to rouse the ire of the people against the foreign presence. Saddam's post-downfall statements were suffused with religious imagery. Of course, he had started down that path more than a decade earlier, but he clearly realized that religion was a great motivational and recruitment tool in the fight against the Coalition. Take the message he issued on the occasion of Ramadan in November 2003, almost a month before his capture:

O great people, God willing, O magnanimous mujahideen, lovers of martyrdom ... O magnanimous men of our armed forces wherever you are hold on tightly to the weapons of the valiant resistance ... May God's peace, mercy, and blessings be upon you ... Our martyrs are in paradise while the dead of the louts and our other enemies are in hell. Let us make this month of Ramadan the prelude to and foundation of victory as it was during the great (battle), which marked the era of the vanguards of Arabs and Muslims who were honored in you.[65]

With Saddam's capture, it is believed that Izzat Ibrahim al-Duri, one of the former leader's closest comrades, has continued to promote the fusion of nationalist and religious themes as an element of the Ba'thist 'resistance' strategy. Izzat Ibrahim, a former vice-president and member of the top decision-making body in the defunct regime, the Revolutionary Command Council, was always one of the most religiously oriented members of the government. He is on the run and it seems he plays a key role in the Ba'thist resistance to the foreign presence in Iraq. It has even been argued that he is the leader of this clandestine 'Iraqi national resistance'. Whatever the case, he does seem to rank highly in the Ba'th resistance and has been responsible for myriad ideological statements issued by the party, particularly those couched in religious terms.[66]

One of the key questions that has been asked is what motivates the Ba'th Party, or the former regime elements writ large, to fight? It is unclear whether many of the ordinary Sunni insurgents or even the former regime personnel are necessarily motivated to fight for their former leader or even whether he is seen as 'the cause'. In the 1980s the Saddamist cult of personality held Iraq in an iron grip. Saddam was the almost infallible 'necessary leader' under whose helm the country was destined to move forward to a bright future. The aura of invincibility slipped over the years with the disasters that befell the country. Tikrit, near Saddam's birth-place, the village of Al Auja, showed contradictory emotions over his downfall and the entry into the city of US military units in force. One the one hand, in the early days of the occupation there was an eerie quiet in the city, which had been expected to be-come a hotbed of resistance. On the other hand, some of the resi-dents defiantly celebrated the fallen dictator's sixty-sixth birthday on 28 April 2003, causing a fracas with troopers of the US 4th Infantry Division.[67]

Yet it is unclear whether the Tikrit citizens' wariness of US troops had more to do with their affection for their former leader and native son than with sheer humiliation at the US presence and disgust with US standard operating procedure. Some residents ex-pressed their affection for the former leader: 'We love him. He gave money to the poor. He helped every man. And he made the city secure. Saddam Hussein loved God. We want him back.'[68] For many residents who had to put up with the collapse of law and order in the immediate aftermath of the regime's downfall and the ensuing vacuum, Saddam represented the rule of law, while the Americans did not. One city resident said: 'The American people are not good people. They support these people who steal the shirt

off your back.'[69] Loyalty to Saddam in Tikrit was expressed in graffiti on the walls—'He's coming back', 'We are waiting patiently',
'Cooperate with the Americans and die'—and in the sentiments of
men like Hakim Salih Mohammad, a former warrant officer in the
Special Republican Guard: 'This new coalition has dismantled the
military and intelligence offices. Hundreds of thousands of people
are without jobs. Saddam is our symbol, and he is our destiny.'[70]
Many residents, however, were not necessarily sorry to see Saddam
go. The words of Muhammad Abdullah are telling: 'Our lives were
not particularly privileged just because this was his hometown. The
ones close to Saddam could do whatever they wanted. They could
take whatever they wanted. They could kill anyone.'[71]

   Sheikh Majid al-Qa'ud is a wealthy man from a well-known
family in al-Ramadi. He is also a self-proclaimed member of the
Ba'thist element of the *muqawamah*. He is secretary-general of a
political wing of the nationalist-Ba'thist insurgents known as Wahaj
al-Iraq, or Flame of Iraq. Not surprisingly, he is wanted by the
Coalition and is in exile in a Middle Eastern country. In an interview with a Western newspaper, the reporter began by asking:
'The United States considers you to be a terrorist. What do *you*
call yourself?' He replied unequivocally: 'A patriot fighting against
his country's occupation. Unfortunately, history tells us that there
is hardly ever freedom without blood being shed.'[72] When asked
about Zarqawi he responded: 'Listen, I am from al-Ramadi and my
family is from al-Ramadi, yet neither I nor my relatives have ever
seen this al-Zarqawi fellow. Does it not occur to you that he might
be a convenient invention? The embodiment of Evil, one of those
things of which the Americans are so fond?' Majid al-Qa'ud is a
staunch supporter of the former Iraqi president: 'Our president is
still Saddam until such times as we, not Bush, decide otherwise.'[73]

   Saddam Hussein's apprehension by the Coalition in mid-
December 2003 and his less than dignified performance in those

early days was a blow to the Ba'thist component of the insurgency
(from which it was eventually to recover). Ba'thist insurgent leaders and spokesmen tried to downplay the impact of Saddam's capture by arguing that one should not focus solely or primarily on the
role of the leader but on the motivations of the 'resistance' and on
the cause they espouse. Nonetheless, even if they were not directly
fighting for him to restore him to power, it is clear that for many
former regime elements he constituted a symbol of resistance to
foreign occupation. It was important that he was free, even if he
was not in direct control of the insurgency. Unsurprisingly, in January 2004 pro-Saddam insurgent leader 'Abu al-Mu'tasim', who
may be a former army officer, declared candidly that the capture
of the former president hurt the insurgency: 'There is no question
that the capture of the leader President Saddam Husayn dealt a
blow not only to the resistance fighters but to all the Arab nation's
honorable sons. It is not a situation that we can easily bypass. President Saddam Husayn is the symbol and leader of the resistance.'[74]
However, he expressed confidence in victory because justice and
determination was on the side of the *muqawamah*:

[The resistance] represents the sons of Iraq and is an expression of their
conscience ... History, however, will record that it was the Ba'thists who
started this resistance. It continued and escalated when elements of the
Iraqi Army, the RG, Saddam's Fedayeen, Al Quds Army, and members of
the security services joined its ranks...the resistance includes pan-Ara-
bists, nationalists, and Islamists. It also includes Arab volunteers who are
effectively participating in this heroic resistance that is led and adminis-
tered by the Ba'th party.[75]

The Ba'thist element of the insurgency has key strengths such as
the fact that the party continues to be deeply embedded in Sunni
Arab society and that its conspiratorial mentality allows it to operate effectively in a clandestine manner. However, it suffers from
severe weaknesses. First, and paradoxically, despite the Ba'thist

ideology having deep roots in Iraqi society, few people still believe in it. Many of the disgruntled Sunnis who are engaged in violence or who support the insurgency either passively or actively recognize that they cannot say they are fighting to restore the old order. Several insurgent groups went out of their way to deny links to or support for the former regime. In a videotaped statement sent to Al-Jazeera television, a masked man belonging to an unidentified resistance group reads the following statement:

We, your brothers in the resistance, announce to the world at large that we will resist. We will resist the occupier to defend our religion, creed, homeland, and people.

We would like to draw your attention to an important fact. This spreading resistance, which is growing bigger and bigger in an uninterrupted manner, has absolutely no links with the so-called remnants of the former regime. The former regime and its Ba'thist agents lack the courage to sacrifice their blood, funds, spouses, and sons. Had they been so, they would not have surrendered Baghdad so easily. Since they have no values and principles, how could they come back now to defend Baghdad? Worldly possessions are all they think about.

This land is ours and the occupier is an enemy to God and Muslims. You know the United States. Our religion orders us to pursue jihad ... The Iraqi resistance is a genuinely national resistance that has absolutely no ties to any party. Our resistance of the occupation is a legitimate resistance sanctioned by international norms and resolutions. How can we not resist when the occupation authorities detain thousands of Iraqis? How can we not resist when our honor is violated and our land is occupied?[76]

Other seemingly nationalistic insurgent groups, such as the Popular Iraqi Liberation Front (PILF), claimed to have nothing to do with the former regime or its party. PILF distributed pamphlets in the streets of Fallujah in late 2003, in which it announced its active opposition to the Coalition but also declared that there is 'no link between the current popular and national resistance and any oppressive Baath regime resistance'. The resistance in the farming village of Duluiyah in central Iraq, 50 miles north of Baghdad, was largely undertaken by former regime military personnel who show strong nationalist, Ba'thist and Islamist but not necessarily pro-Saddam sentiments. What was strange about this farming community was the presence of as many BMW vehicles as of tractors. The small town had provided the Iraqi regular army with many able-bodied men over the years. A suspected insurgent commander, Abu Abdallah, was a lieutenant colonel in the Iraqi army who professes disgust with the former regime yet refuses to cooperate with the occupation. He will not consider joining the new Iraqi security services: 'An Iraqi Army under US occupation, what is that? It is a militia of back-up troops, like in Afghanistan where the Afghan Army spends its time killing Afghans. The resistance does not operate like an army. There is a mixture of everything, Baathists, nationalists, Islamists.'[77] And Saddam: 'He is finished, it is the country that we, the resistance is defending. All we want, I mean all the resistance wants, is an Iraqi Government, democratically elected, that defends the country's interests, not puppets in the hands of the Americans. I hope our Shiite brothers join us soon.'[78]

There was mutual antipathy between some of the insurgents with a more Islamist orientation and those associated with the former regime. Hareth Yousef, an accountant and a self-described moderate Islamist, was scathing of the Ba'thists: 'They are cowards who use the faith of young Muslims to send them to fight the Americans. But they are acting in their own interests, not for the good of Iraq. If ever our sheikh were to decree jihad, I guarantee you things would be different. The Americans would regret that Saddam Husayn is no longer there.'[79]

More importantly, though, the senior leadership of the Ba'th regime has been incarcerated. The ignominious capture of Saddam in December 2003 and the humiliating pictures of him were a body blow. Take the case of a once-fervent supporter of the Ba'th, Muhammad Ibrahim Oda, a middle-class public-sector employee and a member of the Ba'th Party, a fact of which he was immensely proud. He was not demoralized by the capture of Saddam, stridently stating: 'The Ba'th Party did not die with the capture of Saddam Hussein. It has known other reverses. It will be reborn, it will reform itself, it will change its political outlook and return to its original principles that Saddam Hussein had displaced.'[80] Oda was arrested by the Americans and placed in a tent at Baghdad International Airport with fifty-three dignitaries of the former regime. There he allegedly learned a great deal about the nature of power in the Saddam regime, including the leader's arbitrary exercise of power and failure to listen to advice. Oda's experience in jail among the top officials of the former regime was an eye-opening experience for him. For Oda now, Saddam is 'nothing more than a shameful stain in the history of the Ba'th party'.[81]

Nonetheless, it is too early to dismiss the Ba'th Party. It still terrifies the Kurds and the Shi'a. Many people with whom I talked in Iraq believe that without the US presence the Shi'a parties would have had a hard time dealing with its clandestine cadre. Unsurprisingly, the Shi'a are relying on more professional Iranian security and intelligence personnel to identify and 'liquidate' important members of the former regime. The political activities of the Ba'th Party were evident in the strong statement it issued in support of the deposed leader when he appeared in court in late October. This reveals that he still has a following, although with the incarceration of most of the leadership, including the former president, it does look like a new generation of leaders is appearing. Whether they are united in support for Saddam or are trying to move the party into a post-Saddam phase is as yet unclear. This is largely because the party members have not issued a clear ideological platform, despite having held a couple of conferences outside Iraq. We have

heard a great deal about Muhammad Yunis al-Ahmad, the supposedly rising star of the post-Saddam Ba'th Party, including rumors
that he has had preliminary contact with the Coalition to discuss
topics of mutual interest.[82] Moreover, the Ba'th Party has gone
some way towards reinventing parts of its ideological output to
reflect Sunni fears of marginalization.

Motives of former military personnel

At his first news interview, Jay Garner, the hapless first proconsul,
declared his intention to use the Iraqi army to 'help rebuild their
own country' and 'not to demobilize it immediately and put a lot
of unemployed people on the street. We'd continue to pay them
to do things like engineering, road construction, work on bridges,
remove rubble, de-mine, pick up unexploded ordnance, construction work.'[83] Garner's plan would disappear into the dustbin of
history, with catastrophic consequences.

On 24 May 2003 Garner's successor, Paul Bremer, issued one of
his most important and fateful edicts when he declared the complete
dissolution of the Iraqi armed forces, including the regular army,
special regime-protection units such as the Republican Guard, the
Special Republican Guard and the security/intelligence services,
as well as an end to conscription. This was not an auspicious move,
especially because the situation in the country remained very unsettled, but it was not a spur-of-the moment decision. Some US officials who had worked on setting up the new Iraqi military structure claimed that the Iraqi armed forces simply dissolved themselves and that Bremer's edict merely 'legalized' that self-dissolu-
tion. This assertion is incorrect. The fact that the Iraqi army melted
in the face of the Coalition during the war does not mean that it
dissolved itself. The officers and men merely went home. They did
not go into occultation—spiritual disappearance—like the Twelfth

Imam. The occupation authorities could have issued public statements or decrees telling them to muster in their former bases and
await further instructions. Of course, the incorrigibles and the
die-hard members of the regime security services and 'praetorian'
guards would not have done so. Furthermore, the officers and men
did re-emerge following the cessation of hostilities, to ascertain
their future status. That would have been the time to set up a well-
planned and organized process of demobilization and reintegration
of thousands into civilian society and vetting those who wished to
stay on in a smaller armed force. An estimated 9,000 officers were
senior members of the Ba'th Party; they had to be. Let us assume
that they were truly irredeemable. That still left thousands of other
officers in this army that was top heavy with brass.

Walter Slocombe, a former official in the Clinton administration, who was given the task of helping to build the post-Saddam
Iraqi army, argued that 'the Iraqi army disbanded itself, or with a
certain amount of encouragement from Coalition forces'.[84] It is
unclear how accurate this statement is. As journalist Mark Fineman and his colleagues wrote: 'But that nonexistent army suddenly
materialized by the tens of thousands in the streets of Baghdad before the ink was dry on the decree to disband it.'[85] Unless these
demonstrating military personnel suddenly suffered from collective amnesia and forgot what unit they had served in, it would have
been easy to reconstitute them. As for the reasons behind the dissolution of the armed forces, it was not difficult to enumerate a
few valid ones. Moreover, the edict dissolving the army was not
an impromptu measure. It was deliberate policy formulated at the
highest levels among the civilian defense planners of the Pentagon.
It has been argued that that key officials within the Pentagon and
former Iraqi exiles pushed for the dissolution of the armed forces
in order to remove a threat to the consolidation of power by the
returning exiles. There is considerable merit to this proposition.

Fineman and his colleagues researched the issue before going to Iraq, and wrote that one of the reasons could have been that 'gutting what was once the most powerful Arab army on their doorstep was also a priority for Israel's generals ... The generals routinely visited Defense Secretary Donald Rumsfeld's Special Plans Office as it developed plans for postwar Iraq.'[86] Senior administration officials protested, however, that there was no pro-Israeli agenda. 'This is not a neoconservative agenda,' said a Defense Department official. Another senior administration official explained that 'the army was the main instrument of repression by Saddam Hussein. If we had allowed the army to continue in its present form, we would be losing hearts and minds right now.'[87] Nobody suggested that the army should remain the way it was before the war but, ironically, this last assertion comes closer to the truth than any other. The old Iraqi army was indubitably tied to the institutionalization of Sunni Arab ascendancy in Iraq and the promotion of their nationalist vision from the earliest days of the state to 2003. In short, dissolving the army meant also driving a stake through a Sunni identity that had relied on the armed forces as the primary institutional and *symbolic* support for that identity.

This is also how the Iraqi opposition to Saddam saw the Iraqi army. Unsurprisingly, the dissolution of the Iraqi armed forces was welcomed by the exiles, many of whom were suspected of having proposed or encouraged the measure, and by the Kurds, who had been at the receiving end of the Iraqi army's counter-insurgency campaigns. Jalal Talabani said that the decision to dismantle the old Iraqi army 'demonstrated great wisdom', that the old Iraqi army had a 'record of internal repression and external aggression', and that the decree had 'struck at the roots of the Arab nationalist militarism that plagued Iraq even before Saddam'.[88] One wonders whether he would criticize the development of Kurdish militarism and nationalism among the *peshmerga* forces in the same vein.

During my tour in summer and fall 2005 I witnessed at first hand the virulent nationalism of some of the Kurdish officers. I am not excoriating them for it; they had every right to promote it after decades of iron-fisted oppression.

The edict alienated a large and important sector of Iraqi society, raising to a fever pitch the sense of injured nationalism and suspicions concerning US intentions.[89] An Iraqi officer identified merely as Brigadier General Salah was quoted in a Baghdad newspaper:

After the United States entered Iraq and overthrew the regime for its own political and military calculations and economic interests and to weaken Iraq's combat capability after it destroyed all its weapons during the fighting, it discovered that Iraq in the coming stage does not need a big army. The United States will set up a very small army, the sole duty of which will be to protect the border and control security. *Its dissolution of the army secures its interests and Israel's interests; it does not care about our fate and the fate of our families.*[90]

While the history of the Iraqi army has not been covered with martial glory, the vast majority of Iraqis take pride in their army. I noted this even among Shi'a and Kurdish officers who had served in the former army and had been purged, retired or imprisoned by the former regime, and were now serving in the new army. Indeed, Iraqis, especially the officer corps, believe that Saddam, more than any other leader in Iraqi history, warped the army's noble purpose and honor. In the words of a senior officer from the Sunni Arab Al-Jiburi tribe:

Like all other armies, the Iraqi Army is one of the most important national pillars and a symbol of the homeland and the people's pride and dignity. Our army has always been like this until three decades ago, when it was undermined and suffered organized and deliberate destruction by the ruling regime. The Army's armament and equipment were modernized and its formations enlarged but *it sank at the same time to lower dangerous levels, most noticeably the levels where its hierarchy and rules deteriorated, its exemplary*

discipline turned into indiscipline, and the rules of assessment for promotions were
corrupted. Cronyism and parochial, sectarian, ethnic, and tribal discrimination
became rampant.[91]

Bremer's actions prompted cries of dismay from Iraqi officers, who threatened to take their revenge by conducting suicide operations or by joining the burgeoning low-level insurgency that was beginning to concern the US military. An estimated 5,000 officers and enlisted men staged a demonstration on 26 May denouncing the occupation. Through their spokesman, Lieutenant General Sahib al-Musawi, the officers demanded that the administration rescind the proclamation dissolving the Iraqi armed forces, implement plans to set up a new force structure using elements of the old armed forces, pay military salaries immediately, and accelerate plans to form a new Iraqi government that would be representative of all its people.[92] A lieutenant colonel said: 'If they don't pay us, we'll start problems. We have guns at home. If they don't pay us, if they make our children suffer, they'll hear from us.'[93]

The collapse of professional careers and the loss of income had a disastrous effect on the material and psychological well-being of military personnel. Many ended up hawking cheap goods or foodstuffs as street vendors, poignantly portrayed in the comments of Sergeant Hasan Abu Ali:

After 23 years of service in the army, during which I wasted my youth, I ended up selling tea on this sidewalk. It is true, this is not shameful. But where are my rights and salary? Did US democracy come to devour them? I know officers who, out of despair because they ceased to receive their salaries, have begun to work secretly in areas far from where they live. They take jobs that do not befit army officers, such as selling vegetables or sweets. They also work as bellhops in commercial stores.[94]

An anti-Saddam group of Iraqi officers, the oddly named Free Civilian Officers Movement, which worked with the Coalition, professed to be disappointed with the postwar treatment of the Iraqi army and its personnel. It attacked the Coalition for making promises that it had no intention of keeping. For example, Air Force Staff Brigadier General Riyad Abbas Rida al-Bayati, the movement's representative in Babil Province (home to 18,000 military personnel of various ranks) said:

The coalition forces made many promises on many occasions to pay an emergency allowances [*sic*] to the employees of the Ministry of Defense in Babil. Unfortunately, they did not keep their promises. This created a crisis between the street in Babil and the coalition forces. The military men feel that they are deliberately being treated unfairly and humiliated and that this contradicts the goals which the coalition forces came to Iraq for. The continuation of this situation will lead to serious problems that the coalition forces can avoid by paying the salaries and allowances of the people who have large families and live a hard life.[95]

Little was actually done to mollify the officers and enlistees of the former Iraqi armed forces. The first postwar commemoration of Army Day, 6 January 2004, was a sad and humiliating one for many former Iraqi army veterans. For them, including some members of the new structure, the proposed new security forces were a grave disappointment. 'We are not a proper army,' said a corporal in the Iraqi Civil Defense Corps (ICDC), who had served in the former military. Many veterans marked the day by demonstrating against the dismantling of the old army and demanding their promised monthly stipends. Mudhar Abdul Baqi Badri, a former officer in the Iraqi Special Forces, a unit whose training was very tough and professional, refused an offer of $300 a month to become a private security guard: 'It is so remote from the honor of being an officer.'[96]

Unsurprisingly, the occupation authorities ensured that members of the disbanded military would continue to receive stipends and pensions to prevent them from engaging in armed resistance.

But by early fall 2003 any Coalition effort to mollify many members of the former army was doomed. It was no longer a matter of getting stipends and pensions to take care of themselves and their families; it was now a matter of honor and pride. Many officers joined resistance or insurgent groups either as active participants or as experts and trainers for combatant cells. In early November 2005 the Iraqi government issued a proclamation that urged former junior and mid-ranking officers and enlisted personnel to join the new army. It is not clear how much success they will have. Sunni officers have expressed reservations about this 'sectarian' government. Others fear that they will be ultimately purged, so wonder why they should bother. I was unsurprised to come across Sunni Arab officers in the new army who were intent on leaving and going to Kurdistan, of all places.

US journalist Christian Parenti met with former officers who were in charge of insurgent units. One worked in a normal commercial job and funded insurgency operations. The other was a general in the former military who '[held] forth with a torrent of virulently anti-Shiite, hard-core Sunni Baathism'.[97] Parenti quotes the general: 'The Shia know nothing! The Sunni must govern Iraq.'[98] This is not very different from what one Sunni general also told me in 2003 in a meeting in the Karrada district. But what most irked the general interviewed by Parenti was the dissolution of the army: 'The Iraqi Army was very strong, very important. It was very bad when America destroyed it.'[99]

Parenti also managed to arrange a meeting with a resistance cell in the Baghdad Sunni district of Adhamiya. It was led by a forty-year-old former army officer who said he was in the resistance because of his shame and humiliation at the dissolution of the army, and that the goal of his group was to 'repel the invaders and restore sovereignty'.[100] He claimed to maintain contact with the Fedayeen Saddam, but said that the resistance is highly decentralized and kept that way for fear of spies and lack of secure communications. He added that his group 'believes in the ideology of the Baath Party and of Islam' and that it was loyal to Saddam. He indicated that the former leader's capture did not affect their motivation to continue the struggle: 'We will keep fighting. Our goals are clear.'[101] After the regime fell some former officers who had had to hide their Islamist inclinations were able to display them more openly. They managed to develop a blend of Islamist and nationalist motives for opposing the foreign presence in their country. A Fallujah resident, Sheikh Abu Bashir, a former army officer, argued that the biggest problem for the United States was the dissolution of the army, but augmented his fury at that act with a religious motivation: 'They were trying to damage Iraqi society. So everybody immediately joined the resistance ... [They] have to leave this country, even by force. This is not just my opinion, our God ordered us to resist them as invasion forces.'[102]

Nationalism, honor, revenge and pride

Four key values—nationalism, honor, revenge and pride—dictate the need to fight occupation. In other words, resisting occupation simply because it is an occupation is a major motivating factor. One of the towering figures of modern political philosophy, Sir Isaiah Berlin, on whom I was weaned in Britain in the 1980s (another was Karl Popper), once wrote: 'Nationalism is an inflamed condition of national consciousness which can be, and has on occasion been, tolerant and peaceful. *It usually seems to be caused by wounds, some form of collective humiliation*.'[103] While in Iraq I came across Iraqis who would espouse a vague kind of nationalism as they expressed their distaste for the foreign presence in the country. Others who were more articulate or better educated expounded their disgust from within a framework of a more coherent nationalist ideology.

Both in my mind, however, fell within the rubric of Berlin's notion of an 'inflamed condition' caused by wounds. Many other observers noticed this. CBS news correspondent David Hawkins interviewed Iraqi insurgents and posed the following question: 'Why do you fight? Why do you attack American soldiers?' One responded: 'This is occupation, so we fight against the occupation.'[104] Another, an educated man of the Dulaim tribe, told a French journalist: 'Upon the fall of Baghdad, I assumed my responsibilities as a Muslim and an Iraqi citizen. What human being can stand to watch his country, his house destroyed by people who respect nothing? These people have no motivation except material interests. The members of the former Governing Council arrived on American tanks, violating holy places, injuring people's honor and dignity, leaving many dead.'[105] Anthony Shadid details the spirit of revenge that has animated Iraqis to fight in the insurgency. He cites the example of Saadi Muhmmad Abu Shaiba, who returned to fight and die in Fallujah in mid-December 2004 to avenge the death of his thirteen-year-old son at the hands of US forces.[106]

An Arab journalist, Zeki Chehab, political editor with the Al-Hayat-LBC television station, met in the Ramadi area with insurgents who defined themselves in nationalist terms. Said one: 'We do not want to see our country occupied by forces clearly pursuing their own interests, rather than being poised to return Iraq to the Iraqis.'[107] In Mosul and Fallujah Chehab met with insurgents who were more Islamist in their orientation. He mentioned reports of representatives of Iraqi insurgents meeting in Amman, the Jordanian capital, with representatives of the Palestinian group Hamas to learn from its experiences against the Israelis.

The US behavior and tactics of shooting first and asking questions later, or ransacking homes as they search for former regime figures and insurgents, infuriate Iraqis.[108] A resident of the wealthy Mansur district told a British reporter after an US raid in the area that he was not a supporter of the former regime: 'But I cannot accept the way Americans treat us. When I see things like this I can understand why people want to drive them out of our country. If this happens more and more then I will also join this resistance.'[109]

The US loss of Iraqi support reached its zenith in spring 2004.[110] An outraged and humiliated Iraqi told a reporter that he had been ready to explode for months: 'But in the last two weeks, these feelings have blown up inside me. The Americans are attacking Shiite and Sunni at the same time. They have crossed a line. I had to get a gun.'[111] One poor Iraqi, a laborer in his thirties named Abdul Razak al-Muaimi, said: 'I train my son to kill Americans. That is one reason I am grateful to Saddam. All Iraqis know how to use a weapon ... [US soldiers] searched my house. They kicked my Koran. They speak to me so poorly in front of my children. It's not that I encourage my son to hate Americans. It's not that I make him want to join the resistance. Americans do that for me.'[112]

An Italian journalist had an encounter with Sunni insurgents in Mosul who proceeded to explain to her why they were fighting:

We are the fighters for the freedom of Iraq, we are the sons of Mosul, we are the mujahidin who will halt the US crusaders. We will win because the people of Iraq are with us, because Allah is with us, and because the Americans are gutless dogs ... The Americans are rich, but how many soldiers, how many more vehicles can they afford to lose? They are talking about withdrawal. And do you know why? Because we can place in their path all the bombs that we want to, and we can kill them all any time we want to. They will flee like yellow-bellied dogs, or else we will kill them one by one.[113]

These insurgents were not the elite of the former Ba'th Party but country people from the region around the city. They had taken up arms against the US presence and the favoritism shown to the Kurds. As one of them rather theatrically pontificated:

We are the sons of Mosul. When Saddam fell, we avoided fighting against the Americans in order not to destroy Mosul. But gradually we saw the Kurds becoming bosses in our home, and the American infidels stealing our oil, building ever larger bases, and bringing in an increasing number of vehicles. So we realized that they would never leave voluntarily, and that we would have to hound them out. We got organized. Friends telephoned each other, they met in the diwans [rooms for receiving guests] and they counted the weapons available to them.[114]

Insurgents were motivated by a host of factors to join the fight against the Coalition and the new post-Saddam order. Canadian freelance journalist Patrick Graham stayed with insurgents in the Fallujah area for an extended period in 2004. He became friends with a mid-ranking insurgent leader, 'Mohammed', who struck him as a basically rational and decent man with quite ordinary justifications for his being in the insurgency: '[Mohammed] doubted that the United States had come to liberate Iraq. It had been a strategic war, he thought, designed to threaten Syria and Iran and to protect Israel.'[115] It is possible to distinctly categorize Mohammed's motivations for becoming an insurgent. First, he was enraged by the civilian casualties caused by US troops. Second, he subscribed to a general position that the Koran required him to fight non-Muslim occupiers. But the profile of this relatively articulate insurgent leader did not suggest that he was a religious extremist. Third, Mohammed, like many Sunnis, feared the rise of the Shi'a in the post-Saddam era. Finally, it seems that his principle reason for being an insurgent was simple opposition to a foreign presence in his country:

When we see the U.S. soldiers in our cities with guns, it is a challenge to us ... I don't know a lot about political relations in the world, but if you look at history—Vietnam, Iraq itself, Egypt, and Algeria—countries always rebel against occupation ... The world knows that this is an honorable resistance and has nothing to do with the old regime. Even if Saddam

Hussein dies we will continue to fight to throw out the American forces. We take our power from our history, not from one person.[116]

Another insurgent, a Sunni Arab in his late twenties who was interviewed by Western journalists, claimed that he was fighting not to bring back Saddam, but out of disgust at US behavior in Iraq and the bad treatment of Iraqis: 'We are not doing this for the sake of Saddam. Saddam Hussein is finished. The Americans always say they are against terrorism, but they are conducting terrorism right here in Iraq.'[117] He stated that his group had contact with other insurgent groups but that they did not coordinate operations with one another. They had started their operations with little knowledge of US capabilities but had been able to adapt over the course of the insurgency.

An insurgent leader, Abu Abdullah, a Jordanian, posed the following question to a US journalist:

Can you describe a man who defends his country as a terrorist? Iraq is the land of prophets and the birthplace of civilization. We will fight until we shed the last drop of our blood for this country. I saw what the Zionists did to Palestine, how they destroyed Palestinian homes. I told myself I could never let this happen to another Arab country. The Americans are only coming to occupy Iraq, to drain this land of its natural resources.[118]

The Iraqi National Resistance Movement, a large insurgent group, is dedicated to continuing operations until Iraq is liberated from foreign occupation and has called upon Arab and Muslim lands to provide support and volunteers to fight alongside Iraqis. It argues that its operations have prevented the occupiers from consolidating their position in Iraq. This movement is motivated by religious principles to oppose the foreign presence, as the following statement it issued clearly shows: 'This resistance did not emerge as a reaction to US provocative acts against the Iraqi people or for the lack of services as some analysts delude themselves into believing. It is rather resistance to drive out the occupier based on principles and faith and in order to win nothing but a place in heaven.'[119]

In Amriya, 30 miles east of Baghdad, a Western journalist interviewed members of the Army of Muhammad, who claimed that they had 5,000 fighters and a central command with cells in Tikrit, Baghdad and Ramadi. The 'army' started out as a gathering of tribal fighters, many of whom had served previously in the army and knew how to use firearms. The Army of Muhammad's ideology, says the journalist, is a 'blend of ardent nationalism, Sunni Islamic zealotry, and anti-Jewish bigotry'.[120] Its members claimed they did not want Saddam back. And they were not reticent in expressing their hatred for the United States: 'The Americans have occupied our land under a false pretext, and without any international authorization. They kill our women and children and old men. They want to bring the Jews to our holy land in order to control Iraq, to achieve the Jewish dream.'[121] The members of the Army of Muhammad who were interviewed were from the Dulaim tribe and had joined the resistance because US forces had attacked the tribe.[122]

Tribal motives

Given the social importance of the tribe in Iraq, it is worth asking what motivates its members to fight. For example, in the Fallujah area the 50,000-strong Albueissa clan has played a prominent role in the tribally based insurgency. Its members claimed that their fighters in early November 2003 shot down a US Army Chinook, which resulted in the deaths of seventeen US troops.

First, there are the intangible motivations such as the reluctance of conservative Islamists and nationalists to submit to foreign infidels. There is also the traditional tribal reluctance to submit to onerous, strong central authority. Saddam often had trouble with

Sunni Arab tribes. The idea that most of the insurgents were former regime dead-enders can be dispelled by the incidents that
took place in the mid-1990s between the Dulaim tribe, living in
and around the Ramadi area, and Saddam's regime. Ramadi was
a stronghold of the 750,000-member Dulaim tribe. Its members
are also to be found in the cities of Hit (Heet), Fallujah, Haditha,
Kubaysah, al-Qaim and Rutbah. It was an influential tribe that contributed significantly to the political, military and economic life
of the country even before the rise of the Ba'th regime. Its members consolidated their positions in the security services under the
Ba'th regime; many held positions in the intelligence services and
the Republican Guard. But relations between the regime and the
Dulaimis began to unravel when Major General Abd al-Karim al-
Hamdani allegedly led a small group of other Dulaimis in an abortive coup in 1992. Then, to the shock of the regime, segments of the
Dulaimis rose in rebellion in Ramadi in 1995. The events leading
to this rebellion started months before in late 1994, when Iraqi Air
Force General Muhammad Madhlum al-Dulaimi and three other
Dulaimi officers were arrested at the al-Bakr military base near
Samarra because they had deigned to criticize the regime and the
actions of Saddam's dissolute and vicious oldest son, Uday. In May
1995 the officers were tortured and executed, and their bodies
were sent home. The city erupted in violence, which was put down
by regime security forces. From then on Saddam viewed the Dulaimis with suspicion, but because they were so well-entrenched in
the state apparatus he could not rid himself of them without causing a serious tribal eruption. Yet the Dulaimis have been among
the most consistent supporters of the insurgency. Surely this is not
because they are regime dead-enders.

    Second, there are the tangible material incentives to fight, which
can be fixed by the Coalition. These include the lack of economic
opportunities, security, and law and order. Most sheikhs do not

view these as civic necessities for the benefit of the people. Rather, they often want financial and material rewards to benefit them and that they can also hand out to their tribes. Many expect the simple process of patronage to operate, and in the early days of the occupation a lot of money was thrown their way. Things are a little more complicated now, but not necessarily efficient. This, however, has not prevented some of the sheikhs from coming to the nearest US forces or authorities and brazenly requesting rewards.

I recall with considerable mirth that one sheikh came into a meeting dressed in a shiny Western suit and wearing a Rolex. He proceeded to demand that we help set up a police force for his small town—'town' being a kind description—and surrounding rural area. The total population encompassed not more than 3,000 souls. Yet he wanted close to 200 policemen. A 'town' of 3,000 simply did not require 200 policemen. I told my superior, who was sitting next to me, that the sheikh wanted to provide employment, salaries and brand new Glock pistols to the young men of his tribe. We said no, and the commanding officer said that we had to get recruits from other areas too. The sheikh continued to insist that his people 'deserved' to have the police force. He had the audacity to present the illogical argument that the town down the road from his was composed of 'bad elements' in cahoots with the insurgents and that they do not need a police force! I stared at him in sheer amazement, and then I replied: 'It is precisely because the other town is "bad" that it needs a police force more than you do.' He looked at me with undisguised dislike, followed by a look of 'Hey, get with the program.' It suddenly dawned on me. (Let us say I had an epiphany on the road to Tal Afar.) The sheikhs simply no longer have control over the young men of their tribes. Indeed, on many occasions sheikhs told me that they have no authority or rewards with which they can exercise control over the young men. Saddam had provided them with the wherewithal to exert their authority.

They expected us to do the same. The failure to do so opened the way for these young men to 'stray'. And stray many did—they joined either criminal gangs or the insurgency.

Finally, US missteps and 'boorish' behavior are a key factor. For example, US personnel trample on tribal honor and customs when searching private homes and individuals, and detain suspects for months without providing information or access to detainees. US standard operating procedures in response to ambushes and attacks have caused the deaths of innocent bystanders, infuriating the populace. In June 2003 a Fallujah clan chief expressed his anger thus: 'We will fight them to the death if they keep humiliating us.'[123] Even Iraqis whose tribal sentiments had been 'loosened' by modernization and urbanization argued that there must be revenge for humiliations. 'It has increased our hate against Americans. It also increases the violence against them. In Iraq, we are tribal people. When someone loses their son, they want revenge,' said Ali Hatem, a college student.[124] A member of the Albueissa tribe who lost his two-year-old granddaughter in September 2003 to seemingly trigger-happy US soldiers, said: 'It is their routine. After the Americans are attacked, they shoot everywhere. This is inhuman—a stupid act by a country always talking about human rights.'[125]

These are not isolated incidents. Conflict between Iraqi and American erupted in the equally conservative and tribal town of Hit in May 2003 as a result of what the population saw as over-aggressive responses against the locals, after hit-and-run attacks by insurgents. In an extensive discussion with several retired Sunni Arab officers I was told in no uncertain terms that one of the biggest factors promoting hatred for the US was its cultural ignorance and arrogance, and its disdain for the Iraqis. The evidence lay in the daily treatment of Iraqis and of detainees.[126]

In the tribal and conservative towns along the Euphrates valley, intense hatred of the presence of foreigners was enough to make members of the tribes fight. But again it was US methods that often tipped the scales. For example, an aggressive house-to-house search of homes in Hit after a grenade attack on US forces resulted in a major riot the next day, when thousands assaulted the local police station. An infuriated resident claimed: 'They are provoking us. This is a violation of our dignity. They have no right to enter our house and search it. I'm not a soldier, I'm not a policeman, I'm not a party member.'[127] Another resident added: 'We will defend our houses, our land, our city. We are Muslims, and we will defend Islam. The first thing we will do is defend our houses.'[128]

Relations between the Coalition and the tribes in the Samarra area were destined to be hostile. The collapse began when US soldiers shot up a group of fifteen wedding guests headed to the festivities in a truck. They killed four of the passengers and wounded nine others. Sheikh Ahmed Ali Yasin, head of the Albu-Abbas tribe, said: 'We have our tribal and Islamic laws which say that if someone kills one of our family, we must kill one of them. The only way to settle this is to pay a *diya* [blood money] and the Americans have told us they will not do this. Our people have been refused their rights under our law, and so they are angry.'[129] Attacks against US forces began shortly thereafter. The attackers were tribal insurgents whose ability with mortars and rocket-propelled grenades (RPGs) left a lot to be desired.[130]

Religion

Traditionally the Sunni clergy have not been as politically active as their Shi'a counterparts in mobilizing the populace against perceived injustices or inequities. This has begun to change in Iraq as in the rest of the Arab world.[131] In Iraq we have witnessed a rising tide of political activism among the mainstream clerical establishment and the emergence of younger politically active clergymen (*imams*) with clear-cut Salafist tendencies—that is, those who seek a purist interpretation and application of Islam. In Iraq the process of re-Islamization began in the 1990s. Mainstream and extremist Sunni Islamist tendencies have emerged in the country. The reasons for this will require future detailed sociological analysis, but we can at this juncture provide tentative answers to account for their re-emergence through the examination of two structural factors: first, the sociopolitical and cultural conditions prevailing in the 1990s; and second, the conditions in Iraq after the ouster of the Ba'th regime in 2003.

Sunni Islamic activism has a longstanding but checkered history in Iraq. The Iraqi branch of the famed Jamaat al-Ikhwan al-Muslimun (Society of Muslim Brotherhood, a Sunni Islamist movement started in 1928 in Egypt) was founded in 1947 by Sheikh Muhammad Mahmud al-Sawwaf, a religious scholar. Its stronghold was the northern city of Mosul, where it immediately threw itself into the political life of the country then under a thoroughly discredited monarchy. The Brotherhood in Iraq expanded rapidly in the 1950s and attracted significant numbers of adherents in Baghdad, Mosul, Kirkuk, Irbil, Sulaymaniyah, Basra, Tikrit and Samarra.[132] Many of its members were of the middle class. Its strength contrasts greatly with that of the current Iraqi Islamic Party, which claims it as mentor. The Iraqi Muslim Brotherhood had to contend with a more nationalist current within the Sunni Arab population in the 1960s and with the suspicions of the Iraqi army officers. Nonetheless, the constituency for such activism existed among very conservative Sunni Arabs living within the Sunni triangle bounded by Baghdad and Ramadi in the center and Mosul in the north. Moreover, a significant number of officers in the 1960s, particularly under the regimes of the Aref brothers, were conservative and quite religious. The secularism of the Ba'thist regime at the height of its power in the 1970s hindered the ability of Sunni Islamist movements to play a role in the political process, and the cashiering of Sunni officers with ties to Sunni political movements further removed such groups from the center of power. After the catastrophic defeat in the 1991 war many people, particularly within the officer corps, became more pious.

Despite its original allegiance to militant secularism, Saddam's regime began in the early and mid-1990s to promote the re-Islamization of Iraqi society to buttress its legitimacy.[133] Saddam implemented an official policy of religious revival so that the regime could control the rising tide of faith. This was symbolized by a number of religious policies undertaken with the official sanction of the former regime in the late 1990s. In 1999 the regime launched *al hamla al-imaniyah* (Enhancement of Islamic Faith) campaign. This 're-Islamization from the top', as one observer referred to it, saw the restriction of drinking and gambling establishments, the narrowing of secular practices, and the promotion of religious education and the propagation of religious programming in the media.[134] The regime even allowed Sunni clerics to politicize their sermons so long as they focused their ire on the forces that kept Iraq under debilitating sanctions and on criticizing the machinations of the Western powers that sought to destroy Iraq and Islam.[135] Those clerics who strayed from the official line were quickly reminded that the regime was in charge of the re-Islamization process. Take, for example, one of the insurgent *imams* of Fallujah, Sheikh Abdallah Abd al-Aziz al-Janabi, *imam* and preacher of the Sa'ad Ibn Abi Waqqas Mosque and professor at the Islamic Institute in Fallujah. He was banned in 1998 from delivering Friday sermons because he had bluntly declared from the mosque's pulpit: 'I see the American tanks roaming the streets of Iraq. Saddam is the strongest supporter of Jews and their positions. All Arab leaders are Jews, if not by religion then by affiliation.'[136] After the downfall of the regime he blamed the violence in Fallujah entirely on the Americans and

the personnel of the former regime, and added that the response
of the Fallujans to the US presence was justified on religious and
nationalist grounds. He accused Saddam of having been an agent
for the US.[137] Remarkably, even die-hard formerly secular Ba'thist
institutions that had been formed in the 1970s were transformed
into bastions of officially sanctioned Islam. A striking symbol of the
rising tide of officially sanctioned Islam in Iraq under Saddam was
the Umm al-Ma'arik mosque in central Baghdad, which was built
at a cost of $7.5 million. Islamic studies were added to the second-
ary-school curricula and in 1998 the regime opened an all-male
university, the Saddam University for Islamic Studies. A professor
at the university said: 'Iraq is witnessing a religious renaissance.
There was religious stagnation and a tendency toward material-
ism here. Nightclubs, bars, and pubs were spreading. Saddam has
helped correct that.'[138] An Iraqi sociologist at Baghdad University
indicated that the religious revival in Iraq took root because 'when
a society is in crisis like we are, with the embargo and all, religion
plays a greater part in soothing the psyche of the people and giving
the people greater strength to face the crisis'.[139]

The sanctions regime that existed between 1991 and 2003 promoted the return to religion among the Iraqi population. The destruction of the Iraqi middle class, the decline of the secular educational system and the rise of illiteracy, and the growth of despair
and anomie have resulted in large numbers of Iraqis seeking succor
in religion. Iraq's once large, well-educated and relatively affluent
middle class had collapsed by the end of the 1990s. Dr Humam al
Shama'a, a professor of economics and finance at Baghdad University, explains why: 'The state made a tremendous effort to rebuild
the infrastructure of the country after the war ended [in 1991].
With no financial resources, it was forced to resort to emission of
currency, which accelerated the rhythm of inflation four and a half
times a year until 1995. Wealth disappeared under the inflationary

pressure. The currency deteriorated. People depending on salaries [i.e. the middle class] were gradually impoverished. Tens of thousands of Iraqi families now rely only on government rations to survive.'[140] Unlike most developing countries where there is constant rural to urban migration, in Iraq there was a reverse process in the 1990s, as a result of sanctions. People went back to the countryside. As one observer said: 'There are no jobs in the cities. Jobs are in agriculture. Many people left the cities to work in the countryside, raising cattle and poultry.'[141] This extensive destruction of Iraq's infrastructure and of its middle class was well-documented during the 1990s.[142] While the regime focused mainly on reviving religion among the minority Sunni population, many Sunni Iraqi activists saw the regime's strategy as a move from 'infidelity to hypocrisy', said a senior Sunni Islamist, Dr 'Usamah al-Tikriti.

There was a major surge in the influence and power of the Sunni clerical establishment, largely due to several factors: the absence of any secular Sunni politicians or political parties to represent the community's interests; the spiritual needs of a community that had lost its bearings and felt that its identity was threatened; and the perceived integrity of the clerics, who refused to legitimate or cooperate with the occupation when there was an absence of Sunni politicians who could stand up to the foreign presence. 'I have more confidence in the religious leaders now. We are Muslims, and I believe religion is the truth. During this crisis, it was the religious leaders who tried to solve things,' said a Baghdad Sunni.[143] A professor at Baghdad University argued that the clerics had become a 'safety valve' for Iraqis. But above all the Sunni clerics were propelled into the limelight by the 'discriminatory' treatment of the Sunni community at the hands of the foreign presence and the outbreak of the insurgency. It is true that the Sunni clerical establishment adopted a hostile or wary attitude towards the occupation in the early days. Consider Sheikh Nadhim Khalil, who represents the new generation of Sunni clerics, mostly of Salafi background. Not yet thirty years old, he leads prayers at the Masjid al-Khulafa in Duluiyah, and argues with conviction and convincingly that 'only the mosques represent the Sunnis'.[144] He has convened weekly gatherings of the clerics of Duluiyah's seventeen mosques, at which they discussed political and local issues. Khalil condemns the occupation—'The occupation is like a cancer, and it has to be removed'—but rather prudently adds that the clerics 'are fighting with tongues'.[145] Others, like Mu'ayyad al-'Ubaidi, a preacher at the Abu Hanifa Mosque in Baghdad, preached caution while at the same time formally denouncing the foreign presence. At the height of summer 2003 he suggested that it was not yet time to declare a *jihad* and instead to judge the US by the speed with which it returns Iraq to the Iraqis. Others saw the foreign presence in the darkest terms but did not venture to offer any dramatic solutions. Qasem al-Abdali, *imam* and preacher at the Abu 'Ubaida Mosque, was emphatic on why the US was in Iraq: 'The occupation has two aims. The first is economic—to establish a base in the Arab Islamic countries. The second is to attack Islam.'[146] He concluded that the Coalition 'will continue to do harm to us until we convert to their religion'.[147]

But Sunni clerical moderation declined as the summer of 2003 wore on. The manifest inability of the United States to restore law and order, security and basic services was galling. The perception that the Coalition was targeting the Sunni community deliberately was shared by the Sunni clerics. The seizure of Sunni mosques by Shi'a political groups was perceived as having been aided and abetted by the Coalition's manifest failure to maintain public order and to prevent insidious Iranian influence from infiltrating Iraq.[148] Finally, the arrest of clerics—those who tended to be Salafist in orientation and were seen by Coalition forces to be promoting resistance—galvanized the Sunni clerical establishment and moved its members either to seek a more activist political role or deeper and more active involvement in the insurgency itself. These events served to raise the stature of the Sunni clerics, who became unswerving in their opposition to the US occupation. Sheikh Mahdi Ahmed al-Sumaidi, *imam* of the Ibn Taymiyah Mosque in Baghdad, was detained in early 2004 after a weapons cache was discovered in the mosque. His release from detention did not diminish his virulent opposition: 'Neither the occupation forces nor the government they installed is acceptable. The legitimate power is the resistance … America's brutality has caused many to understand that Islam is the answer to our problems. The only solution is Islamic government.'[149] He has often issued withering denunciations of the United States and the Bush administration, accusing the United States of leading a 'crusade' against Islam. He poured scorn on the idea that foreign Arabs were involved in the insurgency, and countered by saying that any Arabs who were involved in the insurgency had lived in Iraq among the Iraqis for decades and that it was natural for them to support their Iraqi brethren in their time of need. Sumaidi concluded with the advice he would give to young Iraqis: 'Resist the occupation. To protest openly against the occupation, with words at first. And if words are not sufficient, by war.'[150]

Sheikh Fakhri al-Qaisi, a Salafi cleric in the Yarmouk district in southwestern Baghdad, loathes the Americans who arrested him as they had Sheikh Mahdi al-Sumaidi. Before his arrest, al-Qaisi stated that there was no need to issue a *fatwa* calling for *jihad*: 'Infidels are occupying a Muslim country, the jihad is therefore automatic as a right of legitimate defense. We have no need to launch a general appeal for a holy war.'[151]

The Sunni *awqaf* (endowments) office claimed in 2004 that there were 7,000 known and officially sanctioned Sunni mosques in Iraq. The Friday sermons have been a traditional way of channeling political and social discontent in Muslim societies. In Iraq the Friday sermons by Sunni and Shi'a clerics resonate with a population that has no notable or charismatic politician or lay leadership to turn to in this time of stress and humiliation.[152] While most of the preachers at the mosques are careful to avoid direct incitement to violence, they are not loath to attack the foreign presence and to present Coalition goals and motivations for coming to Iraq in the darkest of terms, as do the nationalist insurgents. Many of these mosques have served as major mobilization and recruitment centers for the insurgency, particularly in Fallujah, where the vast majority of mosques served either as insurgent strongholds, command-and-control centers, and storage points for supplies, weapons and ammunition. Posters were hung on the mosque walls, urging people to wage a *jihad* against 'the evil people who bring evil things to Iraq'.

With the downfall of Saddam many Sunni Muslims began to express their religious freedom more openly.[153] Young Islamist men who had once hidden overt symbols of piety from the regime 'came out of the closet', so to speak. Abu Mojahed—mid-thirties, a laborer and adherent of Salafi Islam who was jailed four times under Saddam's regime—would gather like-minded friends for secret Salafi classes and discussions. He did not fight for the regime when the United States invaded, but did not welcome the Americans either: 'I didn't fight. I stayed at home. If you fight for Saddam and he wins, you are not winning. If America wins, you are not winning. They freed us from evil but they brought more evil to the country.'[154] Ultimately, clerics in the mosques instructed him and his friends to take up arms. Why does he fight?

We fight the Americans because they are nonbelievers and they are coming to fight Islam, calling us terrorists ... We fight for our land, against those who are fighting Islam, for our country and for our women. Our goal is to fight whoever fights us and not just the Americans. And we want this country to be ruled by the Tawhid and Sunna. If that doesn't happen, that means all of us die because we fight until the last breath.[155]

Once harassed and often arrested by Saddam's security forces, the Islamists of Mosul made serious inroads into the political and social life of the city right under the noses of the Americans, and the attitudes of their preachers towards the occupation are unfavorable. An *imam*, Sheikh Ibrahim al-Nama'a, who had a considerable following began preaching a very political sermon against the occupation from the earliest days:

In invading a Muslim territory, the objective of the infidels has always been to destroy the cultural values of Islam. With them they bring nationalism, democracy, liberalism, communism, Christianity … Today the Iraqis suffer. Now Iraq is occupied precisely because it has forgotten the divine teachings and has not followed the principles of Islam. We have been delivered of the injustices of one man [i.e. Saddam], but this does not mean we must accept the American-British domination …[156]

The religious radicalization of the Sunni Arabs deepened with the collapse of the regime as many in the community sought to find answers to their sudden marginalization. In this context, they have not merely become more religious, but rather have turned to Salafi Islam believing that a return to the pristine purity of Islam as it existed in the time of the Prophet Muhammad and the two generations after him would constitute salvation. Salafists founded the so-called State Council for the Sunnis in December 2003. 'The Islamic movement is now replacing the national secular movement. The secular leaders have done nothing. Now the young men want the Islamists. Now you have no choice,' said Sheikh Mahmud al-Mashhadani, a founding member of the council.[157] Other Salafist groups have proliferated in Iraq. One such group, the Mujahideen Battalions of the Salafi Group of Iraq (Kata'ib al-mujahideen fi al-jama'ah al-salafiyah fi al-iraq), whose leader is Abu-Dajanah al-Iraqi, issued a statement in which it praised Abdullah Azzam, the spiritual leader of the Afghan Arabs, and Osama Bin Laden. The statement described the personnel of the former regime of Saddam as 'the soldiers of tyranny and the devils of darkness. Thousands of Ba'thists, fedayeen, special and Republican Guard have vanished, handing over this Muslim country to their American masters.'[158] Some Salafi groups have forged links with the Fedayeen Saddam on the condition that the latter renounce their allegiance to the former dictator. To defend themselves against the nefarious plots of the 'infidels' to subjugate Islam in Iraq, many Salafists actually reached out to the Ba'thists. Many of the latter had allegedly repented of their former sins, discarded their former beliefs and joined the ranks of the believers. However, the Salafists do not reach out to the mainstream Islamic groups like the Iraqi Islamic Party of Muhsin Abd al-Hamid, which they believe collaborates with the occupation.[159]

Many Salafist clerics deny that they were urging their flock to commit acts of violence. They claimed that they became more active in order to minister to the political and spiritual needs of a community that is adrift. However, take the example of Khaled, a thirty-one-year-old insurgent who says he receives instructions from Salafi clerics to fight the Coalition: 'We are fighting for Iraq and for Islam.'[160] The deepening of religious sentiment and the allure of a pugnacious and combative Islam as represented by Salafism has been a major motivation for young alienated men to join the insurgency. Ibrahim, a twenty-two-year-old Moslawi from an affluent commercial family with companies inside and outside of Iraq, was killed during a 23 October 2003 attack on a US forces compound. Ibrahim was an engineer who had married a year before the invasion, but *two* years prior to the invasion had started becoming more overtly religious, attending the mosque and adopting the strict requirements of Islam. His uncle said: 'When the Americans came here he went beyond just being a moderate religious man. What happened to the country made him that way [an extremist].'[161] But his family's pride in his attack on the Americans was viewed in nationalist terms, especially by his mother, for whom her son was a hero: 'We're proud of him. He raised our heads ... He defended his country and honor.'[162]

An Islamist insurgent, Ahmed, part of an insurgent group known as the Army of Right, has provided a description of his group's motives, which seem to be a fusion of nationalist and religious sentiments:

Our fighters are protecting our religion. We cannot allow foreigners to occupy our country. The Americans do not respect us, so we cannot respect them. They are a cancer of bad things: prostitution, gambling and drugs. This struggle is not about Saddam. It's about our country and our God. Our aim is not to have power or to rule the country. We just want the US out and for the word of Allah to be the power in Iraq.[163]

Another young insurgent articulated a confused mix of motives for fighting the occupation, yet he too seems to have been primarily motivated by religious feelings. Abu Abdul Rahman, twenty-five years old, said he fought for his country and religion but could not articulate a concrete vision for the future:

Thanks to the Americans for getting rid of Saddam, but no thanks for staying in Iraq. The idea of jihad came step by step as I watched what the Americans were doing to our country. In the beginning we were only cousins and friends, and later other people came to join us, people who were presented to us by the sheikhs. My group and I, we always race to death, so we may die and go to heaven. Our goal is to get the invaders out of our country, and from all the Arab countries, and I hope that after we get them out we will have a couple of moments of peace in our life.[164]

The Salafists are on the rise within the ranks of the officers and enlisted men of the former Iraqi army. When the regime fell, many officers joined the Islamists in the culmination of a process that had begun in the early 1990s. One former officer said: 'In 1990, many soldiers returned to religion. But we were forced to pray in secret. And we could not grow a beard. If we attended the mosques too regularly, we were thrown into prison.'[165] The Iraqis, he added, had had enough of war:

That is why the regime collapsed without a fight. This was not their war. The United States promised to get rid of Saddam Husayn, to rebuild the country, to restore democracy [sic]. Our soldiers could not win. US technology was too advanced. Why should they have sacrificed themselves to save the power of a tyrant who oppressed his people? ... The Americans did not keep their word ... They placed at the head of the country people who had been in exile and who had never shared our suffering. They gave them the right to pillage Iraqi wealth when, on their advice, they disbanded the army, stopped paying our wages. It was a mistake. For every officer it has become a question of honor to resist the occupation ...

We are fighting under the flag of Islam ... Muslims in several Arab countries have called for a jihad. We can therefore count on internal and external support. Shaykh Usama Bin Ladin has launched an appeal to liberate Iraq. He is a man of principle. If he wants to help us fight our enemy, we will be pleased to accept. Volunteers are arriving from abroad ... We do not accept anyone who comes without a contact as they could be a spy ... Shaykh Madhi and Shaykh Fakhri serve us [sic] our spiritual guides. We greatly value their opinions.[166]

That officers (and indeed other educated Iraqis) have become bona fide Islamists should come as no surprise. Arab nationalism as preached by the Ba'th and Saddam prior to 1995 rings hollow. Religion, an untested movement in a country whose official ideology was secular, has become more prominent. Many of Iraq's Sunni Arabs see no hope in the Arab world itself, which is seen as either neutral or complicit in the destruction of the country. 'All the Arab countries are traitors,' ventured a teacher in Ramadi.[167]

Instead of nationalism, religion has made a comeback, but it can also be argued that the insurgency's virulence also stems from a successful fusion of nationalist and religious sentiment among the Sunni Arabs of Iraq. This is a critical factor that is missed. We often view religion and nationalism as polar opposites. Nationalism and religion have different ideological foundations, and this has been reflected not only in theory but also in practice in the Middle East, where nationalists and Islamists have traditionally excoriated one another. Witness Saddam's traditional policy towards religion until the mid-1990s, or the thoroughly hostile views of Islamists towards secular nationalism in the Arab world. But this has changed dramatically in recent years, although one could argue convincingly that the origins of the change go back to the defeat of the Arabs by Israel in 1967. Egypt and Syria, whose leaders mouthed sterile secular nationalist slogans, were decisively trounced by Israel, a country whose ideological foundations are, arguably, based on nationalism and religion. In the 1973 war religion played a more significant role in Arab motivation. In the case of Iraq, the Iran-Iraq war witnessed a rise of religious sentiment among the Sunnis, but it was not until the catastrophic defeat of 1991 in Kuwait and the imposition of the sanctions regime that many Sunnis began to turn to religion, without necessarily forsaking their deep nationalism. It is also remarkable that in recent years, with the rise of Islamist sentiments in the Arab world, the rhetoric of the Islamists towards foreign political, cultural and socioeconomic domination is similar in many ways to that of the leftists and nationalists of yesteryear. The point I am making here is that it is not difficult for a nationalist in the Arab world—or Iraq—to subscribe to religion with a renewed fervor, particularly in times of identity crises and stress.[168]

This extensive discussion of the origins, causes and motivations of the insurgency cannot be complete without a discussion of what the insurgents want.

The political goals of the insurgency

There is no doubt that the prime goals of the insurgency are to eject the foreign presence in Iraq ('liberation from occupation') and to overthrow the system put in place by the United States and its Iraqi allies ('reversing the consequences of aggression', so to speak). These are what may be referred to as the 'negative' goals. We know what the insurgents do *not* want. They do not want foreigners in their country nor their presumed 'puppets' and allies ruling the country. They have made this clear in numerous public statements and on their websites. The Ba'th Party 'Political and Strategic Program' stated unequivocally that the immediate goal of the *muqawamah*, 'which is led and run by the Arab Socialist Ba'th Party', is to wage a war of national liberation 'to expel the occupation forces from Iraq and preserve the country as a unified homeland for all Iraqis'.[169] Sheikh Majid al-Qa'ud, to whom I have already referred, indicated that the Ba'thist resistance has a political program that envisions the withdrawal of occupation forces under the aegis of the UN, the Arab League and the European Union; the reconstruction of the Iraqi army on a new basis; and free elections under the eyes of international observers. If this were accepted, 'we would be prepared to shake the Americans' hand even tomorrow morning'.[170] This cause (national liberation) should have collected a great deal of support among the populace, but except among the Sunnis it has not, due to the ethno-sectarian dynamics of the country, as we shall see in chapters 3 and 4.

But what do the insurgents want? What are their positive goals? This is where the Iraqi insurgency suffers from deep-seated structural problem. The Ba'th Party, in its 'Political and Strategic Program', states that it is committed to building a modern state, keeping the country's resources free and in national hands, promoting greater economic and social development, and establishing a national political life based on institutions. But the reality on the ground intrudes in a painful way. First, the insurgents, Ba'thist or otherwise, simply do not have the luxury of focusing on the 'post-liberation' phase. Second, the insurgency is not a monolithic united movement directed by a leadership with a unitary and disciplined ideological vision or unified goal or set of goals. Third, this is an insurgency whose members may have calculated that they do not, at this stage, need an elaborate political and socioeconomic vision for a 'free' Iraq; that is to say, to gain the support of the people it is enough to articulate a desire to be free of foreign occupation. Fourth, it is likely that these myriad groups who cooperate with one another and coordinate attacks at the operational and tactical levels, but who may have profound political differences, wish to avoid fratricidal conflicts. As one insurgent leader said: "We first want to expel the infidel invaders *before anything else*."[171] When I talked openly with many Sunnis during my tour in Iraq, none, of course, stated that they were members of the insurgency, but it was often clear where their sympathies lay. They uniformly expressed a desire to see the occupation end but many seemed unwilling or unable to articulate a vision of what else they wanted. It was as if the end of the occupation would resolve everything. Indeed, some seemed to believe that once the occupation was 'made to go away' everything would revert to 'normal', as expressed by a Sunni insurgent: 'Our main aim is to drive the Americans out and then everything will go back to normal, as it was before.'[172] Clearly, there are some who hew to the wishful thinking that the Sunni-dominated past can be recaptured. Some Sunnis with whom I talked were adamant that they constituted the ruling elite of the country and would like to see a return to their former privileges and power. I was struck in particular by the statement of an insurgent leader who was interviewed in early 2005: 'If we do not hold authority in Iraq, then we will allow no one else to hold authority.'[173] This is merely a justification for nihilistic violence, the kind that seeks to destroy just because it cannot get its own way. On the other hand, others realize that the past cannot be recaptured and that they needed to articulate a more progressive vision. In an interview one officer told his interlocutor that the goal of the resistance was to 'liberate Iraq and expel the coalition. To recover our sovereignty and install a secular democracy, but not the one imposed by the Americans. Iraq has always been a progressive country, we don't want to go back to the past; we want to move forward. We have very competent people.'[174]

Sunni Islamist insurgents believed in the establishment of what one insurgent referred to as an 'Islamic government based on justice, individual rights, love, peace and security ... [But] this government will not be composed of religious figures ...'[175] The head of the Iraqi Salafist Ahl al-Sunnah-wa-al-Jama'ah Association, Sheikh Abd-al-Salam Bin-Osman al-Khattabi, called for the establishment of an Islamic government in Iraq as a prelude to the liberation of other Muslim lands and the establishment of the caliphate.[176] In the same interview, he bitterly excoriated the mainstream opposition group the Association of Muslim Scholars because it supported elections and democracy. Iraqi Salafists like Sheikh Khattabi share a similar approach with foreign Islamists for whom Iraq is one of the lands that must be returned to Islam from the clutches of the 'infidel' and of the 'apostates' (as I will discuss in the Chapter 3, in which I address the foreign fighter presence in Iraq). This is a somewhat expansive and ambitious set of goals, the kind of goals that have caused other insurgents, including 'home-grown' Islamists, to argue that Iraqi insurgency must focus on immediate and on realistic objectives. It is also not clear how Sunni Islamists believe that they can look forward to a Sunni Islamic government in a country where the majority are Shi'a. But it is clear that all the insurgent groups—whatever their ideological provenance—share with one another (and with the politically active Sunni political parties/groups) the desire and determination to make the stay of the United States as painful and untenable as possible so that it leaves Iraq. The next chapter addresses the scope of the insurgency, its organizational structures, support from the outside, and the tactical means of causing the United States pain.

3

THE INSURGENTS' WAY OF WARFARE

This chapter first examines the intensity, the geographical scope, the popular base and the social composition of the insurgency. It then turns to the support base provided by foreign fighters and foreign states. Its primary concern is the organization of the insurgency and its way of warfare.

Intensity, geographic scope, popular base and social composition

The situation in Iraq might be called a 'low-intensity, localized and decentralized insurgency', with large numbers of decentralized insurgent groups engaging in violence to disrupt and remove the US presence. We must not confuse the term 'low-intensity' with minimal violence, as people often do when addressing warfare that is below the conventional threshold. Far from being minimal, the violence can be extreme, as in the case of sustained firefights that have occurred in Ramadi, Fallujah, Samarra and Baquba, where US forces and insurgents have exchanged heavy volumes of fire, or in the existence of a 'dynamic state of violence' in a particular region or city. This dynamic state is fueled by internal factors promoting 'resistance' and external factors relating to what the United States did to add fuel to the fire, or failed to do to stem the slide into violence. To be sure, the violence is hardly 'low-intensity' to the US troops on the ground who have at one time or another faced an average of eighty-five to 110 attacks a day. But the tempo of attacks is sporadic, and on many occasions there are seemingly inexplicable lulls in the battle.

Some centers have gone from near normality to an escalation in violence. For example, Mosul went from being relatively stable and calm under General David Petraeus and the US 101st Air Assault Division to being a violent place in fall 2003. After the division arrived in Mosul in spring 2003, order and basic services were restored quite quickly and efficiently. Petraeus was an energetic commander who moved rapidly to rebuild the city and the surrounding areas and to restore economic and commercial activities. The city was also quiet because it acted as a staging ground for attacks elsewhere. Moreover, the former Iraqi army officers and enlistees who were to provide the nucleus for the outbreak of violence took time to study the tactics, techniques and procedures of the US forces and to formulate their responses. In June 2003 the city was peaceful and US soldiers conducted routine patrols in a relaxed manner.

By late 2003, however, the city had descended into a spiral of violence. Mosul was home to tens of thousands of former military personnel. They had had a good relationship with General Petraeus, but their animosity at the treatment meted out by the CPA, including the dissolution of the Iraqi army, finally led to an explosion of fury. A former officer, Major General Said Jiburi, said: 'We didn't do anything wrong. We've been left with nothing. Mosul didn't put up a fight. We expected the Americans to deal with us fairly. Now we are just out in the streets. There are thousands of us, we are running out of money and we are unhappy. That's why there are attacks.'[1]

By mid-December 2003 a well-organized and ruthless insurgency was perpetrating nearly forty attacks a day on Coalition troops and so-called Iraqi collaborators.[2] The assassination of Governor Kash-moula in July 2004 was another blow to US authority in Mosul. His death meant the loss of a charismatic and effective politician who was in charge of dispensing the tens of millions of dollars allocated for reconstruction. Then Coalition forces were attacked daily with a combination of homemade roadside bombs, drive-by shootings and suicide bombings. The religious extremists within the insurgency initially organized themselves and gained a foothold in the rural areas and small towns around Mosul before moving into the city to cause mayhem. Many of them were adherents of the deadly Ansar al-Sunnah terrorist group (see p. 173), the Mosul chapter of which was led by, among others, a prominent Salafi insurgent, Muhammad Sharqawi. The insurgents and terrorists used raw fear effectively to create a permanent climate of psychological terror in Mosul. For more than a year they regularly killed or disappeared people and widely distributed DVDs showing the execution of captives. The violence leveled off and then declined in 2005 due to a combination of effective counterstrikes by the US military and the movement of insurgents out of the city to go elsewhere.

Like Mosul the city of Samarra, north of Baghdad and within the Sunni triangle, has witnessed extensive insurgent violence. Although Samarra has been a hotbed of insurgent activity it cannot be referred to as a pro-Saddam bastion. It is best to consider Samarra's role in the insurgency by examining its socioeconomic make-up. The city traditionally relied on farming, fishing, state employment and religious tourism. The last two of these have provided the city with much of its prosperity. Samarra was traditionally affiliated with the Ba'th Party, helped produce its ideas and was part of the ideological sentiment that gave rise to the party's role in Iraq. It provided the Iraqi branch of the party with its key theoreticians, men such as Abdullah Sallum al-Samarra'i and Abd al-Khaliq al-Samarra'i. The latter was jailed in 1973 and executed on flimsy grounds in 1979. Its leading clans—the al-Bu Abbas, al-Bu-Baz, al-Bu-Badri, al-Bu-Naysan, al-Bu Mahmud, al-Bu-Diraj, and al-Bu Aswad—provided thousands of men for state employment in the armed forces and security services. These clans were punished in 1995 for the defection of Wafiq al-Samarra'i, the head of Military Intelligence. Even before then the city had begun to fall into disfavor, and hundreds of Samarrans were removed from the military and security services or denied further promotion. As General Khudayr Nasser al-Samarra'i said: 'Not one inhabitant of Samarra was allowed to rise to a position befitting his skills in the military establishment. This was an old practice but after Wafiq al-Samarra'i left Iraq, the situation became worse.'[3]

Samarra also houses key Shi'a shrines: the mausoleums of Imam Ali al-Hadi and of Imam Hasan al-Askari. The city was the venue for thousands of Shi'a pilgrims, a situation that worried the regime and many of the city's majority Sunni Arabs. The regime built a vast network of informers, spies and security personnel in the city to ensure that anti-regime violence did not erupt there. It also put supporters in charge of the city's prosperous commercial activities. Samarra's merchants found the presence and corruption of the regime suffocating. The sanctions imposed after the first Gulf war also eroded the prosperity of the city, and the regime's increased control over the movement of Shi'a pilgrims, to whom many of the merchants had catered, worsened the mood. In this context, then, the people of Samarra were not necessarily saddened by the demise of Saddam Hussein or his Tikriti cronies.

Despite its trials at Saddam's hands over the years, however, Samarra remained loyal to Ba'thist and nationalist sentiment, so its people viewed the US presence with undisguised hostility. The inability of the Coalition to restore services or provide employment (there were many disgruntled state sector employees in the city) and reconstruction added more fuel to the fire. A more ominous development was the rise in Islamist sentiment within the city among the young and the former state employees. Their perception of the United States was uniformly negative, and all indications are that the merchant class provided the funding that maintained the insurgency in Samarra, which began in earnest in late fall 2003. The insurgency was sustained not merely by ideological and nationalist hostility to the United States, but also by US military actions and ultimately by the inability of US forces to maintain a permanent presence in the city (see Chapter 4).

As mentioned previously, the insurgency is largely a Sunni Arab affair, and has been concentrated in provinces with an overwhelming Sunni majority or in mixed provinces with significant concentrations of Sunnis. Its epicenter is an area known as the Sunni triangle, an area bounded by Baghdad in the east, Ramadi to the west and Tikrit to the north, and which includes a heavy concentration of Sunni Arab tribes whose members served in the armed forces and security services of the former regime. The term 'Sunni triangle' has, of course, become somewhat of a cliché; the insurgency has struck far and wide in the country. Just north of Tikrit is the small town of Baiji, which is not in the triangle but has been the center of many insurgent attacks on oil pipelines.[4] Nor is the large city of Mosul, whose descent into violence and near-anarchy I have detailed previously, within the Sunni triangle. The small towns along the Euphrates, extending to the border with Syria and also outside the 'Sunni triangle', are not free of violence either. Finally, despite the smug attitude the British have adopted towards the US in the light of the latter's trials and tribulations in the center and north, violence has been a constant partner to the British forces in the Shi'a south. Admittedly, most of it has nothing to do with the Sunni insurgents but with local intra-Shi'a feuds.[5]

The insurgency is still localized in terms of popular national involvement. A letter supposedly written by the fugitive Saddam

Hussein and aired on Al-Jazeera television on 13 August 2003 called upon senior Shi'a clerics to declare a *jihad* against the foreign presence in Iraq. After what his regime did to the Shi'a over the decades, it was naive of Saddam to expect them to rise in rebellion at his behest.[6] The nationalist and secular insurgents like to think that they are truly nationalist and are supported nationwide. A former senior officer, now an insurgent, argued that case with a Western journalist, stating that the resistance encompasses

all movements of national struggle against the occupation, without confessional, ethnic or political distinction. Contrary to what you imagine in the West, there is no fratricide war in Iraq. We have a united front against the enemy. From Fallujah to Ramadi, and including Najaf, Karbala and the Shi'ite suburbs of Baghdad, combatants speak with a single voice. As to the young Shi'ite leader Muqtada al-Sadr, he is, like ourselves, in favor of the unity of the Iraqi people, multiconfessional and *Arab*. We support him from a tactical and logistical perspective.[7]

Much of what the former officer says here is simply hyperbole and propaganda (which he might, of course, genuinely believe). First, while it is true that Iraqi insurgents have come from a wide variety of ethnic and sectarian backgrounds, as revealed in data from Iraqi researchers, the insurgency is overwhelmingly Sunni Arab, with substantial Sunni Turkmen input in the isolated and poverty-stricken town of Tal Afar, in the westernmost reaches of Nineveh Province. One could argue convincingly that for many Sunni Arabs this is their own national liberation struggle against a foreign and domestic enemy seeking to eradicate their identity, and I actually think that they believe this. However, it does not make it so for the Shi'a and Kurds. Second, the former officer was speaking at a time, in spring-summer 2004, when the insurgency seemed to be on the cusp of a genuine Arab (i.e. incorporating Sunnis and Shi'a) war of national liberation against the foreign presence.[8]

The insurgency does not have the support of all Sunni Arabs but its range encompasses all classes and it is urban and rural. Its ranks include students, intellectuals, former soldiers, tribal youth and farmers, and Islamists. Insurgents ranged from simple provincial folk like 'Mu'ayyad', a small-time weapons dealer (like Americans, Iraqis adore their small arms) who joined the insurgency after listening to an *imam*'s exhortations to expel foreigners from Muslim lands, to 'Abu Fayad' and 'Mas'ud', two cousins who had served in the army. These three men were active in the Fallujah area.

'Walid', a student of English literature at Baghdad University, is also an insurgent. At first he positively welcomed the demise of the corrupt former regime, but the behavior of the US forces and their failure to resolve the problems of security and services drove him into the arms of the insurgency. His trainers were former army officers who taught him how to use an RPG.[9]

In Tikrit, several former high-ranking Republican Guard officers vowed that Hussein's capture would not end the insurgency. They would continue to fight on religious and nationalist grounds. One officer said: 'Until now people who joined the resistance were seen as defenders of Saddam Hussein, but not any more. Our fight is not about a person any more—it's about our country and our land.'[10] The tribes have provided considerable support for their kinsmen who have taken up arms against Coalition forces. This extends from providing logistical infrastructure for the storage of weapons and munitions, to *ad hoc* training grounds in orchards, the collection of information on Coalition forces, and transportation.

As Michael Eisenstadt noted in his analysis of the insurgency's demographics, the insurgents 'swim in a largely sympathetic sea'.[11] He then cites three separate opinion polls, taken in 2004–5 by Iraqi and foreign pollsters, which revealed that between 45 and 85 percent of respondents in Sunni Arab areas expressed support for insurgent attacks on US forces in Iraq. With regard to the depth of the insurgency a former officer, no doubt with consider-able exaggeration, stated: 'The resistance is not limited to a few thousand activists. Seventy-five percent of the population supports and helps us, directly and indirectly, volunteering information, hiding combatants or weapons.'[12] Another, 'Abu Ali', a member of the ruthless Ansar al-Sunnah organization, reported that tens of thousands of people cooperated with the insurgent forces by pro-viding information on troop movements, providing safe houses and vehicles, and acting as couriers between insurgent commanders. Insurgents received support and intelligence from the local popu-lace concerning the movements and activities of US forces; locals would even help during assaults on US forces. Troops of the 3rd Infantry Division on patrol in the town of Duluiyah one evening in June 2003 came under attack by an enemy whose actions were aided by locals signaling the presence of the unit as it moved down the roads at night.[13]

People who may not actively support the insurgency are still quite forward about expressing their admiration for the insurgents and their activities. For example, a member of the Fallujah admin-istrative council openly stated:

[The insurgents] are mujahideen (holy warriors). We don't know them ... Al Anbar [the province where Fallujah is located] has a bigger nationalist consciousness than the rest of Iraq. We are also more religious. We con-sider this resistance a religious duty and a nationalist one as well.[14]

Similarly, some members of the Iraqi security forces demobilized by the US have expressed sympathy and support for the insurgents. An Iraqi police officer, 'Jabir Said', works closely with US forces during the day and joins the resistance at night, turning over to the resistance intelligence about his daytime colleagues:

I have good relations with the American soldiers in my work but I live in a different situation. The Americans have given us nothing—no jobs and no hopes. They are thieves. They break into our houses without warning and stand on our heads. This is why the people are getting more hurt and more angry. This is why we want revenge.

The resistance here is growing stronger every day. First, because the American are occupiers and we will fight them until they leave the country, and second we fight to return Saddam Hussein to power because he is the only man who can return Iraq back to safety within an hour. [15]

Given the geographic base and the existence of substantial raw material (popular support of a segment of the population, and a cause), the question arises: did the regime plan the insurgency before the outbreak of the war or did disgruntled Sunnis spontaneously organize it after the occupation? In other words, was the insurrection organized by an elitist conspiratorial group (the Ba'th Party) or was it the result of a Sunni national insurrection fueled by the rage and humiliation generated by the reality of an occupation (and an ineffective one at that) and of Coalition policies perceived as being discriminatory? Certain Iraqi insurgents, usually security personnel and former army officers, have repeatedly claimed that they had been planning the insurgency long before the outbreak of the war. As Iraq was making the transition to the interim government of Prime Minister Allawi in June 2004, one insurgent said:

Americans have prepared the war, we have prepared the post-war ... We knew that if the United States decided to attack Iraq, we would have no chance faced with their technological and military power. The war was lost in advance, so we prepared the post-war. In other words: the resistance ... Opposition movements to the occupation were already organized. Our strategy was not improvised after the regime fell. [16]

This may have been bravado and propaganda for the benefit of the journalist, but Salah al-Mukhtar, a senior Ba'thist official who is in exile in Yemen, said something similar, only in greater detail:

The current resistance in Iraq, to be accurate, has not [sic] made or prepared by Iraqi government, but by Baath party leadership. At the beginning in the year 2002, the Baath party has completed the training of about 6 million Iraqi citizens to fight urban warfare by the so called Al Quds Army. President Saddam Hussein has managed all preparation, including storing about 50 million of guns, big, medium and small sizes with their necessary ammunition to fight against the occupation for ten years. The groups prepared for a guerrilla warfare has included, beside the Iraqi armed forces, organization called Fedayeen of Saddam, Baath party fighters, as well as leaders of Baath party. In the light of what I have said, you can reach the conclusion that the resistance was prepared mainly by the political leadership of Iraq. Of course, it has used the government apparatus to facilitate the preparation for a guerrilla warfare [*sic*].[17]

However, in the light of the regime's manifest incompetence in fighting an irregular war as part of its defense strategy during conventional operations, it might be difficult to believe that the Ba'th Party and the regime could organize an extensive postwar irregular conflict. On the other hand, the formidable organizational capabilities of the Ba'th Party, its extensive finances, and the skills of the many thousands of personnel the regime trained over the years in the huge, coercive state apparatus cannot be discounted as having played a significant role in mobilizing and directing a potent insurgent infrastructure. Indeed, the evidence on the ground over the course of the past two and half years proves that.[18]

On closer inspection it is plausible to argue that the answer lies in the middle. If the Ba'thists did organize for a postwar insurgency, it may have remained relatively narrowly based had it not been for the participation of significant elements of the Sunni population. Many Sunnis only became insurgents after they felt the effects of the occupation and its policies. In other words, after Operation Iraqi Freedom there were those, the so-called regime diehards, who were determined to force a fight. Others joined as a result of post-occupation policies that hurt them or their families. Many of those who ultimately became insurgents initially adopted a wait-

and-see attitude; they wanted to know whether the United States was going to be a liberator or occupier. For example, 'Abu Muja-hid', a former Ba'th Party member, is an insurgent who does not fit the clichéd image of a regime dead-ender or terrorist, having joined the uprising because of what he saw as the US occupation.

Either way, the former regime elements stood to benefit from the wider participation of members of the Sunni community be-cause it allowed them to move and recruit from among a sym-pathetic populace. Indeed, the Ba'th found among Sunnis more willingness and determination to fight than when the regime was in its dying days. The problem for the Ba'thists and other 'national-ist' insurgent groups is complicated immensely by the participa-tion of foreign fighters and transnational Islamist groups who have brought in their own ideology and ethos into the conflict whose agenda extends beyond Iraq and is not merely or even primarily concerned with the saving of Iraq as a national entity, but with the defense of Islam against its key enemies (see below).

External support for the insurgents

State support. The insurgency has few sources of external state support. The insurgents are painfully aware of this, particularly the Ba'thists and nationalists who have disparaged the Arab countries for their allegedly contemptible behavior *vis-à-vis* the Americans. In the words of Salah al-Mukhtar:

The reaction of Arab and Islamic governments is characterized by fear and hesitation, because they see how the American troops and the others are humiliated. We have an Arab proverb saying that (if you have nothing, you can give nothing). So the Arab governments, as well the Islamic govern-ments, are not prepared to fight in Iraq because if the strongest empire is defeated and humiliated, how they can do what America is failed to do. But even if we suppose that some governments are preparing to send troops to Iraq, their fate will not be different from the fate of American forces.[19]

Ba'th Party theorists write that there will be no aid for the insurgency from 'all the Arab regimes for reasons linked to the nature of the entire Arab official order and the roles played by certain regimes, especially the puppet and influential ones, which hope to play or renew the roles assigned to them by the United States with the approval of the "Zionist entity" in order to serve US strategy in the region.'[20] This is a long-winded and tendentious way of saying that the Arab regimes are incapable of independent nationalist action. Nonetheless, the Ba'thists make their rounds of the regimes and exhort the Arab masses to participate in the armed resistance, insisting that it is the Arabs' duty and right to do so.

The Bush administration has accused two of Iraq's neighbors, Syria and Iran, of facilitating or even actively encouraging the crossing of the Iraqi border by foreign fighters. In singling out of these two countries—despite Jordan, Saudi Arabia and Turkey also having porous borders with Iraq—the United States is reflecting the political dynamics at play as it tries to bring stability to Iraq and the wider Middle East.

Syria and Iran fear that the United States will be able to implement its tacit goal of installing a pro-US 'puppet regime' in Baghdad. This would allow the United States to maintain bases in Iraq with which to threaten these countries, whose bilateral relations with the United States are dismal. Tehran and Damascus fear that they will be US targets for regime change. Their logical response is to support anti-US operations in Iraq, thus ensuring that the hostile Bush administration remains bogged down there.

This is, however, a perilous strategy at many levels. Both countries understand that any overt support for anti-US forces in Iraq means they might incur the physical wrath of the United States and not merely harsh anti-regime rhetoric. Not long after Operation Iraqi Freedom ended, the Bush administration warned Syria and Iran not to help the embryonic insurgency—and the warning was issued from a position of strength. They then went out of their way to avoid annoying a United States that was itching for a fight. Indeed, there were even reports of US Special Operations units crossing the border into Syria and clashing with Syrian border guards. So the increasing US problems in Iraq by late fall 2003 and early spring 2004 was the source of considerable satisfaction to Tehran and Damascus alike.

While neither Syria nor Iran could overtly support the insurgency, it is reasonably safe to assume that they have provided covert support or looked the other way when pro-insurgent activities such as fund-raising, meetings, and the transfer of supplies and bomb-making techniques were carried out by Iraqi elements within their respective countries. Moreover, the domestic constituencies of Iran and Syria are thoroughly hostile to the United States and alarmed by Washington's belligerence towards their countries, even if some disparage the incumbent regimes. Syrian Arab nationalists, for example, tend to support the remnants of the Iraqi Ba'th Party. Syrian Islamists, most of whom loathe the minority Allawi regime of Bashar al-Assad and would like nothing more than to see it fall, support the Islamists in Iraq. They have provided the Iraqi insurgents with safe houses and funding, and facilitated the transportation of foreign fighters across the border into Iraq. Iranian groups such as the Revolutionary Guard might support Shi'a insurgents such as the Jaish al-Mahdi, led by Moqtada al-Sadr.

The role of the Damascus regime is complicated. Syria allows foreigners to enter, but once they are in and move to towns like Dayr az Zawr or Aleppo it has no idea of their whereabouts or activities. Moreover, the writ of the Syrian regime in many of the border areas with Iraq has declined due to the rise of Islamist sentiment, which has seen Sunni mosques and clerics rise to prominence in those regions, and to the rampant corruption of border officials who facilitate the crossing of foreigners into Iraq. Smuggling by tribes that straddle both sides of the border also facilitates the movement of people both legally and illegally.[21]

But there are risks to the support of Iran and Syria for Iraq. First, neither Damascus nor Tehran wants ongoing instability on its borders. Second, neither country is especially fond of the Sunni ideological elements responsible for much of the violence in Iraq. Its regime being dominated by the minority Allawis (utterly detested by Sunni extremists), Syria does not wish to see the growth in Iraq of Sunni extremism, the resurgence of which is mirrored in Syria. And secular Damascus would not want to see a theocratic Baghdad, regardless of its sympathy for and traditional alliance with the Shi'a. For its part, Iran is unlikely to support the Iraqi insurgents, who are either Sunni extremists or Arab nationalists, both of which are antithetical to Tehran's agenda. Interestingly, the approach of the United States is more ideological than that of these two regional powers, whose 'support' for the insurgency in Iraq is pragmatic. In effect the United States has told these two countries, particularly Syria, the following: support the insurgency and we will make your life miserable (i.e. regime change or regime weakening); don't support the insurgency, and we will *still* make your life miserable. Regardless of what it does or does not do, Damascus is targeted. Thus Syria has concluded, naturally enough, that when faced with such a situation it is better to fight. Unsurprisingly, Syria is on the record as wanting to see the United States fail in its enterprise in Iraq.

Disgruntled Muslims, Arab nationalists and transnational Islamist networks. Support for the Iraqi insurgency from individuals and Islamist subnational groups has caught the attention of the region and the wider world. Arab nationalists, disgruntled Muslims, foreign fighters and Sunni extremists have played a role in the insurgency since the beginning of Operation Iraqi Freedom I. They chose to use the suicide bombs and massive car bombs that devastated several targets in Baghdad and elsewhere, causing a great many deaths. Yet the influx of foreign terrorists and religious extremists is not a massive one. More important than the relatively small numbers of these foreigners is that they constitute a force multiplier and are willing to engage in operations that most Iraqi insurgents would prefer to avoid, such as extremely bloody suicide attacks.

The question of foreign insurgents in Iraq is particularly thorny. Complex layers beneath an apparently simple surface make it difficult to discern fact from fiction. The Bush administration has maintained that regime dead-enders and foreign infiltrators are behind the attacks, but hard empirical evidence—often from the US military—indicates that the foreign element is minuscule. In 2004, for example, evidence showed that of 8,000 suspected insurgents detained in Iraq, only 127 held foreign passports. In Fallujah US officers concluded that the overwhelming majority of fighters who battled the Marines and US Army in April and November 2004 were Iraqis. By blaming foreigners, the Bush administration and CPA hoped to quash the notion that there was an insurgency within the Iraqi population, in order to frame the conflict as part of the wider war on terror. Even though the horrific acts of foreign fighters continued to be in the spotlight, such men still constituted a minority within the insurgency. In March 2005 Major General Martin Dempsey said the idea that foreign fighters were flooding Iraq was 'a misconception'.[22] A simple head-count does not tell the whole story. The foreign element of the insurgency has had a greater impact than mere numbers would lead us to believe.

The first wave of these 'foreign fighters' (between April and October 2003) mainly comprised Arab volunteers from neighboring countries. Most were Palestinian refugees recruited either by the remnants of the Iraqi Mukhabarat or by any number of terrorist organizations before and during the war in refugee camps in

Jordan, Lebanon and Syria.[23] Arab nationalists, and 'unsponsored' religious extremists made their way into Iraq to fight the foreign occupation. Many Palestinians were recruited to fight in Iraq during 2002, and some joined the regime's irregular force, the Fedayeen Saddam. Similarly, large numbers of Syrian volunteers with close tribal and cultural links to Iraqis across the border felt it was their duty to fight. These individuals received no encouragement from their government. One such fighter, a twenty-six-year-old Syrian named 'Abed', decided to fight in Iraq barely a week after the war began because, as he put it, 'there was something inside that made me explode'.[24] Another, a Saudi captured in Iraq named Mohammad Qadir Hussein, was a poor, disgruntled individual who had no military training, but who was motivated by an abiding desire to help other Muslims in distress.[25] As mentioned above, there has been a growth in Salafist and Islamist feelings in the Syrian towns and rural areas in the east on the border with Iraq, and the inhabitants there have close clan ties with the inhabitants across the border in Iraq. A Syrian who went to fight the Coalition at the beginning of the war stated that there were more volunteers than there were weapons available. Moreover, the vast majority had no military experience. He, however, had served two and half years in the Syrian army and was put in charge of 125 fighters, for whom he received twenty weapons. They had a difficult time finding someone who could operate an RPG. Those without weapons sat in the mosques, praying and waiting for news.[26] The foreign volunteers suffered from a lack of organization in the early days of the insurgency. They struck out in isolated incidents at targets of opportunity. They acted with little or no command structure and in small groups, relying on runners and messengers to carry messages between them.

The second wave of foreigners, which seems to be growing, comprises mostly Islamic militants recruited throughout Europe and the Middle East and then sent to Iraq through the same elaborate human pipeline the *mujahideen* used to send volunteers to the Balkans, Chechnya and Afghanistan in the 1990s.[27] The big danger came when they managed to create 'bridges' or links to those other resistance groups that happened to be Iraqi and had organizational structure, finances and military skill.[28] Volunteers wanting to fight in Iraq have flooded into Syria, where they have received some rudimentary training in the use of AK-47s, RPG-7s and remote detonators for bombs. Once the volunteers are ready they are taken across the border into Iraq, where they are directed to safe houses until such time as they can be attached to insurgent combat teams. According to Lieutenant General Jacob Vines 150 foreign fighters cross from Syria every month.[29] Interestingly, though, as mentioned in Chapter 1, members of some of the more sophisticated and better-organized insurgent groups told Australian journalist Michael Ware that they neither trust the foreign fighters, nor consider then sufficiently well-trained or skilled to be insurgents.[30]

Syrian tribal members with links to Iraqis have gone to fight in Iraq. One Syrian family even drew lots to choose those who would go to fight in the war,[31] while a Syrian Salafi preacher known as Abu Qaqaa has played an important role in galvanizing many young men to go to the *jihad* in Iraq.[32] The resistance by Iraqi forces removed some of the gloom and despair among Arabs. It was also responsible for making some of them decide to go to Iraq to fight what they perceived as foreign aggression on Arab land.[33] The collapse of Iraqi border controls facilitated the entry of unsponsored insurgents into Iraq, while Iraqi middlemen or facilitators provided logistical support (i.e. food, directions, and weapons and ammunition) once these individuals had gained entry into the country. Unsponsored foreign infiltrators are then 'passed on' to Sunni *imams*, who become their mentors. Many of these foreign infiltrators entered Iraq before the start of Operation Iraqi Freedom II.

Although poorly trained and ill-equipped, a substantial number of them fought doggedly and to the death in some of the battles between Iraqi irregular forces and the Coalition advancing from the south. After the end of the operation, some returned home, while others remained and fought in the insurgency. Many of these gravitated towards the more disciplined jihadist insurgents.

There is still uncertainty regarding the level or depth of the Al Qaeda presence in Iraq, due to a lack of nonpoliticized intelligence on the terrorist organization's activities there. Osama bin Laden and his subordinates did not think much of Saddam Hussein and his regime, and there is evidence showing that the feeling was mutual. In the early days of the war, when there was an influx of foreign volunteers into Iraq, Hussein apparently warned the Ba'th party against close links with outsiders, especially religious extremists. A senior Islamist operative (now dead) allegedly authored a text entitled 'The Future of Iraq and the Peninsula After Baghdad's Fall: The Religious, Military, Political and Economic Future'.[34] The work argues that the fall of the Ba'thist regime was 'better for the Islamists than the victory of the Iraqi Ba'athists, because the collapse of Arab Ba'athism means the collapse of the atheist, pan-Arab slogans that swept the Muslim nation ... The demise of the Ba'ath government in Iraq heralds the hoisting of the Islamic banner over the debris.'[35] Such fighters were attracted to Iraq following the war precisely in order to fight the US presence in that country for the sake of Islam. Al Qaeda believed that the United States had 'decided to make Iraq the cornerstone of their so-called Greater Middle East Plan in their attempt to impose the atheist [sic] democracy, westernize the people of the region, and uproot Islam'.[36]

The foreign fighter who has had the greatest impact and caused the greatest amount of devastation in Iraq is the Jordanian Abu Musab al-Zarqawi, known to the Coalition as AMZ. According to several accounts, the mysterious Zarqawi was a notorious tough guy in jail in Jordan in the 1990s. Zarqawi (real name Ahmed Fadil al-Khalayleh) grew up in Zarqa, a crime-ridden industrial city northeast of Amman and home to many Islamists. He was not exactly pious in his youth; instead, he ran afoul of the authorities. In 1989, when he was twenty-two, he made his way to Afghanistan, but the Soviets had pulled out, so he missed the *jihad*. He returned to Zarqa in 1992, a militant, and joined a Salafist group called Baya'at al-Imam, or Loyalty to the Imam. He was arrested in 1993 for keeping a large stash of weapons and explosives in his home. In jail he apparently emerged as a natural leader and became more militant. He was released in May 1999 and made his way back to Afghanistan, where he established a camp for jihadis; whether it was connected to Al Qaeda is unclear. He returned to Jordan illegally via Syria in fall 2002.

The US intelligence apparatus has made many mistaken claims about Zarqawi, which have contributed further to his mysteriousness. For example, he was said to be Palestinian but is actually from the Jordanian Beni Hassan Bedouin tribe. Nor did he have a leg amputated in a Baghdad hospital during the time of Saddam's regime, a claim initially made by the US authorities.

Zarqawi made his way into Iraq during the war and attached himself to Ansar al-Islam.[37] He then formed his own group, Jama'at al-Tawhid wa al-Jihad, with which he proceeded to produce mayhem in the hapless country (abductions, beheadings, and suicide bombings). In December 2004 Osama Bin Laden praised Zarqawi's operations and recognized Zarqawi as the leader of Al Qaeda in Iraq: 'We are pleased with their daring operations against the Americans and Allawi's renegade government … We in the Al-Qaida Organization warmly welcome their union with us. This is a great step toward rendering successful the efforts of the mujahideen to establish the state of right and annihilate the state of injustice.'[38] Al Qaeda leaders and operatives were delighted by Zarqawi's adherence to the organization because it enhanced the geographical reach of Al Qaeda, and because they believed that cooperation and coordination between like-minded Islamist groups was necessary—God had ordained the unanimity of Muslims and the pursuit of *jihad* under a united leadership. Zarqawi then changed the name of his organization to Tanzim Qa'idat al-Jihad fi Bilad al-Rafidain (Al Qaeda Jihad Organization in the Land of the Two Rivers—i.e. the Tigris and Euphrates). Many of the foreign Arab fighters in Fallujah were volunteers in Zarqawi's group. Each of the squads or cells would have an *emir*, or commander, usually an Iraqi, often who had had military training in the former Iraqi army.

The media, namely television, and the clerics played an important role in persuading many Arab volunteers to go to Iraq. For example, one volunteer, Walid Muhammad Hadi al-Masmudi, from Tunisia, who was captured in Iraq in January and interrogated, readily admitted that the media and exhortations of clerics were the primary influence on his decision to go and fight in the *jihad*:

We also watched [Muslim] clerics on television and on Al-Jazirah declaring jihad in Iraq … there was a statement, fatwa, by a list of 40 scholars from the Arab and Islamic world on Al-Jazirah … They used to show events in Abu Ghurayb, the oppression, abuse of women, and fornication, so I acted in the heat of the moment and decided … to seek martyrdom in Iraq.[39]

Masmudi made his way into Iraq via Syria and went to the Jolan neighborhood in Fallujah with the help of Iraqi facilitators.

Another Tunisian fighter, Muhammad Bin Hassan Rabih, also came into Iraq via Syria with the help of facilitators working out of a Damascus mosque. When he entered Iraq another facilitator, this time an Iraqi, directed him to Hit, a hotbed of Sunni dissent. He described his motivation thus:

What brought me, for example, is what I have seen on Al-Jazirah and Al-Arabiyah of people in Abu Ghurayb [prison] torturing naked people, including women ... This is what brought me. How can [Prophet] Mu-hammad's nation suffer in this manner ... This is the reason. It was the heat of the moment. It made me angry; Americans cross 20,000 kilome-ters [*sic*] to kill our brethren here.[40]

Rabih stated that he had never had any previous military training; he claimed that he was disillusioned when he came to realize that you cannot fight tanks and planes with assault weapons and was on his way back to Syria when he was captured.[41]

Recruits for the holy war come from a wide variety of coun-tries, including several in Western Europe, where there is a large population of young and disgruntled Muslim men of fighting age. While the vast majority are immigrants of Middle Eastern descent (mainly North African), there are some white European converts among them. Dutch intelligence argues that recruitment into the jihadist network is an individual development rather than a group development process. The recruiters spend a great deal of effort and time on subverting and seducing each individual:

Recruiters are purposefully searching for potential recruits. Their ap-proaching of these people—in some cases even during detention [i.e. in prisons]—marks the beginning of a process in which the recruiters gradually drive the potential recruit apart from their family and friends in order to be able to control and manipulate them and, to begin with, indoctrinate them with the radical Islamic range of ideas. Recruitment is a gradual process which requires tact and discretion from the recruiter. The process is not completed before a recruit actively devotes himself to the violent jihad, either by means of support activities or by taking part in the fight.[42]

The Dutch conclude that this is a time-consuming process but the result is usually dedicated and committed individuals who then are allowed to proceed to 'paramilitary training'. Many Muslims in Europe are drawn into the jihadist network because they are outraged by Western policies in the Middle East and the Islamic world, and by the perceived humiliation and poor treatment meted out to them in their adopted countries. As the Dutch intelligence report concludes, 'The group of young people who feel treated disrespectfully is a major potential target for radicalization and possibly recruitment processes.'[43]

In this light, consider the case of Omer Yousef Juma, also known as Abu Anas Shami, a Kuwaiti-born Palestinian whose family returned to Jordan in the wake of the Iraqi invasion of Kuwait in 1990. Juma was transformed from a peaceful *imam* into a violent militant following the US invasion of Iraq. He made his way into Iraq and joined Zarqawi's group, and was killed on 17 September 2004 in a targeted US strike while traveling down a road near Abu Ghraib, outside Baghdad. Juma's descent into radicalism was not sudden. As Palestinian refugees by origin, his family were not well-disposed towards the United States but the father had become an accountant in Kuwait. Omar was inspired by religion at an early age, while his brothers pursued careers as an engineer, a taxi driver and a merchant. Omar attended the Al-Medina Al-Munawara Islamic College in Saudi Arabia and apparently made his way into Afghanistan, where he learned to use weapons. In 1991 he returned to Jordan, where he became the low-key *imam* of the Murad Mosque in Sweileh. Some accounts claim that he had contact with radical Islamist circles such as the one headed by Abu Muhammad al-Maqdisi, the cleric who inspired Zarqawi. However, had Omar had much contact with Maqdisi the efficient Jordanian intelligence service would have picked him up. It seems that the US invasion of Iraq woke the latent militancy of Omar Juma. In his sermons he began attacking the Jordanian government for supporting the US. He was arrested, and after his release sneaked into Iraq, where he joined Zarqawi's group and was eventually killed. Such is the depth of hatred for the United States that in Jordan he was regarded as a hero in the struggle against perceived US depredations.[44]

Muhammad Qadir Hussein, a Saudi drifter, got his wish to fight in the Iraqi *jihad*. He made it to a foreign fighter training camp near the town of Rawa, in the vast desert of western Iraq. With two other foreign Arabs, he carried out a suicide attack against a US checkpoint. He survived and was captured. He maintained a diary that provided a fascinating glimpse into the relatively unknown role of foreign jihadists. One journalist accurately portrayed the fact that many of these jihadists appear to be disaffected young men harboring an abiding hatred of the West, 'but having little or no experience in training camps or the battlefield'.[45] This was the case with Qadir Hussein, whom a US intelligence officer described as a 'poor Saudi guy without a lot of prospects'.[46] Once they reach Iraq the foreigners are helped by Iraqi facilitators who direct the young fighters to safe houses where they get provisions, arms and some rudimentary training. Colonel David Teeples, commander of the US 3rd Armored Cavalry during its first deployment, in the western desert, said:

The jihad people who came in had their own agenda. They were not connected to former regime loyalists, but to Islamic extremists. But as this thing evolved, it became obvious that the best network for anyone coming from outside to fight would be to contact former regime loyalists. Those were the people who knew who to call, where to find safe houses, where to get their hands on money, weapons, transportation. They had intelligence on where the coalition troops were moving convoys, where troops were stationed, where mortars could be set up.[47]

Foreign fighters from Arab and Islamic countries went to do battle in Operation Iraqi Freedom on the side of the Iraqi government and then in the insurgency. They were motivated to fight what they saw as the despoliation of a Muslim land by infidels, as exemplified by the case of two foreign volunteers who were on the run in the area around Balad in summer 2003. 'Abdullah' was a Saudi and 'Majdi' was a Syrian. Both hailed from educated middle-class backgrounds. Said Abdullah: 'I came here because it is the duty of every Arab and every Muslim to defend Iraq from foreign invaders. When I left Saudi Arabia, I was ready to become a martyr. That was the path I had chosen.'[48] Abdullah's transformation into a militant came gradually following his completion of college. Unable to find a job he drifted into a small group of religious extremists who provided ideological foundation for his growing outrage with the perceived iniquities of US policy in the region: 'I would listen to the sheik (sic), I would see pictures of Palestinians dying on television and I would get angrier each day. I knew America was to blame for the suffering of the Palestinians and many other Muslims. I wanted to do something about it.'[49] The war in Iraq provided the venue. Majdi also drifted into radical politics when he graduated from college: 'For me, whether or not Saddam remained in power was irrelevant. I came here to defend the Iraqi people form a foreign invasion, and I'm willing to do that until my last breath.'[50]

Salafi thinking, more popularly but erroneously known as Wahhabism (which was suppressed under Saddam), existed underground, according to many Iraqi academics and sociologists. But with the downfall of the regime it emerged into the open.[51] Former regime elements facilitated the entry of Arab volunteers and provided them with the weapons and hideouts. Little did they know—or if they did, little did they care—that many of the volunteers were deeply religious. Over the course of the insurgency the foreign volunteers and the local Iraqi Salafists sought each other out; their shared ideological worldview made them naturally gravitate towards one another. Indeed, the Iraqi Salafists were full of praise for the foreign volunteers: 'These young men who came here from other Muslim countries to defend Iraq are very brave. They left their homes and comfortable lives to protect fellow Muslims. This is the most important form of jihad. These mujahideen are guaranteed entry to paradise.'[52]

In February 2005 the French internal counterespionage and counter-terrorism service, the Direction de la Surveillance du Territoire (Directorate of Territorial Surveillance), took down a jihadist recruitment center in the heavily immigrant-populated nineteenth *arrondissement* (district) of Paris. The recruitment center was located in the Salafist Adda'wa mosque and was run by an Algerian, Farid B., who would give fiery Salafist lessons to recruits before sending them off to Iraq via Syria. The individuals would make their way to a facilitator in a Damascus mosque, an Iraqi people-smuggler named Abu Barra. They paid him cash for passage into Iraq, where they made their way to Fallujah, and from there they were directed to where they were needed, such as the Baghdad suburb of Adhamiya, as Sunni stronghold.[53] Another jihadist network in Europe has been responsible for smuggling Algerians and Moroccans from Spain and Belgium into Syria and then Iraq. Individuals are lured to militant-run mosques where, aside from prayer, they engage in study groups that discuss the trials and tribulations of the Muslim *ummah* (universal community of all Muslims, based on Islamic law, or *sharia*) in Chechnya, Afghanistan and Iraq.[54]

Once in Iraq, 'sponsored' jihadists need to create a logistical infrastructure, because infiltrating heavy weapons and explosives across the borders of Iraq's neighbors is difficult. For this they need the help of Iraqis. Mutual suspicion between Sunni Islamists and former regime loyalists, secular-minded nationalists and tribal elements actively opposing the Coalition does not mean that the latter groups are averse to providing logistical support for the former. Attempts by foreign jihadist organizations to operate in Iraq depend on the resources, protection and concealment provided to their fighters by Iraqis. Without support from within Iraq these foreigners would be unable to enter the country with the resources they need or to blend in with the local population

The importance of the foreign jihadists who adhere to a strict interpretation of Sunni Islam lies in three distinct areas. First, these foreign jihadists have joined with local Iraqi Salafists, now in the open following the downfall of the Saddam regime, to successfully introduce a cohesive and extreme ideology to the public. Many of these groups, like the Mujahideen al-Salafiyah in Balad, have even reached out to members of the former Fedayeen Saddam, so long as the latter drop their allegiance to Saddam. Second, they have increased the prospects for communal violence by waging a campaign of deliberate and focused attacks against leaders of other Muslim communities, promoters of 'moral laxity' and non-Muslims. In the fall of 2003, Islamists were particularly active in Mosul, where they attacked a nunnery, killed a well-known writer, bombed a popular cinema and burnt four liquor stores. Third, they have been responsible for the suicide bombing campaigns in Iraq between early fall 2003 and summer 2005. August 2003 saw three massive car bombings. Some of the most devastating suicide attacks came in mid-November 2003, against Italian *carabinieri* in Nasiriyah, and in mid-January 2004, outside a CPA compound in Baghdad. In March 2004, the Shi'a religious celebration of Ashura saw multiple suicide bombings that killed hundreds.

However, interrogations of nearly 300 Saudis captured while trying to sneak into Iraq, and case studies of more than three dozen others who blew themselves up in suicide attacks, showed that most were heeding the calls from clerics and activists to drive infidels out of Arab land, according to a study by Anthony Cordesman and the Saudi investigator Nawaf Obaid, a US-trained analyst who was commissioned by the Saudi government and given access to Saudi officials and intelligence.[55] A separate Israeli analysis of 154 foreign fighters compiled by a leading terrorism researcher found that despite the presence of some senior Al Qaeda operatives who are organizing the volunteers, 'the vast majority of [non-Iraqi] Arabs killed in Iraq have never taken part in any terrorist activity prior to their arrival in Iraq'.[56] 'Only a few were involved in past Islamic insurgencies in Afghanistan, Bosnia, or Chechnya,' the Israeli study says. Out of the 154 fighters analyzed, only a handful had past associations with terrorism, including six who had fathers who fought the Soviet Union in Afghanistan.[57] US intelligence officials, speaking on the condition of anonymity, and terrorism specialists painted a similar portrait of the suicide bombers wreaking havoc in Iraq. Prior to the Iraq war, they were not Islamic extremists seeking to attack the United States, as Al Qaeda did four years ago. Rather, they were part of a new generation of terrorists responding to calls to defend their fellow Muslims from 'crusaders' and 'infidels.'[58]

Organizational typology

Having a fairly extensive geographic scope, a large popular base drawn all walks of life from a population that is largely sympathetic and comprises between 5.5 and 7 million people, and foreign sympathizers—some with skills, others lacking even the basics—is insufficient for an insurgency. In short, an insurgency needs leadership, combatants, cadres and resources. All of this requires organization, so here we address organizational type and structure.

A word of caution must be injected. We labor under the disadvantage that the organization and support structure of the Iraqi insurgency is very opaque to us. Because myriad groups appeared in the early days of the insurgency, each of which claimed to be the true voice of 'liberation', it was difficult to gain accurate information about the insurgency's organization, infrastructure and ultimate goals.[59] Moreover, the fact that the insurgency is ongoing as this study is being written means that there is still no access to these most secretive aspects of the Iraqi insurgent movement. Insurgents will issue statements and use the media and Internet to promote their motivations and grievances, and sometimes even dissect their tactics, but they generally do not discuss their organizational structure in detail. Nonetheless, there is sufficient evidence to build up a picture of the organizational type, leadership and structure.

We should underestimate neither the ruthlessness nor the organizational capabilities of this insurgency. The words of 'Khalid', a twenty-nine-year-old insurgent with the Fedayeen Saddam, are worth considering: 'We have many people and we're a lot better organized than the Americans realize. We have been preparing for this kind of guerilla war for a long time, and we're much more patient than the Americans. We have nowhere else to go.'[60]

Organizational type.   The Iraqi insurgency has had to contend from the very beginning with the question of the optimal type of organization necessary or available for its purposes, which are to provide direction and marshal resources for an irregular war and, of course, to fight such a war. The organizational type chosen is based on the decision-making of the emergent leaders, and often just as much dictated by the exigencies of circumstances (availability of resources, manpower, geographic scope of the insurgency, and requirements for effective but clandestine action).

The two organizational types are *hierarchical* and *decentralized*. A hierarchical organization has a clearly defined leadership structure, and a 'well-defined vertical chain' of command and control from the leadership to the rest of the organization, in which 'data and intelligence flows up and down the organizational channels that correspond to these vertical chains, but may not move horizontally through the organization'.[61] Such organizations are functionally specialized, with units below the leadership structure that fight, gather intelligence, recruit personnel, and supply money and weapons.

The Ba'th Party in Iraq was a hierarchical organization. When it was overthrown and went into clandestine opposition after April 2003 it largely retained its traditional organizational culture. Given the circumstances, however, it did decentralize its operations. The Ba'thist operators at the 'pointy end of the spear' (i.e. those engaged in insurgent operations on the ground in Iraq) knew much more about the situation than those in exile in Syria or elsewhere, on whom they otherwise relied for financial support and for general directives regarding cooperation and coordination with non-Ba'thist groups. The same logic applies to those members of the former security and intelligence organizations and, of course, the defunct armed forces. These institutions epitomized hierarchical structures. When they engaged in operations members of these organizations generally did not wear their former uniforms, which would readily have identified them as former soldiers, but they did adhere to strict hierarchical chains of command and control. (I know of only a few occasions where insurgents from the former military wore their old green Iraqi army uniforms during operations. Most of these occurrences took place in and around Ramadi and Samarra.)

The decentralized, or networked, organizational structure has been described as 'loose' and 'flat', with fluid or less distinct boundaries between its various subunits. Such organizations have a leadership structure, but it is weak due either to cultural/environmental factors (i.e. kinship or traditional ties within the leadership) or to the lack of any particular skills that necessarily identify one person over another as designated leader. In Iraq some of the early insurgent groups or cells were made up of family members or neighborhood friends who came together to fight the foreign presence. However, none of them might emerge as designated leader because of constraints (i.e. lack of secure communications between leadership and subordinate units) that do not permit strong control, or perhaps even for no discernable reason at all. 'Weak' leadership permits the subordinate units considerable latitude in their daily actions and in the planning and execution of their operations. Decentralized insurgent groups are characterized by the fluidity and lack of constancy in membership. This has been a characteristic of some groups within the Iraqi insurgency, particularly those in the rural areas whose geographic scope, functional specialization and motives for fighting are often limited to a very specific grievance or set of grievances. Some members may be part-timers who literally come and go, or who may even move to another group that is somehow part of or connected with the insurgent network. Others hold jobs (indeed, in the Iraqi insurgency some fighters work in the very state institutions or structures that the insurgency has been trying to topple) and engage in the insurgency as a 'hobby', albeit a serious, if not deadly, one to which they turn up when required.

It should be noted that clandestine organizations like terrorist or insurgent groups, including those in Iraq, rarely adhere exclusively to one or the other type of organizational structure, instead tending to be a mix of the two types. Whether such a body is more hierarchical or more decentralized depends on a host of factors such as its culture, what the organization is required or has tasked itself to do and, of course, the dynamic and highly uncertain environment in which it finds itself functioning. We once heard a great deal about the Iraqi insurgents belonging to decentralized networks. I believe that journalists and observers used the term because it sounded 'sexy' and because being 'decentralized and networked' seemed to be *de rigueur* for terrorist or insurgent groups. The reality is that you simply cannot be a wholly decentralized insurgent group and continue to exist for long or be able to carry out more than very limited operations in a limited geographical locale (e.g. one's neighborhood or tribal lands).

The Iraqi insurgents have exhibited features of both organizational types, with larger, more geographically extended insurgent groups made up of former regime elements tending towards the hierarchical mode, and tribal or neighborhood insurgents tending towards the decentralized. Fedayeen Saddam, for example, exhibits characteristics of both types. This organization was well-placed to play a role in the insurgency because it had existed for some time. Moreover, the Fedayeen became an important element in certain sectors of the insurgency because they had the training, weapons and motivation to fight to 'restore' the overthrown system, which had benefited them. They were founded by a regime that believed in hierarchy, yet no longer have a strong national hierarchical structure themselves. They have formed into small, decentralized insurgent groups spread into various areas. However, the organization still maintains a key characteristic of hierarchical organizations, in that these otherwise decentralized Fedayeen groups have specialized cells: combat cells, cells for the procurement of ammunition and weapons, technical cells for the construction of home-made bombs, operational security (OPSEC) cells and those whose purpose is purely to facilitate communications. The cells are kept separate and know as little as possible about each other, while members within cells try to minimize the amount of information they exchange each with the other.

Leadership.   A leadership emerges from within the ranks of the disgruntled or dissatisfied population to organize and articulate the grievances and to present its goals and/or demands. An insurgency by definition is a violent activity, and like all other forms of violent action against a constituted authority or more powerful force it is costly and stressful. It can lead to capture, injury or death. But if you have a cause and are motivated, and have a leadership that provides strategic and operational direction and is able to develop an organization, you are halfway there in the confrontation with your opponent. The leadership of the Ba'thist-nationalist element of the insurgency is opaque, as is the political leadership outside Iraq, and the middle-ranking leadership that deals with day-to-day operations. The leaders do, however, come from all ranks of the Sunni community. The Ba'thist element of the insurgency's leadership has at its core members of the former security services, army officers, Ba'th Party functionaries, teachers and police. These men, all of whom have extensive training in some form of activity that requires organization and structure (whether it be as party functionaries, intelligence and security officers in charge of recruitment, in operational security, or as army officers with professional skills to pass on to neophytes, such as firing mortars and sniping), have recruited former colleagues or subordinates into their groups, or have sought men from their neighborhoods, tribes or clans.[62] This insurgent leadership presumably pledges allegiance to the remnants of the Ba'th Party political leadership operating outside Iraq.

The biggest problem for the leadership of the Ba'th-based insurgents is that the dilution of the Ba'th ideology has seen the rise of leaders who are more inclined to adopt a fusion or a mishmash of Islamist and nationalist motifs for the struggle. The Al-Ghaylania *fasila* (unit) of the Army of Muhammad (Jaish Muhammad), an insurgent group active near Ramadi, provides an example of how the fusion of Islamist ideology and Ba'thist/army organizational skills has muddied the waters. The Army of Muhammad claims to have 5,000 fighters and a decentralized structure extending west as far as Ramadi and north to Tikrit. The group is organized in cells, the head of each cell often having been an officer in the former Iraqi army. Many members of the Army of Muhammad are Dulaimis, and cells are often made up of members from the same Dulaimi clan or family. This insurgent group lives among the people. Its specialized cells buy weapons from a flourishing arms bazaar in the Shi'a south. The Al-Ghaylania *fasila* denies any connection with or support for Saddam Hussein.[63] However, they do concede that many officers, intelligence personnel and Ba'th Party members have joined the ranks of the Army of Muhammad, transforming it from a set of isolated units and cells into something more professional. The officer in charge admits that former Ba'th Party members direct large elements of the 'resistance,' but said this does not matter because the resistance is moving towards a post-Saddam ideological foundation.[64] It is not clear, however, whether the sentiments of this *fasila* are necessarily representative of the entire Army of Muhammad.

The leadership of the Islamist groups is even more opaque. Apparently, though, it does include former regime types who have become 'born-again Muslims', so to speak, and have migrated into the ranks of 'righteous' resistance, which sees an obligation to fight the occupation on the basis of Islamic precepts. I mentioned before that Islamic piety had begun to make inroads into the armed forces and security forces long before the collapse of the regime. Even die-hard regime-support organizations such as the Fedayeen Saddam had witnessed the growth of Sunni Islamist sentiment within their ranks. In many small towns in the Sunni areas of Iraq, teachers and policemen, public-sector functionaries of the Ba'th regime, had long ago ceased to believe in the ideals of the Ba'th Party and veered towards Salafi Islam. In many instances, clerics have played roles that can be easily defined as leadership-type roles rather than mere spiritual guidance or indoctrination roles. Some clerics have been known to fight but more importantly, in many instances, clerics in leadership positions have used their mosques as storage points for weapons and ammunition, and as command and control centers for the insurgent groups that they either lead or for which they provide behind-the-scenes guidance. Indeed, in many cases, especially in Fallujah, clerics have provided not only inspiration and justification for resistance, but also the 'wise' background guidance and restraint to young and more excitable gangster-style leaders in the Islamist insurgency, particularly men like the electrician Omar Hadid. Hadid fell afoul of the law during the time of Saddam Hussein, when he became a religious extremist. He quickly emerged as a leader during the Fallujah insurgency, and seems to have been instrumental in trying to unite the city's disparate insurgent groups under the umbrella of the *mujahideen shura* (council).

Organizational structures. The next task for the leadership would be to structure the organization to be able to meet your opponent on the field of battle, and to provide the wherewithal to do so. Given the disparity in power between regular and irregular forces, however, you must be able to face the enemy on your own terms. A framework must be set up to allow you to wage irregular warfare, and to conduct all of the subsidiary but equally important tasks of training, developing and maintaining specialized skills, and obtaining arms and financial support.

Combatant cells. The combat components of an Iraqi insurgent group are the individuals who commit the acts of violence against the Coalition. The attackers are usually young men, either former soldiers, whose attacks and ambushes have been the best-organized and most professional, or men without military experience, such as students, tribal youths or the unemployed. They carry out the attacks under instruction from and guidance of older men, usually former regime soldiers, or intelligence or security services officers. Others combatant cells have been composed almost entirely of former Iraqi army personnel led by their officers. For example, in July 2004 a group of insurgent combatants rained thirty-four well-aimed mortar shells on a US army base on the outskirts of the restive city of Samarra, killing five soldiers of the 1st Infantry Division. Many other insurgents are part-timers who participate in actions and then return to their 'normal' daily routines and jobs.

The organizational structure of such combatant cells is simple: a small number of cells report to commanders, often from the middle levels of the former regime. They rely on the tribes to protect and supply them, and act as their eyes and ears: 'We live as a tribe. People protect you even if they don't know you.'[65]

Most of the part-time insurgents come from groups that have little or no external funding. This means that the would-be insurgent has to hold down a legitimate day job. For example, families that are involved in an insurgency cannot afford to have their menfolk work as full-time insurgents. By contrast the former regime personnel and the Islamist volunteers can afford to have full-time insurgents because both groups have external sources of funding.

The most amateurish insurgent fighters were also the 'dumbest', and many were killed or captured in the early days of the insurgency in a process we have referred to as 'combat Darwinism'. Money was their prime motivation for participating in attacks.[66]

The large and well-developed insurgent organizations have combatant groups that they often refer to as squadrons, battalions or brigades. Combatant cells are made up of four to seven fighters, depending on the nature of the operation and the target. Some insurgent groups show great tactical skill in the field, and are thus able to conduct small-unit attacks or use small mortars effectively. Insurgent groups with these skills are doubtlessly either former military personnel or led by them. In and around Ramadi—a town where the Marines suffered significant casualties—US forces had to deal with small and elusive units of expert insurgents, many of them former regular Iraqi soldiers. They were very good with mortars, with which they regularly pestered the Americans. 'What we've learned about the mortar men is they're very good. In fact, they're experts,' said one US Army captain who fought them.[67] The mortar units are backed by a combined reconnaissance and combat team whose task is to spot US targets and to fight off US troops in order to allow the mortar teams to escape. Iraqi mortar operators in this area are careful to avoid civilian casualties; they fire from grassy areas or fields of crops rather than basing themselves within civilian infrastructure.[68]

Insurgents who intend merely to emplace improvised explosive devices (IEDs, on which more below) on roads that are used heavily by US convoys, but do not wish to follow up with ambushes, do not need combatant cells. In such cases specialized cells that deal with bomb-making come primarily into play.

Specialized cells.   Specialized cells (technical and bomb-making, logistics, suicide-bomber support or facilitator cells, reconnaissance, and operational security) exist to support the combatant cells. They would comprise men like Mohammad Khudair al-Dulaimi, a member of the former Mukhabarat (Iraqi intelligence service), who was an expert in sabotage, assassinations and setting up remote-controlled explosions. Dulaimi was issued with several million dollars before the war and became part of the insurgency. He was alleged to have run D9, the sensitive special-operations directorate, which specialized in sabotage and assassination, and was promoted after allegedly killing an Iraqi nuclear scientist who had defected to Jordan. In the lead-up to the war D9 worked closely with the Fedayeen Saddam, teaching covert techniques.

The key specialized cells either deal with a variety of functional issues and provide support for the combatant sections or, as in the case of the IED and suicide-bomber cells, are essentially combatant units themselves. It is important to recognize that only the large insurgent groups that can afford to be functionally specialized contain such cells, which can be divided into five major types.

The first of these specialized types are 'technical' cells (IED and suicide-bomber control), which are found in some of the larger insurgent groups. The two most important types of cells that provide critical and direct support to combat units are the IED and suicide-bomber control cells. Some IED cells are independent operators that hire out their services to the insurgent organizations that can afford to pay them.[69] IED cells often exchange information and transfer skills among one another by sharing videos of their respective exploits for training purposes. The IED unit includes several people, from those who procure the raw materials (usually from ammunition dumps), to the bomb-builder, undoubtedly the most technically skilled individual in the cell, who also doubles as training instructor. He is thus the key person, but if he is 'eliminated' the cell does not cease operation; if it is part of a larger insurgent organization it merely gets rolled into another cell. The cell also includes the 'emplacer', the individual charged with the dangerous job of emplacing the device along, or even buried under, a road. He may or may not undertake this task alone. Finally, there is the triggerman, who explodes the device.

A journalist witnessed an insurgent setting up, for show, a deadly IED while describing the process:

'Look how to make a booby trap for the Americans.' The man crouched down in front the bombs and began to explain out loud the moves that he was making. 'It is easy to build a remote-controlled explosive device. Here, I uncover the detonator at the top and fix the first electric wire, then all I have to do is to bind it to the bomb with adhesive tape and to attach it to another cable at the opposite end of the detonator. It is set off by the electric current of a battery. Once that explodes, all the rest blows up too.'

He bared the copper wire with his teeth, stuck it into the detonator, unscrewed the grenade's fuse, and stuck a second wire into it. In under 10 seconds the two IEDs were ready to be set up by the roadside, waiting for a US convoy to pass by.

'A mujahid stays hidden a safe distance away and he waits. These here, made using wires, are more accurate; but the Americans might see the wires poking out from Heaven knows where. And that might alert them.

'That is why we have often used cell phones. All you have to do is to call the number of the cell phone that you have left on the bomb linked to the detonators, and electric shock of the ring makes the whole thing blow up. But there are problems with cell phones too. Sometimes the lines are too busy, or the call does not get through, or else it gets through too late. So for some months now we have been using remote controls designed for opening garage doors. There is no delay and you can even stay and watch from 20 meters away, with your hands in your pockets and your finger on the button.'[70]

Suicide bombers do not 'just turn up to their target'. They need a logistical infrastructure, which consists of individuals (or sometimes just one person) who provide everything from recon- naissance of the potential target or approximate area in which the operation is intended to take place, to the provision of a safe house and food, and the explosives-laden vehicle or suicide belt.

The second type of specialized cell is for training. Insurgent groups have trained combatant cadres in various locations around the country. It has been claimed that in some cases they have set up quite extensive and elaborate training locations, which Coalition forces have stumbled upon by accident, but I am unsure how valid these claims are. We do know, though, that the insurgents have training centers in many safe houses, farmhouses and mosques, and in the dense farmlands and orchards along the Euphrates and Tigris rivers. At Abu Qaddum, near Madain, they even established a training facility in an abandoned Republican Guard base. Former military personnel of the dissolved Iraqi army and security forces have provided much of the training. The quasi-professionalism of the attacks in the Samarra and Ramadi areas is due to the participa- tion of and/or training by former army officers.

All evidence suggests that the insurgents suffer no shortage of light weapons and ammunition. Iraq is essentially one huge ammunition dump. According to one source, by spring 2005 Coalition forces had uncovered, secured or destroyed 10,000 arms caches throughout the country.[71] Prior to the war, the Ba'th Party cadre and security/intelligence personnel had distributed thousands of tons of arms and ammunition in readiness for the conflict, storing them in civilian areas, mosques, schools and hospitals. There is estimated to be between 0.75 million and 1 million tons of weapons and ammunition in largely unguarded ammunition storage points (ASPs) throughout the country. This have been sufficient to maintain the insurgency at its current level of activity, and also means that most Iraqi insurgent groups have not been forced to conduct operations to seize arms and ammunition. According to one of its members, Ansar al-Sunnah obtains its weapons mainly from the vast stores of former Iraqi army munitions. Some of the better-financed and more technically capable insurgent groups have set up makeshift arms and bomb-making factories in safe houses or underground facilities. Iraqi insurgents describe how they form teams or cells of up to four men to acquire antitank mines either looted from Iraqi army munitions sites or bought from middlemen who steal them. They would daisy-chain three or four together and place them along roads traveled by US convoys.

The insurgents have access to numerous training manuals from the former army. I have seen large numbers of these manuals that have been recovered from insurgent groups. They have apparently sought to learn from more established and successful insurgent groups elsewhere, and have studied the tactics of Hezbollah and Palestinian groups such as Al-Aqsa Martyrs' Brigades and Hamas.[72]

The most interesting phenomenon, however, is the use of the Internet as a medium for combat training. It is difficult to ascertain how effective this has been because it does not have the advantage of hands-on training. But neither does it require an extensive or elaborate training infrastructure, which would mean a big 'signature' and thus susceptibility to detection and destruction by Coalition forces. It is also cheaper and it reaches a wide audience.

Various insurgent groups have, for example, posted instructions on the Internet on how to disable or destroy US armored vehicles such as M1A1 or M1A2 Abrams tanks.[73] The insurgents have used the Web to provide instructions on how to make IEDs and prepare car bombs. The insurgent website Alm2sda.net presented a sophisticated and detailed multimedia presentation with the opening statement: 'My brothers and mujahideen, this is detailed training for booby traps … All of these have become the basics for killing, destroying, and inflicting heavy damages on the enemy, and very important to know.'[74] The presenter, Albashk (Sparrow Hawk), provides painstaking instructions on the types and characteristics of explosives that are best for IEDs. He then discusses different types of detonators and timers before finishing with instructions on how to build a car bomb, which he says is the 'strongest weapon that the mujahideen have used so far, from the viewpoint of tactics, cost, and major impact on the enemy'.[75]

Intelligence and OPSEC cells comprise the third type of specialized cells. A primary task of an insurgent and his organization is to follow Mao's dictum: try to gain as much actionable intelligence on the enemy while making it virtually impossible for him to acquire it about you. Strategic and operational intelligence among insurgents in Iraq has proven to be quite good. Their ability to assassinate or kidnap individuals, and assault convoys and other vulnerable targets has been the result of painstaking surveillance and reconnaissance. Inside information about convoy and troop movements and the daily habits of Iraqis working with the Coalition has been passed to insurgent cells from within the Iraqi security services, primarily the Iraqi police force, which is rife with sympathy for the insurgents, and Iraqi ministries, and from pro-insurgent individuals who work within the Green Zone. The uncanny ability of the insurgency to conduct effective attacks like that on police headquarters in Baghdad in early September 2003 focused attention on members of the security service as likely culprits or intelligence providers. Salah al-Mukhtar provides an analysis of the scope and extent of insurgent intelligence capabilities that is somewhat self-congratulatory yet has to be judged as accurate:

According to information released by both, American occupation sources and the resistance, the Iraqi intelligence service has penetrated all levels not only of the new Iraqi administration, imposed by the occupation, but also the highest command of American army, because the Americans are in desperate needs for translators, guides, workers, technicians, speaking Arabic, and by this way the Iraqi intelligence has infiltrated their ranks. The newly established security forces and the so called 'national guards' have become a very good sources on the Iraqis cooperating with the Americans and the Americans. I can assure you that the Iraqi intelligence has achieved very important operations and as Mr. Paul Bremer, the American colonial administrator, has said, the most painful operations the Iraqi resistance have [sic] made were not the military ones but the intelligence. You have to know that the intelligence of the resistance is the original intelligence service of Iraq, which was selected from the élite of intelligence officers to join the resistance. So the experiences of Iraqi intelligence were used perfectly against Americans and I assure you that the Iraqi intelligence under the resistance leadership has overwhelmed the CIA.[76]

Insurgent operational security has also varied according to the organizational and social characteristics of the insurgent group. Those composed of or controlled by former regime loyalists have developed good operational security. This is hardly surprising in a society that has been subjected to thirty-five years of totalitarian control. Furthermore, the presence within the insurgency of security and intelligence officers of the former regime has ensured that some of the insurgents have been inculcated by the culture of operational security. Cells of the same group or working within the same area know little if anything about one another. A 'cut-out' is used to pass instructions from the leadership to operational cells. Many insurgents in the field have learned to avoid communicating by cell phone or electronic means and use innocuous couriers to pass messages. Insurgents killed or captured during ambushes or firefights are often found to have no form of identification on them, so that Coalition forces are unable to trace them back to their 'roots' or comrades.

The tribally based insurgents around Ramadi, Fallujah and Hit developed operational security based on cultural and social norms rather than on modern and bureaucratic norms that have characterized cells made up of former security and intelligence officers. The clannish structure of some of the insurgent groups—particularly around Ramadi and Fallujah, where the tribal element of the insurgency is strong—ensures that outsiders are viewed with suspicion. There is a reluctance to surrender or inform on colleagues because this is considered to be dishonorable and likely to incur the wrath of other members of the clan or tribe if the informants are discovered.

Propaganda and media outreach functions are the specialty of the fourth major cell type. Almost all large and functionally specialized insurgent groups have sophisticated programs in this area. The insurgents have often stated that, first, much of the battle lies in the mind and, second, because of the resources at its disposal, including the control of the global media networks, the enemy has managed to slant or frame the message in its favor. The insurgents have also argued that their inability to disseminate their message has contributed to the manifest lack of support for them in the world. The Internet has greatly facilitated the ability of the insurgents to fight this media monopoly. Despite Iraq's relatively late entry into the Internet and information technology age, there has been no shortage of technically skilled individuals prepared to set up elaborate websites for the insurgents. Some of the larger insurgent groups have a propaganda or media arm, which they used to castigate the Coalition forces. They have listened carefully to what the Coalition says and the message it seeks to convey, and have responded with withering replies that include graphic pictures of dead and wounded Iraqis. The Islamic Jihad army, for example, released several communiqués, including the following example:

It is our duty, as well as our right, to fight back the occupying forces … We have not crossed the oceans and seas to occupy Britain or the US nor are we responsible for 9/11. These are only a few of the lies that these criminals present to cover their true plans for the control of the energy resources of the world, in face of a growing China and a strong unified Europe …

This conflict is no longer considered a localized war … We will pin them here in Iraq to drain their resources, manpower, and their will to fight. We will make them spend as much as they steal, if no more. We will disrupt, then halt the flow of our stolen oil, thus, [sic] rendering their plans useless …

And to George Bush, we say, 'You have asked us to "Bring it on," and so we have. Like never expected. Have you another challenge?'[77]

The insurgents have used the Internet to provide would-be recruits with directions on how to make their way into Iraq via Syria. For example, two websites, Jihadweb and Al-Firdaws, have presented detailed instructions. Jihadweb posted an Internet leaflet that stated: 'Hadha huw al-tariq ala al-araq: Ala man yarid an yasul ala al-mujahideen fi bilad al-rafidain' (This is the road to Iraq: for the person who wishes to reach the mujahideen in the Land of the Two Rivers). Another posting gave precise details on routes and the best disguises and means of conveyance in order to enter Iraq.[78] The insurgent propaganda machine went into overdrive during the

US-led assault into Fallujah in November 2004. Insurgent Internet postings claimed that the United States had used chemical weapons because conventional weapons had proven ineffective against the well-entrenched and motivated *mujahideen*. As the insurgents continue to battle the Coalition and Iraqi government, the Internet has played an important role in their efforts to coordinate attacks and publicize them after the fact.

Finally, there are funding and procurement cells. Without financial resources the Iraqi insurgency (or any insurgency, for that matter) would come to a standstill. We do not know much about the financial structure of the Iraqi insurgency, but it is clear that there is a group of individuals dedicated to financial operations. There are three distinct sources of finance.

Former regime loyalists hid large quantities of money around the country prior to the downfall of the regime. US forces have uncovered many of these caches and several key insurgents have been captured with large quantities of cash, but the insurgents continue to have access to financial resources. Saddam Hussein's extended family is allegedly supplying weapons, fighters and money to insurgents in Iraq. There is a network that is allegedly run by three of Saddam's cousins, who operate from Syria and Jordan. One of the leaders is reported to be a former officer in the Special Security Organization and a cousin of the deposed president. Two other cousins from the Majid family, who now live in Syria and Europe, are also involved in the operation. Under Saddam, members of the Majid family, among them 'Chemical Ali' (Ali Hassan al-Majid), had key roles in Iraq's state security. US officials say Saddam's cousins have access to tens of millions of dollars, much of it profits from smuggling oil and military equipment. The insurgents have also received donations from private citizens and particularly from rich families, especially those who are in the construction, contracting and commercial sectors in Anbar Province.

In Iraq, as elsewhere, we have begun to see situations where wider acts of violence committed by organized criminal groups exist alongside or have even been integrated into the insurgency. Criminals have already made their imprint on Iraqi society.[79] Organized crime syndicates worldwide have economic gain as their primary motive, and they clearly thrive in situations where the state and its mechanisms are weak, as has been the case in Iraq over the past three years. While crime by individuals has soared, the emergence of organized criminal gangs as a socioeconomic phenomenon is of greater import and concern. Some groups or individuals have developed links with the insurgents for mutual gain. The development of linkages between insurgent/terrorist groups and criminal gangs becomes much smoother if individuals are members of both organizations and if the politics-driven insurgency/terrorist groups engage in economic criminal activity as a matter either of strategic policy (to ensure that the state cannot restore normal economic activity) or of replenishing their coffers.[80]

Many individuals—some with criminal backgrounds—who were to play a role in the insurgency 'prefinanced' their activities by looting the banks in the immediate chaotic aftermath of the Ba'th regime's collapse. The insurgents continue to rely on criminal elements to extort and steal money or to kidnap people for ransom. Some of the money is in the hands of leaders based in Syria. One of the most notorious underworld figures is a Shi'a who was captured in March 2005. In the time he 'worked' he managed to funnel money from Syria, paying off police and other security officials to look the other way. He also helped fund insurgent cells through money acquired from individuals, including the parents of children who had been abducted for ransom. His activities were critical to the operations of insurgent cells in the notorious Haifa Street area of Baghdad. Iraq has also succumbed to a wave of kidnappings by organized criminal gangs, who demand exorbitant ransoms from the families of the victims.[81] They often even have 'sold' these abductees, particularly those from rich families, to insurgents in return for a substantial fee.

Insurgent organizations

There are a remarkable number of insurgent organizations.[82] They vary widely in levels of skill, functional specialization, professionalism, number of personnel, modus operandi, targeting and longevity. Some come and go, some change names and some claim to have merged with one another to form larger and supposedly more effective networks. I have come across numerous instances where insurgent groups have said they have merged or are merging. In fall 2004 three groups, the Mujahideen Battalions, the Islamic Army in Iraq and the Mujahideen Brigades, supposedly merged to form the Islamic Jihad Brigades. Five other, smaller groups claimed that they had merged to form the Imam al-Mujahideen Brigades. This supposedly brought together nearly 7,000 mujahideen from all corners of the country. This chaotic situation, of course, has proven to be a major problem for effective intelligence-gathering about the insurgency and its methods and goals.[83]

The following are secular nationalist/tribal groups:

The General Command of the Armed Forces, Resistance and Liberation in Iraq.   Probably composed of former Iraqi military personnel, particularly from the Special Republican Guards, security and intelligence personnel, and members of the Ba'th Party and the paramilitary Fedayeen. These former regime personnel are not averse to giving their cells Islamic names.

Popular Resistance for the Liberation of Iraq.   Issued a call on 26 June 2003 to all in the Arab and Islamic worlds to come and attack the

United States in Iraq. It criticized Arab and Muslim rulers for turning themselves into local policemen for the United States.

Iraqi Resistance and Liberation Command. Appeared in late April 2003. It is secular and nationalist but has denied that it is an extension of the defunct regime. It issued a communiqué that called for a 'jihad until the liberation of Iraq'. It is quite normal for secular and nationalist groups to use the term religious term *jihad*.

Al 'Awdah (The Return).   Came to prominence in mid-June 2003. It is made up of former security-service members and Iraqi armed forces personnel organized into cells distributed throughout cities such as Baghdad, Mosul and Ramadi. There are reports that the pro-Saddam elements of the Ba'th Party have actually renamed the party Al 'Awdah.

Harakat Ra's al-'Afa (Snake's Head Movement).   Also Ba'thist, it allegedly has links to Sunni Arab tribes around Fallujah and Ramadi.

Nasserites.   A small group of non-Ba'thist pan-Arab nationalists of little significance. Their only claim to fame, apart from allegedly successful attacks on US forces, is their ability to make enemies of almost all other Iraqi political groups, whether insurgent or involved in the political process under the auspices of the CPA.

Thuwwar al-'Arak—Kata'ib al-Anbar al-Musallahah (Iraq's Revolutionaries—Al-Anbar Armed Brigades).   An anti-Saddamist nationalist insurgent group based in Anbar Province.

General Secretariat for the Liberation of Democratic Iraq.   A leftist, anti-Saddam nationalist group that condemns the Coalition authority for failing to provide security and basic services to the population.

The following insurgent organizations incorporate nationalist and religious elements:

Higher Command of the Mujahideen in Iraq.   This is one of the most active resistance groups in Iraq. It is unclear whether it is largely religious or nationalist, or a front for Saddam's defunct regime. The group first emerged on 15 April 2003, when it issued a communiqué that stated it had 8,000 *mujahideen* (holy warriors) within its ranks. This is a huge number and there are indications that it might be an umbrella organization for several groups. Several subsequent communiqués stated that the group had nothing to do with the former regime and was seeking to establish an Islamic state. But other communiqués indicate that it had conducted joint operations with members of the former Iraqi armed forces, nationalist resistance group and even units of Fedayeen. The organization's 'combat units' are referred to as brigades. The best-known, the Al-Faruq and Al-'Abbas brigades, were raised in early June 2003 and might include secular Sunni Arabs and individuals from now defunct organizations within the former regime. The Al-Faruq Brigades have set up small units, or 'squadrons', with Islamic names such as the *Muntasirun bi Allah* squadron, which was active in Anbar Province during summer 2003. Squadrons have different specialties, such as reconnaissance and combat.

Munazzamat al-Rayat al-Aswad (Black Banner Organization).   This organization's propaganda seems to indicate that it has nationalist and religious tendencies. It has called for sabotage of the oil industry to prevent it from falling to the hands of the West.

Unification Front for the Liberation of Iraq.   Little is known about this group except that it is anti-Saddamist and anti-Ba'thist, and has called upon all Iraqi forces to fight the US occupation.

National Front for the Liberation of Iraq.   This sounds like the name of a secular resistance organization, but apparently it incorporates elements of the regime and religious sympathizers, because it has accepted into its ranks Republican Guards and Islamists. It was also one of the first groups to appear during the war. It issued its first communiqués in April 2003, and claimed that it had tried to assassinate Ahmed Chalabi but only succeeded in killing some of his supporters in an attack in Najaf.

The following are defined largely by their religious tendencies:

Jaish Ansar al-Sunnah.   One of the largest and deadliest insurgent groups in the Iraq, it is also one of the most active and uncompromising in its ideology, as reflected in numerous statements by its 'officials', including the following: 'It is known that the jihad in Iraq has become the individual duty of every obligation after the infidel enemy fell upon the land of Islam ... The task is great ... [and] the aim does not end with their defeat but with the application of the shari'ah of Allah and His Prophet.'[84] It first came into prominence on 26 November 2003, when a unit of the 'army', the Al-Mansur Brigade, killed several Spanish intelligence officers in the vicinity of Mahmudiyah, south of Baghdad. In February 2004 it conducted terrorist strikes in the relatively tranquil Kurdish north. It is notorious for its ruthlessness, having executed twelve kidnapped Nepalese hostages whom it had abducted in August 2004, and seventeen Iraqi contractors working for the US military in Tikrit in December 2004.

Mujahideen al ta'ifa al-Mansoura (Mujahideen of the Victorious Sect).   This includes non-Iraq Sunni Islamist elements or even Sunni fundamentalist elements of neo-Salafi background. Its military arm is known as the Martyr Khattab Brigade.

Kata'ib al Mujahideen fi al-Jama'ah al-Salafiyah fi al-'Arak (Mujahi-deen Battalions of the Salafi Group of Iraq).   A Sunni Islamist group that claims as its spiritual mentor the Palestinian Islamist Abdullah Azzam, who fought with the Afghan *mujahideen* with his acolyte Osama Bin Laden.

Jihad Brigades/Cells.   This group emerged in late July 2003 but little is known about it except it has called for guerilla warfare and threatened to execute 'spies and traitors' (i.e. those who are believed to be collaborating with the US occupation).

Armed Islamic Movement of Al Qaeda Organization, Fallujah Branch.   Very little is known about this group except that it has gained adherents in the very conservative and religious town of Fallujah, which has been the scene of confrontations between US forces and local residents. It has claimed several attacks on US forces in the vicinity of the town.

Jaish Muhammad (Army of Muhammad).   This very enigmatic resistance movement was founded by a group of insurgents in Diyala during a meeting in September 2003 between representatives from the towns of Ramadi, Fallujah, Samarra and Baquba. It has repeatedly threatened to blow up the embassies of Islamic states or those of states neighboring Iraq should they interfere in Iraqi affairs: 'We warn you against the gravity of interference in our domestic affairs if you support the infidel gathering by sending troops to Iraq ... The Islamic Jihad Brigades of Muhammad's Army has decided to send you a warning through the destruction of your embassies in Iraq in case you send any military or civilian forces to loot the resources of our great country.'[85] Jaish Muhammad is composed of the follow-ing 'brigades': Al-Husayn Brigade; Al-Abbas Brigade; Islamic Jihad Brigade; 'Abdallah Bin-Jahsh Bin-Rikab al-Asadi Brigade; Walid

Bin al-Mughirah Brigade, whose members allegedly specialize in targeting foreign institutions, including embassies; 'Umar al-Faruk Brigade; and Al-Mahdi al-Muntazir (Awaited Mahdi Brigade). Jaish Muhammad is large and ambitious and has a significant geographical scope, requiring it to develop specialized cells.

Islamic Army of Iraq.   French journalists George Malbrunot and Christian Chesnot were abducted by members of the fanatical Islamic Army in Iraq, which some sources credit with 15,000 to 17,000 members. If this number is accurate, it raises serious questions about the insurgent counts that US officials and media have bandied about since late 2003. Malbrunot's description of his captors was chilling: 'These people will not surrender. They have time, they have weapons, they have money. And, they are fighting at home. I am afraid it will only get worse, that they will get more and more power.'[86] He believes that the IAI is largely made up of Iraqi Salafists with ties to or admiration for Osama Bin Laden. Some told him that they were former Ba'thists, which is very possible, because there have been many reports about former Ba'thist officials switching allegiance and adhering to religious extremism.

The IAI cells are very compartmentalized and have a meticulous division of labor, with distinct cells for kidnapping, interrogation, guard duty and executions. They have also cooperated with Zarqawi's group. Their enemies, they told Malbrunot, were 'American soldiers and other Coalition members, collaborators, which meant businessmen—Italian, American or even French—who are working there, the Iraqi police and spies'.[87] There was a distinct feeling that the IAI would execute the hostages but they did not. It is unclear why. Maybe they got more mileage out of holding them than executing them. It is possible that they thought twice about executing two well-known journalists from a pro-Arab country. The Arab and Muslim worlds were outraged by the abductions, particularly by the clumsy attempts to link the release of the journalists to the headscarf issue in France, where state law disallows the wearing of any religious accoutrements in public schools. IAI issued a statement that they wanted the law banning headscarves rescinded, which occasioned the commentary in the region that this had nothing to do with the 'resistance' in Iraq.

Then there was the peculiar and half-hearted attempt to persuade the men to adopt Islam, which merely served to increase anti-Muslim prejudice in France. By December 2004, IAI had probably come to the belief that the two journalists were more of a liability than an asset. Whether the French paid a ransom or not is unknown. But to provide financial reserves to the coffers of a brutal extremist organization with links in Europe, and when France is facing quite serious Islamist extremism and responding to it ruthlessly, is not wise. The journalists were released on 21 December 2004 with the warning: 'Don't come back here. We don't want you. Iraq is a land of war.'[88]

Malbrunot believes that while the IAI is largely Islamist in mindset and ideological motivation, because of its message and pronouncements by individuals within the group that abducted Chesnot and him, it included members of the former regime. He bases this on his interrogation by what seemed to be professional intelligence officers and because 'during our detention there were meetings of military experts from those who belonged to Saddam Husayn. Probably they were Islamic individuals with Islamic thought and could not express these opinions during the Saddam rule but now were under the banner of the Islamic army.'[89]

Operational goals and art

It is best to begin this section by addressing what the insurgents believe that the United States wants to achieve in Iraq. In brief, as explained in the turgid prose of the Baʻth political and strategic program, the insurgents believe that the United States and the Coalition want to impose certain political and socioeconomic realities on Iraq in order to facilitate their control over the country, which is their ultimate political goal: 'The occupation has produced its own facts, effects, and implications, which stem from and are linked to the program that it seeks to impose and implement in occupied Iraq and the rest of the region.'[90] What does this mean in plain English? The United States, says the Baʻth, has the following policies for Iraq and the region: to develop and perpetuate the military occupation; establish a collaborative elite and puppet institutions; redraw the region's map; terminate certain ruling regimes; impose a new cultural model on Arab society and institutions; and use all of the above 'to energize the global policies of the United States as a living model of a reborn imperialist ideology'.[91] In an interview in summer 2005 Salah al-Mukhtar, who seems to have emerged as an ideological spokesman of the Baʻth Party, strongly restated the deposed party's view of the conflict and the ultimate aims of the United States:

The main objective of the US in Iraq is to transform Iraq from a strong, unified state into a week [sic] one. To do so it has to encourage all kind of conflicts and disturbances, on the basis of sect and ethnic affiliation. Therefore the United States is not interested in harmonizing different agendas, in contrary it is working on an old agenda, which is American-Israeli agenda, to divide Iraq into three tiny entities. Now, it is necessary to keep all parties fighting each other just to pave the way to impose a full control over Iraq.[92]

Of course, fighting this wide-ranging ambitious and 'insidious' plan is ambitious in itself. The battlefield is large, but for the Baʻthists the primary focus is naturally Iraq, because that is where the United States is trying to create the building block for its next move. The Baʻthist insurgents' total rejection of the occupation and its goals naturally follows from this dire view of US goals in Iraq: 'What the occupier has done and is doing, such as establishing councils, ministries, and departments, as well as political, executive, and other bodies to replace the legitimate government of the Republic of Iraq, is considered null and void and illegal. It is an indivisible part of the occupation system and the resistance will treat it the way it treats the occupation itself.'[93] What does this mean? Simply, the insurgents have made their decision to oppose US 'designs' clear. The overriding political goal is to defeat and drive the enemy out. How does one achieve this political goal? In the context of this study the term 'operational goals' refers to the insurgents' formulation and implementation of those intermediate steps needed to achieve the political goal. Operational art seeks to answer the question: how or by what means do we go about bringing about those operational goals so that achieving them leads to the political goal?

What are the operational goals of the insurgents? The primary goal is to make the occupation of Iraq so untenable and uneconomical that the Coalition will have no option but to consider withdrawal. This cannot be done by defeating the Coalition force militarily for the simple reason that there is a massive disparity in the balance of power between the two sides if it is viewed solely in military terms (I will explore this in the discussion of operational art, which follows). The resistance, then, must be able to 'hinder and prevent the occupation administration, and whatever stems from it, from implementing its political, economic, social, cultural, and other plans'.[94] In other words, the 'resistance must prevent the emergence and institutionalization of any state infrastructure from taking shape in Iraq that would facilitate/support the operations of the occupation forces or allow them to achieve their political goals of consolidation their control over the country. A secondary operational goal is to put 'psychological pressure to disrupt the morale of the troops' of the various Coalition countries and to increase the number of casualties among the occupation forces 'in accordance with its awareness and calculated combat policy of heightening human losses to the point of making the authority in charge of the occupation guilty before its own citizens'.[95] In other words, the insurgents hope that the casualty rates in Iraq will have a domestic impact in the countries that have sent troops to Iraq. In short, the operational goal is to make the presence of the Coalition untenable and costly. Ultimately, the Coalition would find the cost far outweighing the benefit and wisely adopt the strategic and political decision to withdraw.

Operational art deals with the 'how'. The insurgents—Ba'thists and Islamists—recognize that they are fighting under conditions of immense geographic constraint and military inferiority. Both—but particularly the Islamists, because many of them have fought in other battlefields—recognize that Iraq's terrain is quite inauspicious for the creation of internal sanctuaries in inhospitable or inaccessible areas. Moreover, there is simply no route to success by trying to meet the Coalition forces in head-on encounters. Of course, neither the Ba'thist nor the Islamist insurgents forgo attacking Coalition, especially US troops.

Ultimately, though, why are the occupation forces in Iraq? In the eyes of the insurgents they are the umbrella under which the consolidation of the US presence and its puppet infrastructure can take shape and plant its roots. This means one must attack the critical infrastructures and the personnel who man them, and whose existence and institutionalization permits the perpetuation of the foreign presence. As a 'national liberation movement', the Ba'thist resistance believes that it has the right to 'target individuals, equipment and infrastructure, installations, camps, HQs, administrative bodies, supply lines, service and support utilities, buildings, security centers, etc.'; to target collaborators; and to 'ban and hamper the occupation's efforts to take action, consolidate its position, and exploit any of Iraq's resources, utilities ...'.[96] Put another way, the insurgents intend to ensure that they pull the administrative, economic and political rug from beneath the feet of the occupiers.

The insurgents have used many tactics (as will described later in this chapter) in pursuit of their operational goals. Given their weaknesses, ranging from lack of advanced weapons through to inferior or nonexistent training, they know that they have to develop and use tactics that function well below the threshold of the utility of Coalition tactics and weapons systems. Among the most noteworthy have been the massive and deadly suicide campaigns in Iraq. The rationales and justifications for suicide bombings as a method have been analyzed ad nauseam in many studies. I will not repeat them here. Nor will I endeavor to list all of the major suicide bombing operations in Iraq. But the suicide bombing campaign in that country has been one of the most brutal, 'successful' and effective to date. As stated in the *Washington Post* in July 2005, 'the numbers in Iraq alone are breathtaking'.[97] By that month the country had been rocked by about 400 suicide bombings since the US invasion in 2003.[98] May 2005 was a particularly grisly month, with an estimated 90 suicide bombings—nearly as many as the Israeli government has documented in the conflict with the Palestinians since the outbreak of the second intifada in 2000.[99] Salah al-Mukhtar explains the rationale behind the adoption and use of so-called martyrdom operations by secular (i.e. Ba'thist and/or nationalist) and Islamist organizations in the following way:

Let me correct some misunderstanding. The matter of martyr operations is not limited to Islamist organizations but also the organizations under Baath party practicing in the martyr operations. This kind of way of acting is the most effective weapon in the hand of the Iraqi resistance: actually it is the Iraqi mass destruction weapon capable of deterring and defeating the American forces occupying the country. The Iraqi resistance has simple weapons, while the other party has highly sophisticated weaponry, such as jet fighters, tanks, missiles, modern technology. Therefore, to neutralize that kind of superiority, the martyr operations are the only effective weapon the resistance has. I would like to remind you that this kind of operations have been used by the Vietnamese and Tamil tigers [*sic*], as well as by Palestinian organizations.[100]

In short, suicide bombings are cost effective, have a small logistical tail, do not require strenuous training and are not easy to combat.

The Islamists in the insurgency, including the Zarqawi group, have no problem with the operational goals and art as defined by the Ba'thists. The situation on the ground—military technological weaknesses and the nature of the environment—leads the Islamists and extremists to follow the same murderous but manifestly rational logic: the promotion of suicide bombing as a cost-effective measure that generates 'more bang for the buck'. The operational goals of the extremists under Zarqawi, however, differ in one major way. The Ba'thists have argued that they will 'seek to prevent the occupation from exploiting Iraqi society's ethnic and religious diversity in a way that promotes sedition, paves the way for partition, or creates opportunities for foreign intervention in the Iraqi people's affairs'.[101] The reality is that the policies of the occupation are not primarily responsible for the widening ethno-sectarian chasms in Iraq. Indeed, Saddam and the Coalition can both be attacked for policies that have contributed to ethno-sectarian tensions. However, these pale in comparison with the deliberate design on the part of Zarqawi—one for which even many Salafists excoriate him—to create sectarian strife by targeting the Shi'a. For Zarqawi, this is as important as targeting the critical infrastructure of the country. The Shi'a are under fire for religious reasons. They are regarded as 'deviants', or polytheists who 'worship' idols. They have traditionally been regarded as a fifth column within Islam; their treachery 'allowed' the Mongol leader Hulagu to take

Baghdad and thus facilitated the destruction of the Abbasid caliphate. By working with the Coalition they have shown themselves
true to form. Zarqawi's language towards the Shi'a is vituperative:
'Do you fear the army of Ibn al-Alqami [a Shi'a minister accused
of betraying the caliph during Hulagu's siege of Baghdad in 1258],
the followers of the White House? By God, nobody is as cowardly
as those people. Their early forefathers were labeled as cowardly
and treacherous.'[102] Finally, by targeting the Shi'a and hoping that
they will respond with violence, Zarqawi hopes to promote a civil
war that will pit Sunni against Shi'a in Iraq, thus rendering it well-
nigh impossible for the Coalition to rebuild Iraq, and ultimately
to set Sunni against Shi'a in the Muslim world. For many of the
local Sunni insurgents, whether they are secular or religious, targeting the Shi'a is bad politics. This is not because they like the
Shi'a—indeed, many do not. Some of the Sunni rhetoric about the
Shi'a is remarkably similar to that of Zarqawi, with the difference
that it is sometimes expressed in nationalist rather than religious
language. But the targeting of the Shi'a prevents the efflorescence
of a truly national liberation movement. Zarqawi responded with
considerable irritation to the Sunni alarm over his targeting of the
Shi'a but in September 2005 offered to leave unharmed any Shi'a,
individually or collectively, who disassociated themselves from the
Coalition and its operations in Iraq.[103]

The Ba'thists say that the 'resistance' has the right to spread the
armed insurgency to cover the entire territory of Iraq. Indeed,
they state that the resistance will strive to create an Iraqi Liberation
Army.[104] In order to increase the effectiveness and widen the geographic scope/reach of their attacks the insurgents realized that
their operational art needed to include a significant measure of
coordination and cooperation. There are two distinct levels of cooperation. The first is at the political and strategic level. I will not
address this in depth here, because it pertains to the discussions of

whether various insurgent groups seek a benefit from institution-alized merging and whether the insurgency will form a political wing composed of 'merged' groups cooperating with one another and with the legitimate Sunni political parties and organizations. This is addressed briefly in the previous chapter, and also at the end of this chapter, as part of the discussion on the political weaknesses of the insurgency. The second area of coordination and cooperation is at the operational and tactical level. Because I am dealing here with the insurgents' way of warfare, I am therefore interested in whether they cooperate and coordinate at this second level, and if so to what extent.

Cooperation and coordination runs the gamut from exchanging information/intelligence and providing 'training tips' and special-ized personnel to another group in order to improve their combat skills, to sharing information about the enemy's modus operandi based on the insurgents' version of after-action reports, and con-ducting 'joint operations'. In the initial stages of the uprising too many insurgent groups could not and did not achieve much out-side their immediate geographical environment. Some insurgents complained of the lack of cooperation and coordination between the various insurgent groups; indeed, such collaboration between groups was rare in the early days. Members of Ansar al-Sunnah gave the Spanish newspaper *El Mundo* an extensive interview in fall 2003, denouncing Saddam Hussein and blaming him for the situation in Iraq: 'He brought us the Americans; he is to blame for everything.'[105] One of the insurgents then admitted that coordina-tion between the various insurgent groups was lacking. 'It's a result of the lack of a single leadership. We hope a leader will emerge to unite us. We believe it will be much better to have one military and another political leadership.'[106] On the nature of the insurgency, he concluded: 'Our aim is not to take power: just to expel the Americans. Ours is a religious, not a political struggle.'[107] There were various reasons for the lack of cooperation and coordination in those early days. First, the insurgents were still quite disorganized. Second, there was considerable mutual suspicion between the various groups that sprouted like mushrooms to fight the foreign presence. Of course, these mutual suspicions—often based on ideological differences or tribal rivalries—still exist, but they have been subordinated by the pragmatic requirement to cooperate against the common enemy. Moreover, early insurgent organizations were 'primitive' and did not have or need much in the way of specialized skills or groups. Their combat cells were small, often no more than three to five men, and their geographic reach and impact was limited to the Coalition targets in their immediate vicinity. Moreover, many of the groups, especially those in the rural areas or small towns were very insular and suspicious of 'outsiders', although such an intruder might be no more than an Iraqi from another town or tribe.

The situation began to change in 2004, most likely because of the growing role of former military personnel in providing training, specialized skills and manpower to insurgent groups. The deposed Ba'th Party had recognized from the beginning that cooperation and coordination with other groups, including even anti-Ba'thist or Islamist insurgents, was essential to their goal of extending the scope, intensity and reach of the violence intended to make the US presence in Iraq untenable. Documents found on the person of Taha Yasin Ramadan, a one-time vice president in the defunct regime, detailed plans for cooperation between Ba'thists and Islamists.[108] Although after their overthrow the Ba'thists were more forthcoming in seeking help from non-Ba'thists or even anti-Ba'thist groups, it took time to organize cooperation and coordination with other groups. From having been in power for so long, and thus having used to giving orders, the Ba'thists suddenly found themselves in the position of needing to negotiate with insurgent groups that were often composed of individuals with very different outlooks, and some of whom had even been jailed by the regime. While some groups shunned any cooperation with the former regime personnel, many chose to cooperate with the Ba'th Party and former regime security personnel because they had intelligence skills, military expertise and funds. A former Iraqi officer known as Abu Mu'tassim was interviewed in a Jordanian newspaper and stated unequivocally: 'Military cooperation be-tween factions of the resistance is extensive and well-organized. There is a unified military leadership that conducts operations in each city ... [The] political program is not our business, but that of the political branch of the resistance; that is to say, the leadership of the Ba'th Party, they have a clear political program that covers all our actions.'[109] The Ba'thist insurgents who continue to believe that they constitute the basis of the so-called *muqawamah* (resist-ance) had no qualms about cooperating with people or groups they had previously viewed as ideologically suspect. Salah al-Mukhtar is enlightening on this point:

After the occupation of Iraq thousands of people have joined the armed resistance: some of them joined Baath party organizations, some others formulated their own organizations. For the time being, we have many different groups fighting against the American colonial occupation, and these organizations have different ideological characters, including pro-gressive forces, religious groups, nationalists, but the main organization is the Baathist one. As for the connection among these organizations, I can say that there is a strong coordination and cooperation

During a liberation warfare it's very important to mobilize all forces to fight against the occupation. All historical experiences have proven that all kind of ideologies and characters were participating in the process of liberating homeland, for example in Vietnam the Buddhist were active against the American occupation. As for Iraq, we are confronting the most dangerous colonialism ever witnessed in the history of the mankind, and because there are no outside support, the circumstances have obliged all forces to be united with each other to guarantee the liberation of Iraq. The Islamist organizations are fighting side by side with progressive and secular forces, which is very important and necessary to kick out the imperialist occupation.[110]

Mukhtar said that the insurgency was drawing from different groups to fill its ranks, and appealed to it to widen its scope throughout the Arab world. He said, 'Hundreds of Baathists who were made to quit, or who abandoned the Baath Party in the past decades … have returned to the party after the invasion.'[111] In an indication that the Baath Party organization possibly is assimilating Islamic militants, he said: 'We are highly confident that welcoming veteran Baathists within the party in Iraq and Jordan will encourage the Party organization in the Arab Homeland to follow the same road, and give the Baath the Jihadi recovery on the pan Arab level, [following] the same Baath Jihadi example in Iraq, and that may play a better historical [sic] required role.'[112] He echoed Mao Zedong's famous comment that 'political power grows out of the barrel of a gun', adding '… for you agree with the men carrying rifles, the guardians of Arabian and Islamic principles in Iraq, and that the legitimacy in the liberation period sprouts from the gun barrel and not at all from the sofas of five star hotels.'[113]

Another Ba'th official, Abu Ali al-Rubay, confirmed that the party coordinates its political and operational activities in cooperation with Salafi and Sufi religious organizations, but denied that it did so with Al Qaeda or groups linked with it: 'The Ba'th Party opposed pluralism in the past. However, the strong desire among current Ba'th Party leaders to open channels of dialogue with other parties led the party to accept this approach.'[114] In this context, the party has coordinated with the Islamist movements in the areas of logistics, recruitment and the execution of military operations.

Ironically, the fact that the Ba'th Party has in many ways reinvented itself and garnered support from among the Sunni community, including a number of former bureaucrats, military personnel and even Sunni politicians working openly and legally in the political process, has thrown into bold relief its cooperation with extremist Islamist groups. Many insurgent groups have seen the former Ba'thists reassert themselves by taking from Islamists and tribal leaders key leadership roles and training, as well as responsibility for cooperation and coordination within the insurgency.[115]

We have begun to see an increase in sustained cooperation and coordination in training, resource-sharing and the conduct of joint operations. There is also a kind of *ad hoc* collaboration for a specific mission against the Coalition forces and critical infrastructure. Moreover, we have witnessed situations where ground with limited target opportunities is 'congested' with insurgent groups. These groups are then forced into cooperation with one another because of the simple fact that they are about to undertake a mission against the same target. This was the case with the Bulgarian helicopter allegedly downed on 21 April 2005 by two distinct groups. The Mujahideen Army, comprising former regime insurgents, claimed it had undertaken this operation in conjunction with the Islamic Army in Iraq (IAI), but that the operation had not been jointly planned. Al-Jazeera received from the Mujahideen Army a video in which the following statement was made:

In the name of god, the merciful, the compassionate. Operation of the downing of an MI-8 helicopter 40 kilometers north of Baghdad in a joint operation and without prior coordination between the mujahidin army and the Islamic army of iraq ... [As for] the heroes of the Islamic army of iraq,]they] were surveying the target without the knowledge of our elements. They struck together as is apparent by the three explosions near the body of the helicopter. The lack of coordination or knowledge of the presence of resistance elements in areas of close proximity has occurred twice before in Abu Ghurayb. The heroes of the Islamic Army disclosed the count of 11 bodies. They are analyzing the disks and everything that was confiscated to establish if there is important information about the security company that used them. This helicopter takes off from Baghdad airport in a semi-daily manner heading north.[116]

Targets and tactics of the insurgency[117]

Targeting of US military forces in firefights.   By mid-June 2003 there were almost daily attacks on US forces by well-armed groups using assault rifles, RPGs and mortars on convoys, checkpoints and garrisons, though they were largely hit-and-run. Sustained small-unit firefights in which the insurgent combatants have stood and 'slugged it out' with US combat units have occurred but are relatively rare because of the insurgents' inability to engage in complex and coordinated fire and maneuver against such forces. But when the insurgents do initiate such encounters, it indicates the existence of a fair degree of professionalism, military skill and training on their part. On 30 May 2003 US troops patrolling near Baiji walked into a three-tiered ambush. As they extricated themselves from the first ambush they walked into a second and then a third. The Iraqis stood and fought instead of running away. They then broke off contact. This mostly likely indicated the involvement of former Iraqi military personnel. Another such battle, in Husaybah in April 2004, lasted fourteen hours and left dozens of insurgents dead, wounded or captured out of a force of approximately 300. However, five US Marines were also killed and several wounded.

Ambushes are complex operations. However, assaults on fortified positions, however small, can be more complicated and tax even well-trained professional forces. In Ramadi, the ramshackle capital of Anbar Province, the insurgents proved that they could conduct a set of complex attacks on US positions. Ramadi did not share Fallujah's reputation for intractability, but the violence there was nonetheless real. The city is the commercial and cultural center of Anbar Province, and the surrounding area was home to many members of the former Iraqi Special Forces and some of its best-trained soldiers, such as the Republican Guard. The US Marines stayed in Ramadi, unlike Fallujah. Their purpose was to prevent the province's key city from falling into insurgent hands. They set up fortified observation posts along the key roads, but heavily armed insurgents continued to attack, and some were well-trained. Marines were impressed by the dedication and motivation of their enemies in this area. A Marine sergeant, who was later to be killed there, said: 'They were young just like me. Fighting for something different, something they believe in. And that's the worst kind of enemy.'[118] Between March 2004, when they arrived in Ramadi, and July 2004, 2nd Battalion, 4th Marine Regiment lost thirty-one dead and 200 injured to deadly insurgent attacks (and IED explosions). In June 2004 insurgents attacked a Marine outpost containing a sniper team and killed four. 'They pretty much hate us here,' one Marine commented laconically.[119] The young former soldiers of the Iraqi army who carried out attacks in the Ramadi area were instructed in mortar use, ambush and assault techniques by senior officers in the former Iraqi military. The insurgents here were able to launch effective flanking attacks, made use of snipers (in one street battle in April 2004 five Marines were either badly wounded or killed with single shots to the head), and undertook the controlled breaking off of contact with US forces.

Sometimes the Iraqis attempted ambushes in parallel with the detonation of IEDs. The teams were originally small, with one man conducting reconnaissance, one setting off the IED, and two to four men firing on the convoy. Later, as the insurgency grew, the insurgents were able to stage more elaborate attacks involving up to a dozen men, many of them wielding RPGs.

An ambush usually started with an IED exploding amid a US convoy, to halt and disorient its personnel. This was followed by heavy small-arms fire to draw the attention of the US soldiers, while the RPG team fired its projectiles to disable the vehicles. The Iraqis could not win the firefight—they were neither as well-equipped as the US soldiers, nor as well-trained in fire and maneuver. US combat soldiers are taught to be aggressive in firefights and will move to contact rapidly. The Iraqis broke off contact and tried to disengage and leave the area. This was, of course, more difficult than carrying out the ambush in the first place. Many died. The Iraqis discovered this the hard way, and learned to keep very limited their contact with US convoys carrying frontline combat troops.

In another example dozens of insurgents tried to overrun a US military outpost in Mosul in late December 2004. Insurgents used a car bomb to try to blow up the concrete barriers at the entrance to the position, and set up IEDs on the approaches to hinder any US military vehicles coming to its aid. A coordinated force of fifty insurgents armed with semiautomatic weapons and RPGs then attacked the outpost. The US forces called in an air strike, which killed a large number of the insurgents.[120] In the final analysis, in these kinds of fights the disparity in firepower between insurgents and US forces is heavily weighted in favor of the latter. On a number of occasions insurgents have actually stood and fought in major firefights against US forces. They have never won, although they can and do inflict serious casualties, as in the firefight in Baiji. They simply cannot overpower more heavily armed and better-trained US forces. It has been disconcerting for US forces, however, that some insurgent groups have shown the logistical and organizational capability and fortitude to engage in such battles.

Suicide bombings are one of the most insidious phenomena in this insurgency, but they have been relatively rare against US forces, having been directed primarily against 'soft targets' (Iraqi forces—see p. 195—and ethno-sectarian groups). It is not easy for vehicle-borne suicide bombers to approach US troops; Iraqis move aside when they see a US convoy tearing down the road at high speed. Nonetheless, they have succeeded on a number of occasions in getting close enough to cause significant casualties. The worst attack occurred in spring 2004, when a suicide bomber killed eight US soldiers south of Baghdad. In June 2005 a suicide bomber plowed into a US military convoy in Fallujah, and in early November 2005 another managed to get close enough to kill four members of the 3rd Infantry Division manning a checkpoint in southern Baghdad.[121]

Targeting of military convoys and vehicular movements by roadside bombs. From July 2003 insurgents began to use roadside bombs detonated by remote control. This type of assault, referred to by the US military as attack by improvised explosive device (IED), is one of the most common and *the* deadliest means of attack on US forces, the key targets being US military convoys and road-bound patrols. Soldiers on foot have also been killed by IEDs. The insurgents have learned to set up painstaking and elaborate IED ambushes along major highways, and IEDs became the number-one killer of US military personnel in 2005. In 2004 IEDs accounted for 189 of the 720, or about 26 percent, combat deaths suffered by the United States.[122] In the first six months of 2005 IEDs accounted for close to 55 percent of combat deaths. The insurgents are also building bigger and better bombs to thwart the armor of US military vehicles. On 5 January 2005 an IED ripped apart a Bradley Fighting Vehicle, killing seven members of the National Guard from the 256th Infantry Brigade of Lafayette, Louisiana.[123]

The evolution of these deadly IED tells a lot about adaptation and lessons learned by the insurgency. The first IEDs were triggered by wires and batteries; insurgents waited by the roadside to detonate primitive devices when US convoys drove past. It did not take long for US troops to realize that something was amiss, and the triggermen, often hiding behind what cover they could find near the road, began to be picked off before the convoy entered the 'kill zone'. The insurgents then replaced their wires with radio signals. In spring 2005 US convoys were equipped with jammers to block the transmissions. The insurgents adapted swiftly by sending a continuous radio signal to the IED. When the signal stops by being jammed the bomb goes off. The solution would be to track the signal and ensure it remains continuous until the convoy moves out of harm's way. The problem is that the signal is encrypted and so far the United States has not been successful in cracking the code.[124]

Ambushing of military convoys and vehicular movements.   Ambushes usually involve a small group of men armed with RPGs and AK-47s. In the early stages of the insurgency, Iraqis were not very effective in carrying out these kinds of attacks; they tended to fire wildly and blindly at convoys and then break off contact immediately. If they lingered too long they were cut to pieces by the better-trained, firepower-heavy US forces. By fall 2003 insurgent accuracy had improved considerably, and they stood and engaged in firefights. And their tactics, techniques and procedures have improved as well. Their 'riflemen'—that is, those firing the AK-47s—would provide covering fire for the RPG squad whose task was to engage the convoy vehicles. When the entire force was ready to break contact they would often do so under covering fire of mortars. At other times they ambushed convoys in conjunction with the explosion of an IED (as described in detail in 'Targeting of US forces in firefights', pp. 188–91).

Apart from being under-trained and outgunned in such engagements, insurgents face the problem that often they do not know each other very well. This is good for security but bad for group cohesion. The paradox of insurgency is that success at secrecy in order to prevent infiltration by the enemy often has unintended and deleterious consequences. Group cohesion among insurgents can be low, particularly between part-timers who come together for a mission or series of missions.

Targeting of senior Iraqi political figures associated with the Coalition. Several senior officials of post-Saddam Iraq have been killed, and others have narrowly missed being killed in ambush. The best-known incidents have been the assassinations of the head of the IGC, Izzedin Salih, in mid-May 2004, and of Bassam Kubba, the Deputy Foreign Minister of the new Iraqi government, in mid-June 2004.

Targeting of foreign companies and individuals working with occupation authorities in Iraq.   Various insurgent groups have promised to attack any individual or company, including those from Jordan and the Gulf Arab countries, working with the United States in Iraq. In summer 2004, at the height of the wave of abductions and killings of foreign contractors, a Ramadi-based Iraqi insurgent group called the Death Squad of Iraqi Resistance, which had snatched four Jordanian truck drivers, warned: 'We will kill anyone, whether, Arab, foreign or Iraq, inside any truck carrying goods to the occupation forces ... As such, we warn Jordanians not to collaborate with the forces of occupation in the future, and if they do, then they have only themselves to blame.'[125]

Western commercial and private-security companies have not been exempt from such threats. In the early days of the insurgency a number of insurgent groups issued threats against the Vinnell Corporation, which had been assigned the twin tasks of helping to raise and train the new Iraqi military.

Attacks against foreign companies and individuals increased dramatically in April and May 2004, when scores of foreigners were taken hostage. The summer of 2004 witnessed a wave of abductions in Baghdad. For example, in mid-June 2004 a car bomb targeted foreign contractors, killing five, three of whom were Westerners working on the electrical grid. The kidnappings and killings managed to drive many private contractors out of the country, and dramatically increased insurance and security costs for most companies and contractors engaged in reconstruction. Foreign diplomats were also targeted. The insurgents were determined to make sure that no country would extend recognition and legitimacy to any 'puppet' Iraqi government set up by the foreign presence.

Targeting of Iraqis 'collaborating' with the occupation authorities.   Insurgents have assassinated Iraqi technocrats and professionals, interpreters and translators and ordinary workers whom they believe collaborate with the Coalition. In early July 2003 assassins killed the first Iraqi officials. Dr Abdul Amin, the chief tax collector under the Ba'th regime, who had decided to work with the Coalition, was executed in broad daylight in a Baghdad market by professional hit men, and Dr Haifa Aziz Daoud, Baghdad's chief electrical engineer, was killed at home.[126] The key motivation here is to prevent the Coalition infrastructure and military forces—which rely heavily on Iraqi employees ranging from blue-collar to white-collar—from functioning effectively.[127] Throughout 2004–5, people working for the occupation authorities and the military were branded as collaborators and traitors. Often they were sent written warnings—Ali al-Haidari, president of a local council in Baghdad's Adil district, received an envelope containing a live AK-47 bullet and the note: 'We've chopped off the head of the snake [referring to a colleague of Haidari who was killed]. You are next. Let us see what your American friends can do for you'—or are visited by ominous-looking types and asked to cease their activities.[128] One insurgent group, led by former generals of the Hussein regime, regards anyone who collaborates with the occupation as a legitimate target for attack: 'Every Iraqi or foreigner who works with the Coalition is a target. Ministries, mercenaries, translators, businessmen, cooks or maids, it doesn't matter the degree of collaboration. To sign a contract with the occupiers is to sign your death certificate. Iraqi or not, these are traitors. Don't forget that we are at war.'[129]

Attacks on Iraqis believed to be collaborating with the occupation were not limited to those with recognized skills or educational capabilities, but included ordinary working-class Iraqis, such as seventeen contractors who were killed in early December 2004 near Tikrit because they worked in a US military program to collect and destroy loose weapons and ammunition.

Targeting of Iraqi security officers and services. The killing in early July 2003 of Iraqi police officers who had just completed a US training course was the first in a series of devastating attacks on the security forces. It was carried out in accordance with the insurgents' operational goal of unraveling the administrative, bureaucratic and coercive structures that the Coalition was trying to set up in Iraq.

In 2004 the insurgents turned their full attention to Iraqi security forces. Anas al-Shami, Abu Musab al-Zarqawi's deputy until his death in an attack near Abu Ghraib, argued that any state built on secular principles is 'in the light of Islamic law a tyrannical infidel and blasphemous state'.[130] Anyone associated with it, especially police and other security units, may be murdered, for 'they do not represent themselves; they are means in the hands of tyrants'.[131] Zarqawi believes the Iraqi security forces are as legitimate a target as the foreign forces inside Iraq: 'Some say that the resistance is divided into two groups—an honorable resistance that fights the nonbeliever-occupier and a dishonorable resistance that fights Iraqis. We announce that the Iraqi army is an army of apostates and mercenaries that has allied itself with the crusaders and came to destroy Islam and fight Muslims. We will fight it.'[132]

In its video of the execution of five National Guardsmen in early January 2005, Tanzim al-Qa'idat al-Jihad issued the following statement: 'We tell the relatives and families of the civil defense, the national guard and the police that you should bid the last farewell to your sons before sending them to us, and when you bid farewell to them you should keep in mind that the only punishment waiting your sons on our land is slaughter, slaughter, and slaughter. God is great and glory is the lot of Islam.'[133]

The most successful tactic used against the Iraqi security forces was the suicide bombing campaign by individuals wearing suicide belts or vests, or utilizing vehicles (vehicle-borne improvised explosive devices, or VBIEDs). A series of devastating suicide bombings against police stations beginning in 2003 devastated the ranks of the police force and the other security services. It was the police who suffered the most. By January 2005 almost 1,000 policemen had been killed, largely by suicide bombings. By early June 2005 car bombs were averaging thirty a week, a huge increase from the one a week average in January 2004.[134] In July 2005, in the twelfth such attack on the very same recruiting depot, a suicide bomber wearing an explosives-laden vest detonated his payload among a group of recruits for the Iraq army at the entrance to the Muthana army base in Baghdad.

Targeting of Coalition resilience.   Insurgents have launched attacks on forces and officials of nations that are part of the US-led Coalition. The goal here is to drive a wedge between those nations and the United States, and ultimately to force their contingents out of Iraq. The populations of most of the nations participating in the Coalition have been very much opposed to the sending of military units. The insurgents believe that if they target soldiers and civilians from Coalition member states, then the governments of those nations would be forced to withdraw their respective contingents. The rationale behind this tactic was frankly explained to a horrified French journalist:

We don't kidnap to frighten those we are holding ... but to put pressure on the countries that help or are preparing to help the Americans. What are they thinking; coming to an occupied country? They come to terms with the United States in the name of their business interests, but their contracts are stained with the blood of Iraqis. Should we just sit there while we're being murdered? It's not a good thing to behead, but it is a method that works.[135]

As part of the targeting of Coalition resilience the insurgents killed seven Spanish intelligence officials in a well-coordinated, professional and highly publicized ambush outside Latifiyah, 18 miles south of Baghdad, in late November 2003. On the same weekend they also killed two Japanese diplomats to send a message to the Japanese government, which was preparing to deploy a contingent of the Japanese Self-Defense Forces. The most effective attack was launched in early November 2003 against the headquarters of the Italian paramilitary force, the *carabinieri,* in Nasiriyah in the south.

Many countries that were never members of the Coalition, and which, indeed, had opposed the march to war, were targeted nonetheless, to dissuade them from providing any support for or diplomatic recognition of the emerging Iraqi government. In late July 2004 the third-highest official in the Egyptian embassy, Muhammad Qutb, was kidnapped by the so-called Lions of God Battalion to make a point during Prime Minister Allawi's official visit to Egypt to seek support for his fledgling government.[136]

Targeting and sabotage of critical infrastructure.   Insurgent groups have attacked and damaged or destroyed power stations, liquid natural-gas plants and oil installations. It should be noted, however, that three types of groups have attacked such critical infrastructure: looters, who may want something of value to use or sell; organized criminals, who wish to resell useable equipment; and politically inspired insurgents, whose attacks keep the occupation authorities from translating their promise of reconstruction into reality. The last of these groups has caused the most sustained damage.

There is considerable evidence to suggest that the sabotage of critical infrastructure by pro-Hussein insurgents was well thought out before the onset of the war. Numerous statements by Ba'th Party insurgents have focused on the importance of the Iraqi oil infrastructure for 'oiling' the foreign presence in the country, for use in reconstruction and for the global economy. The Ba'thists have acted to ensure that none of these come to fruition. Iraq is crisscrossed by more than 4,000 miles of oil and gas pipelines. Some of the pipes are buried, making them less accessible to attacks, but most of them are above ground and easy to sabotage. The attacks on pipelines further cripple an already ruined Iraqi economy, and also hit the Iraqi populace where it matters most: fuel for transportation, electricity for households, water for daily use (the water system relies on electrical pumps to move it into houses) and kerosene for cooking. The first sabotage occurred near Kirkuk on 12 June 2003.[137] This was followed in rapid succession by attacks in other critical oil sectors. Between June and December 2003 there was a total of thirty-five reported major incidents.

The overwhelming majority of the attacks against oil infrastructure and pipelines have been carried out by groups or individuals who knew exactly what they were doing and where the key vulnerabilities of the infrastructure lay. For example, the critical export pipeline from Kirkuk to Turkey has been an easy target because it snakes southwest through Baiji—just above the Sunni triangle—before turning northwards to Turkey. Attacks on the oil infrastructure have been relentless. Coalition authorities and the

Iraqi government have long been convinced that the insurgents have been aided by insiders, which include 55,000 oil industry technicians and engineers with little love for the occupation.[138] Insurgents have issued leaflets threatening to kill anybody who works in the critical industries such as oil.

Targeting of symbols. The attack on the al-Rashid hotel in October 2003 was an example of a successful symbolic attack. The hotel was picked not only in the hope of targeting American personnel (a US colonel was killed) but also because of the media presence. Journalists stay there or often visited to dine or meet CPA functionaries and US military personnel at loud and boisterous parties. As one Iraqi, a used-car salesman with links to and sympathy for the resistance, said:

There is a symbolic touch to it. Because the Americans are living there and the Deputy Secretary of Defense was there, and even if he was only shocked and panicked, this will be registered as a victory for the attackers ... At the beginning, the operations were simple—just to test the American position. Now, day after day, it is getting stronger and more sophisticated. Every operation is now organized; nothing is left to chance. There is planning, surveillance, gathering information, some intelligence ... We can launch these attacks from anywhere, from rooftops, from the other side of the [Tigris] river.'[139]

The most notorious early examples of such symbolic attacks were launched against the Jordanian embassy on 7 August 2003, and the UN Headquarters in Iraq, located at the Canal Hotel. Without a doubt, though, the most impressive example was an attack launched on Abu Ghraib prison on 2 April 2005. It was symbolic because it was against a structure associated with the US occupation and the abuse of prisoners, news about which broke in spring 2004, and because it highlighted the ability of certain groups to collaborate in a sophisticated and well-organized attack.

On 11 June 2005 a suicide bomber wearing the uniform of the Wolf Brigade police commandos infiltrated the unit's compound in Baghdad and exploded his payload, killing three commandos and wounding about a dozen. The insurgents see the Wolf Brigade as a legitimate target because it is made up of 'puppet' security forces, and as a symbol of the Shi'a government's 'oppressive' policies.

In late October 2005 a well-planned and coordinated attack on the Palestine Hotel, Baghdad, by two or more cooperating insurgent groups failed. But it shook the Coalition and the Iraqi government. Had the insurgents succeeded in bringing down the hotel with a massive explosion it would have killed dozens, including many journalists and members of private security companies. The material and psychological impact would have been catastrophic. Even as a failure the attack caused consternation.

Weaknesses of the Iraqi insurgency

Where does the Iraqi insurgency stand in the history of irregular warfare in the region? It is worth comparing it with another insurgency in the Arab Middle East, the Lebanese uprising against the Israeli occupation of their country between 1982 and 2000. Many Arab nationalist commentators have waxed lyrical about the achievements of this insurgency:

In 1982, Israel overran Lebanon to crush the PLO on its northern border. After it accomplished its objective and celebrated its victory by occupying the Lebanese capital of Beirut, it soon found itself immersed in the quagmire of the Lebanese national and Islamic resistance that it had not anticipated. As a result, former Israeli Prime Minister Menahem Begin lost his political career and then lost his life. Israel found itself forced to make several partial withdrawals that were eventually crowned—after 18 years of a war of attrition and guerilla operations—with a hasty and humiliating withdrawal without making any political or security gains.[140]

It is noteworthy that the defeat of the Israelis was achieved neither by conventional military forces nor through the use of weapons of mass destruction, but by means of a popular war of national liberation that had the support of a large segment of the Lebanese population and significant state backing from Syria and Iran. These same very observers point to the quagmire that the United States faces in Iraq with barely concealed glee, but also recognize that the Iraqi insurgency suffers from severe structural weaknesses that may in the end either destroy it or be a critical factor in containing it and preventing its spread. Most of these weaknesses will be addressed here, but one serious flaw in the insurgency—the fact that it is not a national war of liberation encompassing all the communities, notably the Kurds and Shi'a Arabs—is so definitional that it must be addressed in a separate chapter.[141]

Political warfare and political weaknesses of the Sunni insurgency. The pursuit of politics does not come to a halt when cobelligerents engage in violent conflict. War is about politics and we should not lose sight of this, especially in an insurgency where the fight is often carried on in the political arena. For the first year and half of the insurgency, however, the rebels proved inept, incapable of promoting their views by the pursuit of political warfare, or unwilling to do so. First, the insurgency is not a united movement directed by a leadership with a single ideological vision. By September 2004 meetings between various groups, aimed at establishing a relatively unified political face for the insurgency, had been underway for months, but these conferences collapsed beneath the weight of conflicting interests.[142] In the past the groups had managed to cooperate operationally despite their differences, and to gain popular support it had been enough for them to be seen to oppose the Coalition. While this pragmatic approach may have worked in the early stages, however, it has become a major constraint on the insurgents' ability to influence Iraq's political process and future direction. A nationalist insurgent whose *nom de guerre* is Abu Khalil was reported to have said: 'Thinking has started to move toward asking what happens after the Americans leave. So far we have only shown that we know how to act militarily, but the military wing cannot lead the country into the future.'[143]

The attainment of cooperation and coordination between insurgent groups at the political and strategic levels to present joint goals and common demands has proven difficult, and has, at times, led to hilarious situations. Two active Iraqi insurgent groups, the Islamic Army in Iraq and the Army of the Mujahideen (Jaish al-Mujahideen), have supposedly moved beyond mere collaboration at the operational and tactical levels, and have appointed a joint official spokesman, Dr Ibrahim Yusuf al-Shammari. The appointment of such a spokesman was described as a step towards smoothing the unification of their two organizations, coordinating their goals and preventing individuals from claiming to speak for the insurgency. Shammari said: 'There are many people who are fishing in troubled water [*sic*] and who speak in the name of the resistance and want to adopt political plans that do not serve the resistance ... We have been working hard for a long time in the political bureau to unify the political vision of the resistance.'[144] 'Negotiations are part of our political program,' said the 'new' official spokesman, who then stated somewhat grandly: 'We'll accept nothing but an official initiative from the US Congress with a precise timetable [for withdrawal?] and binding decision.'[145] Yet Shammari denied that the groups were involved in negotiations with the US, telling Al-Jazeera television on 28 June that the 'United States doesn't want to negotiate but they want scorched-earth politics'.[146] Somewhat bizarrely, Abu Jandal al-Shammari, the alleged commander of the Mujahideen Army, issued a statement on 4 July denying that it ever nominated a spokesman.[147]

The insurgents' desire to present a political face was perceived as an opportunity by the few Sunni political parties to portray themselves as the political rather than the military front of the Sunni opposition. Instead, these claims revealed in stark relief the political divisions within the insurgency *and* within the parties and groups engaged in the 'normal' political process. Around spring 2004 the Association of Muslim Scholars (AMS) began claiming that it was the political arm of the Iraqi insurgency because of its role in mediating with combatants for the release of kidnapped foreigners. 'We are the political arm of the resistance fighting to evict American forces from Iraq,' said Muthanna al-Dhari, son of Harith al-Dhari, the leader of the association.[148] But the Salafist *imams* and insurgent groups with Salafist leanings deny that the AMS represents anything but itself, and plastered posters around Baghdad denouncing the AMS and warning it not to try to speak for the insurgency. Fakhri al-Qaisi, a representative of Sheikh Mahdi al-Sumaidi, who has emerged as the leading Salafist preacher in Iraq, poured scorn on the AMS: 'The Muslim Scholars Council speaks for no one but themselves.'[149] The Iraqi Islamic Party sees itself as a rival of the AMS for the hearts and minds of the Sunni Arab population, and denounced it. 'These people are good at giving speeches, but they have little impact on the ground in Fallujah,' said Hashim Hasani, deputy leader of the IIP.[150]

No Sunni political group or personality working legitimately in the political arena has been able to reach out to the insurgents and bring them into the process. Why? They have no constituency, strength of personality or positive program to offer the insurgents, just as they lack the political skills, resources and vision to rally the people to their cause. If the politically active Sunni groups had mobilized their population in order to enter the political process, the insurgents may have taken it upon themselves to reach out to those parties and to promote them as their 'political wing'. Moreover, had the parties succeeded in mobilizing a popular base the insurgency would have been forced on pragmatic grounds to reach out to them. But the parties have not done so and the Sunni populace has regarded them with derision. The IIP, for example, lacks the capacity to recruit and mobilize any significant segment of the Sunni populace, as did its predecessor in the 1960s. This rebounds to the advantage of the insurgents, who are often regarded as the saviors of the now dispossessed Sunni minority.

Indeed, the shadowy insurgency leadership had a greater role than the Sunni political organizations in mobilizing and encouraging the Sunnis to come out and vote against the ratification of the draft constitution on 15 October 2005. The overwhelming majority of Sunnis saw this controversial document as a threat to the integrity of Iraq and to their material interests. The leaders of several insurgent groups apparently coordinated a ceasefire to ensure that the Sunnis turned out to vote in droves to try to defeat the passage of the constitution.[151] (Nonetheless, violence by extremist Islamists reduced Sunni turnout in various locations in Anbar.)[152] The Sunnis did not view in dire terms the fact that they were unable to defeat the referendum, even though they hinted darkly that there were 'irregularities' and fraud in the voting process. They are also determined to vote in large numbers for the selection of a 275-member parliament on 15 December 2005.

It is important to recognize that the insurgency leadership may have played a very significant behind-the-scenes role in directing the Sunnis to vote. According to one analysis, Mishan al-Jubouri, a leading Sunni politician who participated in the constitutional process, stated that Salah ad Din Province—a solidly Sunni area—would vote overwhelmingly in favor of the constitution. It did not. Eighty-one percent of the population voted against.[153] This demonstrates that the mainstream leadership in Baghdad has little traction, and that an insurgency leadership guided by elders and clerics and composed of ruthless younger men who have proven their mettle in battle are beginning to flex their political muscles. If this is the case, then any impetus for the formation of a political wing will come from the insurgents, not from the established but essentially powerless groups in the center. The latter will have their uses, though, because they will be the faces promoting the interests of the Sunni community. No doubt the men in the shadows will have a considerable say in determining the precise nature of these interests as they are presented for consideration in the post-electoral political process.

I am assuming here, of course, a relatively benign polity in Iraq and not an increase in political bloodshed and a downward spiral into more violent communal strife. The political leadership of the insurgency may be unable to make that paradigmatic shift into the political process. They may not even be allowed to do so by the United States and the new Shi'a-dominated Iraq. This would leave the Sunni community in the hands of their increasingly irrelevant self-styled political leadership at the center, which would be a recipe for more violence. The insurgent leadership will most likely revert to its violent ways, no doubt believing that violence pays.

Sunni political groups have little or no influence with the real powers in the country, the United States and the emerging Shi'a. Their manifest weaknesses, lack of capacity and popular base, and divisiveness invite contempt and derision on the part of the Coalition and the new Shi'a power base. Their members are often arrested or detained and their headquarters are regularly searched by US forces and Iraqi government security forces. This is not only humiliating, but also a very public slap in the face, and one witnessed by the very constituency the Sunnis are seeking to mobilize.[154]

In late June 2005 Ayham al-Samarrai, a Sunni political figure, claimed to have formed a political group called the National Council for Unity and Construction of Iraq, to provide the insurgents with a political voice. He said that the group would represent insurgents who have not carried out operations against civilians.[155] Saad Jawad Qandil, a Shi'a legislator, dismissed the effort: 'The general terrorist program is to attack electricity plants, water and oil pipelines, mosques, churches and to target the innocents, police and the army. These are terrorist acts, and cannot be represented as acts of resistance.'[156] Nonetheless, Samarrai repeated his claim in October 2005 in an interview with the newspaper *Al-Zaman*, saying that his council was the voice of the 'resistance', and that the Iraqi government and the US forces can use the council to establish contact with the insurgency.[157]

Other Sunni political leaders are not so sure that their embryonic efforts are, at this stage, sufficient to bring an end to the violence. They believe that their increased role in politics may make a difference in integrating the community into the process and putting its concerns on the table. But they are unsure whether the insurgency will slow down or cease until the concrete issues that infuriate the Sunni community and fuel the uprising are addressed and dealt with: a timetable for US withdrawal, the issue of 'deliberate' political and socioeconomic marginalization, the 'deliberate' and humiliating diminution of the Sunni element of Iraqi identity, and the disposition of the thousands of Sunni Arab detainees.[158]

In short, the Sunnis involved in the political process are not central players.[159] As discussed in Chapter 2 (see p. 74), Saleh Mutlak, head of the Sunni political group the National Dialogue Council, acknowledges that his organization has little to offer the insurgents to draw them into the political process. In late October 2005, after the failure of the Sunnis to defeat the passage of the draft constitution, a group of Sunni politicians and parties (the IIP, the National Dialogue Council and the Iraqi People's Conference) formed Jabhat al-Tawafuq al-Iraqiyah (the Iraqi Accordance Front, or IAF).[160] Its leaders declared they had formed the front to ensure that Sunnis will be mobilized effectively to vote in the parliamentary elections of 15 December 2005, and to present a united front in the political arena beginning in 2006. It is unclear whether the IAF will emerge as the political wing of the insurgency, or at least the mainstream and more moderate elements of it.

The IAF does not include the AMS, which unswervingly continues to maintain the line that it will not participate in the political process until the Coalition announces a timetable for its withdrawal. It is generally believed that the AMS is the Sunni group with the most extensive contact with and empathy for the insurgency. Indeed, as Iraqis were preparing to vote in the referendum the leadership of the Ba'thist and Fedayeen Saddam insurgents issued a statement that lent support to the position of the AMS and argued that the adoption of the draft constitution would be 'Sykes-Picot II' (referring to the secret Anglo-French agreement during World War I that divided the Arab lands of the Ottoman Empire between Britain and France).

It can be argued that the nationalist insurgents seem to have overlooked or ignored a key tactic as part of a potential political platform. If they were to issue a concerted statement that they are fighting for a Sunni autonomous region in the country, they would distance themselves from the secular and religious totalitarian and centralizing sentiments of the Ba'th Party and the Islamists respectively. Why would the Kurds, for example, fight against the Sunni quest for autonomy while trying to preserve theirs? Because many Shi'a are expressing autonomous sentiments, this would leave only certain Shi'a groups with the extremist Sunnis as advocates of a centralized Iraq.

Finally, the presence of myriad insurgent groups has made it very difficult for either the Coalition or the Iraqi government to engage in serious negotiations with so-called mainstream Iraqi insurgents. This was evident in summer 2005, when stories of negotiations between the Coalition and Iraqi government and the insurgents were hastily denied by key insurgent groups. However, the large number of such groups not only constitutes a political weakness for the insurgency, but also has an unintended consequence that actually rebounds to their benefit—the US has had a hard time unraveling or understanding the insurgency.

Ideological divisiveness within the insurgency.   The political divisions among the insurgents, and between the insurgent groups and the legal Sunni political groups, are reflected in increasingly serious divisions between the local Iraqi insurgents on the one hand and the foreign Islamists on the other. By mid-2004 it had become increasingly evident that the different agendas and modus operandi of many of the Ba'thist, nationalist, tribal and even Islamist elements of the Iraqi insurgency on the one hand, and their ostensible foreign Islamist allies on the other, had caused considerable tensions between these groups. In early summer 2004 nationalist insurgents in Fallujah were about to assault a group of foreign jihadists based in the suburb of Jolan and led by a Saudi with the *nom de guerre* Abu Abdullah. While they admire the motivation of the foreigners, many mainstream Iraqi nationalist, Islamist and tribal insurgents resent an ideological agenda that has resulted in the killing of Iraqis simply for not adhering to a strict religious line or for being members of a different sect. The foreign fighters' apparent blood lust, which has led to indiscriminate attacks and the beheading of abductees, also angers the local insurgents. An Iraqi Salafi insurgent, whom we would expect to be sympathetic to the foreign Arab fighters who are also Salafist, was even moved to say: 'We are fighting for our country ... In the past several of our operations were cancelled when civilian lives were threatened. When Arabs direct the operations, they care nothing about killing families.'[161] Later, insurgent 'authorities'—largely comprising former military personnel and Iraqi police and led by clerics—in Fallujah evicted a number of non-Iraqi terrorists from the area.

By fall 2004 the considerable strain between the Iraqi insurgents who viewed themselves as nationalists fighting against occupation and the local religious extremists, opportunists and foreign *jihadi* elements was out in the open. The collapse of the relationship began in Fallujah. Many of the foreign fighters, particularly those led by the vicious Saudi Salafist Abu Abdullah, caused a great deal of resentment. Although they were initially welcomed because they were seen as a morale booster and because some did have useful skills and training to impart, by mid-summer 2004 many Fallujah residents viewed them as being out of control. A local sheikh said: 'We are worried that they are part of al-Qaeda. That means that we will have to force them out and it will be hard. But this is our country we are fighting for, and it is our fight with the Americans. They have their own country and their own ideas, which we do not share.'[162]

The barbaric and provocative behavior of the foreigners in the city irritated and alarmed the nationalists, who saw it as detrimental to a positive perception of the insurgency among the populace. Leading foreign terrorist Abu Musab al-Zarqawi came in for particular opprobrium from the commander of the insurgent group the First Army of Muhammad: 'He is mentally deranged, he has distorted the image of the resistance and defamed it. I believe his end is near.'[163] Another insurgent leader, of the Allahu Akbar Battalions, seemed to concur with this assessment: 'It is the Zarqawis and his Salafi group who are going to lead Fallujah, Samarra, Baqubah, Mosul and even some parts of Baghdad to disaster and death.'[164]

Little love was lost between many of the local insurgents—who often referred to themselves as sons of Iraq—and the foreign Arab and Islamist volunteers: '. . . there was the problem of the foreigners, the people linked to al-Zarqawi: Afghans, Jordanians, Yemenis, and Saudis; but also secret agents from neighboring countries. Some help, while others seek only to kill as many people as possible. Al-Zarqawi does not give a damn about Iraq; he is prepared to kill 10 Iraqis if in doing so he can kill one American. So we decided to react.'[165]

By late 2004—in contrast to the situation in April 2004, when there was a sense of unity and brotherhood—there was also a growing gap between local insurgents and Arab volunteers. Anthony Shadid, a US journalist who spent months in Iraq, summarizes the views of local insurgents: 'They had been betrayed by zealous Arab fighters from abroad. One described the foreign fighters as locusts leaving desolation in their wake.'[166] The Iraqis accused the Arabs of cowardice. The local fighters were fighting for Iraq and for *intiqam* (revenge) for slights, real or imagined, committed by the Coalition. Many Iraqi insurgents were not even sure what the foreigners were fighting for. Even by mid-2004 differences between locals and foreigners were evident. Two groups, reportedly based in Fallujah, even threatened to kill Zarqawi.

The Iraqi insurgents seem to be opposed to the incessant targeting of innocent civilians. Some went so far as to denounce attacks on security forces and on infrastructure. For example, Sheikh Abdul Sattar al-Samarrai, a member of the AMS, was asked whether he supported resistance against occupation: 'Yes. Honest and true resistance—that is away from chaos, killing innocents and policemen and sabotaging the infrastructure—should go on to kick the occupation out of the country.'[167] For many insurgent groups the killing of civilians, especially by car bombs and suicide bombers, was a serious problem because it allowed the Coalition and Iraqis to label the *muqawamah* as terrorism and, more ominously, alienated the public from the insurgents. Indeed, there were debates within the insurgent groups concerning the nature of permissible targeting.

Many insurgent groups (and not only the foreign fighters) viewed the pronouncements of Sunni political leaders, such as that of Abdul Sattar al-Samarrai quoted above, with derision. They often responded, 'What then are we to target in order to make the presence of the foreigner untenable?' For the majority of insurgent groups the targeting of so-called collaborators, foreigners and infrastructure was deemed permissible military activity. Some of the more militant groups responded that civil disobedience against a ruthless foreign enemy is simply untenable. In a remarkable mirror image of the attitude of many in Washington, DC, that 'the Arabs only understand force', numerous insurgent groups, including their clerics, have argued that the foreigners 'only understand force' and so must be met with force. Others have argued that there is a difference between conducting an insurgency against a foreign presence and its collaborators, and one that is conducted against an 'unjust' local government that is not overtly buttressed by a foreign power. In the former the list of possible targets must include collaborators and major attacks on critical infrastructure. In short, liberation from the foreigner is the most important consideration. In the case of a latter situation, the insurgents must be more discriminating, for they are seeking to win the populace over to their side against an unjust government.

Another source of problems between the local insurgents and the foreigners, particularly Zarqawi's group, revolved around the legitimacy of targeting the Shi'a. Early in the insurgency, many Sunni groups, such as the Islamic Jihad Organization, Muslim Youth Groups and the Iraq Liberation Organization, warned against attempts to create sectarian sedition and differences in Iraq: 'We are facing today the most serious sectarian sedition. Some weak-hearted elements—which are supported by the occupation troops, infidel countries, and Israel—have infiltrated into Iraq to carry out terrorist actions, like the attack on the house of Sayyid Muhammad al-Hakim in holy Al-Najaf. That was a terrorist action that was aimed at inciting sectarian sedition among the people.'[168] But that was in the early days.

In a reflection of the growing chasm between Sunni and Shi'a in Iraq today, there are very few statements specifically warning against the creation of sectarianism. On the contrary, an increasing number of statements accuse the Shi'a of cooperating with the enemies of Iraq through their service in the state apparatus of the 'puppet regime'. For example, Ba'th Party insurgents issued a statement that argued, much in the line of past thinking, that the growing sectarian discord in Iraq was being fomented by a conspiracy composed of the 'occupiers, whether American, British, Persian or Zionists.'[169] There is nothing extraordinary about this statement. But the Ba'th Party proceeded to criticize Iran for urging Iraq's Shi'a to create 'a Shi'a nation instead of an Arab or Islamic nation' in an attempt to 'destroy Iraq and strip it of its true Arab Islamic identity and will'.[170] This kind of language does not merely highlight the suspicion with which the Sunnis and Shi'a see each other, but actually deepens it. In 2004 the differences between the two communities were reflected in the widely divergent political views of the future of Iraq and the increasingly violent Sunni insurgency, which targeted Shi'a civilians. A sign of the rift lies in the different responses to the violence in Fallujah. Whereas in April 2004 the Shi'a had expressed considerable support and sympathy for Fallujah when US forces attempted their assault, by November 2004, when the city was assaulted successfully, the Shi'a were largely in favor of the attack.[171]

However, the problem for the insurgents *vis-à-vis* the Shi'a question is not only political or ideological, but also operational. Their uprising is faced with a structural dynamic that they cannot resolve: much of their target list of collaborators is implicitly defined in ethno-sectarian terms. For some of the insurgent groups, the targeting of the Shi'a and Kurds was in the beginning an 'unfortu-nate' by-product of the fact that the security services, particularly the army, were overwhelmingly composed of members of those two ethno-sectarian communities. For others, such as Zarqawi's group, the targeting was deliberate. In the final analysis, the grow-ing chasm between the Sunni Arabs and the Shi'a and Kurds (who are not particularly fond of one another either) is starkly reflected in the comments of a Sunni sheikh from Kirkuk: 'The Americans aren't the problem; we're living under an occupation of Kurds and Shi'ites. It's time to fight back.'[172] In other words, as we deal with the Iraqi insurgency we are faced with the ineluctable reality of contending national identities of the other two major communities in Iraq, the Kurds and Shi'a, whose overt alliance with the United States has further strengthened the conviction of the Sunnis that they are fighting a serious threat to their collective identity.

CONTENDING NATIONAL IDENTITIES

THE KURDS AND SHIʿA ARABS

The fact that neither the Kurds nor the Shiʿa Arabs have participated in the insurgency speaks volumes about the nature of the Iraqi state, particularly under Saddam Hussein, and of Iraqi nationalism such as it exists. The nonparticipation of these communities in the Sunni-led insurgency highlights that the insurgency is not a war of national liberation against a foreign presence. More accurately, the insurgency may be about liberation for the Sunnis, but they are only one community and a minority. The Kurds and the Shiʿa saw the Coalition's entry into Iraq in 2003 as liberation from Saddam's tyranny. There certainly have been disappointments within these communities over the past three years. The Kurds' greatest fear is that the Coalition will betray them at the altar of power politics. This has happened twice before in their modern history: first, when they failed to get an independent state built on the detritus of the Ottoman Empire in the 1920s; and second, when their 1975 insurgency against Saddam was throttled when hitherto hostile Iran and Iraq reached accord over their differences, with the full assent of the United States. The Kurds have another fear—the indifference of the international community to their suffering over the past decade. These fears exist together and reinforce one another.

The greatest concern of the Shiʿa was that they would be denied power commensurate with their demographic status. Their secondary concern was that liberation from the despotism of Saddam would turn into occupation; indeed, they suspected that the injustice and tyranny that had been 'their lot' for centuries would continue, and one Shi'a group reacted violently. This chapter claims to provide not a full analysis of the political trajectory of both communities, but merely a brief summary so that we can comprehend their respective responses to the Coalition and to the insurgency.

The Kurds: federalism or independence?

The Kurds constitute somewhere between 17 and 20 percent of the total population of Iraq. I shall not provide an historical analysis of their political evolution as members of the Iraqi state; this has been more than adequately done in a number of well-researched studies.[1] Instead I will briefly address the emergence of their separate national identity, the growth and development of their autonomous region (which has all the earmarks of an independent entity), and the issues that divide them from the rest of the country. Finally, despite tensions and disappointments with the Coalition, the Kurds have felt that the best guarantor of their security and interests is the de facto alliance with the United States. The US presence is also an umbrella under which the Kurds will further develop their own institutions, including the paramilitary *peshmerga* forces, and present their demands to the weak post-Saddam central state.

While the Kurds are part of a country of which they had historically been unwilling members, their sense of alienation from the Iraqi state has increased dramatically in the past decade. They see political matters in ethnic and Kurdish nationalist terms. Ethnicity here is taken to mean the idea of a shared affinity and sense of belonging based on the myth of culture, ethnicity, language and habitation of a particular locale. This applies particularly to the Kurds, many of whom have progressed from tribal bartering with the Iraqi state, through local autonomy-seeking, to the onset of full-fledged nationalism that seeks independence. Twelve years of de facto independence in their enclave, which was formed in 1992 to protect them from Saddam's depredations, has crystallized their nationalism—few young Kurds speak Arabic or are loyal to Iraq.

A number of searing events in recent Iraqi Kurdish history solidified the 'us' versus 'them' phenomenon: the Halabja Massacre of 1988, in which the regime used chemical weapons to kill 5,000 Kurds; the Anfal campaign of 1989, in which more than 180,000 Kurds were killed; the crushing of the 1991 uprising; and the suicide bombings in Irbil in February 2004. Indeed, the slow but steady march towards nationhood is likely to continue. Many Kurds believe it is time to drop the pretence that they are Iraqis; various reports over the years suggest that most do not wish to be. The terrible deeds committed against the Kurds have forged a separate and powerful Kurdish identity, while the emergence of the decade-old enclave has served merely to heighten this sense of a separate, non-Iraqi identity. A statement by a Kurdish novelist to a US reporter clearly symbolizes this feeling: 'We are not Iraqis and we are not Turks and we are not Syrians. We are Kurds and we want an independent nation.'[2] Moreover, during the decade of quasi-independence for the enclave a whole new generation of Kurds emerged having no knowledge of Arabic or connections to the Iraqi state. The Kurdish student population, its tiny middle class and intelligentsia, are unenthusiastic about reintegration with the rest of Iraq, and their views of the Arab south verge on the racist. 'The Arabs from other parts of Iraq are starting from zero, but we've been through all that already,' said a Kurd in his mid-twenties. Joining with Iraq, he continued, 'is like putting a sixth grader in a class with first graders'.[3]

Some young Kurds who have grown up free of Saddam's government know little or nothing about the rest of the country of which they are ostensibly a part. A Kurdish university student asked: 'Are there good Arabs? ... I haven't seen anything good come from them in Iraq.'[4] Saad Othman, Minister for Agriculture with the Kurdistan Democratic Party (KDP), said in an interview: 'I am Kurdish, but also Iraqi, and there doesn't have to be a contradiction.' His young son blurted: 'I hate Arabs.'[5] The mentality and political views of the young are important because it is they who will put their imprint on Kurdish politics, culture and society in the coming years. At a Sulaymaniyah high school a female student was adamant in her belief: 'We want a Kurdish government with a Kurdish leader. We don't want a government led by an Arab, like Saddam Hussein.'[6] While instruction in Arabic is available to the young Kurdish generation it is not popular; indeed, young Kurds speak less Arabic than their parents.[7] Moreover, the Kurds are fearful of the increasing role of religion in politics; as one Kurdish woman put it: 'In the south, you see demonstration for gasoline, for jobs, and they always hold up signs that say, "There is no God but Allah, and Muhammad is his prophet." What's the connection between that and jobs or gasoline? We're all Muslims, but their thinking is old.'[8] 'We are free,' says Azad Seddiq Muhammad, a prominent journalist. 'If you want to go into mosques, you will find a lot of mosques. If you want to go into bars, we have a lot of bars.'[9] Muhammad thinks of himself as Kurdish first and Iraqi second: 'But it is not my fault. This country was never able to enfold me, embrace me. On the contrary, it was always pushing me away.' Irbil and Sulaymaniyah, the two major Kurdish towns, are thriving economically and there is little extremist religious sentiment there.

The massive suicide bombing in Irbil on 2 February 2004, which devastated the party headquarters of the Patriotic Union of Kurdistan (PUK) and KDP and killed scores of high-ranking officials, hardened official Kurdish resolve to move as far from Baghdad as possible without calling for outright independence. The Kurds refer to the event as their 9/11. For their part, many ordinary Kurds viewed the tragedy as an opportunity to move towards actual independence.[10] A KDP official wounded in the blast said: 'We don't feel connected with Iraq. We want independence, not federalism. This attack will make us insist on independence.'[11]

During my time in the north I found a variety of sentiments among the Kurds I met, most of whom, given the nature of what I was doing there were military people. I met a rabidly nationalistic Kurdish officer who demanded nothing but total separation. I encountered many more Kurds who said they wanted a state of their own sometime in the future, but that they would stay in Iraq for now. I met some who even said that they were willing to stay in Iraq so long as there was no religious government and the country recovers and prospers. Many Kurds increasingly appreciate the difficulties of an independent and landlocked Kurdistan. They and their politicians may well choose to remain part of Iraq, not because of any identification with the country that they were forced to become part of more than eighty years ago, but out of prudent consideration of US and Turkish interests.

The Kurds also used their quasi-independence to build some enduring institutions reminiscent of a state.[12] At first, despite their freedom in the northern enclave, the Kurds had considerable difficulty establishing a durable political system. The Kurds and their supporters in the United States have tried to portray the region as having been a paragon of democratic virtue. It was definitely better than Saddam Hussein's Iraq but democratic it was not. The KDP and PUK were intolerant of political pluralism and heavily patrimonial, in that each party provided tangible benefits to those who directly supported them.[13] Instead, intertribal differences and deep personality clashes between leading Kurdish figures Massoud Barzani and Jalal Talabani resulted in the creation of a political system of clientelization and neopatrimonialism, which mirrored but could not rival in terms of resources the similar system that Saddam operated in the rest of the country.[14] This meant in effect that Barzani and Talabani gave rank, position, power and money to those who were loyal to them as individuals.

The Kurds also tend to overestimate the capabilities of their guerilla forces. Moreover, two rival *peshmerga* forces owe allegiance to Massoud Barzani of the KDP and Jalal Talabani of the PUK respectively. Attempts to merge them have yet to come to fruition. However, both Kurdish parties are slowly but surely transforming these guerillas from essentially ragtag militias into quasi-professional forces, which they are using to stealthily acquire territory for the Kurdish autonomous region.[15]

Contrary to popular lore, then, the Kurds are not re-entering the center stage of the post-Saddam polity with greater political maturity or sophistication than their Arab counterparts. Nonetheless, they did enter the new era with a relatively more benign political system, great organizational skills, a better understanding of and interaction with the outside world as a result of their decade-long freedom, and relatively well-organized armed forces. All of these factors have stood them in good stead as they bargained their way through the maze of politics in the new Iraq.

Events of the past three years in Iraq have also further solidified Western sympathy for and understanding of the plight of the Kurds. Kurdistan is another world from the rest of the country, lacking the rampant violence, religious fanaticism and chaos of the south. It is perceived as a region that 'works', that is safe and, despite rampant poverty and corruption, showing signs of economic vibrancy, and that it is more functionally democratic than the rest of Iraq.

Unsurprisingly, the Kurds feel considerable trepidation about being part of a dysfunctional Iraq. Many Kurds whom I met in Nineveh were very keen to invite me to Kurdistan to see how different it is from the rest of the country. They will be loath to give up any of their institutions and freedoms now.

The separate identity of the Kurds and the profound differences between their region and the rest of the country are divisive issues in the new Iraq. In short, at the ethnic faultlines in the north the Kurds find themselves at loggerheads with Sunni Arabs and Turkmen over the issues of territory, resources and to some extent identity. Among the first signs of fissures between Arabs and Kurds was the attempt by the latter—flush with the arrogance of victory—to seize the lands of the Arab farming community of Haifa in September 2003. They could not comprehend that the Arab inhabitants, members of the Jiburi tribe, decided to stand and protect their land.

The Kurds swaggered into Tuz Khurmatu, a largely Turkmen city of 70,000, and claimed it was part of the future 'autonomous' Kurdish territory. The United States attempted to quell the rising tide of violence in the city, but forces in the area appointed Kurds as mayor and chief of police. This inevitably led the Turkmen to complain that the United States was showing favoritism to their wartime allies. The Turkmen claim is probably accurate; there is no reason to doubt that the administration was going to go out of its way to reward the Kurds for their help during the war. The city erupted in violence in August 2003 and the Turkmen turned against the United States. A pharmacist whose twenty-one-year-old son was killed that month in the ensuing riots (subsequently suppressed by US forces) between Kurds and Turkmen, said: 'After the war, I was so happy I was ready to put up a picture of [President] Bush in my house. If I see Americans now, I will try to kill them. I only care about revenge.' About the Kurds he added: 'Five months of them is worse than 35 years of Saddam.'[16]

The gulf between Arabs and Turkmen on the one hand and Kurds on the other increased when the latter began to act as a security arm for the occupation. When hundreds of Arabs of the 36th Battalion, Iraqi Civil Defense Corps, deserted rather than fight in Fallujah in April 2004, the Kurds remained and fought. The Kurds also attracted the ire of the Shi'a for killing their coreligionists during the uprising led by Shi'a cleric Moqtada al-Sadr. Kurdish members of the security forces recognized the problem, saying that they joined not as Kurds wanting to kill Arabs, but as Iraqis wanting to defend their country.[17] I recall conversations with Kurdish officers in the Iraqi army who said that they are not interested in suppressing Turkmen and Sunni Arabs for the sake of a sectarian Shi'a-dominated central government. They said this not because they were 'fond' of or liked Sunni Arabs and Turkmen—Kurdish security forces have been accused of abusing Arabs and Turkmen in the north—but because they thought it was not to their ultimate benefit. And the Kurds will probably have to live with a significant minority of Arabs and Turkmen.

Despite the tactical alliance with the new Shi'a-dominated Iraq, the Kurds have found themselves in conflict with the Shi'a over the nature of government power and the country's identity. In spring 2003, soon after the downfall of the Ba'thist regime, Barham Salih, then a senior official in the PUK in Sulaymaniyah, articulated some of the key demands of the Kurds: Kirkuk, democracy, federalism and secularism.

Kirkuk, with its rich oilfields, is a major sticking point that has embroiled Sunni and Shi'a Arabs and Turkmen against the Kurds. The importance of Kirkuk, which the Kurds have referred to as the 'Kurdish Jerusalem',[18] is reflected in the following statement by Barham Salih, Prime Minister of the Kurdish regional government in Sulaymaniyah:

Historical reality shows that Kirkuk is a part of Kurdistan. It is a city inhabited by the Kurds, but also by Turkmen, Assyrians, and Arabs. When I say that Kirkuk is part of Kurdistan, I do not wish to imply that it is purely

Kurd, because over the course of history, it has been peopled by many different ethnicities. We would like to transform Kirkuk into a model of coexistence and tolerance which would be followed in the rest of Iraq.[19]

Noble sentiments indeed, but the reality on the ground in Kirkuk is a muscular and irredentist Kurdish approach that has raised ethnic tensions between Kurds, Turkmen and Arabs. When the regime fell on 9 April 2003 the main Kurdish political parties, the PUK and KDP, fanned into Kirkuk and took over the key installations and buildings of the former regime.[20] Kurdish refugees returning to the city insisted that it was their home and that nobody will ever again drive them out. City officials—who are drawn from among Kurds, Arabs and Turkmen—also waxed lyrical about the harmony between the various ethnic groups, but the reality among the populace was different. And it is among the masses that politics is made. Ali Mahdi Sadek, a Turkmen member of the provincial council and an official of the Iraqi Turkmen Front, said: 'Our problems are many, but we don't want to use our guns. We want to use our pens. But if everything else fails, we have our guns.'[21]

The success of the Kurds in the Iraqi elections of 30 January 2005 strengthened their hand locally, in Kurdistan and the outlying region, and nationally, in Baghdad. They won 59 percent of the vote in Kirkuk, gleefully celebrating the victory as being indicative of the Kurdish character of the city, a claim vehemently denied by the other major ethnic groups, the Arabs and Turkmen.[22] The relationship between the Arabs and Kurds in Kirkuk and its surroundings is destined not to be peaceful. The Kurds are suffering from the hubris brought on by the support, explicit or implicit, of the Bush administration and by their showing in the election. They are flexing their muscles and have adopted a strongly anti-Arab and nationalist agenda. For example, Mayor Abdul Rahman Belaf of Makhmur, a small town near Kirkuk, proudly boasts of having reversed local demographics in less than a year. His area used to be 80 percent Arab but is now 80 percent Kurd: 'We made sure there wasn't a single Arab left who came as part of the Arabisation program and we haven't stopped yet. We have more land to take back.'[23]

Arab leaders, Sunni and Shi'a, made extraordinary efforts to prevent Arab residents from departing Kirkuk and thus leaving it to the Kurdish PUK and KDP, who strode triumphantly into the city followed by thousands of Kurds whom it was alleged had been forcibly ejected under Saddam's regime. One Arab resident received a menacing visit from a man who told her: 'If you choose to leave Kirkuk, you will never arrive home. The Arab hold on Kirkuk must be preserved against the Jews, the Kurds and all the collaborators with the infidels and occupiers.'[24] There were reports that former officials of the Ba'th regime were collaborating with Shi'a of Moqtada al-Sadr's militia (the Jaish al-Mahdi, or Mahdi Army). Adherents of the militia had come to protect the city's Arab inhabitants, many of whom were Shi'a who had settled there as a result of incentives provided by the former regime.

The Kurds claim Kirkuk, but in 2004 even the deputy mayor, a Kurd named Hasib Rojbiyani, admitted: 'It is a microcosm of the country. All the nationalities and religions are here—Kurds, Turkmen, Arabs, and Christians.'[25] If that is the case, what makes the city specifically Kurdish? The reluctance or inability of the Jaafari government to deal with the issue of Kirkuk's future status, providing compensation for 'returning' Kurds and encouraging the 'voluntary' departure of Arabs, has infuriated the Kurds. The Kurdish authorities have taken it upon themselves to encourage the overt and rapid 'Kurdification' of the city. They have provided financial support for Kurds to settle in and around the city, and changed the names of streets and buildings from Arabic to Kurdish.

The Kurdish parties were also accused of exacerbating ethnic tensions in Nineveh Province in 2004. The CPA did nothing in response, while in the United States the supporters of the Kurds seem to have implicitly encouraged their increasingly muscular behavior. As one Western journalist said:

In Ninevah Kurdish leaders are helping thousands of Kurdish villagers move back inside the province after Saddam Hussein's forces expelled them over the last two decades. In some cases, Arab settlers are fleeing ahead of the influx, often hastily selling their land to the advancing, well-armed Kurds. In other cases, Kurds are closing in on multi-ethnic villages that had—prior to Saddam's manipulations—been models of good ethnic relations. [26]

While stationed in Tal Afar in the latter part of 2005 I noticed the growing Kurdish presence in the region. The Kurdish parties were opening offices in several areas, and the logos of the Kurdish political parties were commonly seen on buildings and walls. The Kurds were also trying to mobilize the Yezidi Kurds in the Jabal Sinjar region, to the west of Tal Afar. Sunni Arabs and Turkmen, of course, accused the Kurds of all kinds of nefarious activities, including a stealthy encroachment on Nineveh Province with the intent of incorporating it into the Kurdish region. Indeed, the US offensive in Tal Afar (see Epilogue) in early September 2005 was perceived by the insurgents and Turkmen not only as an attempt to 'suppress' the Sunnis on behalf of the central government, but also as a means of facilitating Kurdish control of the region.

The Kurds have argued for an ethnically based federalism from the very beginning of the post-Saddam era. Kurdish officials have stressed continuously that the Kurds will decide what powers the central government will have over their region. As Barham Salih pugnaciously stated: 'We will not have the Iraqi bureaucracy decide our priorities here. Those days are over.'[27] From the earliest days of the occupation the Kurds had made it known that they wanted the widest autonomy possible consistent with them remaining part of Iraq, including control over their own security, taxes and oil revenues from Kirkuk. To many other Iraqis this sounded suspiciously like a step towards independence, part of a strategy of seeking statehood incrementally. In the early months of post-Saddam Iraq, Kurdish talk about their right to an ethnically based federalism alarmed Iraqi politicians and officials, who argued that this would be a recipe for a disastrous disintegration. As one Iraqi politician stated: 'You know what the largest Kurdish city in Iraq is? It's Baghdad. It isn't like you could draw a line in Iraq and say the Kurds live here or the Assyrians, the Chaldeans or the Turkomans or the Shiites or the Sunnis live there. In the supposedly Shiite south, there are a million Sunnis in Basra.'[28]

In response to angry denunciations by others that they are making too many demands, the Kurds say they are seeking nothing more than they already have in the post-Saddam state, and are making no further demands on the state. Some argue that by seeking reintegration into Iraq they are actually giving up their quasi or de facto independence. This was the argument of Barham Salih: 'Right now, we are almost independent. By seeking reintegration into Iraq, we are giving up things; we are not asking for more.'[29]

Unlike the Shiʻa, the Kurds can never be the dominant political group in the country, and as such their distinctive imprint—formed partly by their tragic history and partly by a decade of living in relative freedom in their quasi-independent enclave—on state and society will never be the deciding identity for the new Iraq. They obviously oppose Iraq being seen as an Arab country. Rather, they favor its identification as a multiethnic state. Many Kurds believe that the militant Arabism of past governments, along with the nationalistic ideologies that underpinned it, was responsible for the attempts to suppress Kurdish identity. A form of secularism is important, and they are clearly against the formation of a religious government in the country. Even if they were to split from the rest of Iraq, one Kurd told me, a Shiʻa-dominated theocracy in the south would be unsettling for Kurdish security. The 'politicization' of religion in the rest of the country—which many Kurds say has contributed enormously to the violence there—has made the Kurds more adamant that the central government cannot dictate the imposition of theocratic rule, at least not in the Kurdish region. Moreover, religious governments have the tendency to be ideologically rigid and totalitarian—that is to say, they seek to make the entire society conform to their vision. The Kurds want none of that.

The sincerity of the Kurdish claim that they wish to stay in a federal and secure Iraq is questionable. On the one hand, I met Kurds who say, quite sincerely, that they wish to stay in Iraq. Indeed, I encountered a couple of Kurdish officers in the Iraqi army who said they are Iraqi and wish to see the country remain intact. When I asked them why they expressed such sentiments, they said that independence would be difficult—an independent Kurdistan would be landlocked and in conflict with its immediate neighbors, including the rump Iraqi state or states. But they included a number of provisos for their belief in Iraq. While it is overwhelmingly Arab, it must be multiethnic, secular and federal. And, importantly, the Arabs must stop viewing 'us as an alien implantation in the heart of the Arab world as they do Israel'.[30] 'We are not settlers or colonists,' and Kurdistan, they state, has been Kurdish since ancient times.[31]

On the other hand, it can be argued that the Kurds will use their presence within the central government to expand as much as possible their autonomy and the resources at their disposal. This constitutes their stepping-stone to independence, because sometime in the future they will use the power they have marshaled to declare their sovereignty.

The Kurds have voiced constant threats to use force to get their 'rights'. The deputy commander of the *peshmerga* general staff, Mustafa Sayed Qadir, warned: 'Kurds insist on their rights, and if Kurdish rights are not recognized and respected, Iraq will never

know stability.'[32] They have also threatened to withhold cooperation with the central government or to secede if their concerns
are not taken care of. But much of this is bravado. The Kurds have
a strong paramilitary force, but it is neither a unified nor an offensive force yet. They can and have used it quite effectively to gather
intelligence for themselves and the Coalition, and to consolidate
control over territories they claim rightfully belong to them. Their
most powerful weapon, however, has been the threat of secession.

While it is unclear whether the Kurds actually can secede in the
face of 'disapproval' on the part of the United States, and possibly
violent opposition on the part of Turkey, the mere threat to do so
alarms the rest of the country. However, I am not so sure that this is
the case anymore. The Sunni Arabs once viewed with apprehension
Kurdish talk about ethnic federalism, but I did not sense this during
the time I spent in Iraq in 2005. The Shi'a, who have been seriously
considering the feasibility of an autonomous region in the south,
seem decreasingly concerned by Kurdish designs for self-government. Indeed, Sunni and Shi'a Arabs, both of whom have their own
problems with one another, increasingly resent the Kurds. They
are seen as making too many demands, and as anti- or non-Iraqi.
Many senior Iraqi officials—Shi'a in the Jaafari government—have
privately indicated that Iraq's Arabs and Kurds are destined not to
live together and that the latter are intractable.[33] Finally, the Kurds'
constant threats to secede began to backfire when in August 2005
one lawmaker actually challenged them to do so.[34]

Much has been written about the evolution of separatist thinking and action within the ranks of a minority ethno-sectarian
group. However, we still do not fully understand the rise of sentiment within the center acceding to the separation of that minority
group. One Sunni Arab with whom I talked seemed to no longer
care anymore whether the Kurds 'left'. He did say, however, that
Mosul, a largely Arab city despite claims to the contrary, was a 'red

line'. Surprisingly, he did not mention Kirkuk, but did speak of 're-source-sharing'. This is, of course, the sentiment of only one person. Generally, however, the Sunni Arabs and Turkmen with whom I spoke were little concerned whether the Kurds left or not, so long as they grabbed no more territory than they already have in the autonomous region.

Where does all of this leave the Kurds? They see no option but to stick with the United States. 'How long is Kurdish patience for a new Iraq? That's based on how long American patience is. Without the Americans there will be no democratic Iraq,' says Rowsch Shaways, Speaker of the regional Kurdish parliament and a one-time official in the former IGC.[35] Regional Interior Minister Osman Mahmoud has accepted wholesale the canard that democracy in one place can have a demonstrative effect elsewhere in the region, with the added twist that Kurdistan is the example to be held up: 'A real push should be given to democracy in the region. Kurdistan can be held up as a good example. If this were done, people in the rest of Iraq and the Middle East would be able to see that the US is not just here for its purposes, but to help them.'[36] The reality, however, is that Kurdistan is having little demonstrative effect on the rest of the failing country. Indeed, the Kurds are doing their utmost to prevent the violence from migrating north.

Most Kurds do not see the United States as an occupier, but rather as a friend and an ally. As Barham Salih says:

We have made a strategic choice. We are partners with the US to bring about a democratic transformation of Iraq. We will not be on the fence. This is not gimmicking—it is how we read our interests. But I am worried, as so often US policy people tend to take their friends for granted while attempting to win over opponents. The thugs of Fallouja, who represent the same value system that gave rise to the tyranny of Saddam, cannot and will not like the Kurds. And most probably they will never forgive us for opposing Saddam and working with the US-led Coalition.[37]

The United States enlarges the Kurds' freedom to maneuver within Iraq, and protects them from the attempts of outside powers (i.e. Turkey and Iran) to undermine or curtail that freedom. Ironically, however, the US umbrella acts as a brake on further or more expansive Kurdish ambitions, namely independence. That the United States has pressured the Kurdish leadership to curtail any talk of independence or self-determination is well-documented, but the question is why? Are there any US strategic interests in insisting that the Kurdish enclave remain part of Iraq? In my estimation, unless we take into consideration Turkey's interests in preventing the emergence of a Kurdish state in northern Iraq (which makes this US strategic position a derivative one), there are none at all. The main US interest in the post-Saddam era is ideological and is implicitly propagated by the neoconservative administration hawks, for two reasons. First, the retention of the Kurds within a united but decentralized Iraq is seen as a test of the idea of promoting a multiethnic democracy. Second, and more importantly, the retention of the Kurds within Iraq allows the dilution of Iraq's Arab identity. Iraq is ethnically at least 75 percent Arab. This 'low' percentage of Arabs has allowed some observers in the United States to propose that Iraq should emerge as a non-Arab multiethnic society. It is not clear why they would propose such a strategy, but it is unlikely to succeed even if the Kurds do not secede. It will definitely be a non-starter should they obtain their independence, because Iraq without the Kurds would then be about 90 percent Arab ethnically. A negative attachment to the Iraqi state is hardly a foundation on which to build Kurdish loyalty to the new post-Saddam Iraq.

In conclusion, the Kurds are likely to continue to seek a greater expansion of their political and economic room for maneuver over the next several years as expressed by the Minister for Foreign Affairs of the Patriotic Union of Kurdistan, Shalaw Ali Askari, who said of independence: 'It is the dream of every Kurd and I believe we will reach it.'[38] Even senior officials like Talabani and Barzani, who have made a strategic decision, for the moment at least, to work within a united Iraq, do not bother to hide the fact that they dream of an independent Kurdish state. Barzani states: 'The people of Kurdistan has the right to have a state and one day there will be that state, but we do not know when … I hope I would see that happen while still alive. The most important thing is that this will become a reality, and I am sure of that. As for when that will happen, I do not know.'[39] They could hardly have been expected to be part of the Sunni Arab insurgency against the Coalition. The reaction of the majority of the Iraqi population, the Shi'a Arabs, was more complicated, a fact of little solace to the insurgency or indeed to the Coalition, although the non-participation of the majority of the Shi'a in violence has helped the Coalition maintain its presence in the country.

The empowerment of the Shi'a Arabs

Iraq's Shi'as constitute roughly 60 percent of the country's total population. Historically they have been the 'marginalized' majority. Like the Sunni Arabs they do not constitute a homogeneous bloc or view the unfolding events of the past three years through a single lens. The overthrow of Saddam Hussein was welcome news to the vast majority of them, except perhaps those who had been associated with the Ba'thist regime and even members of the party.

The United States went into Iraq with little or no understanding of the Shi'a factor in Iraqi politics. Often what little 'understanding' exists would have us believe either that the Shi'a would be eternally grateful to the United States for liberating them from the horrors of the Saddam regime, or that they were under the control of the Islamic Republic of Iran, the region's major Shi'a power. Jay Garner, the first proconsul of occupied Iraq, was astounded that the level of anti-US sentiment on the streets—particularly among the Shi'a—was of a 'little more magnitude than I had expected'.[40] Indeed, a number of Shi'a clerics and spokesmen made it clear over the course of spring 2003 that they expected the United States to leave Iraq now that it had accomplished the goal upon which everybody opposing the Ba'th regime had agreed: the overthrow of Saddam.

Yet in my estimation—based on working on the Iraq situation for up to six months prior to the outbreak of the war—most policy-makers showed little understanding of the Shi'a issue. Indeed, those junior and mid-ranking 'policy wonks' whose job was to provide senior-level policy-makers with short, pithy policy information did not do so when it came to the Shi'a. These senior officials were clearly neither interested in nor had any clue about the historical formation of the Iraqi Shi'a or the dynamics of their political and socioeconomic emergence. Occasionally a senior administration official would unwittingly and prominently display ignorance of the politics of the Shi'a, as in the case of one who stated that the Iraqi Shi'a belong to the Akhbari school, whose rivals the Usulis dominate in Iran. The individual in question probably does not know the differences between the two, but more to the point he was wrong. Both Iran and Iraq are dominated by the Usuli school of Shi'ism.

Moreover, as will be demonstrated in the next chapter, there existed a supercilious 'Shi'aphilia' among certain academics, Iraqi political exiles, policy wonks and policy-makers linked to the Bush administration. This is a remarkable turnaround from the 1980s, when the rise of Shi'a power in Lebanon and the Islamic Republic of Iran was viewed with alarm in the United States. Indeed, anti-Shi'a sentiment and actions became the leitmotif of the 1980s.

But matters began to change, at least where it concerns the Iraqi Shi'a—Iranian and Lebanese Shi'a are still 'suspect'. The Shi'a of Iraq (I have not yet heard them being referred to as 'our Shi'a' in Washington, DC, and do not think I will because, as a well-known Australian journalist told me, 'Shi'aphilia' there has begun to die down a tad) were believed to be pro-American. Why? Was it simply because they were anti-Saddam, or was it because they saw the United States as the instrument of their salvation? The Shi'a clerical establishment, it was declaimed breathlessly from the oracles of neoconservative thought, was more 'democratic' than the Sunni clerical establishment, such as it was. The pronouncements of the senior Shi'a clergy (see below) in favor of majority rule and of elections were proof positive of the democratic leanings of the Shi'a. The reality is more complex. And had we been aware of this complexity, we would have been on firmer ground in implanting our presence in Iraq. In short, from the very beginning of its enterprise in that country, the United States, through its ignorance, faced a potentially formidable Shi'a problem.

A primer on Shi'a history in Iraq is a useful introduction to understanding that they are not monolithic, are not united on the kind of polity they want, and are certainly not all controlled or manipulated by Iran. It will also help explain why, despite condemning the insurgency against the foreign presence, they are not part of it. Who are the Iraqi Shi'a? How and why did they emerge? What is their relationship to their Arab *ethnic* identity? What is the relationship between the clergy and the Shi'a population? What has been the relationship between the clerical establishment and the state in Iraq? What are the major Shi'a movements or parties in Iraq and how do they see the eventual relationship between the clerical establishment and the contours of the emerging state? These questions and more are key to understanding the Shi'a, rather than platitudinous, self-serving, superficial observations such as those coming out of certain government institutions and think-tanks, and well-heeled former Iraqi opposition groups. And certainly, while the literature on Shi'a of Iraq is not as extensive as that on their Iranian coreligionists, neither is it sparse.[41]

The division between Sunnis and Shi'a began over the issue of who was to succeed Muhammad in the new Islamic state, and erupted in Arabia after the Prophet's death. A group of devotees, later to be known as Shi'a Muslims, believe that Ali—Muhammad's cousin and son-in-law—should have followed the Prophet as his direct successor and leader of the Muslims. Another group, later to be known as Sunni Muslims, believes that Abu Bakr, the first caliph, or successor, to hold power after Muhammad, was the legitimate successor, as then were the two individuals who succeeded Bakr. Ali did become the fourth caliph, and Sunnis regard him as the fourth and last of the 'rightly guided caliphs', after Abu Bakr (632–4), Umar (634–44) and Uthman (644–56). The *Shi'at Ali* (partisans of Ali) argue that Ali should have been the first caliph and that the caliphate should pass only to direct descendants of Mohammed via Ali, the *imams* who are endowed with qualities and values that ordinary mortal men do not have.

When the third caliph, Uthman, was murdered Ali finally succeeded to the leadership of the caliphate. But this was not the end of the controversy. Ali faced considerable opposition and turmoil during his rule. Mu'awiya Umayyad, Uthman's cousin and the powerful governor of Damascus, refused to recognize him until Uthman's killers had been apprehended. Ali made compromise after compromise with the Umayyads, much to the dismay of some of his followers. He was assassinated by a disgruntled follower in 661. Mu'awiya then declared himself caliph. Ali's elder son Hassan, allegedly a weak man, was persuaded not to pursue his claim as successor. Ali's younger son Hussein was made of sterner stuff but deferred his claim to the caliphate until Mu'awiya's death.

However, when Mu'awiya finally died in 680 his son Yazid usurped the caliphate.

Hussein felt that he had to act, and though he knew his position was hopeless he led a tiny army of seventy-two men against Yazid's forces, which overwhelmingly outnumbered him. They met on a field outside Karbala on the tenth day of Muharram, or 20 October 680. Hussein, his men and most of the women and children with them were slaughtered. Shi'a believe that Hussein was deliberately going to his death in a remarkable act of martyrdom to highlight a manifest injustice.

This battle on Ashura (the tenth day of Muharram) is commemorated by the Shi'a, for whom injustice, victimization and martyrdom are intricately linked in this tragic event. Karbala is thus one of the most holy cities in Shi'a Islam. Hussein's infant son, Ali, survived the massacre but the line of Mohammed through Ali and Hussein became extinct in 873 when the Twelfth Imam, Muhammad al-Mahdi went into occultation, or extended hiding from his enemies. During his absence all temporal power is viewed as illegitimate, and when he returns he will do away with injustice and oppression. The central belief of Twelver Shi'ism (Ithna 'Ashariyah), which holds sway in Iran and Iraq, is the occultation of the Twelfth Imam. In the meantime, the Shi'a community's affairs are taken care of by their clerics, the *ulema*. The Twelfth Imam is considered to be the only legitimate and just ruler, and therefore no political action taken in his absence is legitimate. The religious authority of the Shi'a clerics is derived from their role as deputies of the absent Twelfth Imam. They are as such the recipients of the *khums* religious tax, a source of substantial economic autonomy.

Shi'a clerics are often referred to as *mullahs* and *mujtahids*. The most prominent clerical position is that of *marja' al-taqlid*, or 'source of emulation'. A *marja' al-taqlid* emerges as a result of learning and prowess in scholarly debate, as well as of their ability to gain a following among the faithful by virtue of their pronounce-ments on questions of religious law. *A marja' al-taqlid* can also is-sue edicts that are binding on his followers. Ironically, while the Shi'a clerical establishment is considerably more hierarchical than that of the Sunni Muslims, the Shi'a have never developed a formal mechanism to choose a 'source of emulation'. Scholarship, piety and purity were the traditional requisites. But more important is the number of followers who consider a *marja' al-taqlid* or ayatollah (a purely honorific title) their spiritual guide. The religious taxes paid to the *marja' al-taqlid* translate into finances that bring prestige and, of course, power.

Shi'ism is intricately tied to Iraq. Indeed, no other place, includ-ing Iran, the giant of the Shi'a world, has been so closely linked to the fortunes of Shi'ism. Yet paradoxically, apart from those in the enclaves of Najaf and Karbala, which have been the centers of Shi'a learning for centuries and were dominated largely by Farsi speak-ing Shi'a from Iran, the Iraqi Arabs are relatively recent converts to Shi'ism. This was well-documented in the work of Yitzhak Nakash, Pierre-Jean Luizard and Hanna Batatu.[42] For centuries the coun-tryside around the holy cities of Najaf and Karbala was dominated by nomadic tribes or tribal confederations of nominally Sunni Arab Bedouin who had migrated *en masse* from the Arabian Peninsula.[43]

A variety of cultural, environmental, and sociopolitical factors, which have been described in rich detail elsewhere, allowed the thin layer of Shi'a clerics that existed in Iraq at the time to con-vert these increasingly sedentary nomads to Shi'ism, beginning in the eighteenth century. Within a hundred years Iraq had become a majority Shi'a province of the Ottoman Empire and the south-ern Arabs of Iraq showed a keen attachment to their new religion. Historically, the Bedouin wore religion lightly, but adherence to Shi'ism represented a wonderful vehicle for instigating and widen-ing a gap between the tribes and the ever-centralizing Ottoman authorities in faraway Baghdad. In short, Shiʻism provided the tribes of southern Iraq with the ideological strength to resist the central-izing tendencies of the Sunni Ottoman rulers of Mesopotamia, and the clerics with a demographic reach into the hinterland beyond the holy cities and with bodies of armed men to ward off maraud-ing Sunni fanatics from the Arabian Peninsula.

But the Shiʻism of the southern Iraqi tribes was not at the ex-pense of their Arab and specifically Bedouin values, and some tribes witnessed the anomalous situation of their sheikhs remaining Sunni in orientation, while the rest of the tribe 'converted' to Shiʻism. Iraq's Shiʻa are Arab, despite historical attempts to cast doubt on their *ʻuruba* (Arabness) by the majority of the state's rulers from its inception to the present. This point emerged in my discussions with Iraqi Shiʻa, particularly with those who had no qualms about telling me that they followed Moqtada al-Sadr, who has strongly espoused Iraqi nationalism (see pp. 249–50).

Iraq's Shiʻa were never able to parlay their majority status into a key role in the country's politics. Even though they participat-ed in the nationalist uprising against Britain's attempt to directly colonize Iraq, the Shiʻa lost out during the first phase of nation- and state-building in the 1920s.[44] Power devolved to the former Sunni Ottoman elite—almost all Arab but with a smattering of Sunni Kurds and Turkmen—who controlled the monarchy, the bu-reaucracy and the armed forces. The Iraqi Shiʻa clerical establish-ment has never been endowed with some of the classic strengths of its counterpart in neighboring Iran.[45] More specifically, it has not been blessed with the level of resources available to its Iranian equivalent. Also clerics have never managed to establish an im-portant symbiotic relationship with the Iraqi commercial classes. Historically, commerce in Iraq was—as in another key example, Egypt—dominated by foreigners.[46] In Iraq, the Jews constituted the predominant commercial class. When they migrated *en masse* to Israel after 1948, partly as a result of prejudice and partly due to encouragement by the new Israeli state, the rich Shi'a emerged as the leading commercial sector. However, they did not create bonds with the clerical establishment, as is the case in Iran, where the clerics and the *bazaaris* (merchants) have had longstanding social, familial and financial links. Finally, over the past three decades government policies have decimated the clerical establishment. These policies have reduced its size, cut down its influence and further curtailed its former financial independence.

The Shi'a were largely excluded from power, even though in time some notable Shi'a individuals rose to prominence. Moreover, prejudice against the Shi'a was strong among Sunnis, many of whom, particularly the early educators of the Iraqi state who incorporated Arab nationalist ideals into the education system, viewed them with unalloyed suspicion as a fifth column for Shi'a Iran.[47]

The second nation- and state-building experiment came in 1958 with the overthrow of the monarchy and the rise of the republic under 'Abd al-Karim Qasim. The growth in the political awareness of the Shi'a masses, their adherence to mass parties like the Iraqi Communist Party (ICP), and Qasim's sympathy towards them led the Shi'a to believe that they would become an important political force. The ICP emerged as a potent force among the urban poor in Shi'a neighborhoods where the inhabitants were relatively recent migrants from the rural hinterlands. The Shi'a did go into pan-Arab parties like the Ba'th Party and Shi'a members played a prominent role in that party's emergence in Iraq. But the Shi'a could never use the ICP as a vehicle for their political and social integration into the state. The party did not attract sufficient Shi'a members, and its leadership in the early years was dominated by very leftist Shi'a and was characterized by severe intraparty ideological bickering. Moreover, it was viewed with suspicion by the Arab nationalists in power.

Conflict between the ICP and the Ba'th was rampant and often bloody in the late 1950s and early 1960s, and was played out in rival urban districts that represented the strongholds of one party or the other.[48] The mass arrests of Ba'th Party members in the early 1960s, however, diluted the Shi'a percentage of the party base. Slowly but surely, Sunni Arab members took over and the Ba'th Party became the stronghold of the Sunnis, particularly of their urban poor and lower middle class.[49] After the overthrow of Qasim in 1963 Iraqi politics degenerated into military dictatorships. And because the senior officer corps was overwhelmingly Sunni Arab this meant control of the state by that minority. Moreover, one of the early post-revolutionary leaders, General Arif, was a conserva- tive Sunni Muslim who despised the Shi'a.

From the early 1960s, Shi'a Islamist parties began to play a more prominent role within their community. This was done partly to offset the strong presence of communism among young Shi'a and partly as a response to the Arab nationalism of the Sunnis, which tended to delegitimize the 'Arabness' of the Shi'a. Ayatollah Mu- hammad Baqir al-Hakim, a leading clerical opponent of the Ba'th regime, elaborated extensively on the rise of the Shi'a Islamist cur- rent in Iraq in an interview with the Iranian newspaper *Seda-ye- Edalat* in August 2002, when he was still in exile in Iran. He argued that the emergence of Marxist-Leninist ideology played a major role in energizing the *ulema* and making them play a political role:

Communist parties were extensively active in the Arab world, particu- larly in Iraq. The danger that the ulema sensed from that quarter and fear of the influence of that ideology upon the Islamic societies' mental and cultural dimensions were the other factors that brought the ulema into the political and cultural arena.[50]

The third nation- and state-building experiment came with the takeover by the Ba'th Party in 1968. This was the most secular and radical nation-building experiment undertaken by an Iraqi ruler and was dominated by a small element of the Sunni Arab population from the formerly sleepy and poverty-stricken town of Tikrit and its rural hinterland. No matter how hard he tried to project a national project that encompassed the entire Iraqi people, Saddam Hussein never succeeded in winning the active allegiance of the Shi'a and Kurdish populace to his peculiar amalgam of ancient Mesopotamian, Arab and Iraqi identity.[51] The Shi'a did not look favorably upon this regime because of its pan-Arab ideology, its early militant secularism and its policy of weakening the power of the clerical establishment.[52]

The Shi'a clerics and the regime were bound to clash because of these deep ideological differences overlaying a sectarian one—and clash they did from the very early days of the regime. After the Iranian Revolution in 1979, the Shi'a opposition to Saddam's regime turned actively militant and called for the overthrow of the godless Ba'thists and for their replacement by an Islamic government. The rise of political Islam, particularly the Shi'a variant, was a mortal threat to the secular orientation of the Ba'th Party and its views on the 'proper' relationship between religion on the one hand and state and society on the other, as defined by the leader himself and by various party documents and statements. In the words of Saddam Hussein: 'Our party does not take a neutral stand between faith and heresy, it is always on the side of faith. However, it is not and should not be a religious party … *We have to resist the politicisation of religion whether by the state or by others in society.*'[53] In short, the politicization of the Shi'a via the vehicle of religion constituted a national security threat, a threat to the construction of a seemingly progressive and modernizing Arab power—whose despicable acts and corruption were well-hidden, as were its victims—and to the national identity of the country as defined by the Ba'th. Not surprisingly, the regime organized to meet the challenge and did so with its customary brutality and efficiency.[54] The result was a sanguinary confrontation in which thousands of Shi'a—laypersons and clerics—lost their lives or were deported to Iran. It came as a surprise to many observers when the overwhelming majority of Iraqi Shi'a fought bravely and stubbornly in defense of their country in the latter half of the Iran-Iraq war, when confident Iranian forces launched offensive after offensive in Iraqi territory. It was loyalty not to Saddam but to Iraq that drove the Shi'a to fight. The Shi'a rank and file and officer corps had not lost their pride in being Arabs because they were Shi'a. This was an observation that neither Sunni Arab in Iraq nor neoconservative policy-maker in Washington, DC—obsessed as both were with the idea that the Shi'a were somewhat less than Arab—seemed to acknowledge.

With the collapse of the Ba'th regime in April 2003 the Shi'a were all agreed upon one thing: the post-Saddam situation in Iraq constituted the best opportunity for them to play the key role in state- and nation-building for the first time in Iraqi history. Within hours of Saddam's fall tens of thousands of Shi'a poured into the streets of Baghdad, fanning out first from the Shi'a shrine in the Khadimiya district, chanting, 'The oppression is gone, however long it took. The tyrant is gone.' The Shi'a tried to allay the fears of Iraq's ethno-sectarian groups—particularly the Sunni Arabs—who watched their re-emergence onto the political stage with some trepidation. Signs went up on placards, posters and mosque walls saying: 'No Shiites, no Sunnis, Islamic unity, Islamic unity.' But underneath the tenuous current of so-called unity in the early heady days of the overthrow, many on all sides knew that the competition for power and resources was unfolding. There are many Shi'a groups, political parties and movements (see Table 1 for examples), but only four that really matter.

The first is centered on the most senior ayatollahs in Iraq. As I mentioned above, the Ba'th regime did considerable damage to the Shi'a clerical establishment from the 1970s until its downfall in 2003. Fearful that the senior Shi'a clerics would endorse the Khomeinist notion of rule by clerics, Saddam Hussein kept a close watch on the theological establishments in Najaf, the Hawza al-Ilmiyyah, and the senior clerics like Ayatollah Al-Sayyid Abu al-Qasim al-Musawi al-Khui. Khui groomed Ayatollah Ali al-Husseini al-Sistani, Iranian by birth, as his successor. Ayatollah Sistani—a recluse who weathered intimidation in the Saddam era and assassination attempts since the US-led campaign in Iraq began, and who rarely speaks in public—has often shown that his influence can trump the plans of the United States and its Iraqi allies. He played a decisive role in Iraq's transition after Saddam's downfall and won most of his battles with US officials, as I will briefly summarize in the next chapter.

It has been argued that Ayatollah Sistani adheres to a 'quietist' tradition in (Twelver) Shi'a Islam like his mentor, Ayatollah Khui. The so-called quietist tradition is viewed as a classical, non-activist tradition, which discourages the *mujtahids* from any interference with political matters at the state level. There has been a distinguished line of such quietist *mujtahids*. The quietist tradition posits that the *mujtahids* engage in study and teaching. The senior cleric's main goals are to ensure that the principles of Islam, revealed in the holy scriptures and traditions of the Prophet and the Imams, continue to be respected in public life. However, the clergy neither demands the right to participate in government nor presumes to exercise control over the state, which is in the hands of laypersons. However, at a time of moral decadence and political corruption, or of great injustice, the *mujtahid* can become more active in politics by limiting himself to advice, guidance and the implication of sacred law in public life.[55] Sistani, like many senior *mujtahids*, has long rejected the radical ideology of Ayatollah Ruhollah Khomeini, who lived in exile in Najaf before leading Iran's Islamic revolution

Table 1.1. POLITICALLY ACTIVE SHI'A GROUPS

Name	Leader	History and current status	Web and media sites
Supreme Council for the Islamic Revolution in Iraq (SCIRI)	Muhammad Baqir al-Hakim. (His brother, 'Abd al-'Aziz al-Hakim, who has assumed considerable prominence in SCIRI following its return to Iraq, at one point headed a group called either Harakat al-Mujahideen al-'arak or Harakat al-Muqatilun al-'arak.)	Formed in November 1982 in an attempt to create a united and coordinated bloc of all religious political parties. Many eventually seceded from SCIRI. Under Hakim's leadership SCIRI became known as most pro-Iranian Iraqi Shi'a group. It established its own militia, the Badr Corps (now the Badr Organization), which is trained by the Iranian Revolutionary Guard Corps.	http://www.majlesala.com* *Nida al-Rafidayn* (Arabic-language weekly), http://www.nidaa-arrafidain.* *Liwa al-Sadr* (Arabic-language magazine), http://www.lewasadr.com* Office of Ayatollah Al-Sayyid Muhammad Baqir al-Hakim, http://www.al-hakim.com
Hizb al-Da'wa (Islamic Dawa Party)	Ibrahim al-Jaafari	Oldest Shi'a religious political party; observes 1957 as its founding year but came into official existence in 1962. Ayatollah Muhammad Baqir al-Sadr was one of its key figures; he insisted on the creation of a conspiratorial and centralized Leninist-type party. Dawa launched a number of large-scale attacks on installations and leaders of the Ba'thist regime. Decimated in conflict with	http://www.daawaparty.com *Al-Jihad* (Arabic-language political weekly), http://www.daawaparty.com/aljihad80/index.htm *Al Mawqif* (Arabic-language political magazine), http://www.daawaparty.com/almawkif/index.htm

Munazzamat al-'Amal al-Islami (Islamic Action Organization, or Islamic Task Organization)	Political section headed by Ibrahim al-Mutayri; spiritual leader is Ayatollah Muhammad Taqi al-Mudaressi	Ba'th regime between 1970s and 1980s. Held its third major conference in Tehran, May 1983, where its members emphasized that the party's goal was the 'application of lofty Islamic law, as a system of governance and program of state'.	http://www.amalislami.org* *Al-Shahid* (Arabic language weekly), http://www.alshahid.com* *Office of Ayatollah Muhammad Taqi al-Mudaressi*, http://www.almodarresi.com *Office of His Eminence Hadi al-Mudaressi*, http://66.221.74.102
Islamic National Front	Muhammad Taqi al-Ha'iri and Sadiq al-Husseini al-Shirazi	Emerged in 1968 but organized at the beginning of 1970 by Hasan al-Shirazi. Headed in the 1980s by the brothers Mohammed Taqi and Hadi al-Mudaressi. From earliest days put great stress on military action against the Ba'th regime, and made assassination attempts against leaders of the regime.	http://www.iraqinf.com*
Iraqi Islamic Jihad Movement, or Jehad Islamic Organization of Iraq		Established in 1979.	http://www.jehadparty.tk

Table 1. POLITICALLY ACTIVE SHI'A GROUPS (continued)

Name	Leader	History and current status	Web and media sites
Jamaat al-Sadr al-Thani, or Al Sadriyyun	Moqtada Al-Sadr	Hitherto a little known radical political faction that is named after the late Ayatollah Muhammad Sadiq al-Sadr who was murdered along with two of his sons by the regime of Saddam Hussein in 1999. Sadiq al-Sadr's youngest son, Moqtada, leads this organization, which opposes the political quietism of Ayatollah Sistani. Because Moqtada is too young to be a *marja*, he and his followers profess allegiance to Ayatollah Kazim al-Ha'iri who was born in Karbala but who resides in Qom, Iran. The organization has a strong base in Medinat Sadr, Baghdad, where its radical young clerics have managed to build up a strong following. Al Sadriyyun has a 5,000-man militia based largely in the holy city of Najaf.	No further information available

Note: *Website not active, September 2005.

Sources: *Der Spiegel*, 7 June 2003; *Al Mustaqbal*, 16 April 2003; *Yawm al-Akhbar*, 5 June 2003, p. 2; *Al Jaridah*, 4 June 2003, p. 2; *Al Nashrah* 5 (1983), 23–5, and 13 (1984), 16–19; Pierre Martin, 'Le clerge chiite en Irak hier et aujourd'hui,' *Maghreb-Machrek* 115 (1987), 29–52; 'Opposition—Ad-Daawa Party,' *Middle East Reporter*, 10 August 1991, pp. 12–14; Pierre Martin, 'Une Grande Figure de l'Islamisme en Irak,' *Cahiers de l'Orient* 8–9 (1987–8), 117–34; Arnold Hottinger, 'Die Zukunft des Iraks heisst Schia,' *Neue Zurcher Zeitung*, 11 May 2003; John Lee Anderson, 'Dreaming of Baghdad,' *NewYorker*, 10 February 2003; Irak: le Jamaat al-Sadr: nouvel acteur politique chiite,' *Monde*rebelles.com; Michael Collins Dunn, 'Competing to Lead Iraq's Shia: A Guide, Part I,' *Estimate*, 16 May 2003, and 'Part II,' 30 May 2003; Juan Cole, 'Informed Comment: Thoughts on the Middle East, History, and Religion,' May and June 2003, <http://www.juancole.com/2003_05_01_juancole_archive.html> and <http://www.juancole.com/2003_06_01_juancole_archive.html>.

and developed the philosophy of *velayat-e faqih*, or the guardianship of the jurisprudent, which called for clerical rule.

Despite the myths swirling around the notions of quietism, however, Sistani cannot be a believer in a strict separation of church and state. As Babak Rahimi pointed out in his excellent article on Sistani's political role:

However, the key point to bear in mind is that the degree of authority that a *mujtahid* can exercise in political matters has never been clearly defined in the history of Shi'i Islam. *This is predominantly the case because what determines the level of political participation by a Shi'i cleric primarily depends on the particular historical and social settings the* mujtahid *confronts, giving him a certain leeway in creatively overcoming problems according to his use of reason (*'aql*) regarding the best application of divine law.* In other words, discussing the politics of Shi'i Islam in terms of dichotomies, namely 'activism' or 'quietism,' can be misleading.[56]

Sistani has also written about the need for clerical influence in political life.[57] 'Sistani in his *fatwas* does talk about ... the guardianship of the jurisprudent in social issues,' says Juan Cole, Professor of History at Michigan University, adding that Sistani's preference is 'that clerics mostly leave running the state to lay persons'.[58] But the implication is that Shi'a laypersons will be influenced by the clerics.

What is important to stress here is that Sistani emerged as the most powerful man in Iraq not long after the collapse of the regime, and that his goal was to ensure the mobilization and participation of the Shi'a in the political process so that they would finally receive their just rewards. Iraq was clearly in a time of distress and political instability. Staying aloof from politics would not do. Apparently certain Shi'a clerics have said that there has been one principal concern behind most of Sistani's political pronouncements: that the country's majority Shi'a population must never be excluded from Iraqi politics again. In the early 1920s, the British devised a bogus election to legitimate their control of Iraq. At the time, the most important ayatollahs in Najaf issued *fatwas* telling their followers not to vote because they felt the process would lead only to an unfair order. But the upshot of their abstention was that the clergy lost all influence over the process and played a minor role in the formation of the state. As an aide to the Ayatollah stated: 'The *marjiya* [Shi'a religious leadership] have studied everything surrounding the 1920 revolution—the British ended up writing our constitution. Now we insist that the same mistake not be made again.'[59]

The emergence of Sistani from political quietism was, of course, viewed with elation by the Shi'a, who heeded his rulings and mobilized themselves for participation like never before. But the Sunnis viewed Sistani's emergence balefully and in many quarters with deep-seated suspicion. First, he 'unfairly' opened the way for the Shi'a to seize the state that *they*, the Sunnis, had built. Of course the United States was the other party to blame, but part of its culpability was that it bent over backwards to accommodate Sistani and his interminable demands. Second, the Sunnis believe the Ayatollah wants to implement a Shi'a theocratic system of government on Iraq. He does not, but it was amazing for me to discover how little Sunnis generally knew about the Shi'a. Third, Sistani is Iranian and in the eyes of the Sunnis represents Iranian interests. As in the early days of the split from Rome, when Protestants came to view their Catholic countrymen as a fifth column for the Pope, many Sunnis view the Shi'a clergy—many of whom coincidentally happen to be Iranian—as agents of Iran. This view is prevalent among Sunnis, irrespective of education or locale.[60]

The second Shi'a group of note is the Islamic Dawa Party. The Dawa was Iraq's first Shi'a Islamic political party, headed by one of its most popular Shi'a clerics, Grand Ayatollah Muhammad Baqir al-Sadr, who was executed by Saddam's regime in 1980. Jaafari, the current Prime Minister, was a member of the party and fled in 1980 amid a fierce crackdown by Saddam's forces against a bloody Dawa Party uprising that began in the late 1970s and was crushed in 1982. The group said that it lost tens of thousands of members in its war against the former Iraqi ruler. Given its immense losses it is not surprising that party members are not particularly forthcoming about truth and reconciliation with the deposed Ba'thists and former regime elements. Dawa is not particularly pro-Coalition, and despite the evisceration of its militant cadre in the 1980s it still has sufficient organizational skills and motivation to wage a campaign of irregular warfare. However, there has been no need for that as Dawa has been fully integrated into the post-Saddam political process.

The third such group is the Supreme Council for the Islamic Revolution in Iraq (SCIRI),[61] also known as the Supreme Assembly of the Islamic Revolution in Iraq (SAIRI), which was formed in Iran in 1982. SCIRI grew out of a breakaway faction of the Dawa Party. Ayatollah Muhammad Baqir al-Hakim led the faction, which left Iraq in 1980 and eventually settled in Iran. Hakim had been a member of Dawa since the 1960s and was imprisoned three times in the 1970s. He established the Mujahideen fil-Iraq, which was renamed the Office for the Islamic Revolution in Iraq in early 1981 and then SCIRI in November 1982. After the Iran-Iraq war, the organization continued to operate with the aim of toppling the regime of Saddam Hussein. SCIRI was directly supported with funds by Tehran and with arms by Iran's Pasdaran (Revolutionary Guard). The movement advocated theocratic rule for Iraq and conducted a low-level, cross-border guerrilla war against the Ba'th regime.

By the late 1990s SCIRI had from 4,000 to 8,000 fighters, composed of Iraqi Shi'a exiles and prisoners of war, operating against the Iraqi military in southern Iraq. Iran's Revolutionary Guard continues to provide weapons and training to the SCIRI militia, the Badr Corps, which changed its name to the Badr Organization soon after the downfall of the former regime in order to portray itself falsely as a social welfare organization. Its open alliance with Iran during the Iran-Iraq war caused enormous damage to SCIRI's credibility inside Iraq. Even within the Shi'a community SCIRI came to be seen, undeservedly, as an Iranian puppet. Its lack of a presence in Iraq was debilitating and the Ba'th regime's intelligence apparatus easily contained whatever influence SCIRI commanded.

Militarily SCIRI performed little better. Torn between two different philosophies of war, the council leadership did not know whether to develop a quasi-regular military force or simply maintain a guerilla warfare or militia capability. This also may have been a reflection of the turmoil existing with the military structure of its patron, Iran, where two rival forces, the regular army and the Revolutionary Guard, clashed over different approaches to war and competed for scarce resources. In any event, Iran's Revolutionary Guard—which became progressively more professional after the end of the Iran-Iraq War—selected and trained Badr units, and strong ties have persisted between the organizations for more than two decades. Indeed, SCIRI participated in the war against Iraq alongside the Guards. Its units were deployed in bases in Iran's western Khuzestan, Ilam and Kerman provinces, and its main training center was located in a Revolutionary Guard center outside Dezful at Vahdati Air Force Base.

The Badr Corps claimed it could field a 15,000-man army. But in contrast to the professionalism and dedication of its trainers, the Iranian Revolutionary Guard, the Badr Corps proved ineffective against the army of Saddam Hussein. It did, however, develop an effective intelligence service and this has helped it consolidate power in post-Saddam Iraq and allowed it to wage a war of assassination against former Ba'th Party regime officials. It is not clear what role Iranian intelligence officials play in this, but it is clear that the Sunnis have shown a profound hatred for the Badr Corps. Many in the latter community view it as the key instrument that Iran is using to finally dominate Iraq. Several Iraqis told me that Faylaq al-Badr (Badr Corps) has provided the Iranian intelligence service with the seventh-floor of the Ministry of Interior. 'Why would they do that?' I would ask. I would then be given pitying looks. My interlocutors would then slowly explain that this was part of the Iranian design to take over Iraq. Unsurprisingly, the Sunnis applaud the insurgents' tactics of gunning for Badr Corps members. Indeed, it seems there are Sunni insurgent groups, including Zarqawi's 'Umar' unit, dedicated primarily to hunting down the corps. Its clandestine paramilitary activities in post-Saddam Iraq have aroused the hatred and fear of many Iraqis, Shi'a and Sunni. As one Iraqi told me, 'It is only able to act in the swaggering manner it does because of the presence of the Coalition forces. Had it not been for that particular fact, we would have exterminated it and its Iranian masters in the country.'[62]

Ideologically SCIRI is committed to the *velayat-e faqih* doctrine prevailing in Iran, which mandates clerical intervention in political affairs. Its strong Iranian links have ensured that some former and current SCIRI leaders and cadres are loyal to the theocratic component of the Islamic Republic. SCIRI representatives take pains to assert they are not interested in establishing a theocracy in Iraq. Spokesmen have the unenviable task of reconciling the organization's ideology with its practical agenda. Recently SCIRI pledged its allegiance to a democratic system in Iraq. One of the council's most erudite and articulate representatives, the UK-based Hamid al-Bayati, said in a May 2003 interview that a Shi'a-led theocracy was inappropriate because it would not fully represent Iraq's diverse communities.[63]

The fourth Shi'a group of note, whose emergence is relatively recent, is the Sadrist movement of Moqtada al-Sadr, which did rebel.[64] Its uprising gave the Coalition authorities considerable trouble in 2003 and 2004 and caused an intra-Shi'a rift in 2005. Moqtada derived much of his legitimacy from his deceased father, Ayatollah Muhammad Sadiq al-Sadr. As a bona fide Iraqi, Ayatollah al-Sadr was the incarnation of the Iraqi nationalist current among the Shi'a clerical establishment. Indeed, the Sadr family has had a long history of political activism. Mullah Sayyid Muhammad al-Sadr was active in the anti-British independence movement along-side Ayatollah Mirza Muhammad Taqi Shirazi in the 1920s. This led the Ba'th regime to view Ayatollah Muhammad Sadiq al-Sadr as a useful counterweight to the Iranian-dominated Shi'a clerical es-tablishment. But Ayatollah al-Sadr had different ideas. He was not interested in being the political puppet of a hated regime. He al-legedly had 'taken receipt' from the Iraqi security services of the bodies of his famous and revolutionary uncle, Muhammad Baqir al-Sadr, and of his activist aunt, Bint al-Huda, following their torture and execution by the regime in 1980.

Ayatollah Muhammad Sadiq al-Sadr was arrested in 1991 after he allegedly came out in support of the Shi'a intifada following the Iraqi defeat in Desert Storm. After his release he was kept under surveillance. He transformed the mosque in Kufa into an anti-regime bastion and began to recruit followers among the des-titute Shi'a of Saddam City, next to Baghdad. Sadiq al-Sadr used the wealth generated by religious taxes and the *sahm imam* (the Imam's share) to establish a widespread charity network for the dispossessed. His experiment did not last long, however. He was assassinated on 17 February 1999, along with his two oldest sons, which precipitated days of rioting in Saddam City. The younger Moqtada went into hiding. Following the overthrow of Saddam he re-emerged and entered the political fray, launching inflammatory anti-US and anti-Coalition tirades during Friday prayers from the pulpit of the mosque in Kufa.[65]

It was against the Coalition forces that Moqtada began his campaign of political mobilization of the masses. Soon after the formation of the IGC in July 2003, he launched into a well-rehearsed attack on its legitimacy. In an extensive interview with Dubai's Al Arabiya Television he dismissed the interviewer's suggestion that all classes of Iraqis were represented in the make-up of the council: 'No, that is not true. Many parties, communities, and currents did not participate in it. Therefore, it does not represent all classes of the people.' Its lack of representation was not only the IGC's problem from Moqtada's perspective: 'It was formed under the direct supervision and flagrant intervention of the United States … So, what is the value of the council? They make decisions and their big one [the United States], so to speak, then comes and contradicts this decision as if nothing has happened.' Moqtada also vehemently denied that he wanted to establish an Islamic state: 'I have not advocated the establishment of an Islamic state. I said that the shariah laws must be implemented, whether there was an Islamic state or not.'[66]

The Sadrist group went to great lengths to allay fears that they wanted to establish a theocratic state in Iraq. A senior Sadrist political official, Sheikh Ali Sumaysim, told the widely read and respected Arab newspaper *Al-Hayah* that 'Islam is our religion and that of the majority in Iraq, and hence it is essential that it should be the primary source for legislation and rules'.[67] He added that while they would prefer to see the emergence of an Islamic state, it was not possible given Iraqi conditions: 'We want to establish an Islamic state because this is our first objective. However, anyone taking a serious look at the Iraqi situation and closely examining the make-up of the Iraqi people and its factions will realize that it is difficult to establish an Islamic state in this country.'[68] Moqtada concluded: 'We are not calling for establishing an Islamic state but we want the Islamic religion to be the source of legislation.'[69]

The emergence of Moqtada al-Sadr caused consternation among the hapless personnel of the CPA. Neither the CPA nor the Bush administration understood that the Sadrist organization was a social movement of the dispossessed. The initial approach to Moqtada, either dismissive or castigating him as a 'bad guy', a 'thug' or a 'hooligan', simply denoted a lack of understanding of the social environment in this devastated country. There is a clear class and social basis to Moqtada al-Sadr's insurgency. He caters to the most dispossessed elements within the long-suffering Shi'a community. His constituency is the young disgruntled men of towns such as Sadr City, where the unemployment rate hovers around 70 percent, and Kut, which faces a similar unemployment problem.[70] Even if the Shi'a did not welcome the advancing Coalition forces with open arms as was promised by the civilian architects of the war and their exiled Iraqi advisers, without a doubt the Coalition did have considerable goodwill among many of the Shi'a in the early days of the occupation.[71] My own analysis of the situation on the ground and the statements of various Shi'a clerics confirm the view that the Shi'a were prepared to challenge the authority and legitimacy of the Coalition if the gap between its promises and its achievements was too great. And the Shi'a political leader best prepared or able to undertake that challenge was none other than Moqtada al-Sadr. As Hasan Zirkani, a pro-Sadr cleric in Sadr City, bluntly stated in a November 2003 prayer meeting: 'We had hoped that some of the problems might have vanished by now.'[72] What Zirkani was referring to included lack of law and order, rampant unemployment, lack of basic services in Shi'a urban areas and Coalition disregard for the cultural and societal norms of the population.[73]

The Moqtada phenomenon is not only religious but also populist. Thus, attacking his nonexistent religious credentials simply because he is young and has yet to attain a level of religious learning within the Shi'a clerical establishment is beside the point, a waste of time, effort and resources. During the summer of 2003, while Moqtada had shown himself to be disdainful and critical of the CPA and of the Iraqis on the Governing Council, he was shrewd enough to avoid inciting violence. Instead, he focused his energies on revitalizing his father's extensive political network among the poor Shi'a and building up the power of the young clerics who were loyal to him in Sadr City. This neighborhood is the model of Shi'a disenfranchisement. Its people missed out on Iraq's days of wealth in the 1970s and 1980s because the regime devoted few resources to building up the infrastructure or the public services of a suburb it viewed with unalloyed suspicion as a hotbed of Shi'a radicalism.

While all of Baghdad suffered during the decade-long era of sanctions, Saddam City suffered the most. Its families are falling apart, its children malnourished, stunted and ignorant. More ominously its young men are angry and volatile. Their disgruntlement increased enormously during Operation Iraqi Freedom, when they fell prey to the depredations of Saddam's Fedayeen, who invaded the neighborhood and bullied its inhabitants. The young men took up arms but their arsenal could not match that of the regime's thugs. Unsurprisingly, when the war officially ended in April they flocked by the hundreds to join the militia forces of local clerics or those set up by the major Shi'a political movements. Many who have had to conceal fervent displays of faith are now free to do so openly to profess support for their clerics and for an Islamic-oriented form of government. The Shi'a clerical establishment sees considerable benefit in mobilizing the raw power that Sadr City represents. Indeed, clerics from the *hawza* (schools for traditional Islamic studies) are competing with those linked to Moqtada in the provision of services and security in exchange for loyalty.

A cadre of young clerics who are devoted to Moqtada and his movement act as the backbone, or religious noncommissioned officers, of the budding movement. They have emerged as the decisive political force in that slum and in other cities in the south that were sympathetic to Moqtada.

The Shi'a clerical establishment sprang into political life from the instant the regime collapsed. They restored municipal services in many places, paid salaries and brought stability, particularly in southern cities like Karbala and Najaf. Religious and political indoctrination were also promoted, but they were not particularly friendly to Coalition forces or their presumed goals. An activist cleric in Karbala, 'Abdel Mahdi Salami, did not mince words in a sermon in May 2003: 'Muslims, beware! The foreigner is trying to enter the mind of the Muslims with false ideas. He is trying to take religious leaders out of society and to build walls between religious leaders and the people.'[74] Abdul Jawad al-Issawi, a twenty-two-year old cleric, wields immense power in impoverished Kut, overseeing a network of social services, maintaining security, collecting taxes and dispensing justice—all independent of the US-backed local government. He said: 'We have told everyone from the start that only failure awaits the occupiers if they try to interfere in how we run our lives. Occupation is humiliation, and we cannot accept humiliation. We never trusted the Americans and we never will.'[75]

Moqtada also created his own Jaish al-Mahdi militia. This was not an original step in itself in a country where militias were proliferating in an atmosphere of violence and menace. However, he cleverly argued that his group would be unarmed and devote itself to social work in the neighborhoods. The members of the militia merely hid their arms, which they had acquired from looted Iraqi military stores, at their homes. The ammunition was supplied by the central offices of the Sadrist movement and militiamen were able to drill and practice their marksmanship in the numerous garbage-filled open fields that dot Sadr City. The militia was made up largely of disgruntled and unemployed young Shi'a men who would stand at street corners for hours on end every day. 'I am a volunteer, I will do whatever Sadr tells us to do. I'm not sure what the aim of the army is or when we will fight, but I will follow Sadr's order,' said an unemployed twenty-nine-year old local.[76] That was precisely the point—many were aimless young men seeking an identity and direction in their lives. A representative of Ayatollah Sistani in Sadr City echoed this: 'Young Shi'a are looking for an identity and Sadr's call for a jihad has moved them.'[77] I met many of these young men in the streets of Sadr City in November 2003 and March 2004. Some were hanging around literally doing nothing; others were huddled around a pool table incongruously placed outside a shop. Eventually they would be enticed to attend Friday sermons, after which their entry into the movement began. Few of the 'rank and file' within the lower levels of the militia—often young illiterate kids who had migrated from rural areas into urban centers—had any training whatsoever in arms or small-unit tactics.

The political and socioeconomic situation in Iraq after the invasion provided the perfect opportunity for an emerging social movement to herald its entry into the political process. The Shi'a south was seething with discontent in late summer 2003. It started as anger over the manifestly poor socioeconomic conditions in the south; it quickly became political. Shi'a expressed considerable anger over fuel shortages and the lack of electricity in an oil-rich country. In the words of one resident of Saleh Qasr, near Basra: 'We haven't had any electricity since the war. The British promised us everything, and they have given us nothing. We were happy when the Coalition forces got rid of a big tyrant, but if they don't help us, we are all going to become like Fallujah people.'[78] Protests over the dismal economic conditions broke out in the Shi'a cities of Kut, Amarah and Basra in early 2004. Many of the demonstrators were former military personnel and ordinary workers distraught at the lack of employment opportunities and the rampant corruption in the new Iraq. As one Kut resident said: 'I was a policeman before the war. When I went back to rejoin my station, they said I had to pay $150. Every single department is asking for bribes, and they are all followers of Saddam. People have gone without jobs for a year, and they are ready to tear down buildings.'[79] Low-level violence erupted in the southern part of the country as Shi'a militia groups vied for power and fought each other and Ba'thist remnants, while vigilantes meted out street-style justice and organized crime groups to engage in kidnapping and smuggling.[80]

On 9 October 2003 several hundred of Moqtada's followers ambushed a patrol of 2nd Squadron, 2nd Armored Cavalry, in Sadr City. This put into doubt several months of civic activity and local construction projects undertaken by the regiment, the 2nd Squadron of which I visited in November 2003 and March 2004. The next day three mortar shells landed on Camp Marlboro, the dilapidated and peculiar-looking cigarette factory that serves as 2nd Squadron's headquarters. (The roof of the building provides an excellent panoramic view of Sadr City.) The lieutenant colonel in charge of the squadron sent a company of tanks rumbling through the slum in a show of force. The Sadrists upped the ante by occupying the building used by Sadr City's US-sponsored and newly created district council.[81]

Moqtada suddenly backed down in late October 2003. He softened his tone towards the Coalition, saying he was an enemy of Saddam Hussein and was willing to work with the US occupiers to move Iraq more quickly towards self-governance. This move was only tactical, though, and came in the wake of the arrest of some of his followers by US forces and the lukewarm response to his call to establish a government independent of the foreign occupiers. The response of the senior clerics was to advise the Shi'a population to be patient, an implicit criticism of Moqtada's rabble-rousing.[82]

In a long interview with Lebanese Hezbollah's television station, Al-Manar, Moqtada complained bitterly about being harassed by the Coalition because of his strident opposition to the occupation of Iraq. But in a tone of injured innocence he also claimed: 'I oppose the occupation, but in a peaceful way. I do not advocate violence, resistance, or anything of the kind. I call for peaceful demonstrations, which fall under freedom and democracy, and the formation of an army that is equipped only with the weapon of faith.'[83] On the Jaish al-Mahdi, he argued: 'I established the army for the sake of enjoining what is right and forbidding what is wrong; second, to combat corruption and terrorism in Iraq by peaceful means; and third, to protect holy places, religious authorities, and leaders whoever they may be.'[84] In the light of the chaos engulfing Iraq, it made eminent sense to create some form of force to help maintain law and order, protect holy places and fight terrorism. It is not clear, however, how Moqtada intended to do this with an unarmed militia, as he claimed it would be. In any case, Moqtada, who had serious political aspirations, was not about to create a force armed only with faith when other groups or political parties in the country had their own well-trained forces.

But Moqtada was impatient, saying in mid-December 2003: 'The situation [in Iraq] cannot be stabilized except when power is returned to the Iraqi people.'[85] By the end of March 2004—and to everyone's surprise—significant elements of the Shi'a community rose in open rebellion against the Coalition when the firebrand Moqtada unleashed his militia against it. Suddenly the Coalition was faced with the unsavory prospect of a two-front war. The precipitating factors of the Shi'a insurgency were again the mistakes and failed policies of the CPA, but as with all conflicts there were underlying causes for the uprising.[86]

The factors underpinning Moqtada's revolt seemed simple enough. For months as he built up his organization the Coalition and the CPA had debated what to do about the Sadrist movement, particularly after Moqtada's sermons began to sound like they were

preaching violence against the United States. In March 2004, when
the CPA decided to close down Moqtada's newspaper and arrest
one of his chief aides, Moqtada concluded that the United States
was going to move decisively against him. He decided to preempt
this by calling out his supporters, arming them and throwing them
into battle against the Coalition forces.

During two days of patrolling with members of the 2nd Armored Cavalry Regiment in early March 2004 I got a full flavor of
the rising tide of anti-US sentiment among the young, especially
among young men who claimed that they were members of Jaish
al-Mahdi.[87] By way of contrast, on my previous visit to Sadr City in
November 2003 the inhabitants were still quite friendly and open.
This was despite a serious contretemps between some of them
and US military personnel in October 2003 that had led to overt
expressions of hostility among segments of the district's inhabitants.[88] Moqtada's launching of a revolt in spring 2004 coincided
with the immense difficulties that the Coalition was facing *vis-à-vis*
the Sunni insurgency in the center of Iraq.

Moqtada adopted a policy of challenging the occupation and
backing down after he had made his point or when he felt that
the situation would tip decisively against him. In summer 2004
he went back on the verbal offensive. In an extensive sermon in
Kufa on 30 July 2004 Moqtada ripped into the interim government, warning them about the dearth of services that had beset
the country, notably the lack of electricity, potable water and fuel.
He advised the government to renounce the occupation and the
Iraqi people to demand their rights by demonstrations, sit-ins
and strikes:

Let us together condemn what the occupation forces are doing. Let us
proclaim disobedience to the occupier ... Know, too, that jihad against the
unbelievers is both military and ideological, for their war is both military
and ideological. So we must struggle against them ideologically also. They

do not want our religion to endure ... We have seen over the space of many years the overall policy of wars, occupation, and invasions that America has followed in Iraq or in the other countries reached by America's weapons that spare neither young nor old. For they bear hatred against peace and Islam, and their souls love domination through bloodshed, expulsion, and other means approved neither by religion nor reason.[89]

Israel comes in for a great deal of opprobrium, a tactic popular with Iraqi Arabs, Sunni or Shi'a, because many believe the war was undertaken for the benefit of Israel:

See how Israel is sucking up the wrath of noble resistance fighters and converting it into infighting between sons of the same people. It does so by planting traitors and spreading love of power in order to consolidate its imperialistic planning and spread beyond Palestine by any means ... All of this is increasing the tension in the Middle East. If (America) claims that it wants to spread peace in the Middle East, why doesn't it threaten (Israel) with occupation and war? Or is it only equal to dealing with the Arabs and Muslims and fears and even stands in awe of Israel? America supports Israel in all its decisions and its attacks against our oppressed people, the people of oppressed Palestine. America is for violations against the Arab and Islamic countries, such as Lebanon and Palestine.[90]

Strengths and weaknesses of Moqtada's movement.   Moqtada's revolt has won support and admiration among Sunni insurgents, who have plastered his picture on the walls of Sunni-dominated towns. This would have been unheard of much before late 2005. Members of Jaish al-Mahdi have begun to cooperate with the Sunni insurgents and there are rumors that a number of Moqtada's militiamen tried to infiltrate Fallujah.[91] The evidence of mutual Sunni and Shi'a sympathy has evoked memories of the 1920 revolt, when the two communities cooperated in their rising against the British. However, while there have been signs of cooperation in the insurgency, it has not been at a serious level.

Moqtada has undeniably gained influence with many Shi'a be-cause of his perceived courage in standing up to the Coalition. Whether he did this in self-defense or because he saw it as an op-portune time to act, his defiance struck a chord with the Shi'a. By late March 2004 many within that community had begun to believe that the 30 June agreement to transfer sovereignty to Iraqis was bo-gus and that Iraq would continue to remain under barely concealed US control beyond that date. A Shi'a radio outlet reported: 'The supposed restoration of national sovereignty, of course, should be preceded by an end to US occupation. The plan, however, en-trenches the occupation and legitimizes its presence.'[92]

Nonetheless, Moqtada was unable to foment a widespread re-volt among the Shi'a.[93] Many were simply terrified of his politi-cal vision of an Islamic government ruled by politicized clerics. Moreover, while his pugnacious statements calling upon Iraqis to launch a nationwide revolt and telling the Coalition to leave have allowed him to make some headway towards becoming a more na-tionally recognized leader, this has not been enough. He has yet to transcend the bounds of his own uncouth constituency. The class distinction between his followers and the inhabitants of Najaf and Karbala, where his militia chose to make a stand, is evident in the anger with which the petty bourgeoisie and commercial class of these towns reacted to the downturn in business occasioned by the fighting. In the aftermath of the collapse of the Ba'th regime, these two holy cities both witnessed a massive revival in commercial ac-tivity and construction of housing and hotels as a result of the surge in pilgrim traffic from Iran and further afield in the Shi'a world.

While there was tension between the native Iraqis of these towns and the influx of richer Iranians (many of the former blamed the latter for the dramatic increase in prices and rents), such pres-sures were subordinated to the fact that many locals were either making money or benefiting from the economic upsurge.[94] It was thus unlikely that Moqtada would gain much influence in that city. As one Najaf resident put it: 'Moqtada al-Sadr does not represent most Shiites. He's too young to lead us. He doesn't yet have the wisdom of a leader.'[95] Unlike many Iraqi cities, Najaf had electricity twenty-four hours a day, relative security and thriving commerce. Much of this stability was traceable to the influence of the senior clerics and to the presence of 1st Battalion, 7th Marines, which enjoyed good relations with local leaders from the moment it arrived.[96] Many Najafis began to fiercely resent the presence of Mahdist militia. The fighting there between US forces and the militia killed innocent people, caused property damage, and suffocated commerce in the city.[97]

Finally, if the Maoist adage that political power grows out of the barrel of the gun is true, then Moqtada has the least number of barrels in Iraq. His Jaish al-Mahdi is the weakest militia in the country; it does not begin to compare with the militias of SCIRI (the Iranian trained and commanded Badr Organization), the Dawa Party and Iraqi Hezbollah. While Jaish al-Mahdi has several members of the former Iraqi army, it also numbers many young men who have few or no military skills (including those who had avoided the draft under the former regime by disappearing from sight).

Tactics of Jaish al-Mahdi. During the firefights of April 2004 many outraged but inexperienced young Shi'a men heeded Moqtada's repeated call to arms and were simply thrown into the fray. Thus it is not surprising that their casualties have been very high, despite the fact that the militia deliberately chose to confront US forces in urban environments of holy significance. Some of Jaish al-Mahdi's 'commanders' knew well that they had no option but to fight in the time-honored manner of irregular forces. As one thirty-eight-year-old 'commander' said: 'When the Americans advance, we harass and retreat, fire from new positions and then retreat again. If the attacking force is too big, we call for support.'[98] But Jaish al-Mahdi could call upon no support other than ill-trained RPG and mortar teams. This is why the militia sought and received some training and advice from Sunni insurgents. It is unclear whether this cooperative relationship survived the growing sectarian violence between Sunni and Shi'a over the past two years.

While it is an incontrovertible fact that urban warfare is tough for conventional soldiers—most armies avoid it if they can—it is also tough for insurgents, particularly inexperienced ones. An insurgent force that chooses to make a stand in the 'urban jungle' has to be well trained and dug in. It has to have well-constructed and concealed and easily accessible means of egress from fighting positions so that it can fall back (e.g. tunnels connecting buildings). It has to have very good intelligence, which means that its soldiers have to be from the city or neighborhood they will be fighting in or have a sophisticated network of human intelligence available to them. Such a force needs liberal quantities of weapons and ammunition and, finally, must be imbued with a tremendous level of cohesion and self-sacrifice.

While many of the Sadrist militiamen showed great courage and spirit and were well-armed, they were clearly not prepared for intensive and extensive, block-by-block urban combat (while the insurgents in Fallujah were). Many were not from either Karbala or Najaf but had been shipped in from elsewhere, and were thus unfamiliar with the lay of the land and did not have good relations with the locals. Indeed, they managed to alienate many of the latter as a result of the physical destruction and disruption of commercial activity they caused in the two cities. Finally, the Sadrists had no sniper teams—a force multiplier in an urban environment—while most had little training in light weapons or instruction in small-unit tactics against opposing forces, and had not had time to dig adequate defensive positions in those towns.

Even as the United States and the Iraqi authorities insisted that Moqtada disarm his militia, the cleric and his followers were quietly and efficiently extending their control over Sadr City, which it polices effectively, directing traffic and arresting criminals and drug dealers.[99] The Coalition's call on Moqtada to disarm his militia or integrate it into the official security forces was met with a peculiar riposte: 'I cannot dismantle it, because it is not I who commands it [the militia] but the Mahdi [i.e. the Hidden Imam].'[100]

In July 2004 it looked as though relations between Moqtada on the one hand and the United States and interim Iraqi government on the other would settle down. Sheikh Raad al-Kadumi, one of Moqtada's representatives in Baghdad , said: 'If the Allawi government dispatches its duties properly … we will be happy to cooperate.'[101] This conciliatory announcement came only days after Moqtada himself issued a statement from his headquarters in Najaf, labeling Iyad Allawi's government 'illegitimate' and vowing 'to continue resisting oppression and occupation to our last drop of blood'.[102] The battles between the Mahdists and the Coalition in Najaf also disrupted commerce and the flow of pilgrims.[103]

In early July 2004 Sadr City seemed to be heading for another showdown between the Sadrists and the Coalition. A truce that had held for nearly a month began to fray under Moqatda's constant political exhortations and attacks on the newly formed interim government, which he deemed 'illegitimate'. By then he had consolidated control over much of the slum with the help of his clerical network and his militia. The Jaish al-Mahdi continued to police the neighborhood and pursued criminals and 'immoral' people. A Mahdist militia commander, Ammar al-Sa'adi, said: 'The Iraqi police are so weak, they have perhaps 10 per cent of the power in our community. When people ask them for help, they must ask us to help them. We have excellent relations, because almost all of the police are from Sadr City. They are the same as us. And a few of them are also members of al-Mahdi.'[104] In Sadr City in summer 2004, hostile jeering mobs, largely of rock-throwing young children and youths, would often greet US soldiers on patrol or trying to help in the reconstruction of the decaying neighborhood.[105] This, of course, was an improvement on the gunfire that had often been directed towards US troops. In fall 2004 even the rock-throwing had disappeared, replaced by indifference or sullen looks.

By late 2004 the bitter military confrontation between the Sadrists and US forces had transformed itself into a battle over hearts and minds. The United States worked frantically to reconstruct the dismal and decaying suburb of Sadr City, spending millions on what military units refer to as SWET—sewerage, water, electricity and trash disposal. The Sadrists, for their part, continued to provide social and spiritual welfare, mass politics and policing. This organizational development allowed the Sadrists to emerge in full force in summer 2005, as I shall briefly mention in the conclusion. But as Karim Abed, a Sadr City cab-driver, pointed out, it was easier for the locals to interact with the Sadrist officials: 'With the Mahdi Army, we understand their language. If they don't do something for us, we'll complain to the Sadr office. How do we complain to the Americans? Whom do we complain to?'[106]

Intra-Shi'a conflict.   The Sadrists spent the remainder of 2004 reinforcing their organizational capabilities, expanding their social programs, building up considerable loyalty and leverage among the poorer Shi'a inhabitants, and protecting Shi'a against the murderous rampages of extremist Sunni Islamists. The movement's clerics have become masters of political mobilization, and many who were released from detention returned with a renewed vigor to continue their political and social activities. Jaish al-Mahdi's capabilities are still those of a poorly trained militia, but it has new arms and brand-new green military uniforms. The intrepid Anthony Shadid wrote a vivid description in late August 2005 of the maturation of the movement. Shadid relates that the newly freed aides were surprised by the dramatic organizational changes: 'Clearer lines of communication, a more structured hierarchy and a sprawling social services network.'[107] The movement's new, two-story stucco building boasts floodlights, air conditioners and a cluster of seven 'agitprop-style' megaphones on the roof.[108] The movement has come a long way, and its growing strength has allowed it to play an increasingly confident and assertive role in local and national politics, often in opposition to Shi'a groups it disdains.

The significant victory of the unified Shi'a slate, the United Iraqi Alliance, in the elections of January 2005 may have given people the erroneous impression that the Shi'a form a monolithic bloc. However, considerable tensions exist within the Shi'a community. The key conflict is that which pitted Moqtada against the Shi'a hierarchy and later against the Shi'a political parties returned from exile. Moqtada's differences with Sistani were over politics, resources and national identity. Initially, following the downfall of the Saddam regime, Moqtada castigated the senior clerics in Iraq because of their political quietism, particularly in the face of the results of the foreign occupation of the country. Of course, this was not a line of attack that he was able to keep up for long because Sistani did rouse himself to checkmate Coalition plans for Iraq. Indeed, Sistani may have succeeded too well from Moqtada's point of view. In this context one could argue that Moqtada's periodic confrontations with the Coalition were partly a means by which to take the limelight away from the senior cleric. Moqtada's political and mobilizational activities among the Shi'a, which brought him into confrontation with the senior clerics of Najaf, were designed to enlarge not only his recruitment base, but also that of his finances, to compete with that of well-established endowments such as those of Sistani.

Sistani, as has been pointed out, has considerable financial resources. His association consists of thousand of members and activists who operate a vast network of social services—from schools (*madras* or *hawza*) to public endowments (*waqf*), from hospitals to libraries that extend throughout the south of the country. As the most senior of the Shi'a *ulama* in Najaf's Hawza al-Ilmiyyah, or major seminary center, the revered grand ayatollah controls most of the seminaries and has a large following of students in Iraq. These seminaries are funded through donations, which since May 2003 have grown larger through the influx of foreign capital to Iraq's southern regions and of contributions from pilgrims and Shi'a throughout the world.[109]

Finally, Iraqi Shi'a Arab nationalism is evident in the disdain shown towards Ayatollah Sistani, who is Iranian and is suspected by young Iraqi clerics of showing little interest in the plight or future of Iraq. He is also perceived to favor Iranian *tullab* (students) over homegrown Iraqi *tullab* in the seminaries of Najaf.[110] Indeed, among the reasons behind Moqtada's distaste for Sistani is that the latter is Iranian by birth.[111] In this context, we must also view Moqtada's uprising as a struggle within the Shi'a hierarchy—waged largely between the 'nativist' Iraqi Shi'a such as the Sadrists on the one hand and the returning exiles on the other—for political and socioeconomic paramountcy over the Shi'a population, and thus by extension (because the Shi'a are the majority) over the future of Iraq itself.[112] Whether Moqtada expected a wider rallying of the Shi'a population to his side is not clear, but he knew that no Shi'a leader or organization could openly take sides with the United States/Coalition against him without losing legitimacy or being considered an open collaborator.

Many Iraqi Shi'a have also been embittered by the manifest political and socioeconomic failings of the Islamic Republic of Iran and even by their own experiences while in exile in that country.

Iranians do not like Arabs, even if they are Shi'a. Many Iraqi exiles return the disdain with equal fervor and could not wait to leave Iran when Saddam fell from power. Some returned to their homeland with tales of woe suffered at the hands of 'arrogant' Iranians. But many seem devoted to Iran and are pro-Iranian, and have accordingly been accused of following an Iranian agenda in Iraq. This is where it is pertinent to speak of the deep differences between the native Sadrist movement and the returning exiles represented by Dawa and SCIRI.

There was considerable class and political tension between Moqtada and his movement on one side and the Hakims and their movement, SCIRI, on the other. The former represented the Shi'a who had stayed in Iraq and borne the brunt of Saddam's megalomania and brutal tactics. The Hakims represented those anti-Saddam Iraqi Shi'a of the commercial middle class who had managed to go into exile in the relative safety of Iran. Moqtada also claimed that SCIRI's military arm, the Badr Corps, had promised to stage an uprising in 1999 against the regime after his father, Ayatollah Muhammad al-Sadr, was assassinated: 'After this happened, we lost trust in them. Since the people don't trust him, I also do not trust him.'[113] SCIRI returns the dislike and contempt. 'He's a young man who hasn't finished his religious studies. He's trying to use his family name to get ahead,' said Ali al-Abudi, a spokesman for SCIRI.[114]

Then there is the class difference. Moqtada represents the lower Shi'a classes, the poorest of the poor—the *mustazafin* (dispossessed).[115] The tensions between the two groups, which was complicated by the deadlock over the constitution, boiled over in August 2005. SCIRI's surprising call for weak central government, federalism and a greater share of the oil resources for the south was fiercely opposed by the Sadrists who saw it as an Iranian design. Its implications for the Shi'a denizens of the center—particularly in Baghdad, where much of Moqtada's constituency is—were understood by the Sadrists. As Ellen Knickmeyer and Anthony Shadid point out in dramatic fashion, over the course of three days the Sadrists showed the power that they could bring to bear.[116] After clashes with the Badr Organization in Najaf, Moqtada's armed followers flooded the streets in Baghdad and six other cities. Twenty-one members of parliament and three cabinet ministers loyal to him suspended their work in protest. They also organized some of the biggest demonstrations in recent years; ostensibly protests over government services, they were effectively shows of strength.

To complicate matters, interesting alliances, which cut across class and sectarian considerations, have emerged as a result of these deep Shi'a differences. During the era of Saddam Hussein the Shi'a may not have been in the upper echelons of the regime's elite, but they did constitute a large part of the middle class in Iraq and were tied to the state. Even though the middle class in Iraq has collapsed as a material sector in terms of their salaries, as mentioned above, it exists in the sense of the values and beliefs held by a group of Iraqis who consider themselves middle class. While it is correct to argue that years of sanctions have eroded the clear-cut lines between classes, it is still true to say that deep fault lines exist between the haves and the have-nots. It is equally clear that the most obvious group of have-nots, even if not defined in sectarian terms, are the Shi'a dispossessed, who are gravitating towards radical religious politics.[117] For the middle class the prospect of a theocracy is unappealing and the antics of puritanical firebrands who have sought to shut down restaurants, bars and movie theaters have alarmed the professional classes of the major urban centers.[118] In this context, while the Shi'a state middle class has little in common with their dispossessed brethren in the urban centers, most are Iraqi Arab nationalists and resent immensely the 'Iranified' returnees.[119] This is a stance they share with the Sadrists. Both these groups share this disdain for the 'Iranians' with the Sunni Arabs and Sunni Turkmen, for whom the 'Iranians' have taken over much of the machinery of government in Iraq.[120]

In conclusion, the insurgency in Iraq has suffered from the contending national identities of the Kurds and the Shi'a. The insurgents never thought that the Kurds could be seen as part of the so-called national liberation movement, or *muqawamah*. There was some regret among nationalist insurgents that the Shi'a had not joined in the 'national resistance', particularly when it seemed that such a possibility existed in spring 2004. But apart from the fact that Sunni extremists managed to alienate the Shi'a by their terrorist activities, there was never a chance that the Shi'a or the Kurds would join in fighting the Coalition presence. For both groups the overthrow of Saddam was a liberation from tyranny, a chance to express their identity—indeed, to imprint it on the state—and to bring about a redistribution of resources in their favor. The Coalition facilitated this, and as long as that international presence did not act as a hindrance there was no reason to take up arms. Of course there were issues within each community over the rightful distribution of resources, political and economic. This is one of the reasons for conflict between the Sadrists and SCIRI.

The nonparticipation of the Shi'a and the Kurds, which together comprise almost 80 percent of the population, in the insurgency has significantly benefited US efforts in Iraq. The Kurds could not be expected to join an insurgency against the very forces that protected them for more than a decade and then liberated them from the potential reimposition of Saddam's tyranny. They know full well that the Coalition did all this for them primarily out of self-interest, but they made the strategic decision to throw in their lot totally with their liberators. Moreover, the Kurds do not care about Iraq; they care about Kurdistan. They are not going to fight to throw off a foreign presence that has allowed—indeed, encouraged—them to gain as much as possible in post-Saddam Iraq.

The Shi'a are a more complicated issue. As I discovered in my tours of duty in Iraq, the manifest failure of the Shi'a to overthrow Saddam themselves and to see it done by others was a huge source of embarrassment and dismay. For many or indeed most of them the foreign presence turned very quickly from liberation to occupation. But many chose to work through the Coalition in order to consolidate their power. Why fight the hateful presence in any case, when it was bending over backwards to accommodate your emergence onto the political scene? Moreover, it was easier for Coalition forces to deal with the threats posed by the remnants of the former regime. Indeed, the newly emergent Shi'a parties and organizations simply did not have the capabilities or organization to handle such a formidable insurgency. And nor were the Shi'a united; deep differences existed between them over the nature of the post-Saddam state, the characteristics of Iraqi nationalism and the distribution of resources.

It is in this context that one must view the opposition mounted by the Sadrists against Iraqi returnees (particularly those exiles coming back from Iran). The Sadrists constitute a social movement of the disenfranchised but increasingly mobilized and politically aware Shi'a lower classes. They are fighting not to maintain or restore privileges, as are the Sunni insurgents, but to acquire privileges that had hitherto been denied them. They do, however, share Sunni fears of the dilution of Iraq's Arab identity. While the nonparticipation of the Kurds and Shi'a in the insurgency has been beneficial to the US counter-insurgency campaign at a military level, the convoluted political evolution of both communities and their power in post-Saddam Iraq has complicated the overall US effort immensely, as will be discussed in the next chapter.

IDEOLOGY, POLITICS AND FAILURE TO EXECUTE

THE US COUNTER-INSURGENCY CAMPAIGN

'Great nations do not have small wars,' Arthur Wellesley, the Duke of Wellington, is reputed to have said. If true, it is a surprisingly inept remark from the victor of Waterloo. Indeed, Wellington had played a role in and observed the impact of a vicious guerrilla or small war on a great power, namely the French imbroglio in fighting the brutal counter-insurgency campaign against the thoroughly roused Spanish population. Moreover, as he said this his own country was about to embark on a major series of 'small wars' for much of the course of the nineteenth century, during the long reign of Queen Victoria. The United States became a great power in the mid-nineteenth century and has fought its share of 'small wars', within its borders, against Mexico, and in the Philippines and Central America. From the mid-twentieth century its focus was major conventional wars and its armed forces were designed to wage and win such conflicts. Yet in the same time frame it has also found itself either conducting or helping local allies wage long, bitter counter-insurgency campaigns. The United States is clearly no novice at fighting or helping allies fight small wars.[1] It has a wealth of experience, as a victor and a loser. But this experience has not stood it in sustained good stead in the Iraqi irregular campaign.

So why has it done so poorly in Iraq to date? Some may become indignant and retort angrily that the United States has not done badly in the campaign, as have the numerous officers who have written e-mails or given off-the-record interviews to journalists in which they have uniformly claimed that the US military has won every single engagement against the insurgents, and that the latter simply cannot match the training, fire-power, equipment and dedication of the selfless US forces. Indeed, from the vantage point of fall 2005 US troops have improved dramatically their tactics, techniques and procedures. But ultimately all of this could be beside the point in a counter-insurgency campaign. Small wars are not primarily or merely about winning battles. They are about winning the political fight and not necessarily or mainly by 'kinetic methods', a US military term for military action. The US may well win the counter-insurgency campaign in Iraq through sheer attrition of the insurgent forces. But it will not be a graceful victory. The Iraqi insurgents are not the Viet Cong, yet after three years the United States still cannot be certain of any meaningful victory.

The US counter-insurgency campaign in Iraq deserves a complete study of its own (as does the corresponding campaign in Afghanistan). The purpose of this chapter is to argue that US policy and the counter-insurgency campaign have played a key role in the outbreak and perpetuation of the insurgency. In previous chapters I argued that factors internal to the Sunni community led to the eruption of violence. In this I address how the external factor—the United States—added fuel to the fire. I make no explicit claim in this chapter to propose solutions to US counter-insurgency failings (although the negative aspects I highlight should put into stark relief what we could refer to as 'worst practices')[2] because this important issue deserves considerable study.

The counter-insurgency in Iraq has been the subject of considerable discussion in the United States, in the open and classified realms. The primary focus of these debates is the efficacy or lack thereof of the counter-insurgency effort. Most observers, including this author, lean towards the view that there have been serious problems and they must be remedied. However, I will not be discussing this angle here. It is a vast topic and would require extensive analysis of military campaign plans, and of operational and tactical after-action reports (AARs). Instead, the approach will be to address the question of how bad or incoherent policy and counter-insurgency approaches further inflame and perpetuate insurgencies. My goal is to point out that bad or inefficacious policy choices and counter-insurgency approaches drive up the cost enormously. However, this is not the same as saying that counter-insurgency lasts a long time. The historical evidence shows that, as in the cases of the British in Malaya and the French in Algeria, even if and when you do succeed in devising an effective counter-insurgency plan, success either takes a long time (the British won in 1960) or is not guaranteed (the French won militarily but lost politically).[3] To simplify the argument that bad policy and counter-insurgency practices, as opposed to 'best practices', inflame insurgencies, and to understand how they do so (at least with respect to the Iraqi case), I have developed a three-tiered conceptual framework.

First, there is the problem of adopting a rigid and inflexible ideological approach and of continuing to see the world through such a lens. But we need to take a step back. This war was about ideas, as George Packer points out in his excellent analysis of its genesis: 'The Iraq War started as a war of ideas, and to understand how and why America came to be in Iraq, one has to trace their origins.'[4] But the ideas were not all that mattered. Most states or governments begin a counter-insurgency campaign with an unbending ideological formulation and approach, one of the most insidious impacts of which—and which trickles down to the operational and tactical levels—is the refusal to face reality and accept that an insurgency has erupted. Arguing that the insurgency is made up of regime dead-enders or foreign terrorists who cannot possibly have the support of any 'sane' element of the populace may actually boost the violence. The British in Malaya and Kenya (and, incidentally, during the Iraqi revolt of 1920; see pp. 323–4), and the French in Vietnam and Algeria suffered this problem.

But the above problem is a 'minor' failing compared to an entrenched three-tiered, manifestly ideological theology adopted by the senior policy-makers responsible for the Bush administration's Iraq transformation project: democratic transformation, 'Sunniphobia,' and 'Shi'aphilia'. There is nothing wrong with wanting to see a country that had suffered the ravages of tyranny for most of its existence transformed into a democratic polity. It is unclear, however, whether those who promoted this transformation actually fully believed in it. Moreover, even if they did believe in it, we know not whether they actually prepared for it. Unsurprisingly, the Iraqis and others were skeptical, and their skepticism increased as the political dynamics of the country unfolded. For the Sunnis the US invasion was not liberation, nor was it designed to deliver a democracy in which the rights of the communities would be respected. This perception received further impetus by pronounced, seemingly anti-Sunni patterns of behavior and policies applied by the United States. It is odd that two mutually incompatible tenets—bringing the joys and benefits of democracy to a whole nation, and the marginalization of one of that nation's communities—could coexist. By the same token, there was considerable concern to ensure that Kurdish rights would be protected under a federal system. It was necessary from the very beginning to project a determination that the rights of all the minority groups were going to be protected and guaranteed under the rubric of democratic transformation. Moreover, the Sunnis needed to be shown from the outset that their adherence to the notion of a centralized state was obsolete. To this end they should have been engaged from the first. Instead they were marginalized as the state was seemingly reconstructed along central lines, and in the hands of their 'enemies'.

Second, there was a failure to implement the basics of state rebuilding in the wake of conflict. Moves to implement effective democratic governance and restoration of basic services were tardy, shoddy, *ad hoc* or nonexistent. The failure to prevent the chaos that ensued after the collapse of the regime, and to promote the promised restoration of basic services and reconstruction, contributed to the disdain and contempt with which Iraqis viewed their 'liberation'.[5]

Third, there is the US military's failure to have an effectively prepared counter-insurgency strategy. The reasons are numerous but the culprit is primarily the organizational or military culture, defined here as those values or beliefs that promote a conventional-warfare mindset to such an extent that little or no consideration is given to the study and effective preparation for the prosecution of small wars. Numerous analysts have addressed this issue in great detail and with profound originality.[6] Why the US military adheres to a particular mindset that promotes conventional warfare has been and continues to be studied. The key question here is what is the impact on the ground when the military is faced with an insurgency when it is prepared neither organizationally nor in terms of frame of mind of the officer corps? In simple terms it means that the United States will do badly. But that is not the only negative result. The military will make the situation worse for itself by relying on conventional 'kinetic' methods to deal with the situation it faces. Its actions—born of a lack of understanding of this type of warfare and magnified by its frustrations—will further alienate the population and reinforce the insurgency. Of course a military can learn, adapt and change. But will these changes be *ad hoc* and incremental or will they be extensive changes that affect the organizational culture and mindset?

These three structural defects—ideological rigidity born of certain predispositions, failure to implement reconstruction, and the organizational culture and mindset of the US military—promoted the outbreak of and perpetuated the insurgency. Indeed, they seem to be interconnected in some insidious yet intangible manner.

Ideological lens versus political pragmatism

What goals did the US articulate for Iraq?   Did we truly have a clear and well-articulated goal for post-Saddam Iraq? While this is a controversial issue and I do not wish to dwell on it, it must be addressed because it lies at the political heart of the counter-insurgency campaign. Senior administration officials stated explicitly that the key goal of Operation Iraqi Freedom was to liberate Iraq and bring it democracy and the rule of law. After the terror acts of 9/11 had seared the US psyche and imposed enormous material costs, the Bush administration was resolved to deal decisively with regimes and terrorist organizations that were perceived to be arming themselves with weapons of mass destruction and allegedly considering cooperating with one another against their main mutual enemy, the United States. The administration's group of key thinkers and policy-makers, collectively known as neoconservatives, created the ideological construct for its new approach to the Middle East, which called for, among other things, the use of unparalleled US military power in the post-Cold War era to supposedly transform Middle Eastern states from authoritarian regimes—which oppress their peoples, seek weapons of mass destruction and support terrorism—into 'peaceful', pro-US democracies. Iraq under Saddam Hussein topped the list of most dangerous authoritarian and oppressive regimes. This was symbolized by the President Bush's focus on Iraq in his State of the Union address in January 2002, in which he castigated Iran, Iraq and North Korea as an 'axis of evil', ready to harm the United States. But of this pantheon of 'evil' it was only Saddam's part that was to be toppled by pre-emptive military action, which entailed striking before the actualization of the threat.

In formulating a strategy to deal with Iraq, the Bush administration, despite its philosophical abhorrence of nation-building, settled on an expansive set of goals: the transformation of Iraq, via an audacious process of reconstruction, into a democracy that would act as a beacon for the rest of the largely autocracy-ridden region.[7] President Bush stated this clearly at a dinner hosted by the hawkish neoconservative think-tank the American Enterprise Institute in February 2003: 'A liberated Iraq can show the power of freedom to transform that vital region, by bringing hope and progress to the lives of millions. A new regime in Iraq would serve as a dramatic and inspiring example of freedom for other nations in the region.'[8]

In an ideal world the democratization of Iraq is a noble vision for that country and for the Arab world, whose experiments with sundry totalitarian ideologies ranging from parochial nationalism, pan-Arab nationalism, socialism and Islamism have brought nothing but misery, aggressive militarism, defeat and retarded development. Indeed, if there is a single factor that truly justifies this war by any yardstick, it *is* the fact that the war has rid the world of one of the most depraved totalitarian regimes since the Nazi regime of Adolf Hitler. Its leaders mouthed slogans about Arab nationalism and their commitment to the well-being of the Iraqi people, yet they and a small 'upper class' of nouveau riche parasites lived in ostentatious splendor while the rest of the country suffered the traumatic effects of past wars and deadly sanctions.[9]

The world and key Middle Eastern states were alarmed by the expansive ideological tendencies of the neoconservatives. One of their leading exponents, Deputy Defense Secretary Paul Wolfowitz, argued that the United States was trying to create not a 'domino effect' but rather a 'demonstration effect', or even an 'inspiration effect', that would be felt as far away as Morocco.[10] He saw the military conquest of Iraq as a lesson to regimes that threaten US interests, and envisioned Iraq as a model for an undemocratic Arab world. He also argued that 'the real point is that removing this regime will be so liberating for the United States in the Persian Gulf. Our whole footprint can be much lighter without an Iraqi threat.'[11] The US presence in Saudi Arabia is one of 'Osama Bin Laden's principal recruiting devices.'[12] His entire argument is full of flaws that neither the US media nor the public sees. Wolfowitz envisioned US bases in Iraq as a post-Hussein friendly ally. Why would Iraqis or other Arabs not be recruited into fighting such a presence in Iraq, just as they have been recruited into fighting it in Saudi Arabia?

Moreover, the neoconservatives' claim that they want to help the Arab world democratize and develop is debatable. Numerous people, including me, were simply never convinced that the neoconservative thinkers and policy-makers who have advocated revolutionary transformation in the Middle East after regime change in Iraq are concerned about bringing genuine democracy to Iraq and the region.[13] Only a few years ago they cast scorn on the idea that the region could be democratized.[14] Their protestations in the media, before and after Operation Iraqi Freedom, that they were genuinely concerned by the plight of the Arab peoples and sought their well-being may have fooled the US public and media. They did not, however, fool those who have paid attention to the evolution of neoconservative views of the Middle East and its denizens. Indeed, the neoconservatives have been seen as less interested in building a 'better Arab',[15] one who is democratic and modernized, than in seeking a pliant one. But the neoconservatives are the very same thinkers and policy-makers who have repeatedly argued, since Saddam Hussein invaded Kuwait in 1990, that the only thing the Arabs understand is force. Does this mean that they can only be brought democracy at the point of a gun? Or is it an ineluctably congenital condition that renders them incapable of progress towards democracy?

Having interacted with many neoconservatives or individuals close to high-ranking neoconservatives for the past decade, I can attest to the fact that genuine interest in or empathy for the peoples of the region are the furthest thing from their ideological mindset. Frankly, I simply do not see any neoconservative welcoming an economically vibrant, politically mature, free and confident Arab world linked to the West. I recall a rather unfriendly encounter during a break at a conference on the Middle East in Washington, DC, in 1998, when one of the better-known neoconservative thinkers and I fell into an argument over the underlying motivations for his hawkishness towards Iraq. He became increasingly strident due to my apparent obtuseness, and concluded with characteristic superciliousness: 'We intend to get Iraq out of the Middle Eastern strategic line-up for at least a quarter century.'[16] Not once did he mention that he was motivated by a desire to bring the fruits of democracy to the Iraqis. Before I could ask to what purpose was Iraq to be removed from the strategic line-up (whatever that meant), he walked away in a huff because I had dared question his ideological construct.

Neoconservatives lament the fact that 'Arabists' (i.e. those US government experts on the Arab and Islamic worlds who have immersed themselves in the languages and cultures of those peoples) doubt that the region is ready for democracy and then excoriate them for being racist, precisely, in the opinion of many observers, to hide their own barely submerged disdain for the inhabitants of the region. Indeed, neoconservative attitudes towards the Arabs and Muslims are seen by many as racist, disdainful and dominated by the view that the only thing 'these people' understand is the

salutary application of force against them. To those who have witnessed the evolution of the neoconservative-dominated policy towards the Middle East, Neil Clark, British journalist and Middle
East observer, may well seem correct when he says: 'Scratch a neo-
con and you find an Arabophobe.'[17]

'*Sunniphobia*.'   But the matter is clearly more insidious and dangerous to the US effort in Iraq than mere Arabophobia. Many
learned people with whom I talked in Iraq and the United States
have argued that the neoconservatives, their sympathizers in the
media, think-tanks and the instant experts have also transformed
the US war in Iraq into a sideshow against the Sunni Arabs of Iraq.
In this context, it is little wonder that I am not surprised by the
deep animus that seems to motivate many in the US against the
Sunnis of Iraq. Indeed, as one Iraqi Sunni said to me in Baghdad,
'Why do they hate so, should be our question.' I mention this because if a deeply racist attitude exists at the policy and ideological/
intellectual levels in the center (Washington, DC), then it will inevitably color the nature of the enterprise in the periphery (Iraq).
It will also influence events on the ground or help promote similar
views among those at the pointy end of the spear (at the operational and tactical levels). In short, the ideological underpinnings of
any enterprise such as that taking place in Iraq have strategic, operational and tactical consequences, and often not positive ones.

The US administration totally discounted the Sunni reaction to
the destruction of the regime. Just as we believed that the Shi'a
would rise joyfully to embrace us, we also thought that the Sunnis
could be treated with disdain, discounted and swept aside with little in the way of adverse reaction. The unfavorable reaction of the
Sunnis acted to reinforce preexisting prejudices. This is no exaggeration. The anti-Sunni sentiment that existed among policy-makers
filtered down into the CPA in Baghdad. It increased as the Sunnis

clearly failed to hew to the script that was assigned to them. The slow pace or even absence of reconstruction fueled the discontent in Sunni areas. The chaotic situation also had an adverse impact on the Sunni Arab commercial class and aroused the fears of the Sunni Arab middle class. Both groups would have been an asset of inestimable value to the Coalition had their grievances and worries been addressed from the outset. The Sunni Arab community as a whole was well placed to contribute in the post-Saddam era under US guidance and support. Although they had been hard hit and virtually destroyed by Saddam's policies and by a hard decade-long sanctions regime, the large Sunni Arab middle class/technocratic elite and other members of the huge public sector constituted a cadre that could have been co-opted to play a role in reconstruction and the restoration of law and order. This did not happen. Coalition failures and policies were responsible. As one Sunni observer, Qais Ahmed al-Na'imi, a local council leader in the Baghdad district of Adhamiya, put it to a journalist: 'If the Americans came and developed our general services, brought work for our people and transferred their technology to us then we would not have been so disappointed. But it is not acceptable to us as human beings that after one year America is still not able to bring us electricity.'[18] Larry Diamond, a respected political scientist and former senior adviser to the CPA, added: 'Much of the Sunni resistance was an expression of Iraqi nationalism. They objected to the occupation and especially the presence of foreign troops. This grievance will only be fully alleviated once foreign troops are gone.'[19]

US policies in Iraq hurt not only Sunni material interests, but also their identity. In the eyes of the Sunnis the latter was the more dangerous threat. Claims that the Sunnis were not taken into account are true. The question is why. Was it clumsiness, ineptitude or oversight? I am no believer in conspiracy theories but clearly there was an element of deliberateness in this. The neoconservatives

viewed the Sunnis—traditionally strong supporters of Arab nationalism and of Iraq's involvement in pan-Arab issues—as a threat
to their vision of a new post-Hussein Iraq. They thought they could
safely ignore or marginalize the Sunnis and rely on the Shi'a Arabs
and the Sunni Kurds—who together constitute 78 percent of the
population—to build the Iraq they wanted. If there is any doubt
about this I would refer to the extensive debates occurring in
Washington, DC, among policy-makers, in think-tanks with supposed Iraq experts, and among Iraqi exiles concerning the de-Arabization of Iraq and the transformation of its identity prior to the
launching of Operation Iraqi Freedom. Granted, the Sunni Arab
imprint on Iraq had to change—after all, they made up only 20
percent of the population—but there is a difference between that
and the policy of marginalizing them politically, culturally and in
terms of identity.

It became very clear from the beginning of the occupation that
the CPA was not interested in reaching out to the Sunni community. According to Robin Wright, 'there was also no outreach to the
Sunni minority, nervous about their future after dominating power
since modern Iraq was created about eight decades ago.'[20] 'The key
from the beginning was political inclusion,' said Larry Diamond.
'The CPA did a poor job of including Sunnis with real followings
in the Iraqi Governing Council and in the emerging structures of
power. The CPA should have reached out from the beginning to a
wider circle of Sunnis from the vitally important tribes.'[21] The Sunnis saw themselves as being discriminated against. As one English-
speaking Iraqi put it, the Coalition and US military's Sunni engagement strategy was, 'When you see a Sunni engage him' (militarily,
that is). Morbid jokes began to appear among US officers and soldiers, such as 'Arrested while Sunni'.

I witnessed at first hand in the Green Zone this tendency to
view the Sunnis as irrelevant or undeserving of reincorporation

into a new Iraq. I also recall one officer based in a rather obstreperous Sunni town asking the CPA for money to buy electrical generators. CPA officials told him, 'We cannot be seen rewarding
them.' As the insurgency took hold in late fall 2003 and early winter 2004, there were frantic attempts to institute a Sunni engagement strategy. The military recognized the virtues of this from the
start. One of the primary tasks of a counter-insurgency is to try to
bring to your side those who are susceptible—or who have already
succumbed—to the siren song of the violent groups. It is no good
saying, 'We have the Shi'a and Kurds on "our" side', and then proceeding to use these groups against the Sunnis. Had we managed
to swing 78 percent of the Sunnis to our point of view early in the
occupation, it would have been a significant measure of success in
those early days of the insurgency.

Leading Sunnis saw the US hostility towards the community
that had held the reins of power for more than eighty years as a
calculated step to fully marginalize them in the new Iraq.[22] History has conclusively shown that those who stand to lose privileges
and power will often react violently. And those who are threatened
with a disruption of their identity—their particular conception of
themselves—will often choose to fight.

Shi'aphilia.   There is a curious caveat to the dim view of the Arabs
among the neoconservatives, and this is their 'soft spot' for the
Iraqi Shi'a, who are also Arab. Writer and journalist Tony Karon
cites a *Newsweek* report: 'Bush administration officials now talk
about Iraq's Shiites as a vital component of their plans to reorganize and democratize the Middle East. They claim that traditional Shiite Islam, as opposed to Ayatollah Ali Khameinei's kind
that rules in Iran, has a "thick wall" between mosque and state.'[23]
Some neoconservatives held the odd notion that democracy intrin-
sically appealed to the Iraqi Shi'a because they had been oppressed

and knew the value of freedom, and because the Shiʻa clerical establishment was democratic. This notion was very quickly laid to rest in Iraq after the invasion. As Karon remarks, 'anyone suggesting that Ayatollah Sistani is staying behind a thick wall separating the mosque from the affairs of state ought to check in with Paul Bremer', who has had to suffer constant intervention in the political process by the senior member of the Shiʻa clerical order.[24]

More to the point is that the thoroughly reactionary worldview of some members of this clerical establishment reveals the bankruptcy of the neoconservative approach. Consider the comments of some young Iraqi clerics in the Shiʻa areas. For example, during a Friday sermon barely a month after dozens of US soldiers had died to give him the privilege of free speech, Kadhim al-Ebadi al-Nasseri shouted: 'The West wants to distract you with shiny slogans like freedom, democracy, culture and civil society. Infidel corruption has entered our society through these concepts.'[25] The views of another cleric, Muhammad al-Fartusi, who claimed adherence to Moqtada al-Sadr, illustrate the depth to which reactionary religious thought dominates Iraqi society. A Western journalist had the privilege of listening to the progressive ideas of this religious luminary:

[Fartusi] said he was particularly concerned about the sale of alcohol, which he insisted was forbidden under Christianity and Judaism.

When challenged on that point, he expressed astonishment that anyone could possibly dispute his convictions.

'Islam and all religions forbid alcohol,' he said. 'Did you ever read that the prophets Jesus or Moses drank alcohol? No. Only the atheists from Christianity drink.'

When informed otherwise, Sheikh Fartusi was cheerfully dismissive and defended his recent religious rulings that ban alcohol, require all men to grow beards and condemn all women who chat with the foreign soldiers here as prostitutes.

'I'm just ordering what God already ordered,' he said. 'I didn't forbid Christians or Muslims from taking a walk under the trees by the river or having a picnic.'[26]

Instead of focusing on helping his downtrodden citizens to find a way out of their suffocating lives, he was more concerned with banning alcohol and labeling as prostitutes Iraqi women who interacted with the Coalition. We have given Iraq to individuals not with democratic impulses but with obscurantist and reactionary ones. Despite my own realist impulses, I would have supported the neoconservatives had their platitudes about modernizing and liberalizing Iraq been more than simply that—platitudes.

Two facts present themselves for further analysis. First, I wonder why the neoconservatives are so enamored of Iraqi Shi'a clerics, but so bitterly hostile to the corresponding Shi'a clerical order in Iran that they seek its downfall? Is it because of the supposed difference between the quietist school in Iraq and the political and ruling clerical establishment in Iran? This 'difference' is false and absurd. As I pointed in Chapter 4, the political impulses of the Shi'a clerics are anything but quietist in extraordinary times. Second, the Sunni Arabs and neoconservatives do share one thing in common—they both view the Iraqi Shi'a Arabs as somehow 'less Arab' by virtue of being Shi'a. The Arab political scene, particularly in Iraq, has witnessed several occasions when the Sunnis questioned the *uruba* ('Arabness') of the Shi'a, to the extent in Iraq that they were even seen as a fifth column for Iran. For Sunnis the suspect Arabness of the Shi'a is a tragedy. For the neoconservatives, doubts about the Arabness of the Shi'a are an opportunity to 'de-Arabize' Iraq, as they obliquely repeated ad nauseam in the run-up to the war.

The lukewarm reception that the advancing Coalition received from the Shi'a in the south was one of the major shocks of the war. Muhammad Baqir al-Hakim sent a message to his supporters in the south that the Shi'a population must not support Saddam's regime nor extend support to the foreign Coalition. Hakim, while welcoming the imminent demise of a regime that had brutalized the Shi'a population and killed dozens from his family, warned: 'Foreign troops must leave Iraq at the earliest possible time. The Iraqi people will resist by all means available means, including armed struggle, if these foreign forces turn into occupiers.'[27]

The United States had expected the Shi'a to rise against Saddam. Political exiles in the Iraqi National Council under Ahmed Chalabi, and noted policy experts on the Arab world, had convinced senior administration officials that the overall Iraqi reaction to the invasion would be one of delirious joy. However, as US journalist Mohamad Bazzi wrote at the height of Operation Iraqi Freedom: '... instead of being greeted with cheers and flowers, Coalition forces have met stiff resistance in the south, and they have yet to capture any major city there. While most of the opposition has come from ruling Baath party militias and Republican Guard units loyal to Hussein, the Shi'i civilian population has largely remained on the sidelines.'[28]

The Shi'a simply did not trust the Coalition, for two reasons: they did not believe that the United States was overthrowing Saddam to bring democracy; and they remember how the Americans had betrayed them before, when they rose against the regime in 1991 and the United States sat by and watched. 'The Americans and their allies betrayed the Shiites of Iraq once before, and they might do it again. This time we know better than to trust the Americans,' said one of Ayatollah al-Hakim's senior advisors.[29] Hakim told Bazzi what he expected to happen in post-Saddam Iraq: 'If the Americans enter Iraq because they want to rescue our people from this evil regime, and then they leave matters to the Iraqi people, themselves, then everyone will be pleased. But if the Americans come in with the intention of controlling Iraq, its wealth and its resources, then they're going to face strong opposition from all the Iraqi people.'[30]

No wonder many people in the United States, Europe, Iraq and the rest of the Middle East believe that the enterprise known as Operation Iraqi Freedom had nothing to do with bringing Iraqis and others liberty from oppressive government and poverty. Racism towards Middle Easterners in general and Arabs in particular, as well as pronounced prejudice against Islam as a religion, is rampant in the United States. It has had a significant impact on the US ability to understand the region in general and Iraq specifically, and to wage an effective counter-insurgency there. Unsurprisingly, many think that the plan to bring a liberal democracy to Iraq was a 'bright shining lie', to borrow the title of Neil Sheehan's renowned book, which is a masterly description of the disillusionment of US Army field advisor Lieutenant Colonel John Paul Vann with the US experience in Vietnam.[31] In other words, those who formulated the policy never believed in the platitudes they were mouthing. As a former member of the CPA told noted US journalist Christopher Dickey, the administration's cherished goal from the outset had been to 'create a stable, friendly, Israel-recognizing, [US military] base-tolerating and oil-producing friend who will allow us to thumb our nose at the rest of the region with impunity'.[32] There is nothing particularly democratic about such a pliant nation, but obviously such an end-state could not be articulated as the US goal for Iraq.

If this reading of the neoconservative political goal is accurate, it is unsurprising, as Dickey points out, that the 'Iraqis just haven't bought into our vision for their country, which is precisely why quite a few are fighting us, and why so many more are tolerating or supporting them'.[33] The Bush administration's failure to present a future that would promise all communities a stake in the political system and that would have made a genuine effort in the direction of democratic governance set the stage for the political vacuum in the country in 2003, and ultimately for forces that the administration did not understand to step into the breach.

Political development, basic services, rehabilitation and reconstruction

This is not the study in which to discuss the sad story of Iraq's nation-rebuilding and reconstruction after three wars and a decade of sanctions. Historically, however, few counter-insurgency campaigns have ever succeeded without political reforms, and a socio-economic plan to remove the causes of popular dissatisfaction and to rehabilitate a damaged or unstable country and society.

Failure to institute democratic governance and political development.   This is a vast topic that is being addressed by many observers and analysts. I am concerned here with the perception among the Sunnis that, despite high-sounding statements about bringing democracy, the United States and the Coalition has 'given' the country to a defined ethno-sectarian majority. The Sunnis, particularly the middle class, the technocrats and former army officers, watched in alarm as the country was increasingly held hostage, in their view, to a more assertive Shi'a clerical establishment. There were no solid or cohesive Sunni political groups in the center to press the case for the displaced community, which was 'out of favor' in any case. The Kurds, by contrast, were able every step of the way to press effectively for consideration of their rights as a minority.

To begin with, most Iraqis did not buy the idea that many of the former exiles who returned home as part of the logistical accoutrement of US military forces constituted the democratic foundation of the new Iraq. Supremely self-confident, the former political émigrés salivated at the prospect of running the country they had returned to after decades in exile. On 28 April 2003 the United States and Britain sponsored a political meeting of 300 Iraqi political figures and supported their call for a national conference to meet by the end of May to select a transitional government. On 5 May 2003 Jay Garner, the man appointed to bring things back on track in Iraq in the immediate aftermath of the war (see pp. 17–18), indicated that the core of such a government would emerge later that month.[34] When the returnees' alleged popularity proved to be nonexistent, they were deeply irritated that their chance to run the country was being sabotaged by the United States. They lashed out at the plan of Garner's successor, Ambassador Paul Bremer, to appoint an interim governing council instead of convening a national conference to choose a transitional or provisional government that would, naturally, be in their hands. In a meeting on 16 May 2003 US and British officials told the exiles that the occupation authorities were going to shelve plans for a provisional government and would create, instead, an 'interim authority'.[35] British diplomat John Sawers argued that legal and social institutions needed to be rebuilt before vesting a government with sovereignty. Why the reversal? According to reports, Bremer did not view as sufficiently representative the exiles who had expected to take over—'[you] don't represent the country,'[36] he reportedly told them in a meeting in early June 2003—and too disorganized to take over. He was right on both counts. Taking advantage of a UN Security Council resolution that legitimized and gave broad powers to the Coalition presence in Iraq, Bremer scrapped the original plan.[37]

Just as the US misjudged the popularity of the exiles, so did it fatally misjudge the power of the Shi'a clerical establishment, which had moved into the political vacuum occasioned by the collapse of the hated regime and the impotence exhibited daily by the occupation powers. Unsurprisingly the Shi'a clergy were able to steal the show from the Bush administration and the hapless CPA.

As US administrator Paul Bremer was promoting an Iraqi constitution written by US appointees in the summer of 2003, the most
senior Shi'a cleric, Ayatollah Ali al-Sistani, issued a *hokm* (edict)
emphatically stating that only an elected body could write the constitution. He called the CPA plan to appoint drafters as 'fundamen-
tally unacceptable' because 'There is no guarantee that the council
would create a constitution conforming with the greater interests
of the Iraqi people and expressing the national identity, whose basis
is Islam, and its noble social values'.[38] In early July, Bremer decided
that the best way forward was to form a council, a twenty-five-
member body made up of US allies and exiles. Thus was born the
Interim Governing Council.

Bremer thought the IGC would be able to form a commission
that would identify the best way to select those who would draft
the constitution. By August 2003, following intense discussions, the
CPA and IGC came up with the idea of a 'partial election'. Instead
of allowing anyone to stand as a candidate and having to compile
voter rolls for general elections, the occupation authorities would
organize caucuses in each governorate. Local influential figures approved by the occupation authorities would select the drafters.

In mid-August the IGC selected a twenty-five-member constitutional commission that began discussing ways to choose the drafters. Although holding caucuses would take longer than appointing
the authors of the proposed constitution, Bremer accepted the idea
of a partial election, as did several members of the IGC. But, to the
consternation of the IGC, CPA and US government, the commission selected by the IGC voted on 8 September 2003 to endorse
general elections. It submitted its final report on 30 September, but
this did not resolve the impasse. The commission presented three
distinct options—direct appointment, partial elections and general elections—without opting for a choice. Attempts were made
to persuade Sistani to endorse partial elections, but he would not

budge and declared emphatically that there could be no substitute for general elections. In November 2003, when Bremer was seeking to choose an interim government through appointments and indirect voting, Sistani ruled that only direct elections would do. The US said Iraq was too turbulent for full elections and that a vote could not be held until a complete national census was held. Sistani's aides countered that food-ration cards issued to every Iraqi family could be used as registration documents for the election.

The CPA yielded. On 10 November Bremer hurried back to Washington to confer with President Bush and his advisers, returning two days later to Baghdad. On 14 November he met with senior members of the IGC and handed them the new plan. Iraq, he said, would be given sovereignty before it had a permanent constitution. Instead the IGC would draft a basic law (the Transitional Administrative Law, or TAL), which would serve as an interim constitution to enshrine basic rights such as freedom of speech and worship, separation of powers, and so on. Each province would hold caucuses to choose representatives to a 250-member transitional national assembly. The process would have to be completed by 30 June 2004, after which Iraq would move to an interim government.[39]

On 28 June 2004 the CPA dissolved itself. Bremer left Iraq somewhat unceremoniously and Iyad Allawi, a former Ba'thist, took the premiership. Allawi came into office with great expectations, and many people were attracted to various aspects of his persona. Some Sunni professionals liked him because he was a secular Shi'a and a former Ba'thist. Some secular Shi'a liked him for the same reason. Still others liked him because of his tough image—people thought he would return law and order to the country. There were those, however, who were suspicious of him. The religious Shi'a groups disliked him because of his secularism, and more importantly because he returned former Ba'thists, Sunni and Shi'a, to power. Allawi certainly deserved a great deal more support than he received from his benefactor, the Bush administration, but of course this is hindsight. Allawi's biggest problem was his inability to put an end to the rampant violence that Iraq witnessed in 2004. He also lost a tremendous deal of popularity among the Sunnis when he backed the attack on Fallujah in November 2004.

Restoration of basic services, reconstruction and socioeconomic development. The reconstruction of Iraq has been a tragic failure. The Pentagon's, or rather the neoconservatives', insistence that the postwar effort be run by the Department of Defense was a miscalculation because the department lacked experience, experts on nation-building and sufficiently detailed plans. Ambassador James Dobbins, an expert on nation-building and an advisor on the Iraq postwar reconstruction phase, said: 'The decision to transfer civilian aspects of reconstruction from the State Department to the Pentagon imposed immense costs as Defense had not handled anything like it for at least 50 years, while State had garnered considerable experience over the previous decade.'[40]

In January 2003 the Bush administration set up an organization called the Office for Rehabilitation and Humanitarian Aid (OHRA), headed by Garner, whose goals were to ensure law and order and the restoration of basic services, and to begin the process of putting Iraq back on the road to political and socioeconomic rehabilitation after the war. ORHA's tenure in Iraq between mid-April 2003 and mid-May 2003 was an unmitigated disaster. ORHA failed to establish law and order and ensure security in the immediate aftermath of the war. Iraq descended into chaos, with widespread looting and vandalism of infrastructure, the emergence of pervasive organized crime, and massive increases in the incidences of assaults, rapes and homicides. To be fair, while ORHA can be blamed for not 'gaming' the possibility of such a scenario, it cannot be blamed for the disappearance of the police from the streets and for the fact that US combat personnel are not trained for the maintenance of law and order.

ORHA can be blamed for failing to restore basic services to the Iraqi people or distribute humanitarian aid effectively.[41] The country had less electricity than before the war and during the decade of sanctions. This was not an optimal situation to have in spring as the heat of the Iraqi summer loomed. As the regime collapsed hospitals were extensively looted of medicines and supplies, and were also in worse shape than before the war. The effective rationing system collapsed after the war but humanitarian assistance could not reach the people in a sustained manner because planners in the Pentagon did not work with NGOs. Moreover, NGOs that were keen to go into postwar Iraq were loath to send their workers because of the absence of law and order. Unsurprisingly, the political, economic and social situation in Iraq under the auspices of Garner and ORHA in spring 2003 could be said to approximate—with a little hyperbole—Thomas Hobbes's state of nature where there were 'no arts, no letters, no society, and, which is worst of all, continual fear, and danger of violent death; and the life of man, solitary, poor, nasty, brutish and short'.[42]

Like the unexploded ordnance littering Iraq's landscape, ORHA—which arrived with great expectations—proved to be a dud. Why? The problems began in Washington, DC. While many of ORHA's cadres were dedicated, disciplined civilians and military personnel who represented the 'best and the brightest' the United States had to offer, many were not. I had the honor of working with many of the former, in Washington, DC, in the lead-up to the war and later in Baghdad. There was simply no real planning for dealing with postwar Iraq. The briefings and PowerPoint presentations were amateurish, pathetic, shoddy and heavily politicized. (Some planners mounted presentations that represented the sum of their corpus of knowledge about Iraq, a state of affairs that was no doubt responsible ultimately for the gallows humor among officers that went: 'His knowledge about XYZ is no more than PowerPoint deep.') ORHA activities between January 2003 and the onset of the war were characterized by slipshod work, bureaucratic wrangling and constant interference by individuals with patently transparent political agendas, many of whom ensconced themselves in Baghdad and interfered with the work of dedicated individuals. Because ORHA was set up only on 20 January 2003, planning for postwar Iraq was nothing compared to the two and half years of solid and exhaustive professional work during the course of World War II to prepare for the postwar occupations of Germany and Japan. As one noted authority on postwar nation-building said in a recent study:

By May 1945, Allied occupation of German territory was complete. Within days of full occupation, US civil affairs units sent detachments into every town, establishing security and US authority in each population center within the US sector ...

Much the same occurred in Japan. US forces began entering Japan just days after Emperor Hirohito surrendered, on August 15, 1945. Within weeks, General Douglas MacArthur established his command in Tokyo and began an astonishing round of reforms. He too sent troops and civil affairs officers on rounds of motorcycle diplomacy throughout the country to establish security and to explain US intentions ...

In both occupations, combat troops transitioned into a governance presence.[43]

Not only was ORHA ill-prepared, but it did not even hit the ground running. Thus it was unable to garner momentum (no pun intended!) from the very first day it was in Iraq.

The failings mentioned above had an impact on the ground in Iraq in spring 2003, when ORHA staff ensconced themselves in Baghdad in some of Hussein's palaces, having little contact with the rest of the city let alone the rest of Iraq. The organization's understanding of Iraq was also stymied by a shortage of Arabic-speakers and regional experts. According to one source, there were seventeen Arabic-speakers and even fewer Iraq experts in a staff that had between 600 and 800 personnel in the Republican Palace in Baghdad. Instead, ORHA relied on 'Iraq Kremlinologists'—mid-ranking policy officials who had read enough on Iraq to suffer delusions of adequacy about their knowledge of that country—more often than it did on the smattering of genuine Iraq experts in the United States.[44] The organization came to be known derisively in Baghdad as HAHA. The verdict of a senior ORHA official based in Baghdad a month after the organization's arrival in Iraq is devastating: 'The planning was ragged and the execution was worse.'[45]

Well-meaning but out of his depth, Garner fared so miserably that Rumsfeld replaced him in May 2003. His suave successor, Ambassador 'Jerry' Bremer, strode into Baghdad on 12 May making MacArthur-like statements: 'This is not a country in anarchy. People are going about their business. Across most of Iraq, life is clearly getting better.'[46] But as journalist Daniel Eisenberg pointed out at the time, most of Baghdad's residents 'might beg to differ'.[47] A US intelligence official remarked in late May 2003 that the amount of political inspired opposition to the US presence was 'remarkably low'.[48] This faith-based belief that things were fine and were getting better each day was a problem from the very beginning.

The CPA would have succeeded in degrading the impact of ill will and of the insurgency had it restored law and order, had it not implemented certain policies that either humiliated Iraqis or added to the level of unemployment, and had it begun an effective reconstruction of the country. The lack of basic services and the patent inability of the occupiers to rebuild infrastructure fueled much of the emerging discontent.[49] The confrontation between the inhabitants of the southern and Shi'a-dominated city of Basra and British troops in mid-August 2003 stemmed not from nostalgia for the former regime, but rather from the deterioration in civic amenities and services.[50]

But the CPA had little more success than its hapless predecessor. Even as early as summer 2003, a very senior British official who was part of the infrastructure stated bluntly that the US-led reconstruction effort in Iraq is 'in chaos' and suffering from 'a complete absence of strategic direction'.[51] He added, for good measure: 'This is the single most chaotic organization I have ever worked for ... We are faced with an almost complete inability to engage with what needs to be done and to bring to bear sufficient resources to make a difference.'[52] It is unsurprising that Iraqis rapidly lost faith in the abilities of the CPA to do anything constructive in their ravaged country.

The CPA's efforts to implement basic services and engage in reconstruction were also plagued by its inability to work effectively with the organization that was, in the initial stages of the occupation, best-placed to help in these tasks: the US military. The latter was, of course, by nature not set up to engage in these kinds of tasks, but it was in place in areas that the CPA had neither the manpower nor the resources to reach effectively. The CPA talent pool was unimpressive, as a former CPA aide admitted.[53] In November 2003 in an Iraqi city I sat through a four-hour briefing given by irate officers who complained about the CPA's lack of responsiveness to their requests for resources. In many cases the CPA had the money but not the people to implement the projects, while the military had the people but not the finances. In other cases the military had access to financial resources through what came to be known as the Commanders' Emergency Relief Funds.

Skyrocketing security costs forced the United States to slash about $1 billion from reconstruction projects and put the money into security. William Taylor, a US diplomat who oversees the reconstruction efforts, said the violence in Iraq had created a 'security premium', wherein the money slated for clean water, sanitation and electricity is diverted to providing security.[54] When the US Congress approved $18.4 billion in November 2003 to help rebuild Iraq, the majority of the money was intended for projects designed to improve the lives of the Iraqis. Now the largest chunk of money—about $5 billion—is slated to pay for weapons, uniforms and other equipment to help build the Iraqi security forces. Security costs now take up anywhere from 5 to 25 percent of the total costs of a project.[55] The effect of the violence ripples through construction projects. US officials had originally estimated that 10 percent of the money slated for reconstruction would go to security. As of February 2005 roughly $8 billion of the $18.4 billion (around 43 percent) was allocated to this need.[56]

The *Iraq Living Conditions Survey 2004*,[57] a three-volume report jointly produced by the UN Development Program and the Iraqi Ministry of Planning and Development Cooperation, was based on a survey of more than 21,000 households in the country from April to August 2004. It showed that the Iraqi people were suffering from a widespread collapse in their living standards and conditions, exemplified by war-related injuries, chronic malnutrition, low life expectancy, declining health, declining literacy, and significant setbacks in women's rights. This is hardly a foundation for the creation of a democratic society. Electrical supply to 85 percent of houses was unreliable, 46 percent lacked access to clean water, and only 37 percent were connected to a sewage system. Nationwide, unemployment was 20 percent and the median household income was $144, down from $255.[58] Lieutenant Colonel Anthony Brown, an Army reservist and delegate in the Maryland State House in Annapolis, has had his energy sapped by the immense difficulties of rebuilding Iraq: 'You can't make a democracy in that kind of environment. It is going to take much longer than I ever anticipated to reestablish an Iraqi government, the organizations, entities and bureaucracies that are going to have sustain this population. Things just move very slowly.'[59]

The situation had not improved a year later. As of summer 2005 it was reported that major reconstruction projects were grinding to a halt because of the lack of funds. Moreover, security continued to eat into funds that were dedicated to water, electricity and sanitation. 'We have scaled back our projects in many areas,' James Jeffrey, a senior State Department adviser on Iraq, told a congressional committee in Washington, DC. 'We do not have the money.'[60] Water and sanitation have been particularly badly hit. According to a report published by the Government Accountability Office, the investigative branch of Congress, $2.6 billion had been spent on water projects, half the original budget, after the rest was diverted to security and other uses: 'The report said "attacks, threats and intimidation against project contractors and subcontractors" were to blame. A quarter of the $200 million worth of completed US-funded water projects handed over to the Iraqi authorities no longer worked properly because of "looting, unreliable electricity or inadequate Iraqi staff and supplies", the report found.'[61]

The US government too often presents a rosy picture of the reconstruction and nation-building efforts in Iraq. There is often little or no merit to these pictures. As one Marine civil affairs officer, whose knowledge was based on his seven-month posting to unstable Ramadi, said, 'goodwill physical infrastructure projects, while generating some positive public sentiment, are poor measures of success against the insurgency'.[62] There were often simply no trained personnel or staff to man them or equipment to supply them. And because of the pervasive insecurity the Marines were unable to convince nongovernment institutions to establish a presence in the city to institutionalize the benefits of reconstruction. Morgenstein was simply pessimistic about the Iraqi security forces in his area, and with good reason: they were ill-trained and often worked for or with the insurgents.

Creation of legitimate coercive state apparatus

One of the most important functions of any state is to establish and maintain control over the instruments of violence. Max Weber recognized this long ago: 'Today ... we have to say that a state is a human community that (successfully) claims the *monopoly of the legitimate use of physical force* within a given territory.'[63] This becomes doubly important in a state facing considerable internal turmoil, including the collapse of former forces, the rise of militias and, of course, ongoing violence. The post-Saddam state is struggling to deal with numerous militias, whose existence serves to widen the ethno-sectarian gap between the communities. It is also finding difficult the complex task of forming a professional, cohesive and national military that can replace the militias, and is able to combat the insurgency so that US forces can scale back their presence, transform their roles to those of training and logistical support for the host nation military, and ultimately leave a legitimate government with effective forces in place. Is this happening? I am not sure. We may succeed in the end, but the beginning was inauspicious, given the dissolution of the former army and reluctance to deal with the militias.

State power and the roles of militias.   Militias are quasi-official paramilitary units formed either by the government or by forces loosely allied to the government. Officially they owe allegiance to the state, but in reality it transfers to an individual leader or warlord, a tribe or an ethno-sectarian community. The government may or may not fund and equip them. The closer such forces are to the official government the more they look like official forces, and they are supposed to act as regular security forces or under their aegis. Such militias are among the greatest obstacles to political stability and economic reconstruction in societies trying to recover from conflict or seeking to prevent a descent into incipient civil war.

Militias sponsored or supported by the Coalition and the Iraqi authorities have proliferated in post-Saddam Iraq. At one point the CPA indicated its intention of doing something about them. As the violence spiraled out of control in April 2004 a CPA official said: 'Our objective is the complete elimination of militias. While the CPA cannot expect to achieve this by July 1, it can set in train a process whereby the goal can be achieved in the first six months of Iraqi permanent government.'[64] This was easier said than done. In July 2003 Barzani indicated that the Kurds had no intention of dissolving the *peshmerga*: 'We've faced genocide in the past and we need guarantees.'[65] By retaining their militia, the Kurds believed they could have a major input into the restructuring of political power and the coercive apparatus of the state in the post-Saddam era.

In March 2004 members of the largest and most powerful political groups in post-Saddam Iraq, SCIRI and the Kurds, provisionally agreed to disband their respective militias, the Badr Organization and the *peshmerga*. The agreement offered the personnel of these groups membership in the new security forces or substantial retirement benefits. Hamid Bayati, a high-level SCIRI official, said: 'We believe that all militia members should be part of one national army and police force.'[66] Larry Diamond commented: 'You can't have a free and fair election unless parties can mobilize their following, candidates can campaign and people vote free of intimidation and violence. We know from experience in other post-conflict situations that it is very difficult to achieve that kind of climate of freedom and security when there are substantial armed militias.'[67]

A Coalition official stated emphatically in April 2004 that 'no state can exist in which sub-national entities are allowed to have their own private armies or armed forces. Our job is to create a single nation in which the government has the control of armed forces. And in order to do that, all these sub-national forces have to be absorbed.'[68] Brave words. But neither the CPA nor the Coalition forces showed the ruthlessness or determination to disarm militias. Indeed, there was a reluctance to push one group in particular, the Kurdish militia. This did not go unnoticed by others, particularly the Shi'a parties with militias of their own. 'The Americans do not want to dissolve the Kurdish military, but they want to dissolve the Badr Brigade? Do they think we will accept such a thing?' asked Sheikh Abbas Hakim, spokesman for the political wing of the Badr Organization.[69] The Kurds made it abundantly clear that they had no intention of dissolving the *peshmerga* or its intelligence organs. They point to the tranquility and vibrancy of the Kurdish region as evidence of *peshmerga* effectiveness.[70]

Kurdish officials have insisted that a stillborn agreement of June 2004 to disband militias does not apply to them. So the *peshmerga* remain, but where and to what end becomes a critical issue. If they persist as a wholly *peshmerga* force in the autonomous region, they will form the nucleus of a future Kurdish army. If the units are integrated into the Iraqi army they can be used more extensively in fighting the insurgency. Kurdish officials declare publicly that because they are part of the country, there is no reason not to use these relatively well-trained forces in the counter-insurgency campaign. Privately, however, many Kurds worry about the use of *peshmerga* in conflicts outside the autonomous region. Their deployment in the counter-insurgency campaign poses two risks: the fighters could desert and return home, arguing that they are not interested in fighting and dying in conflicts outside Kurdistan; and/or the use of the *peshmerga* could raise ethnic tensions with Arabs or Turkmen if they are deployed to suppress the insurgency.[71]

The United States wanted to begin disarming militias early after the end of the war, but ethnic and sectarian groups with militias proved very reluctant to disband. The Kurdish *peshmerga* units in Mosul proved to be more of a problem than a solution, as the 101st Air Assault Division discovered. But the United States was reluctant to crack down on the Kurds, who had been allies during the war against Saddam.[72] More than that, though, the neoconservative policy-makers are almost instinctively sympathetic to the Kurds and their aspirations to gain as much power and as many resources as possible at the expense of Sunnis.

Nonetheless, the US military understands the dangers of militia forces. In August 2005 the Director of Operations for Iraq and Afghanistan at United States Central Command, Major General Douglas E. Lute, expressed his concerns about the continued existence of 'local militias not under central Iraqi command', saying that they are an obstacle to the achievement of 'ultimate peace' in Iraq.[73] Lute stressed that Iraq's stability and future depend on it building up its armed forces and regulating them under centralized control. He explained that 'many parts of local militias remain outside the Ministry of Interior's control. Our view is that ultimately the Iraqi political system will have to contend with these militias.'[74] The militias 'are an important "open business" item for the emerging Iraqi government. They have to be dealt with.'[75]

Making militias go away has never been easy in post-conflict societies, and Iraq will be no exception. Militias justify their existence by stating that they provide protection for their neighborhoods, communities, and ethnic and religious groups. This view is understandable if the state cannot provide security and law and order. They also justify their reluctance to disband or disarm by stating that they are provided with no incentive to do so. In Iraq, the state or Coalition forces have faced considerable challenges in providing nationwide and equitable security and have offered no inducements for the militias to lay down their arms. Instead of trying to force them to disband immediately, we could implement a phased disarmament process. The militias would be asked to surrender their heavy weaponry, reduce their numbers and then relinquish their light arms. This would, of course, depend on the state being able to steadily increase and expand its security functions, implement basic community services and provide monetary incentives for the surrender of the arms.

The difficulties of dealing with the militias are reflected in the fact that the US has essentially accepted the reality of their existence and indeed often legitimized that existence by working with them in Fallujah, Najaf and Karbala.[76] Even before the formal constitution of the new government of a 'sovereign' Iraqi state, however, the Prime Minister designate, Iyad Allawi, declared in early June 2004 that the nascent government had reached an agreement with the various parties and communal groups under the terms of which they would disband their powerful militia forces.[77] It is unclear, though, how the interim government intended to go about decommissioning such forces.

Building effective Iraqi security forces.   To succeed in a counter-insurgency campaign the local government must build effective, efficient and professional security forces. And if the state has help from a foreign power the latter must ensure resources are provided to ensure these goals are met. The evolution and effectiveness of the new Iraqi security forces has been the subject of numerous analyses. The purpose here is not to repeat these but to assess whether the local government and the Coalition are succeeding in raising well-trained, professional, national and effective Iraqi security forces capable of conducting a counter-insurgency campaign, at first under foreign tutelage and supervision and then alone. The prognosis is worrying, and not only because the forces are still not fully trained or are poorly equipped, but also and largely because the US has created official ethno-sectarian militias in uniform.

In July 2003 General Abizaid, who assumed command of CENTCOM early that month, said it would take years to create new professional Iraqi forces but: 'In the interim we need civil defense forces that can cooperate with coalition forces, and eventually alone.'[78] By late July 2003, the US began considering the raising of a new Iraqi army and a civil defense force. A recruitment drive launched in three Iraqi cities in late July attracted long lines of young men. Many were members of the former military and indicated that they were willing to join because there were no other jobs available.[79] A host of problems bedeviled the Iraqi security forces from the outset. There was a tug of war between the CPA and the IGC over control of recruitment. 'We are not completely happy with the way recruitment has been handled,' said Adel Abdel Mahdi, a spokesman for SCIRI. 'We have to keep an eye on who is going into the security services, especially those who worked for the old regime.' Iraqi Shi'a were concerned that many former regime loyalists were returning to positions of power in the security services and the Interior Ministry.[80]

The loyalties of the new Iraqi security forces and police were also a problem from the beginning. The uncanny ability of the insurgency to conduct effective attacks like the one on the police headquarters in Baghdad in early September 2003 focused attention on members of the security service as likely culprits, or at least providers of intelligence to the triggermen. Motivation and morale in those days were low. Moreover, the recruits were interested less in the mission than in access to a regular paycheck. A soldier in the former military volunteered for the new Iraqi army on purely practical grounds: 'I am coming back for the money of course. There are no other jobs, and I don't know how I will feed my family.'[81]

The Iraqi security forces leak like a sieve. It is almost impossible to keep secrets among soldiers who have members of their family, clan or tribe on the other side. Thus operations may turn up many weapons but few insurgents. This is a problem to which even Iraqi officers admit. 'We still don't have secure operations. When we go on a mission, this gets leaked out to the people,' said Colonel Tha'ir Dhia Ismail Abid al-Tamimi, commander of the 205th Battalion in Diyala Province.[82] Moreover, Iraqi personnel often have no sense of national cohesion or loyalty to government and country. The first loyalty of too many soldiers in Iraq's myriad armed forces is not to the government, but to their close-knit extended families, larger tribal units, ethnic fellows or coreligionists. One US officer said, 'They're like gangs.'[83]

The demographically dominant Shi'a and Kurds also dominate key units of the Iraqi security forces. Commando Unit No. 36, which went into Fallujah in November 2004, largely comprises personnel from Shi'a militias and the *peshmerga*. Sunnis have been reluctant to sign up for such units, and when they do so they are regarded with immense suspicion.[84] Unsurprisingly, there are ethnic and sectarian tensions within the police force. In one notable instance officers barged into the home of an Iraqi in a Sunni-dominated district, held a gun to the head of his mother and said to the family: 'We're Shia, and we can kill any Sunni in this area.'[85]

Iraqi police express resentment towards US personnel, who they say are better-protected and less vulnerable to attack. 'Take a look at the American bases. They are hiding behind barricades while we are here in the streets with not even guns to protect ourselves,' said a twenty-five-year-old police lieutenant in Baquba.[86] Others say they sympathize with the insurgency and call it a *jihad*. One police captain expressed the sentiment that everyone involved in the resistance 'is a proud Iraqi fighting for his nation'.[87] Others said that they would not notify the US troops if they knew of an imminent attack against Coalition forces.[88] The same sentiments were echoed by General Ismail Turki Bou al-Khalifah, the Khalidiya police chief who vowed that he would fight crime wherever he could find it but indicated that he would neither fight resistance fighters attacking Coalition forces, nor would he share intelligence about them with US intelligence officers.[89] He justified his position thus: 'If you had a brother in this country in my position, and his country was occupied by foreigners, would you be happy that your brother would take reports to the Americans?'[90] In 2003 the culture of the Ba'th regime was still very much in place in the Iraqi police, as were sympathies for the former regime. Major General Hamid Othman, who ran the Iraqi national police from 1997 to 2001 and continued in his position as a police officer, would speak in respectful tones about 'President Saddam Hussein'.[91] While many Iraqi policemen are dedicated and brave, not to mention highly motivated, 'it's not unfair to say that the quality of Iraqi police work in the past ran the gamut from actively dreadful to passively dreadful'.[92]

For many Iraqis who volunteered for the New Iraqi Army, money—not patriotism—was the prime motivator. Nasser Hashim, a twenty-three-year-old former conscript, said sarcastically: 'I'm looking for a better salary, of course. And defending the nation is also one of the reasons.'[93] Another Iraqi, a former officer, voiced his suspicion concerning the purposes of the new security forces: 'The Americans will use this army to strike against the Iraqi people. I do not encourage Iraqis to join.'[94] In early 2004 there was considerable concern that the Iraqi security forces were simply ineffective. The extent of that impotence became evident in the fierce fighting of April-May 2004. In early 2004 there were 14,000 to 15,000 supposedly trained Iraqi Civil Defense Corps (ICDC) personnel, far short of the target of 40,000.[95] No overall command structure was being built from the ground up in the platoon-sized units. They receive one week of training in basic first aid, one day at the firing range, a discussion about ethics and rules of engagement, a day of practicing tactical formation, and practice managing a traffic-control point. When I visited two separate units, one in Tikrit and another in Sadr City, the American trainers told me the corpsmen received three weeks training. The performance of the trainees was relatively bad, even though there were some first-class former military personnel in the units. There was little or no communication or trust between the police and ICDC in either city. Both forces suffer from the suspicion with which many in the general populace view them. In the words of a political science professor at Baghdad University: 'For me, and other Iraqi people, the ICDC are followers of the occupiers of Iraq.'[96]

Indeed, Iraqi personnel in the Sunni areas have had to ask themselves agonizing questions for which there are no easy answers: are they fighting for Iraq or for the Americans? Are they traitors or patriots? What do they do when the United States withdraws and leaves them to face the wrath of the population and insurgents? 'We have children, we have families and we need to live. We don't love the Americans, but we need the money. It's very difficult, but there's no alternative,' said an ICDC member in Baiji, a Sunni town north of Baghdad.[97] Another said: 'We can quit working with the Americans. Fine. But will the clergy give us salaries?'[98] According to these security-services personnel, their friends and relatives in the town want nothing to do with them, either because they view them as puppets or because being seen with uniformed Iraqis can make them targets too. Wathban, a Baiji resident with a relative in the former ICDC, said: 'Their destiny will be the same as it was in Vietnam. The Americans left their allies there and they were killed. I think the same will happen here.'[99] As mentioned above, some Iraqi security forces personnel have links with the insurgents. In fall 2004 the US military arrested an Iraqi National Guard officer based in Diyala Province, Brigadier General Talib al-

Lahibi, suspected of being associated with insurgents.[100] This came in the wake of the arrest of a senior police chief, Jaadan Muhammad Alwan, in Anbar Province in August of that year.[101]

Most US troops who accompany Iraqi security forces on operations are not exactly effusive in their praise of the latter's performance. A journalist who went out on a joint US-Iraqi operation with the Baghdad-based 303rd Iraqi Army Battalion was moved to say: 'I don't know what effect the Iraqi soldiers will have on the enemy, but they terrify me. An eagerness to pull the trigger gleams in their eyes as they wave their Kalashnikovs about. They have a reputation for spraying bullets all around them if fired on, and two Americans have been killed by such stray rounds.'[102] The journalist quotes a US soldier: 'I'm more scared of going out with these guys than clashing with the insurgents. They have no concept of identifying friendlies, and let loose at anything.'[103] (The tendency of Iraqi soldiers to fire in every conceivable direction when they come into contact with the enemy has been referred to as the 'death blossom' by US troops. In the 1984 science-fiction film *The Last Starfighter*, the Death Blossom is a weapons system that fires a massive volley of death rays in all directions.)[104] Moreover, that unit was anywhere between 75 and 95 percent Shi'a in composition, which made them unwelcome in Sunni Arab neighborhoods. Captain Eric Massey of the 82nd Airborne Division, whose troops were attached to the counter-insurgency operation in Haifa Street—a one-time notorious insurgent sanctuary in the middle of Baghdad—said: 'The Shi'a love them. The Sunnis here are either neutral or less excited.'[105]

The embryonic Iraqi security services collapsed, refused to fight, went over to the insurgency or went home during the spike in violence in April and May 2004.[106] This highlights the complete bankruptcy and failures of previous approaches to building security forces in Iraq. The contractors supposedly training the security forces and police could have done better. General Paul Eaton, the US Army officer overseeing the training program, said the instruction 'hasn't gone well. We've had almost one year of no progress.'[107] The training by the Vinnell Corporation and others was declared to have been less than wholly effective. Indeed, in December 2003—even before the horrendous spike in violence in spring 2004—more than half of the first battalion trained by Vinnell deserted.[108]

The Iraqi security forces faced a tough time in 2004. The 630-strong 2nd Battalion of the Iraqi army chose not to support US Marine Corps units battling for control of Fallujah in April. On 6 April US troops detained roughly 200 of the 340 members of the Baghdad-based 36th Security Brigade of the ICDC for refusing to participate in a night assault on insurgents in Fallujah. One of the soldiers reportedly stated: 'How could an Iraqi fight another Iraqi like this? Nothing has changed from the Saddam days. We refused en masse. They were bombing the city and using cluster bombs. I could not be a part of that.'[109] In the south several units of the police and ICDC refused to engage the Mahdi militia. The incidents came as a shock and lesson to the United States. Even the ever-optimistic Bremer was forced to concede on 18 April 2004 that: 'It's clear that Iraqi forces will not be able, on their own, to deal with the threat of insurgents by June 30 [when authority was to be transferred to a provisional government].'[110] Five days later, Bremer announced that the CPA would start recruiting senior officers from the former Iraqi army.[111]

'Our military exit strategy requires a fully effective, credible, reliable Iraqi security force,' said Brigadier General Mark Kimmitt in June 2004, as the CPA was preparing to fold its operations.[112] By mid-2004 about 40 percent of the total on the force at the time, 90,000 police officers and cadets, had received basic modern police training.[113] Their morale was at rock bottom because of the constant terrorist toll on their numbers. In March 2003 the CPA had created the Civilian Police Assistance Training Team (CPATT), which was responsible for coordinating the training of every police officer.[114] Brigadier General Andrew MacKay, the head of CPATT, was frustrated by the lack of progress as of mid-summer 2004. He saw it as one of the most complex police training programs in the world. The assistance provided to local police forces in Kosovo and Bosnia could not compare in size and complexity with the effort to reconstruct the Iraqi police force.[115]

A considerable amount of focus was beginning to be put on 'Iraqization' of the security situation by training and equipping Iraqis to take on the task of fighting insurgency and terrorism. The United States unfortunately fell into the trap of measuring success in this endeavor by means of a single key and obvious indicator: the number of personnel it can claim to have been trained. But as an astute journalist pointed out in early fall 2004:

There are, however, considerable grounds for skepticism over the extent to which the training of Iraqi forces can transform the situation ... The rate of desertion among Iraqi forces is high, as is the rate of infiltration of these units by insurgents.

The fundamental challenge in transferring security responsibility to Iraqi forces is political. The U.S. must convince Iraqi personnel that they're fighting for Iraq, rather than fighting under the command of an unpopular foreign army ...[116]

In mid-2004 the United States was ambivalent about the state of the Iraqi security forces. The disintegration of many units during the worst of the insurgency crisis in April 2004 had shocked many. Looking back, many US officers and officials realized that the forces were clearly inadequate. As of mid-2004 there was still a lack of trust between Iraqi and US personnel. The former were loath to go on patrol with Americans. They were still under-equipped and inadequately trained. A unit in Miqdadidiya, 20 miles north of Baquba, had made some strides by July 2004, according to 1st Infantry

Division officers.[117] Their corrupt commander, who was skimming a third of the salaries, was arrested. The security forces opened a joint command center to improve coordination between the various security forces. But there was a tendency to bolt at the slightest sign of heavy insurgent assault. Discipline was inadequate, and US trainers ruefully admitted that most of the Iraqis in the security forces were 'doing it for a paycheck'.[118] Senior Iraqi officers treated their men as flunkies, and often would not do jobs that they considered 'menial', such as cleaning their own weapons. They are hesitant to delegate authority to their subordinates, as if authority was some kind of totemic symbol that needed to be hoarded.[119]

Poor motivation, particularly among the Sunni Arab personnel, was a serious problem plaguing many units. In Samarra on 6 July 2004 a car bomb exploded outside a US outpost that housed US troops and Iraqi National Guardsmen. It killed five US soldiers and three Iraqi guardsmen. The incident scared all but fifty of the town's 500 guardsmen into resigning.[120] But the problems had actually started in April 2004 when the 202nd Battalion, mainly comprising local Sunnis, collapsed as the uprising broke out in Fallujah. The battalion started with 750 men but in the space of one day, 11 April, it was left with merely forty.[121] It was rebuilt but collapsed again after the car bomb on 6 July. The police folded too; their remnants fled after a night attack by insurgents on 6 November 2004. The US was forced to bring in three battalions totaling 1,000 men from other areas. Two of the battalions were largely Shi'a and the residents of the town resented them and did not provide information about the insurgents—most of whom happened to be relatives—to the Iraqi or US forces. Lieutenant Colonel Eric Schacht of Task Force 1-26, who was stationed in Samarra, summed up the problem as he saw it thus: 'Until they make the decision that they want a better society—and that means their uncle, their cousin, their brother needs to end up being detained—then this is going to continue.'[122] This betrays a lack of understanding of the culture of the country. In a society where traditional kinship ties are so strong, why would someone inform on their relatives for the uncertain promise of material handouts by a foreign entity they do not trust?

According to some reports, training of Iraqi security forces had improved by late December 2004. General Babikir Shawkat Zibari, the Kurdish commander of the Iraqi armed forces, insisted in January 2005 that the capabilities of the armed forces were steadily improving: 'God willing, during this year, our units will be fully armed, trained and have enough soldiers. After all this is finished, I am very optimistic that the Iraqi army will be able to protect the territories and border.'[123] It is possible that Zibari had to exude a sense of optimism for political reasons. But his confidence flew in the face of facts and of statements by General George Casey, commander of the Multinational Force-Iraq, who doubted that the Iraqi armed forces would be ready in 2005 to take the primary brunt of the fight against the insurgents.[124]

A US State Department report on the Iraqi security forces, issued on 5 January 2005, paints a bleak picture. It states that Iraqi forces have been 'rendered ineffective' in many areas, and that due to intimidation and attacks by insurgents a large number of security personnel 'have quit or abandoned their stations'.[125] In January, Lieutenant General Thomas Metz offered a blunt assessment: 'There's areas where the Iraqi security forces have performed well. There's been areas where they've performed sub-optimally. There's areas where they've been overwhelmed by their opposition and have had to step back and live to fight another day. And there's areas where they've plain not participated in the fight.'[126]

The US planned to revise its approach to the insurgency after the Iraqi elections. It would beef up the new Iraqi military by bringing in more former army officers and enlistees, and by putting the

Iraqi forces in the front lines of the counter-insurgency. As of the end of January 2005, Coalition forces were averaging 12,000 patrols a week; Iraqi security forces were managing only around 1,200.[127] With this in mind retired US Army general Gary Luck was sent to Iraq in early January 2005 to assess the Iraqi security forces, and to make recommendations on how to accelerate their training and shift to them responsibility for security.[128] His team concluded that US forces must hasten and strengthen the training of Iraqis by assigning thousands of additional military advisers and trainers to work directly with their units. The team endorsed a plan by US commanders to shift the emphasis from fighting the insurgents to training Iraqis to do it, ultimately allowing the United States to draw down and then withdraw forces. The plan envisages a doubling or trebling of the number of trainers working with the Iraqis, up to 8,000 to 10,000.[129] But the training would take a step-by-step approach over months if not years, proceeding at different paces in different parts of the country, depending on unit performance. Luck also recommended that US forces be freed to become quick reaction forces backing up their Iraqi counterparts, or to help tighten Iraq's borders with its neighbors.[130] Part of the reorganization of the Iraqi forces included rationalization. In early January 2005 the Iraqi army activated nine divisions and the National Guard was formally merged into the army.[131] It is unclear whether the recommendations of General Luck will be enough to make a difference, because there remain many structural problems within the Iraqi security forces.

The immense problems of the Iraqi armed forces were also addressed in a sobering report by a journalist for the British *Guardian* newspaper, who spent two weeks with a supposedly elite unit of the Iraqi military in the Baquba area. He was unimpressed. They suffered from a lack of equipment despite having matching uniforms, boots, flak jackets and helmets.[132] The unit was quite unconcerned with the human rights of detainees or suspects. One could argue that they do not have the luxury of treating suspects with kid gloves in a time of rampant violence, much of it directed at themselves. But it is not a winning strategy, for it further alienates the Sunni Arabs (and Sunni Turkmen in the north), who bear the brunt of this treatment by forces largely made up of Shiʿa and Kurds. An Iraqi junior officer, a Shiʿa from the south who served in the former Iraqi army, readily admits that this is a sectarian conflict: 'This is a sectarian war. These Sunnis, they have the right to resist.'[133] The men are members of the 2nd Brigade, 4th Infantry Division. They face a tough fight in the Baquba area, which is overwhelmingly Sunni, with an enclave of Shiʿa and Kurds. The unit has suffered several casualties due to ambushes, IEDs, car bombs and drive-by shootings. Yet they are reluctant to man checkpoints effectively. The attitude of the Iraqi troops seemed to be that the entire exercise of having checkpoints was a waste of time. US troops came upon a large number of sleeping soldiers and others who had simply ditched their equipment and were walking around in T-shirts and shorts.[134]

I can confirm such occurrences. In late July 2005 in Tal Afar, I accompanied a unit of the 3rd Armored Cavalry Regiment on patrol and paid an Iraqi army traffic control point an unexpected mid-morning visit. The troops checking the vehicles seemed to be doing a relatively good job, but the command post, which was set away from the main road, had little or no protection against attack. It was also dirty: the living quarters stank, trash lay everywhere, and the stench from the latrine was unbearable. The commander, a lieutenant, was fast asleep and seemed irritated when woken to explain why his troops were wandering around half-dressed (some in their underwear) and without their weapons.

The forces seem to be riddled with ethno-sectarian tensions. According to Iraqi and US officers, the Kurds have taken over the

Ministry of Defense, a traditional domain of the Sunnis. The fact that the Minister of Defense is a Sunni is actually irrelevant. Saadoun al-Dulaimi is a lone Sunni voice in a government dominated, as Sunnis see it, by separatists on the one hand and sectarianists on the other. Moreover, Dulaimi is no Ramon Magsaysay (Philippines Defense Minister and later President, who rebuilt the Philippines military and Ministry of Defense and took them to victory over the Hukbalahap Rebellion in the 1950s). But from personal observation in northern Iraq in the summer of 2005, I found few Iraqi officers with much energy, professionalism or initiative. Even the much-vaunted Kurdish officers were less than meets the eye in terms of military professionalism, although they were dedicated and politically aware in a strategic sense. One Iraqi officer, whose ethnic or sectarian background remained unspecified, told a journalist: 'The Badr Brigade is the biggest terrorist group and they run the interior ministry. The Kurds are running the MoD. The first thing they ask you when you want to become an officer is, "Are you an Arab or a Kurd?"'[135]

Kurds and Shi'a constitute the majority of the new Iraqi forces. They are deeply suspicious of one another, says Ferry Biedermann, an Israeli journalist who spent time with the Iraqi forces in the north, but are bound by a mutual hatred for the Sunnis whom they label *irhabi* (terrorist). The Kurds, says Biedermann, are 'even more ferocious in their attitude toward the local Sunni Arab population. They refer to Sunnis as murderous "dogs," two-faced liars, animals and other epithets that indicate a deep distrust and even hatred of a group clearly regarded as an enemy.'[136] The 104th Battalion, 23rd Brigade of the then Iraqi National Guard was stationed at Al-Kindi military base and entirely comprised Kurds. But their integration into the Iraqi army has been in name only; these soldiers see themselves as *peshmerga* first and foremost. Brigadier General Muzaffer Derki, commander of several *peshmerga*-ING units, including those in Mosul, has the same attitude towards Arabs as do his men, and does not bother to hide it saying: 'They need to be treated rough. You need lots of force when dealing with the Arabs. Otherwise they don't respect you—they think they can rise up against you.'[137] The fact that under the Ba'th regime, the Arabs, particularly Saddam's brutal henchman 'Chemical Ali' (Ali Hassan al-Majid) used to say the same about the Kurds escapes Derki, who is savoring the reversal of fortunes.

The 104th is based next to the 101st, a battalion that used to be made up of Sunnis. It now includes Kurds, but the battalions do not mix. The attitude of the Kurds is: 'Stay away from them. They are Arabs and you can't trust them. But don't worry, we keep an eye on them.'[138] A Kurdish officer said of a Sunni Arab colonel: '... I still don't trust him. And he still has a choice, but you and I, we will have our heads cut off if his brothers get their hands on us.'[139] With this statement he has created that bond between Us on the one hand, and Them on the other. Derki, the Kurdish officer, has no intention of letting Sunni Arabs command him or his men: 'These Arab officers, Kurds don't have to listen to them. Even the division commander is an Arab. But I only take my orders from the peshmerga.'[140] I noticed this mentality over summer and fall 2005. Many Kurds were disparaging of the Shi'a, and in this they were no different from the few Sunnis who were there. In the old Ottoman fort in central Tal Afar, I met with a number of Shi'a in the Iraqi army who were also supporters of Moqtada al-Sadr, and who were from Samawah, Nasiriyah and Basra. They were Iraqi nationalists who accused the Kurds of irredentist designs and being racist.[141]

Another structural problem continues to roil the Iraqi security sector. A 'tidal wave of corruption' has engulfed the entire security sector. The Iraqi military is full of what are referred to as 'ghost battalions', units in which officers pocket the pay of soldiers who do not exist or have simply gone home. 'I know of at least one unit which was meant to be 2,200 but the real figure was only 300 men,' said Kurdish parliamentarian Mahmoud Osman.[142] The army and police are poorly armed despite heavy expenditure over the past two years. 'The interim government spent $5.2bn on the ministry of defence and ministry of interior during six months but there is little to show for it,' said a senior official who chose to remain anonymous.[143] The Iraqi Ministry of Defense is being investigated for corruption that occurred during Prime Minister Allawi's tenure. It allegedly squandered more than $300 million buying faulty and outdated military equipment. More than forty questionable contracts allegedly resulted in huge chunks of the ministry's budget disappearing into the pockets of senior defense officials and their foreign business partners.[144]

The slow equipping of the Iraqi security forces has caused irritation among the Iraqi officer corps. 'Soldiers with Kalashnikovs and pickup trucks is not an army,' said Gen. Abdul Qader Muhammad Jassim, commander of the Iraqi ground forces, during an August 2005 interview with the *New York Times* at his office in Baghdad. 'To make the Iraqi Army stand on its own without American or coalition forces, we need command and control equipment, transport vehicles and training.'[145] He added that he wanted helicopters and artillery, more powerful guns and bigger tanks. These are the kinds of weapons the US says he does not need now. Clearly, what he does need is somewhere in between what his army has—which is pathetic—and what he and other officers like him think he *needs*.

Finally, the prospect of widespread purges in the security sector as the majority Shi'a seek to consolidate their power continues to hang over the heads of military personnel like the sword of Damocles. Any extensive purge of the security forces by the new Shi'a government could lead to its collapse and the emergence of militias masquerading as national forces. About half of the troops and 75 percent of the officers in the new Iraqi military had served under the old regime, according to a Defense Ministry spokesman, Saleh Sarhan.[146] If the new government purges them, mostly Sunnis or secular Shi'a, it risks increasing the level of violence. Hadi al-Ameri, head of the Badr Corps stated: 'All the ministries, especially ones that concern security, like defense and interior, need reformation. All the bad elements should be removed.'[147] One wonders who he, a member of an organization that fought against their own alongside the forces of the Islamic Republic of Iran views as a 'bad element'? Captain Ahmed Dawood, an infantry officer under the old regime, is now an officer in the 505th Battalion of the new Iraqi army. He has expressed doubts as to whether he will keep his career intact under the new government of Jaafari and stated that the Shi'a in charge refuse to reach out to Sunni officers of the former military: 'They've already removed those who committed crimes against Iraqis, and if they keep pushing, the entire security services will collapse. The new government wants to dismantle everything and start from zero. And from where will they bring officers and soldiers with the experience we have? From the moon?'[148]

Creating effective Iraqi security forces to take over the counter-insurgency campaign from the Coalition will continue to be a long, difficult and painstaking task. Observers and reporters made a series of devastating indictments of the Iraqi security forces in spring and summer 2005. These have cast considerable doubt on the uniformly positive claims made by the Bush administration about the capabilities of those forces. In conclusion, while the formation of an effective and offensive-minded local security force is essential to winning the counter-insurgency campaign, until they are ready we simply cannot throw the Iraqi security forces, particularly the ones we have raised, into the the counter-insurgency fray, because they are not trained, equipped or cohesive enough as forces.

The US military's approach to counter-insurgency

Despite the rich history of the United States in insurgency and counter-insurgency warfare, the US military, particularly the army, has a mind-set peculiarly geared to fighting conventional or regular warfare. Moreover, its organizational culture is highly resistant to change and accepting that insurgency or 'small war' is going to be an almost constant future challenge. This is an area that has been and continues to be explored by a significant number of defense analysts and thinkers. What has it meant on the ground in Iraq?

Understanding the enemy I: Importance of accurate and professional strategic intelligence.   The old real-estate adage in the United States (or anywhere for that matter) goes 'location, location, location'. Similarly, success in counter-insurgency is about intelligence, intelligence, and yet more intelligence. The Coalition clearly failed to anticipate the insurgency in Iraq, as admitted by the British Defense Secretary, Geoffrey Hoon: 'The Americans were thinking of a benign environment in the post-conflict planning. We did not take as much account as we should have done of the issues of security.'[149] General John Keane, the US Army's deputy chief of staff during Operation Iraqi Freedom, said in testimony—after his retirement—that the US military had been unpleasantly surprised by the insurgency because it had believed the assurances of the exiles that the United States would be welcomed in Iraq. He told the House Armed Services Committee: 'We did not see it coming. And we were not properly prepared and organized to deal with it ... Many of us got seduced by the Iraqi exiles in terms of what the outcome would be.'[150] But this is only part of the story. The United States military also lacked an understanding of the country in question and of the cultural context within which counter-insurgency was to be waged.

In this section I will address solely what I call strategic intelligence, which I define here as our knowledge based on thorough education and language training of a general 'area of responsibility' (AOR), and of a particular country and its mores, culture, strengths and vulnerabilities, peculiarities and idiosyncrasies. Strategic intelligence analysts must be able to make sober assessments about the particular country in which we are engaged. Each step of the way, they must be cognizant of and ready to accept the fact that they could be wrong or that their extrapolations will not necessarily lead to the result they desire. This is very difficult for human beings; nobody likes to be told that they could be wrong. Bureaucratic and office politics also often act to propel analyses in a desired direction. Moreover, even if we develop a formidable strategic intelligence capability the experts' analyses will not be worth the paper they are written on if policy-makers are addicted to a rigid and inflexible ideological frame of mind that is further reinforced by listening to the 'instant experts' who sprout like poisonous toadstools during times of crises. While we all see the world through an ideological prism, the so-called worldview, the prosecution of effective counter-insurgency requires a flexible and ruthless professionalism shorn as much as possible of overt biases and ideological predilections. I am not sure the United States is capable of that. It is a self-professed moralistic country that sees the world in black and white rather than shades of gray, and it conducts crusades. Its victory in the Cold War reinforced that, as did the terrorist tragedy of 9/11. It is in effect, as currently constructed, congenitally incapable of waging effective counter-insurgency. [151]

Understanding the enemy II: Operational and tactical intelligence. The lack of understanding of the enemy at the strategic and operational/tactical levels gave rise to theological statements that bore no resemblance to reality. In summer 2003 an unfortunate US colonel reportedly declared the insurgency to be the last 'gurgling gasp' of former regime henchmen.[152] Even by fall 2003, when the insurgency was intensifying, the US military and policy-makers were still at a loss as to whom they were fighting. On 30 October, Undersecretary of State John Bolton told the BBC that 'elements of the previous ... regime' had linked up with 'international terrorists' and were responsible for the rampant violence.[153] A few weeks earlier, General Ricardo Sanchez had told reporters: 'We believe there is in fact a foreign fighter element.'[154] Ground commanders in the field expressed skepticism about the importance of foreign fighters. Brigadier General Martin Dempsey, commanding officer of the 1st Armored Division, which controlled Baghdad at the time, told reporters that he had not seen any 'infusion of foreign fighters', while Major General Ray Odierno, commanding officer of the 4th Infantry Division said: 'We haven't seen them yet. We continue to look for that every day.'[155]

Intelligence for fighting an insurgency is often very different from conventional forms: 'Enemy countermeasures [to American tactics]—concealment, dispersion, deception, intermingling with civilian populations, etc.—place certainty in the fight outside the reach of technology. The information we desire the most about the enemy—his real fighting power and his intentions—lie in the psychological and human dimensions rather than the physical.'[156] This also pertains to having effective knowledge of the culture of the society in question. In the type of irregular conflict in which we are increasingly likely to be engaged, we simply cannot divorce operational and tactical intelligence (the lower levels) from an effective understanding of the enemy at the higher level of strategic intelligence. When intelligence officers find themselves immersed in gathering information for actionable intelligence in a 'small war', they become amateur sociologists, cultural and negotiation experts, and a host of other things. This is not a topic that can be dealt with in an open-source format, particularly because it relates to the operational and tactical levels. Suffice it to say that while some US forces have done an excellent job of building up a localized picture of insurgent groups and activities within their particular area of operations, others have not. While based there in 2003 the 1st Armored Division began to send sources deep into Baghdad's neighborhoods to collect information on insurgents. Foot patrols also began to visit neighborhood homes posing as water and sewer survey teams, when they were actually gathering information. 'Everyone is an intelligence officer—that's sort of our theme,' said one officer. 'You have to see everyone you come into contact with as having intelligence value.'[157]

Other problems abounded, of course. The Center for Army Lessons Learned (CALL) published a scathing report about the army's intelligence gathering and analytical capabilities with regard to the insurgency. Apparently younger officers and enlisted personnel were unprepared for their assignments as intelligence specialists and possessed 'very little to no analytical skills'.[158] A network that was supposed to link intelligence teams and convey time-sensitive information among them—as well as permit them to tap into an evolving database—worked so poorly that it was virtually non-existent. There were not enough interpreters and many of those who were available were misused.[159] Furthermore, during my time there I noticed that many were not good at translating from Arabic into English or vice versa, either because they lacked a ready fluency in one or both languages, or because it was difficult to engage in simultaneous translation.

Coercion and enforcement strategy.   Operationally and tactically the US counter-insurgency approach can be characterized as one of coercion and enforcement rather than a hearts and minds policy. The former focuses on collectively punishing those who deign to rise up in revolt. The latter seeks to address the rebels' grievances, figuring out which are legitimate and which are not, and slowly but surely looks to incorporate the disgruntled community into the political process.

It is worth exploring the British response to the Iraqi revolt here, however briefly. Their experience in the 1920 revolt remarkably foreshadowed the current insurgency in a number of ways. First, the British, who viewed themselves as bringers of the benefits of civilization and progress to the 'poor benighted heathen', as Rudyard Kipling would have it, could not conceive of the reality that the locals actually hated them or would deign to raise up arms against the vastly superior British. In an original and historically rich analysis of the 1920 revolt Daniel Bernard, a US Army captain with whom I had the pleasure of serving in Tal Afar for a short while, wrote: 'Due to an internal logic whereby British forces had cast themselves as liberators, officials had difficulty in ascribing the causes of the revolt to domestic discontent.'[160] As with the latest insurgency, which is blamed on outside forces, the British blamed everybody but themselves, including all of Iraq's neighbors, except Transjordan, which they controlled.[161]

Second, the British believed that the only thing the locals understood was the salutary application of force, as best articulated in a notorious statement by General Sir Aylmer Haldane (British General Commanding Officer Mesopotamia, 1920–2), who wrote: 'The Arabs of Iraq respect nothing but force, and to force only they will bend.'[162] And if they did not submit, one must apply yet more force. A similar sentiment seemed to be rampant in Washington, DC, and was, and continues to be, played out on the ground in Iraq. Its ideological articulation continues to be strengthened by the anodyne claim that the Sunni Arabs have not understood that they are defeated. It seems that before the start of the insurgency very few people had referred to memoirs dealing with past

colonial history. After US forces had become mired in the uprising, Haldane's memoirs were dusted off the shelves of the few institutions that claimed it in their collections, and it was supposedly
made into required reading for policy-makers and officers in the
Pentagon. While I am not sure that this is accurate—although the
dramatic 1960s French film *The Battle of Algiers* was shown to Pentagon audiences—Haldane's memoirs were allegedly reprinted to
reach a wider audience. I should note here that I do not think Haldane's negative views of the locals were imbibed by the officials
who supposedly read him; such views existed among the latter before they even knew of the British general. Reading him, however,
reinforced their prejudices and provided yet another ideological
buttress for the stereotypes. It was as if in Haldane the officials
found the evidence that allowed them to say: 'Look, even decades
ago the British knew that these people only understood force. It
worked for the British so it will work now.'

The problems associated with this elevation of racism as a deeply
embedded ideological construct in counter-insurgency are many.
I am going to discuss not the argument's moral or ethical aspects
but its logic and the evidence for its ultimate efficacy. The British
view that the locals only understood force contributed in no small
measure to their harsh policies, which included collective punishment of entire tribes and towns.[163] Naturally, the 'treachery' and
atrocities of the insurgents further reinforced the views of the British. The population often views the descent of the state into 'illegitimate violence' in a far worse light than it views violence by insurgent groups. We need to avoid such an outcome in dealing with
the current Iraqi insurgency. But I am not sure we will succeed in
preventing it because the ideological underpinnings of the British approach are still strong within the overall context of the current *ad hoc* approach to counter-insurgency in Iraq. The efficacy of
the practices based upon Haldane's views was open to doubt even

among British officers and officials. The words of Arnold Wilson, who at the height of the revolt wrote to London, are instructive:

I am having a most difficult time. Our military forces are at their lowest ebb; religious and political excitement is on the increase, and I am confronted with the usual dilemma: To do nothing is to encourage brute force which we are unable to control and is purely anarchic; to suppress it by force may precipitate grave troubles which we are not in a strong moral position to meet.[164]

Similarly, the Iraqi Arabs seem unable to understand the use of force in the insurgency. Why? Frederick Kagan, an assistant professor of military history at the United States Military Academy, West Point, says it is because they have not grasped the fact that they are defeated.[165] What are the implications of this line of argument? In polite circles it is mentioned implicitly, in less polite and more right-wing circles more explicitly: more 'brute force' is needed until 'they' submit. This is not counter-insurgency; rather, it is in lieu of counter-insurgency. We have come full circle. The ideological approach of the neoconservatives functions in parallel with the US military's adoption of the same view on the need for force, except for the military that view is less ideological than based on its frustrations with a lack of effective or coherent counter-insurgency doctrine and with the situation on the ground.

The US military's response to the insurgency has been uniformly muscular, its weapon of choice the blunt military instrument. This is necessary to a degree, but the existence of deep cultural misunderstandings and the pervasive US tendency to view peacekeeping and policing with disdain in favor of a 'robust' (force protection) approach means the missions invariably manage to enlarge the circles of alienation within the populace.[166] The British have expressed considerable alarm and revulsion over the US approach, and the Poles have taken to calling it the 'baseball bat' strategy. An alienated populace provides tacit or active support for insurgents, as well as a ready supply of recruits. These weaknesses in the US approach were recognized by senior US officers, including the recently 'retired' Colonel Douglas McGregor, one of the most charismatic and outspoken officers in the US Army in the 1990s:

Most of the generals and politicians did not think through the consequences of compelling American soldiers with no knowledge of Arabic or Arab culture to implement intrusive measures inside an Islamic society. We arrested people in front of their families, dragging them away in handcuffs with bags over their heads, and then provided no information to the families of those we incarcerated. In the end, our soldiers killed, maimed and incarcerated thousands of Arabs, 90 percent of whom were not the enemy. But they are now.[167]

Interactions between US forces and Iraqis were characterized from the early days by profound psychological and cultural gaps. The vicious cycle is exacerbated when Iraqis and Americans begin to view each other as merciless and brutal savages, and then to act upon these perceptions, inflicting atrocities that further widen the gap. 'God, I hate these people,' a comment from a disgruntled US Army sergeant in mid-summer 2003, was the expressive formulation of US alienation from the Iraqis and their apparent ingratitude and hostility.[168] Having interacted intensively with Iraqis from 2003 to 2005, it pains me to admit that I can, to use a cliché, understand where he's coming from. The war of graffiti on walls also provides a good indicator of the cultural gap and the depth of mutual contempt. In one Fallujah schoolroom US troops had written 'I [love] pork' (the word 'love' being represented by the picture of a heart), and a drawing of a camel was labeled 'Iraqi Cab Company'.[169] The following observation by a Western journalist on the scene also deserves citation:

It's a bad day at Camp Cancer. The angry crowd is pushing forward in the hot sun. The crush of bodies between the curled barbed wire on both sides adds to the oppressive 47-degree heat. The American GIs holding the crowd back are visibly sweating, the black antiglare paint on their faces smudging until they look like heavily armed pandas ...

'No food!' shouts one man, his white, button-down shirt sticking to his back, although it's not yet 8 a.m.

'No fruit!' yells another.

The burly GI at the head of the line has clearly heard all this before, and isn't moved by their pleas. 'Get away!' he shouts at the man in white, who has pushed his way near the front. 'I don't want to hear your voice!'

The crowd tells the soldiers barring their way that they need jobs.

'I don't care!' the GI responds at full volume. 'Go find jobs then. In the city. Away from here.'

To emphasize his point, he unlatches the safety on his assault rifle. The crowd takes a step back. A few start to drift away, and eventually the crowd dissipates, returning to the streets and souks of nearby Sadr City. Few hearts and minds were won this morning.[170]

By early 2004 the US was trapped by its primarily coercive approach to the counter-insurgency. The USMC thought it could adopt a different tack. The 1st Marine Division, in particular, believed that the Sunni triangle was ripe for the kind of Combined Action Program (CAP) that had been instituted during the Vietnam War. Prior to its deployment to Iraq in March 2004 the division had begun to train select units to live in Sunni villages along with ICDC personnel. The goal was to build trust among the locals and convince them to provide effective human intelligence. General John Mattis, commander of the division, ordered his troops to patrol on foot in Sunni cities rather than in buttoned-up armored vehicles. The army naturally believed that the Marines were overoptimistic. One army officer said: 'In Fallujah, you can put out all the foot patrols you want, and you could turn a corner the next day and they'll still try to kill you.'[171] The Marines' approach did not last long. There was simply not enough manpower, and the chasm between the locals and the US military was too deep.

By September 2004 many within the US military establishment believed that the situation on the ground in Iraq was far worse than the Bush administration—then facing elections—was willing to admit. These officers would not identify themselves by name for fear of reprisals by vindictive civilian superiors. One officer, in a rather dramatic and overstated claim, expressed the following view: 'We are losing the war. Since the transfer of authority in June, attacks all over Iraq have increased dramatically.'[172] Many officers believe that the attacks on Iraqis and on nascent institutions have set back reconstruction efforts tremendously. 'The enemy's intimidation and assassination campaign is very mature,' said another officer. 'Terror does work when employed ruthlessly, as in Iraq.'[173] The war, many officers admit, is about political success, not military victory. 'This war cannot be won militarily. It really does need a political and economic solution,' said General John Batiste, commander of the 1st Infantry Division, based in the Sunni triangle.[174] Many officers argued that the US tendency to overuse physical force often backfired. A Marine officer said: 'Every time we go kinetic, we actually play into the evil-doers' hands.'[175] This is true. In November 2003 Operation Iron Hammer, which targeted the insurgency and its sympathizers in Baghdad and took place while I was there, temporarily succeeded in reducing the number of daily attacks. However, it also created fresh enemies because of the rough treatment allegedly meted out to the people who were caught up in the sweep. One Iraqi woman said: 'I used to feel sympathy for the soldiers. They looked young and were away from their families. But not anymore. If the people had some mercy for the Americans before, they don't anymore. God bless the resistance.'[176]

By fall 2004 the outlines of another theme in the coercive and enforcement-based counter-insurgency strategy had become apparent. It involved enticing more Sunnis into the political process as a prelude to their participation in significant numbers in the elections of January 2005, splitting the mainstream insurgent factions from the former regime and the Islamist extremists. These last two groups were targeted for destruction. A senior US policy-maker said: 'The aim is to drive a wedge between the Sunni Arab rejectionists and the incorrigibles. Many in the rejectionist group feel disenfranchised and are being intimidated. They need to be re-lieved of that yoke and engaged, while the extremists need to be iso-lated, captured or killed.'[177] In fall 2004 Defense Secretary Rums-feld alluded several times to the plan when he spoke of attempts by the Coalition and the interim government of Iyad Allawi to reach out to and negotiate with mainstream insurgent groups.[178]

Rectitude and ethical conduct.   Anthony James Joes approvingly quotes famous British counter-insurgency expert and practitioner Sir Robert Thompson on the issue of rectitude, which means that the government or counter-insurgent side should act in 'accor-dance with the law of the land, and in accordance with the highest civilized standards'.[179] Irregular warfare descends into barbarity, cruelty and planned dehumanization of the enemy much faster and more easily than does regular warfare. The rules of irregular war-fare are not as well-codified as those for regular war because the ir-regular force does not follow them. Members of the latter often do not wear uniforms, and hide among the populace and hope govern-ment forces commit heinous crimes against the people. The irregu-lar force sometimes goes out of its way to commit its own 'barba-risms' to highlight the fact that the government forces are incapable of providing security. Of course the insurgency must balance this descent into barbarity against the possible loss of support among the people when it engages in such acts. It is incumbent upon the government/counter-insurgency side to prevent such a descent from taking place because it will rebound negatively against it. If the government/counter-insurgency side uses its security forces to engage in barbarities it loses the right to claim that it is on the side of law and order, or of morality and ethics. If it fails to prevent the insurgency from committing atrocities against the people or security forces, then it has failed to protect those it is supposed to. The Abu Ghraib torture and abuse scandal, about which much has been written, is a particularly egregious example of the failure to function within the bounds of rectitude and the rule of law.

Foreign forces are not the only ones to have engaged in 'immoral' and 'illegal' activities. The fact that local forces have also done so is unsurprising because they are in contact with and trained by the former. If the foreigners show no respect for rectitude and the rule of law, then neither will the locals. Another insidious factor has an impact in this case. The deep-seated ethno-sectarian divisions that fracture a society will be reflected by the local security forces in their daily interactions with the society that they are supposed to serve and protect without bias. Torture and abuse have become routine procedures among Iraqi security forces. Robert Perito, an expert on post-conflict security at the US Institute of Peace, said: 'In the long run, with the assistance of the US military unfortunately … [we are creating] a security force which is very much like the old Saddam security forces. That's not what we set out to do.'[180] Almost 40,000 police officers from the Saddam era went through a twenty-one-day program that was little more than a superficial introduction to western policing standards in human rights and effective law enforcement practices. Another 20,000 trained in Jordan for two months in a course modeled on one that had been established for the Kosovo police. In Kosovo, however, the training lasted five months, with an additional four months of fieldwork under careful guidance.[181]

On the issue of rectitude and the practice of rule of law among the local security forces, it is sad to say that as a whole they have inspired little trust from the Iraqi population. One Iraqi policeman complained that members of what used to be known as the Iraqi National Guard broke into his house, beat him up and stole money from his car, which actually belonged to the government. (The rivalry and mutual contempt between the National Guard and the police were intense, partly due to bureaucratic rivalries and partly because in many places the regular police are Sunnis and the National Guard are Shi'a.) He was arrested and accused of being an insurgent, and was finally handed to the Americans, who treated him courteously and released him. His final comment was, 'I tried to follow up on the incident and get an explanation but no one would talk to me. This isn't a police force—it's a bunch of thugs in uniform. Unless the government sorts this out quickly, the National Guard will become useless and corrupt.'[182] Many Iraqis viewed the National Guard with well-deserved derision and contempt. A traffic policeman in Baghdad said:

It is as if some of them want to be like the Americans, but you can tell the Americans are professional and well-trained. Their uniform looks quite like the US military's and they've started wearing black sun glasses and cutting their hair really short too. They also try to act like them, holding their rifles with their fingers on the trigger and using sign language rather than talking.[183]

In Fallujah, where the insurgency is once again rising from the rubble, the local residents initially welcomed the defeat of the radical insurgents but 'after the unfairness and injustice with which the city's residents have been treated by the American and Iraqi forces, they now prefer the resistance, just so they won't be humiliated'.[184] They hate the Iraqi army personnel, most of whom are rural Shi'a from the south. 'The Iraqi Army is not trained. They're killing people. They're shooting people in the head. You're not in the street. You don't see what's happening,' a Fallujah sheikh told a US Marine officer.[185]

While stationed in Tal Afar during summer and early fall 2005, I found the situation curiously different. The local Sunni Turkmen flatly declared that they were content with the presence of Coalition forces and Iraqi army units, but they were not going to support the entry of or work with Interior Ministry forces. Tal Afar locals showed a preference for the Iraqi army units, most of which were former Kurdish *peshmerga* with a smattering of Sunni Arabs from the north. (There were some Shi'a units from the south, many of whom spent their time complaining about pay and the difficulties of going to the south on leave.) The Interior Ministry forces, however, were overwhelmingly Shi'a, and from what I witnessed in Tal Afar they were there not to protect and serve but to extract revenge against the Sunnis.

I talked with dozens of Iraqi security personnel—most of whom were Shi'a and Kurds—in Nineveh province in the run-up to the September 2005 offensive in the city, and was struck by the more deeply primitive and atavistic approach of the Shi'a. At a traffic control point a bedraggled and smelly 'soldier' with rotting teeth and several days' stubble told me he was from Nasiriyah and that he wished to see 'a Fallujah' done to Tal Afar (i.e. for the city to be reduced to rubble). Other Shi'a joined our conversation. some agreed with him, and others, to be fair, disagreed vehemently. What struck me even more was that a couple of Kurdish soldiers in the same unit took me aside and indicated that the Shi'a are intoxicated by religion and a sense of victory. One of the Kurds, a young and handsome man from Dohuk, Kurdistan, who was incongruously wearing his camouflaged battledress top but not the trousers, had a thoroughly bored demeanor and a disconcerting habit of scratching himself at regular intervals. This young fellow told me that the best leader in his platoon was a Sunni Arab Jiburi from Mosul, and that he would follow him but not the somnambulant Shi'a lieutenant who had been thrust upon them. Suddenly the Kurd became more voluble, heaping scorn on the Shi'a. He told me that he did not want to be there, had no interest in waging a war to increase the power of the religious Shi'a, and wanted to return to Dohuk, which, he said, was very different from Iraq. As was I was leaving he dropped his bombshell: 'Can you help me get a green card to get to the United States?' he asked plaintively. I apologized profusely, telling him this was way above my pay grade and not part of my job description.

Sunni complaints about the 'irregular' behavior of the Iraqi security forces were particularly loud during summer and fall 2005. For much of June 2005 US and Iraqi forces stormed through largely Sunni neighborhoods, arresting thousands in a series of sweeps designed to put a halt to the suicide bombing campaign. Sunnis viewed Operation Lightning as a form of collective punishment of the entire community. Those who were detained and then released because there was no evidence against them complained of being tortured by Interior Ministry security forces. A sweep of Abu Ghraib was perceived as indiscriminate and the general in charge admitted as much. He reportedly told detainees who were about to be released, 'The fire burns the wet leaves as well as the dry ones' (the innocent suffer with the guilty).[186]

Maintaining a presence.   Counter-insurgency forces must maintain a presence in an area they have cleared of insurgents. If the foreign or local government cannot or does not maintain such a presence in a secured area then its initial battle to clear the insurgents will have been in vain. It is a mistake to clear an area or city of the enemy and then to declare victory. Victory comes after the re-establishment and consolidation of normality, security and stability, under which people can go about their everyday lives without fear of disruption.

It is unclear whether in the beginning US officers necessarily saw the value of maintaining a long-term presence in an area. The modus operandi was cordon and search operations: sweeping neighborhoods looking for weapons and 'bad guys' and then returning to base. The insurgents would return after the soldiers and the marines had left. The US troops would then have to repeat the procedure all over again.[187] In the middle of November 2003 Major General Charles 'Chuck' Swannack, commander of the 82nd Airborne Division, announced that security had improved so rapidly in Ramadi that the US could withdraw and leave the city at peace. This abdication of initiative was a major mistake of a type that should never be made in a counter-insurgency campaign. Swannack and his officers deemed that Operation Iron Hammer had subdued the insurgency in the region north and northwest of Baghdad: 'I believe our joint patrols with the police between now and January 1 will allow us to move to a second stage in regards to security in Ramadi where American forces step back.'[188]

The US military continues to pound insurgent positions in and around Ramadi, while the insurgents are able every day to launch a dozen significant attacks in the city. Army Sergeant First Class Tom Coffey commanded a platoon of the Army's 28th Infantry Division, conducting patrols along Ramadi's southern border. His unit was hit by roadside bombs almost daily. 'There's no way I can control this area with the men I have,' the sergeant told a US journalist. 'The reports are that the insurgents are using these southern control points because they're open. We can't keep them closed because I don't have the manpower.'[189]

The implications of not maintaining a presence can be seen clearly in the difficult time the US is having in key areas. Iraq's insurgency has concentrated much of its fight against US and Iraqi forces in towns along the murky waters of the Euphrates River, beginning with Qaim on the Syrian border and running through places such as Haditha, Haqlaniya, Hit, Ramadi and Fallujah. These are all in Anbar province, the heartland of Iraq's Sunni Muslim minority. In the cities where US forces have set up bases—such as Ramadi, the provincial capital, and Fallujah—the fighting has destroyed much of the infrastructure but failed to completely secure the areas. In smaller towns, US forces launch repeated raids to clear the streets of insurgents only to see them return as soon as the Marines and soldiers are gone.

Three weeks of reporting by Tom Lasseter, a journalist embedded with US troops in Anbar's main centers of guerrilla resistance, found that US forces are failing to make headway, and some commanders feel that much of the military's efforts are wasted.[190] 'It doesn't do much good to push them out of these areas only to let them go back to areas we've already cleared,' said Lieutenant Colonel Tim Mundy, commander of the 3rd Battalion, 2nd Marine Regiment. 'We're successful at taking some of his equipment and killing some insurgents, but the effectiveness is limited because we can't stay … we go back to camp and then we get reports that they've come back in.'[191]

In Fallujah, a city that Marines and soldiers retook from insurgents in November 2004 in what Lasseter describes as 'the heaviest urban combat since Vietnam',[192] fighters have begun to return to try to re-establish a presence. The fact that insurgents in Fallujah have twice blown up one police station under construction, and kidnapped and executed a contractor who was involved in the project, is ample evidence of continued insecurity and instability. Such attacks also signify that the counter-insurgents have not yet established a presence in the city and its environs. Indeed, the area is attacked from four to nine times each day, including by roadside bombs, RPGs and sniper fire.[193]

Western Anbar has proven to be a continuing problem. US Marines have repeatedly launched raids and mini-offensives on the small towns of Karabila, Haditha and Haqlaniya. But as soon as the Marines leave, usually after a few days of conducting sweeps through houses, the insurgents return and set up their base again. 'If you go to an area and you don't stay in that area, the insurgency will return to that area and intimidate the local population,' said Lieutenant Colonel Lionel Urquhart, who commands the 3rd Battalion, 25th Marine Regiment.[194] When Marines re-entered Haqlaniya during an operation in mid-2005, the front of practically every store in the main street had pro-*jihad* messages spray-painted on it, such as 'Allah is our God, Jihad is our way', 'Long live the mujahedeen', 'Long live jihad', 'It is your duty to fight for jihad in Iraq', or 'Death to those who collaborate with Americans'.[195]

The small Sunni town of Haditha, a farming town of 90,000 people on the Euphrates River north of Ramadi, is a further example of what happens when government forces fail to establish a permanent presence. In early 2005 Marines launched Operation New Market to clean up Haditha, but after they left the area returned to lawlessness and insecurity. In August 2005 insurgents killed twenty Marines just south of Haditha in an ambush and a roadside bombing.[196] Lieutenant Colonel Urquhart, who was responsible for Haditha, said he did not have enough men to maintain a permanent presence in such towns. 'You're going to have this constant need to go back in and clean it up again ... we have to go back in and make it clear to everybody that the insurgency does not control this country.'[197]

A three-day visit to Haditha by a reporter for the *Guardian* newspaper in August 2005 established what neither the Iraqi government nor the US military cares to admit: the town is run by insurgents.[198] They have established there a sanctuary in which they are the sole authority, maintaining and running the town's security, administration and communications, and proscribing that which they deem 'un-Islamic', such as alcohol and certain types of music. The insurgents apparently cut mobile phone network links with the rest of the country, but retained their walkie-talkies and satellite phones.[199] Hospital staff and teachers are permitted to collect government salaries in Ramadi but other civil servants have had to quit. The insurgents have been lauded by locals for allegedly pressuring managers of the local power station to supply electricity almost twenty-four hours a day, unheard of in the rest of Iraq. Insurgents, say the reporter, 'decide who lives and dies, which salaries get paid, what people wear, what they watch and listen to'.[200] Haditha lays bare the limitations of the Iraqi state and US power, which seem, and indeed are, far away and almost totally irrelevant to the daily lives of the local populace, except when the US military periodically sweeps through.

The journalist described the steady transformation of the town into an insurgent stronghold: 'A year ago Haditha was just another sleepy town in western Anbar province, deep in the Sunni triangle and suspicious of the Shia-led government in Baghdad but no insurgent hotbed.'[201] Then the government sent in heavy-handed Shi'a police. This highlights another problem with maintaining a presence: you cannot do so in an oppressive and punitive manner, because that will only arouse support for the insurgents. Attacks against the police intensified, and finally they fled. Into the vacuum thus created stepped the insurgents.[202]

Three times in 2005 Marines backed by aircraft and armor swept into the town to flush out the rebels. There were skirmishes, and a few suspects killed or detained, and the military, as was its habit, would release information on the number of insurgents killed as proof of their claim of success. The reality was different. The insurgents would withdraw and watch patiently for a few days as the US forces expended their energy and resources and then left, at which point, locals told the *Guardian* reporter, the insurgents returned.[203] During their operations the US military would not have destroyed the insurgents' infrastructure, simply because it is 'opaque' to them and does not have a heavy footprint. Nor would they have succeeded in breaking the invisible link that ties the locals, willingly or not, to the insurgents.

The insurgents' ability to establish and institutionalize a presence in a town or region has another insidious outcome. If they are not on the run, they can renew hitherto broken links, or establish new ones, and begin to coordinate and cooperate with other groups. In evidence of increasing collaboration between rebels, a group in Fallujah, where the resistance is said to be regathering, wrote to Haditha seeking background checks on volunteers from the town.[204] Tribal elders said they feared but respected insurgents for keeping order and not turning the town into a battleground.[205]

Why did the US fail to establish presence in areas cleared of insurgents? Although I cannot answer this question within the confines of this study, I can say that it is tied to the twin, controversial issues of whether the US had enough troops in Iraq and of the culture of troop rotation after one year. Logically, if you have insufficient troops in the country it becomes very difficult to maintain a significant presence in cleared areas. Even more insidious is the troop-rotation policy that leaves little time to develop and institutionalize knowledge of the particular area. And although a unit that has maintained presence for a year in one area does accumulate a considerable amount of knowledge and human intelligence about that place, other problems might still arise. The unit might, for example, be unable to transfer that institutionalized knowledge to the one taking over from it. There may simply be no mechanism for doing so, or, as is often the case, the unit's knowledge may be limited to a very small group of harried and harassed officers who simply do not have the time to pass information to their successors, or are not tasked effectively to do so.

Yet another problem may occur when the rotating unit is replaced by another with a smaller footprint because the military feels that its predecessor has successfully dislodged the insurgents. This is simply wrong. The tipping point is *not* removing the insurgent presence and then claiming success. David Galula, the much under-appreciated French counter-insurgency theorist, whose writings are making a comeback, said we must beware of a 'Sisyphean trap'.[206] In Greek mythology Sisyphus was the young man condemned by the gods to roll a rock up a mountain, only to have it roll down again under its own weight, at which point he would have to roll it up again, and so on, *ad infinitum*. Failure to maintain a presence in cleared areas means our gains can be reversed very easily and condemns us to returning again and again, as US troops have had to do in western Anbar.

Moreover, an area cleared of insurgents can only remain so with the support of the populace. Thus our presence must not be an oppressive one 'imposed' on the population (although initially that may be necessary, because the first task is policing and establishing security). The population must also be complicit in the establishment and effective maintenance of the forces of the government in the area, and in the center's attempts to implement basic services and reconstruction. In other words, the 'permanent isolation of the insurgent from the population,' is not 'enforced upon the population but maintained by and with the population'.[207]

I am addressing here not what the United States can or cannot do to deal with these problems, but merely what they have meant for our ability to prosecute a counter-insurgency campaign. *The inability or unwillingness to maintain a presence, to ensure security and stability and allow a legitimate political process to take root and reconstruction to proceed, has been of inestimable help to the insurgency, allowing it to take root and perpetuate itself in key regions or cities.* The local inhabitants are not going to support the forces of law and order if such forces merely conduct sweeps and either leave or merely maintain a token presence.

The inability to maintain presence is a major problem in itself, but it also has serious negative consequences for the counter-insurgents' ability to turn the tide in their favor. It requires returning and fighting again and again in an area that is well-known to insurgents and in which they have links to the population that are broken only temporarily by the ineffectual sweeps by US forces. Between March and August 2005 insurgents killed or wounded more than a third of the men in the two companies that during that time were the two main fighting forces in Lieutenant Colonel Urquhart's battalion. Twenty-two of Lima Company's 156 men were killed in action and thirty-one wounded. Kilo Company, with about 150 men, had four killed and at least fifty wounded.[208]

Sealing and policing Iraq's porous borders.   A counter-insurgency campaign in Iraq will have a greater chance of success if the counter-insurgents are able to seal the country's borders, which are wide open and about which Iraqis complain bitterly. The new Iraqi border guards face considerable challenges: they are ill-trained, poorly equipped and few in number. The influx of foreign terrorists and insurgents has not been great in terms of quantity, but what matters is their quality. The infiltrators have had a combat multiplier effect. Finally, control over the country's borders will affect the burgeoning drug trade into Iraq, which is being run by organized criminal groups.

Much of the onus for patrolling Iraq's particularly porous border has fallen upon US troops. The 3rd Armored Cavalry Regiment was rotated to Nineveh province in spring 2005. Its personnel have complained with considerable justification that they simply do not have troops to patrol and maintain a presence in the 'badlands', the deserts of northwestern Iraq, near the Syrian border. The area, which they often refer to as Iraq's 'wild, wild, west', is a major transit point for weapons, money and foreign fighters. From October 2004 to April 2005, when they were relieved by the 3rd Armored Cavalry, 400 soldiers of the 25th Infantry Division patrolled this 10,000-square-mile region. About 3,500 men of the 3rd Armored Cavalry took control of the area in May 2005, along with 4,000 Iraqi troops of questionable quality. Officers of the armored regiment say that even with this increase, they are still understaffed.

The town of Tal Afar lies within this region, and seems to be a staging post for fighters and weapons filtering into the rest of Iraq. Contrary to official and journalistic perception, the foreigners do not stay in the city and integrate themselves into the insurgency, which is overwhelmingly local in origin, as we discovered during an operation in September 2005. The infiltrating fighters move on to the center of Iraq. To the west of Tal Afar, the small and even duller town of Biaj for a very long time had no police or mayor—they had simply vanished—until the 3rd Armored Cavalry made heroic efforts to rectify matters. The same was true for the town of Rawa, south of Tal Afar and home to many officers and enlisted men from the Iraqi army. A brief firefight in Rawa in late May 2005 between armored cavalry troopers and foreign fighters underscored the gravity of the problem of infiltration in a poorly policed town and region. Four insurgents, three Saudis and a Moroccan, were killed; while four others, from Syria, Jordan and Algeria, surrendered.[209]

The US counter-insurgency campaign in comparative context.   No discussion of the US counter-insurgency campaign in Iraq can be considered complete without comparisons to Vietnam or other counter-insurgency campaigns. I do not intend to wade into the Vietnam quagmire, but I wish to address the superficial comparisons that have often been made to successful counter-insurgency campaigns. Many on the neoconservative right point to the British success in Malaya (1948–60) as worthy of emulation by the United States. They do so, however, without a thorough understanding or analysis of the similarities and differences.

The similarities are remarkable. First, in Malaya as in Iraq the British and Americans face an insurgent that comes from a minority within the population. In Malaya the British faced an insurgency instigated and led by Chinese communists within the Chinese minority. In Iraq the insurgency has been instigated and led by nationalists and Islamists within the Sunni minority. Second, in neither case did the insurgents have extensive or extended regional or global support. The Malayan insurgents had little or no sanctuary, while that of the Iraqi insurgents is shaky. Foreign fighters from a global network have infiltrated Iraq, but in the case of Malaya few, if any, outside communist adventurers went to fight for the so-called 'common masses'. Third, the ragtag insurgents in both cases faced two of the most technologically advanced military establishments of their time. Fourth, both Britain and the United States suffered intelligence failures and were taken by surprise when the respective insurgencies broke out. Such surprise was totally inexcusable for Britain,[210] which was hardly a newcomer to Malaya. It had been the colonial power there for decades, and its settlers and colonial officers were well-versed in the intricacies of Malaysian politics and culture. As for the United States on the eve of going into Iraq, I forcefully reiterate my view that, because of the grip of ideology at all levels, it knew nothing and had learned nothing.

The contrasts between Malaya and Iraq are just as remarkable. First, Britain was a bankrupt nation in 1948. World War II had been financially ruinous and more than anything else the cost of that war had destroyed its great power status. This was brutally confirmed by the Suez Crisis of 1956, fought alongside another 'geriatric' imperial power, France, as well as Israel. The United States, on the other hand, is the world's richest and most powerful nation. It has 'everything going for it', a sentiment made abundantly clear in a panegyric offered by the *Economist* little more than a year before the war with Iraq.[211]

Second, Britain was unsuccessful at the beginning of its counter-insurgency. In fact, it was facing failure. It took a paradigm shift, or epiphany, on its part, which was forced by some remarkable officials, to turn the tide. Because the Iraq conflict is ongoing, it would be unfair to say that the United States has failed, is failing or will fail. But I do not see any 'epiphany' taking place on how to win this war (or have the Iraqis viewed as Iraqis, rather than as divided ethno-sectarian communities) with the minimum goal being the emergence of a relatively stable and legitimate state entity.

Third, the British implemented an effective intelligence organization to make up for their past failures. The US has not to my knowledge really gained a full understanding of this insurgency. Fourth, while the British did implement a harsh and ruthless counter-insurgency campaign, they also carried out political and socioeconomic reforms. Moreover, although the Malayan conflict was seen as part of the ideological struggle against communist takeover, Britain did not take an ideological approach towards the Chinese population. They sought to integrate them into the future of the country. British officials knew that ethnic cooperation and integration into the political process was critical to the emergence of Malaya as a successful and independent country. They ultimately developed a vision and a plan for the implementation of that vision. The US lacks that 'vision thing' for Iraq, and unsurprisingly has no plan, although there is plenty of ideology and *ad hocism*. While that may sound counterintuitive in theory, in practice it is not so. This has left us with a situation where, at the operational and tactical levels, we have success after success, but this has no bearing on or relationship to the fact that such successes occur as Iraq seems headed towards the division of its peoples.

CONCLUSIONS

WHITHER IRAQ?

It is difficult to venture any conclusions about an ongoing conflict. I feel I can, however, make summary remarks in two distinct areas. First, what conclusions can we make about the Iraqi insurgency itself, and the counter-insurgency campaign? Second, in the light of the tragedies and travails that have befallen Iraq, and which it is still suffering, what does the future hold, for the Coalition presence in the country, and for Iraq itself?

The Iraqi insurgency

Origins and motivations of the insurgency.   The origins and motivations of the Iraqi insurgency lie in the material, nonmaterial and policy realms. The collapse of Sunni Arab privileges and positions, even in the straitened circumstances of sanctioned Iraq, was a body blow to members of that community. However, I am not convinced that the key promoter of the insurgency was the loss of material positions (although one could argue with convincing evidence that the perceived attempts to deny the Sunni region its share of Iraq's oil wealth will help perpetuate the conflict). We must not believe that conflicts are caused or motivated only by struggles over tangible and material issues. In other words, while it is true that states and peoples go to war rationally for the express purpose of maximizing gains or minimizing losses, there are other reasons that are not so readily apparent or so easily identified or explained. Put simply, often states and peoples act not only to win things or to prevent the loss of things, 'but also in order to defend a certain conception of who they are'.[1] The Coalition overthrow of the regime in April 2003 saw the collapse of the Iraq that the Sunni Arab community had built and known for almost eighty-three years. This assault on Iraqi national identity as shaped by the Sunnis could have been mitigated had there been a post-Saddam policy of reconciling the Sunni Arabs to the new order. Indeed, many Sunnis were willing to play their part in the new regime, as I discovered in numerous discussions in Baghdad in fall 2003 and winter 2004.

Instead it could be argued that an insidious set of policy options were adopted by the Bush administration to deepen this assault on the Sunni Arab community and to ensure its marginalization in a future Iraq where the Kurds and the Shi'a were the favored partners. These policy options have undoubtedly been key factors in the outbreak and persistence into 2006 of the insurgency. These policies have affected the Sunnis materially and in terms of assaulting and undermining their identity. Many observers have no doubt that this was a deliberate strategy crafted by the policy-makers who gave us the war. However, they did not expect the Sunni Arabs to react the way they did by sparking an insurgency that has had a widespread and significant impact.

In the light of their unfavorable views of the Sunni Arabs the policy-makers reacted in the only way they thought that community would understand: with force. The United States made more enemies than it needed to with its perceived harsh operational and tactical measures in the Sunni heartland. Not surprisingly, the old canard that the only thing the Arabs understand is force proved its inefficacy with the intensification of the insurgency and the depravities of Abu Ghraib. As the situation worsened in Iraq there was a belated attempt to reach out to the Sunni Arabs and re-engage them. But it was too late. First, it was an effort that was insincere, deprived of resources, unsustained and too narrow in scope to encompass the majority of the community, including the technocrats and those members of the armed forces and the Ba'th Party who had not committed crimes.[2] The Bush administration's attempts to engage the Sunni Arab population intensified during the negotiations over the drafting of the new constitution in summer 2005. But this was perceived not as a sincere effort to re-engage with the thoroughly disgruntled community, but as merely an attempt to convince the Sunnis to accede to a constitution so that the administration can claim that progress is being made.

Characteristics, methods and goals. From the vantage point of late summer 2005, what can we say about the Iraqi insurgency, or even insurgencies? I have used the phrase 'low-level, localized, and decentralized insurgency'[3] to describe a situation in which myriad political groups that are not necessarily connected or coordinated with one another have engaged in acts of violence to disrupt and remove the US presence in Iraq. The above description of the insurgency merits further clarification. The low-level nature of the Iraqi insurgency has already been discussed in Chapter 3 (see pp. 125–6). It is also pertinent to add here that the IRA insurgency of the 1920s waged by Michael Collins in Ireland was even more low-level than the Iraqi insurgency, yet ultimately it achieved many of its objectives. In short, while this insurgency is not the Vietcong or the Algerian FLN in terms of resources, legitimacy and support from external sources, it has been potent.

The insurgency is localized in terms of geography and of popular/national involvement. At its height the Sunni insurgency was largely confined to one part of the country, the center, and to a particular part of the center. Yet we must not ignore the fact that the insurgents have often struck beyond their base locales and caused considerable destruction and death. The insurgents do not look unusual or act differently from the majority of Iraqis and can blend in quite easily with the rest of the population. Nor is the Sunni insurgency is national in the sense of being popular nationwide. The Sunni insurgents have argued that they have support among *all* sectors of the population. This is not credible; neither Sunni Kurds nor Shi'a Arabs are going to fight to return the former regime to power, or to bring about Sunni fundamentalist rule. And Kurds and Shi'a alike have issues with the Arab nationalist orientation of some of the insurgent groups. Similarly, when Moqtada's insurgency broke out it also remained localized. He managed to gain some sympathy and cooperation from Sunni insurgents but, more importantly, no nationwide Shi'a uprising occurred. By late 2005 Moqtada had shifted gears and devoted his attention to grooming himself as a major player in the Iraqi political scene. He has not, however, neglected the Mahdi Army. In a land where the writ of the central government hardly extends beyond Baghdad, militias are rife, and increasingly a symbol of community power and providers of basic services. The Mahdi Army has better training and weapons, but in a vicious firefight on 27 October 2005 proved it was still no match for Sunni insurgents.

Should we stay or should we go?

The insurgency has devastated Iraq. There is next to no socioeconomic development, reconstruction or security. The security situation deteriorated over the course of 2004 and worsened dramatically during the first eight months of 2005. We have seen in Iraq in 2005 the emergence of 'complex warfare patterns' in which the norm has become a 'national resistance' by one community, violence by organized criminal gangs, and incipient civil war pitting ethnic and religious groups against one another in a massive fight over 'who gets what, when and how'. The insurgency has not only exacerbated ethno-sectarian tensions in the country, but also highlighted and solidified the mutually exclusivist nationalisms of the three main communities. As a result the prospects for US success in Iraq, in bringing about security as a stepping-stone towards reconstruction and political stability, are not good.

However, no analysis of the Iraq imbroglio is complete without a discussion of the various options available to the United States and the potential scenarios for Iraq's future. While these are two distinct issues, they are, as things stand in Iraq, intricately related.

First, the 'grand vision'—the idea that US presence will promote a stable, secure and democratic Iraq—persists among the ranks of the ideologically 'pure and virtuous'. We can dismiss from the outset the prospect of Iraq moving towards a stable and secure democracy with the help of the US presence. Based on my experiences in Iraq I do not envisage a progression towards the 'higher stage' of political development (i.e. democracy) in Iraq. There is no democracy; there is ethnocracy. The latter has been defined as a political system that is 'instituted on the basis of *qualified rights to citizenship*, and with *ethnic affiliation* (defined in terms of race, descent, religion, or language) as the distinguishing principle'.[4] Iraq was an ethnocracy for eighty-three years under the Sunnis. After the demise of the Ba'th regime the domination of one ethnicity was merely replaced by the domination of another. There was no circulation of elites in the past, merely intra-circulation within one ethnic group, and often by violence. I do not see anything changing much in coming years. The country is raising not a national army but distinct mini-armies and a host of official and unofficial militias. The human glue for democracy, an educated middle class, was shredded during the sanctions regime and much of its remnants have been fleeing to neighboring countries. Politics is either a zero-sum game or about moral absolutes. While some individuals and think-tanks keep promoting this theology, it is safe to say that even the more realist-oriented within the Bush administration have lowered their expectations. We could stop in midstream and decide to organize ourselves for a massive all-out effort to ensure the success of the grand vision. But do we have the resources, the energy, the patience and that 'vision thing' across the spectrum in the United States? I do not think so. The failures to date have soured many people. Nor should we further dissipate our resources on a project whose outcome is uncertain.

There is the 'muddle through' approach, in which we are engaged now. It is *ad hocism* across the board. Like Pangloss in Voltaire's *Candide*, we proceed grimly, dealing with the setbacks and hoping for the best. We implement piecemeal solutions and salves to the festering problem and measure progress by quantifiable indicators (how many insurgents were killed, how many Iraqi army battalions have been raised). There are many problems with this strategy, including the fact that we allow the legitimate Iraqi government to abdicate responsibility and let us do the majority of their 'dirty work' (suppressing a quasi-nationalist insurgency among a defined minority). The approach promotes the implementation of a coercive counter-insurgency approach born of a priori ideological assumptions and fury and frustration over things not going right.

We can withdraw, though I for one do not support this option. The United States cannot cut and run. The loss of prestige and power for the world's most powerful country—already battered by global unpopularity and glee over its difficulties—would be incalculable. The impact on Iraq and on the region, and to the global political economy, would be devastating. Why? Iraq would most likely descend into civil war, the ingredients for which exist. It would take little to spark violent confrontations if we were to depart. Barely submerged ethno-sectarian animosities are bubbling to the surface. There are confrontations over resources and territory between various communities. And finally, there are political elites—some functioning legally, others illegally—who are definitely bent on the 'social construction' of ethno-sectarian hatred of the Other, for a variety of reasons including mobilization of their respective communities and strengthening of their political base. There are, of course, others who have gone out of their way to denounce and prevent the social construction of ethno-sectarian violence. For example, Ayatollah Sistani has implored the Shi'a not to fall into the trap of responding to the sectarian violence of some Sunni groups, despite the constant visits by some Shi'a leaders to implore him to allow them to respond.

Many Iraqis and their supporters in Washington, DC, suffer from wishful thinking and repeatedly claim that civil war could never happen in Iraq. When pressed as to why such a war is unlikely they reply that Iraqis would never do such a thing to one another and, in a disparaging and supercilious manner, remark that 'the Iraqis are not Lebanese'. Another hoary argument often advanced by Iraqis is that their compatriots of different ethnicities and religions have intermarried and lived in harmony for generations. This is true, but supposedly idyllic societal harmony can break down, and when that happens it can do so with barbaric violence. Yugoslavs of all stripes lived in close proximity and intermarried, as did Rwandan Hutus and Tutsis, long before their civil wars became bywords for post-Cold War barbarity. To assume that the Iraqis are immune from the catastrophic factors that lead to internal or civil war is to imbue them with superhuman characteristics that they simply do not have. Indeed, why is it possible for Iraq to witness a decades-long war of secession by one ethnic group, the Kurds, many of whom lived in amicable proximity with their Arab neighbors, but it is not possible for it to witness sectarian conflicts? Many observers have now discarded their naivete and acknowledge that Iraq could be headed towards civil war or, indeed, is already in the midst of a low-level one.

The reason why a full-scale civil war between Iraq's various ethnic and sectarian groups has not taken place is the presence of the Coalition, and such a conflict is unlikely while Coalition forces remain. It is the US military that specifically constitutes a formidable deterrent to such an eventuality. In any case, reality—which the faith-based believers in the Iraq enterprise disdain—has the depressing habit of intruding on wishful constructs. People from the various Iraqi communities are increasingly seeking succor, support and security within their own. People who are not of the same faith or ethnicity are seen as the outsider. One Iraqi observer put it: 'A tide of religious and ethnic sentiments was reborn by the war. Everyone now calls himself a Kurd or Arab, Shiite or Sunni and sticks to his side. Everyone feels the tension; the smallest incident could make things degenerate.'[5] A worried Sunni Arab member of the Association of Muslim Scholars said in late February 2004: 'The people are not safe. The people have started to gather along sectarian lines. The ethnic and sectarian divisions threaten to fragment the country into small parts.'[6] Saddam claimed to have wanted to abolish sectarian and ethnic affiliation as an organizing principle, yet he practiced it. Indeed, he institutionalized it by his policy of favoring a select group of Sunni Arabs from his ancestral area of Tikrit.

The political climate of post-Saddam Iraq has further contributed to this by allowing sectarian and ethnic affiliation to continue to be the organizing principle of Iraqi politics. The struggle over resources, namely land, water and oil, has exacerbated ethno-sectarian differences. Clashes have taken place between the ethnically Turkish Turkmen minority in the north and the Kurds both in the oil-rich town of Kirkuk, over the 'correct' division of resources and political power, and in the poverty-stricken western areas of Nineveh Province, around Tal Afar and Avghani. The traditional conflict between Iraq's Arab majority and its large Kurdish minority over the level of self-autonomy the latter can have within a united Iraq has not flared into open violence ... yet. But localized clashes between Arab and Kurd over land and resources have already occurred in the northern part of the country.

While the prospects for a civil war between Arab and Kurd do exist should the latter decide they would prefer to secede and take territories and resources that the Arabs and Turkmen feel belong to them, many observers are also worried by the dire prospect of an inter-Arab civil conflict between Sunni and Shi'a. Sectarian tensions between the Sunni and Shi'a Arabs were already apparent in 2003. A minor attack on a Sunni mosque, Ahbab al-Mustafa, in the largely Shi'a Baghdad suburb of Hurriyah in mid-December illustrated the slow but steady rise of mutual antagonism. A Sunni worshipper automatically blamed the Shi'a: 'It was the Shiites who did this. The Shiites are worse than the Jews.'[7] It was merely one of a series of attacks against Sunni mosques and reinforced the belief that the Shi'a were engaging in ethnic cleansing.[8]

When I was in Iraq between November 2003 and April 2004 I received mixed responses to the question I posed concerning the possibility of a *harb madani*, or civil war, between the sects. Some said it was looming on the horizon and was only a matter of time. Others claimed it was simply impossible. Still others repeated the mantra that Iraqis of all stripes had to work actively to prevent such an eventuality. But the fact is that a low-level civil war—in all but name—and ethnic cleansing are already taking place between Sunni and Shi'a in parts of Iraq, with brutal tit-for-tat killings by death squads. This has been a particular problem in the small towns and villages just south of Baghdad and extending into the city's southern suburb of al-Doura.[9] The 'low-level' sectarian conflict in such suburbs is dwarfed by the barbarities inflicted on Shi'a by Sunni extremists in the so-called 'triangle of death', an area south of Baghdad bounded by the poor and nondescript towns of Mahmudiyah, Yusufiyah and Latifiyah, which lie on the road to Najaf. While most Shi'a deferred to their clerics, who told them not to engage in vigilantism, naturally, other Shi'a created their own retaliation squads and responded, further worsening sectarian relations. Indeed, the Shi'a are not the innocent and aggrieved party that they make themselves out to be. In many cases the retaliation is encouraged and coordinated by the Badr Corps.

Tensions between the two sects became worse in 2005 when senior Sunni scholars and leaders such as Harith al-Dari accused the Badr Organization and Ministry of Interior troops of harassing Sunni Arabs, torturing detainees and killing Sunnis, including clerics. Badr Corps leaders say they are part of the solution to the insecurity plaguing Iraq. Members of the Sunni Arab community disagree, arguing that the Badr Corps is part of the problem. Indeed, Harith al-Dari accused the militia of killing Sunni clerics, including Sheikh Hasan al-Naimi, who was murdered on 17 May 2005. Al-Dari stated that members of the Iranian-trained Badr Corps militia had joined the Ministry of Interior's so-called elite Dhib (Wolf) police commando battalion, whose logo is a snarling wolf. However, Brigadier Abu al-Walid, their commander and an officer of the former Iraqi army, responded: 'The Badr Organization has not supported us in our assaults on militant strongholds. Our duties are independent of any party or organization. And we don't interfere in Badr's affairs.'[10] While this is a good answer, it is simply not true; the Shiites have made every effort since 2003 to secure control of the Interior Ministry, which is charged with internal security. Moreover, Abu al-Walid—who was the target of a failed assassination attempt in early June—may not interfere in the affairs of the Badr Organization, but this does not mean that this well-trained militia with its extensive Iranian-trained intelligence apparatus does not interfere in Interior Ministry affairs.

Although al-Dari called upon all Iraqis to exhibit patience in the face of 'those who seek discord' in order to avert the 'shredding of the social fabric', he also warned that the Sunnis would begin to defend themselves more actively. As if to lend credence to his statement, hundreds of Sunni demonstrators stood outside the mosque where al-Dari was speaking and chanted 'We will take revenge on the brigade of shame', meaning the Badr Organization. The head of the Sunni *awqaf* (religious endowments), Adnan al-Dulaimi, stated: 'We do not want discord, and we emphasize brotherhood in Islam, but we shall not stand by with hands folded in the face of the killing of mosque Imams.' The Sunni community proceeded to close their mosques between 20 and 23 May in protest. SCIRI and the Badr Organization responded by denying that they were seeking sectarian strife and accused al-Dari of stirring it up.[11] Other prominent Sunnis joined in accusing the new government's interior ministry security forces of singling out clerics and killing them, including Imam Dhia Muhammad al-Janabi in July.[12]

Unfortunately, clerics have not been innocent of precipitating the growing chasm between the Sunnis and Shi'a. On both sides of the sectarian divide they have not been averse to whipping up tensions between the communities. After a bombing of a Shi'a mosque in the largely Sunni neighborhood of Adhamiya in Baghdad, a Shi'a cleric thundered: 'They were aiming to target as large a number of Shiites as possible. The suicide bomber wore the devil's beard, and he wore clothes from the people of hell ... Those who want you to have a peace agreement with these criminals, they are telling you that they are carrying explosive materials and they want to kill you; and you think you should have a peace agreement with them?'[13]

A devastating suicide bombing on 16 July 2005 in Mussayib, south of Baghdad, in which 100 died and more than 150 were injured, led many Shi'a began to call for the activation of local militias to protect vulnerable communities from terrorists. The matter was even raised before the Iraqi National Assembly when Shi'a member of parliament Khudayr al-Khuzai called upon the government 'to bring back popular militias. The plans of the Interior and Defense Ministries to impose security in Iraq have failed to stop the terrorists.'[14] This view was echoed by Saad Jawad Kandil of SCIRI, which controls the Badr Organization of roughly 7,000 militiamen.

The tension between the two sectarian communities of Islam can be found at three distinct levels. First, there is the traditional disdain that they hold for each other and their respective rituals. This has been compounded by the Sunni Arab view of the Shi'a as either actual or potential fifth columnists for their coreligionists in Iran. It is nothing more than ingrained Sunni prejudice against the Shi'a, which existed at the time of the Ottoman Empire, was magnified for much of the monarchical era (1921–58) and reappeared in a thinly veiled manner during the republican and Ba'thist eras (1958–2003). Prejudices can lead to vicious sectarian clashes and fulfill significant roles in (civil) wars. Indeed, political leaders can harness prejudices effectively for use against other ethnic and sectarian groups. But mutual historical prejudice is not enough reason for a civil war. Such conflicts break out as a result of clashes over concrete political and material and resource issues, over the future direction of the state and its organizing identity, and, of course, over who receives the largest share of political power. All of these ingredients for civil war exist in present-day Iraq.

Second, there is the role played by a large part of the Sunni Arab community in the discrimination against, and oppression and wholesale massacre of Shi'a under the Saddam regime. The mixed Sunni-Shi'a Baghdad suburb of Ghazalia was a microcosm of all the ethno-sectarian ills, conflicts and suspicions that plague Iraq. Saddam had the suburb built in the 1980s for army officers and members of the Ba'th Party, the latter being provided with choice parcels of land in the southern part of this new suburb. There they began building large and quite often imposing homes. The northern end of the suburb was a different story altogether, a dirt-poor sprawl inhabited by lower middle-class Shi'a. The Ba'th regime refused to allow the Shi'a there to build a mosque, while the Sunni section of Ghazalia had a dozen.[15] The Shi'a have little reason to overlook these recent events, and my first-hand observations in Iraq over the course of November and December 2003 indicate that many Shi'a are not too eager to forget and forgive.[16] The collapse of a regime that had brutalized the Shi'a for more than thirty years was a key victory and, furthermore, it opened the way for their rise to power. The Sunnis believe that they are entitled to rule because they see themselves as the authentic voice of the country and as having its best interests at heart. Moreover, they are among the most skilled and educated segment of the population, along with a significant Christian element. Both groups are leaving the country *en masse*.[17]

Sectarian tensions existed long before the US invasion and occupation. Many Sunni Arabs who were part of the regime viewed the Shi'a as religious obscurantists. 'We're civilizing the zealots,' said a Sunni Ba'th Party official on the eve of the war in March 2003.[18] Outside observers also detected a growing anti-Shi'a rhetoric emerging from the Salafi mosques of Iraq's Sunni population. Some Shi'a apparently boasted that as soon as the United States attacked the regime, they would strike at the Sunnis in revenge for decades of oppression and for the brutal suppression of the Shi'a intifada of 1991.[19]

Sunni and Shi'a political groups have little in common in post-Saddam Iraq. This is bound to continue causing political tensions and problems in the Iraqi body politic. Even Sunni political parties that participated in the political process, like the IIP, are separated from their Shi'a counterparts by a vast gulf. Fuad al-Rawi, a member of the IIP's political committee, stated: 'Sunnis ruled Iraq from 1921 until 2003, and they were efficiently ruling it. They have their intellectuals, their religious scholars, their politicians, and they have the elite people. They also have political awareness, and they have the capability to run this country.'[20] This sense of entitlement is widespread among Sunni Arabs and will not be easy to eradicate. Al-Rawi also adamantly insisted that the Sunnis constituted the majority of the population. If he means the Sunni Arabs constitute the numerical majority, then this is delusional or wishful thinking. Even Sunni Arabs and Sunni Kurds combined make up barely 40 percent. This is not an inconsequential minority—it is almost half of the population and would clearly dilute the power of the Shi'a. More to the point, however, is the inescapable fact that the Sunni Arabs and Sunni Kurds are not a unified bloc, and nor are they likely to be. For many Sunnis, the rise of the Shi'a means domination by Iran, a country that they excoriated for decades under Saddam. The Shi'a fiercely resent any aspersions cast on their 'Arabness', their alleged subordination to Iranian interests and their supposed lack of readiness to rule Iraq. These views to them smack of a colonial mentality on the part of their Arab brethren.

The Sunni sense of entitlement causes both mirth and anger among some Shi'a. Sheikh Abd al-Jabbar Menhal, a Shi'a cleric, was scornful of the Sunni Arab resistance: 'These people do not defend the interests of Iraqis. They defend their own interests because their future is being buried together with Saddam Hussein.'[21] The Shi'a, he argued, have a right to run the country: 'We also have thinkers, we have philosophers and [ruling the country] is not a matter of Sunni or Shi'a. It is a matter of justice. We believe in justice, and we follow the leader who leads Iraq in a just way and does not waste the fortune of Iraq to kill millions, as Saddam Hussein [did].'[22]

I heard almost the same sentiments expressed by a couple of Shi'a clerics in Al-Hilla in late November 2003, when a group of my colleagues and I piled into a couple of armored suburbans and drove at high speed with a military escort of Humvees for a day visit to Babil Province. The CPA headquarters in Al-Hilla was based in a decrepit and seedy hotel done up in the ubiquitous Stalinist-style architecture so beloved of dictatorial Middle Eastern regimes. There an Arab-American officer with the US army took us to meet and have lunch with the Shi'a cleric Farhad Qazwini, a big bear of a man who rambled on about a wide variety topics ranging from social and political to cultural issues. He was, however, quite unequivocal about the rising power of the Shi'a, as was one of his followers, another cleric engaged me in a spirited discussion. He was unfailingly and obsequiously polite, in the way that only Shi'a clerics seem capable of, but he saw the world through the lens of a chilling and smug self-righteousness. Any scenario that I posed to him concerning Iraq's future was met with a polite 'It cannot happen here', or 'We will not let it happen'. I knew beforehand that Iraq had its own adherents to faith-based reality; here was an interview with the real thing. As we talked in the clichéd carpeted receiving room of Sheikh Qazwini, a thuggish-looking man with an ample girth but huge arms walked in and sat down. I knew right away that this was not a cleric. Indeed, as I recall he introduced himself as an engineer. I discovered, to my consternation, that he spoke relatively fluent French. This man, whose relationship to Qazwini I did not know or care to find out, was out for sectarian power and revenge for what he saw as decades of humiliation and oppression. He claimed that he had recently come from the uncovered mass graves in which were buried Shi'a victims of Saddam's perennial bursts of anger against that community. This may have accounted for the state of his emotions, yet I could not help but think that people like this, on both sides of the divide, were in the ascendant.

Managed de facto *or* de jure *partition?*   If outright civil war is not possible while Coalition forces remain in Iraq but the country does not move forward in a manner that is to the benefit of all the communities, is it possible to bring about a managed partition?[23] It has been discussed extensively in recent months as a viable option by some and excoriated by others.[24] In the theoretical literature, scholars continue to argue the pros and cons of partition by looking at examples in recent memory. These debates notwithstanding, there is much to be said for this option. Indeed, some believe it may ultimately be the only one open to us. And it is the option that can allow us to leave with honor intact. By 'managed partition' I mean a process that could be mediated by the Coalition and the international community in negotiations with the major ethnosectarian communities in Iraq. The Coalition would then guarantee the agreement reached between the major groups in the country. It could be a 'soft partition', enshrining a confederal system wherein the communities would be free to develop their respective identities and quasi-national entities. They would need to sign ironclad agreements on territorial boundaries and resource-sharing. On the other hand, it could be a 'hard partition', which splits the country into distinct and independent entities. The mere mention of partition is viewed with distaste by the international community, genuine horror regionally, and a wide variety of responses by Iraqis. It would be best if the Iraqis were to walk back from the abyss and find a way to coexist. What is most important, however, is what the Iraqis themselves say.

In early 2004 Sunni and Shi'a Arab leaders and groups alike were adamantly opposed to the Kurdish demand for federalism, which would have given their autonomous region greater control of its own affairs. Iraq's Arabs saw it as a prelude to Kurdish separatism and ultimately the partitioning of the country. In the words of Moqtada al-Sadr: 'We all belong to one country. The north cannot be separated from the south because we are all Iraqis, the Arab is an Iraqi and the Kurd is an Iraqi.' Others, like veteran Sunni Arab politician Adnan Pachachi, who did dismally in the January 2005 elections and is rumored to be retiring, stated in early 2004 that there had been in-principle acceptance of federalism but that the structure would need to be worked out over the course of time. Flush with their success in the elections the Kurds lost no time in putting forth a series of demands to solidify a strong degree of freedom from central control in the new Iraq. They want control of oil in Kirkuk, the right to retain the *peshmerga* paramilitary and the right to control taxation in the north

In a statement that reflects the Kurds' new strength, Massoud Barzani, the head of the KDP, said: 'The fact remains that we are two different nationalities in Iraq—we are Kurds and Arabs. If the Kurdish people agree to stay in the framework of Iraq in one form or another as a federation, then other people should be grateful to them.' Kurdish poet Pire Mughan perhaps reflects the viscerally anti-Arab sentiments that they generally wish to hide—though they are not very successful at doing so—as they continue to maintain a façade of reasonableness while they remain officially part of the country: 'Iraq is a beast. Arabs are beasts, because their entire history is one of killings and massacres. I didn't vote for anyone in the elections, because I believe in independence, not in federalism. If I had voted, it would have meant voting for federalism, and that would have been treason for future generations.'[25] The fact that Jalal Talabani became president—a symbolic post—was in itself a symbol for men like Nechirvan Barzani, Prime Minister of the Kurdish region, for whom it represents a key step in the plan to 'de-Arabize' Iraq: 'This [the elevation of Talabani to the presidency] would show that there are people who are not Arabs in this country, that Iraq is not part of the Arab nation, and that it will never be a part of it.'[26] Adnan Mufti, a senior PUK official, was adamant: 'We must have a federal system, with, if possible, two states, a Kurdish state and an Arab state. In the end, with four or five Arab states—this would make central power much weaker—but in any case with one Kurdish state.' In fact, it is not so much federalism that the Kurds want, but a confederal system—which would allow them to opt out of Iraq—as a pit stop on the road to eventual independence. Article 5 of the constitution of the Kurdish region proclaims that Kirkuk will be the capital of that region. A senior KDP official close to Barzani had the following to say about Jaafari, the Shi'a doctor who became prime minister:

Jaafari is like the Ba'th, he will seek to use his position to construct an Islamic state. He wants all of Iraq to be an Islamic state, with a modern face. That is why we do not like him. If the Shiites would like to live with us, the constitution must be secular, otherwise we will separate. We cannot oppose what they choose to do in their part of Iraq, but we can oppose what they wish to do to all of Iraq, or Kurdistan. That is why we would have preferred as Prime Minister Allawi, Chalabi or Adel Abdel Mahdi. But again it all depends on their platform for governance. If we obtain the guarantees we want on federalism and the contested territories, we will be able to sleep with one eye shut![27]

Such statements must have been greeted with frissons of delight in certain Washington, DC, policy circles, in which during the lead-up to the war the 'de-Arabization' of Iraq was raised as a new identity for the country post-Saddam. This is not as strange as it sounds. Iraq's Arab identity was closely and intricately tied to the Sunni Arabs, whom the war planners in Washington wanted out of power. But de-Arabizing Iraq also meant marginalizing the Sunni Arabs. How feasible the policy of de-Arabization is with 76 to 78 percent of the population being Arab is a good question. Not surprisingly, there are some Sunni Arabs who would welcome the Kurds choosing to opt out of Iraq, because the Arab portion of the population would increase to 90 percent. However, this ignores the chasm between the Sunni and Shi'a Arabs.

In any case, it seemed inevitable that the Kurds and the Shi'a, the latter seemingly favoring strong central government, would clash over the issue of federalism. During the intense negotiations over the future shape of the country, conducted largely among the victors of the January 2005 elections, the governor of Irbil Province said of the Shi'a politicians: 'They're hard negotiators. They're inflexible. The Shi'a do not want to admit the federal system for the Kurds.'[28] By way of contrast a senior SCIRI official said: 'There is a sense that the Kurds have taken more privileges than the others. So we advise the Kurds to be more Iraqi.'[29]

But in the summer of 2005 political developments began to impinge on the debate over federalism in a manner that rebounded to the advantage of the Kurdish position. The story begins in fall 2004, when leaders in Iraq's oil-rich southern provinces began considering plans to set up an autonomous region as a reflection of their growing frustration with what they perceived to be the central government's indifference to them and their concerns. The three provinces—Basra, Misan and Dhu Qar—account for 80 percent of the proven oil reserves of Iraq. Members of the Basra municipal council initiated the idea when they held talks with officials from councils in the two other provinces on establishing a federal region in the south. The inhabitants of the southernmost provinces have traditionally felt marginalized and many feel they would do no better even under a Shi'a-dominated government.[30]

Matters on this front began to move ahead in 2005. Renewed efforts to create an administrative federal region or super-province in the governorates surrounding Basra reinvigorated debate on the overall issue of federalism in the country as a whole. Shi'a defenders of the proposal say that the federalism they envision is purely administrative. Detractors, Sunni and Shi'a Arabs, say the proposal, like its counterpart in Kurdistan, poses a serious threat to the unity of Iraq and was encouraged by the United States and other 'foreign parties'. After a sumptuous dinner at the home of an upper-class Sunni Arab in Baghdad in early December 2003, I was treated to a raucous and fascinating debate among Sunni intellectuals concerning the future of the Sunni community and of the country. Surprisingly, though, and possibly not wanting to be outdone, some Sunni groups began advocating the creation of a Sunni super-province as well, one to counterbalance the existence of the Kurdish entity in the north and the possibility of the emergence of a Shi'a super-province in the south. If it is a serious idea, it is remarkable because it comes from a group that has hitherto traditionally cherished the notion of a strong nationalist and centralized state.

But the idea of an autonomous Sunni Arab area has not caught the imagination of a sufficient number of Sunni Arabs or their politicians. They fought bitterly against the notion of federalism in the long and painstaking drafting of the constitution over the summer of 2005. Instead of bringing peace the constitution may ensure years of war, says Nabil al-Dulaimi, a Sunni political scientist from one of the tribes leading the insurgency: 'If you're going to convince [insurgents] to leave violence behind, you have to give them something valuable, something they think is good for the community and the national interest. This doesn't give them anything.'[31] The Sunnis are still wedded to the old notions of a powerful centralized state. This is a mistake on their part. Such a structure in the new Iraq will not rebound to their benefit because it will be in the hands of those Shi'a who believe in it. The Sunnis need to develop a new paradigm, one that promotes their autonomy or even independence and allows them to turn their attention westwards, towards the Sunni Arab heartland and Turkey.

The situation looked bad from the vantage point of late summer 2005. As veteran journalist Trudy Rubin, who has spent much of 2005 in Iraq, said, 'the Iraqis aren't even close' to being able to handle the insurgency.[32] The 'government is ethnically split and includes few representatives of alienated Sunnis. Many soldiers are more loyal to ethnic or religious factions than to an Iraqi nation.'[33] At the height of summer 2005 a senior US officer told Rubin: 'In many respects, the whole endeavor will increasingly rest on the ability of Iraqi leaders in the security forces and government to foster cooperation among factions. It will rest on their ability to convince as many Iraqis as possible—especially Sunni Arabs—to support the new Iraq and oppose the insurgents.'[34] But what is the new Iraq he is talking about? The various Iraqi interests seem incapable of resolving, or unable to resolve, their differences or even reduce their maximalist demands *vis-à-vis* one another for the sake of the greater good. The only reason that they have not fallen upon each other in an orgy of violence is the presence of the Coalition. But that very presence also allows the victors of the January 2005 elections to expand their gains at the expense of the marginalized Sunnis, leaving them as a thoroughly disgruntled and recidivist population. Moreover, it is doubtful that the thinly-stretched Coalition forces would be able to handle the situation if vengeful Sunni and Shi'a Arabs go head to head should, say, another senior Shi'a figure be assassinated.

How long the Coalition will continue to have the resources and willingness to keep the situation simmering at a manageable level—as is taking place now—before it leaves and watches Iraq fall apart is still unknown, despite intense speculation in summer 2005 about a US military draw-down. By late August 2005 the country was in political deadlock as fierce debates ranged on key constitutional issues. Either way the Iraqis' short-term future may be either civil war or partition—or both. Civil wars can break out and last years without one side or the other gaining the advantage, and ultimately peter out as a result of exhaustion. This is unlikely to happen in Iraq because too many outside forces have a keen interest in intervening and tipping the balance towards their favored party. An Iraqi civil war could escalate to new heights of violence and descend to new lows of depravity. Of course an Iraqi civil war could lead to partition rather than exhaustion, but it will be a messy partition with much bloodletting and regional interference.

On the other hand, why can the Coalition not bring about a managed and relatively humane partition that offers the maximum benefit and least discomfort to all? I am unwilling to discuss the parameters of such a partition here. And to those who would argue that I am, in effect, promoting a couple of US neoconservative alternatives for Iraq (i.e. either a weak state controlled by their favorites or a break-up), I would say that the presence of disgruntled minorities within a country allows insidious and long-term meddling by outsiders and perpetuates police-type regimes. It was, I think, Lord Carrington, a former British Foreign Minister who became the first European Union peace envoy at the time of the bloody Yugoslav crisis in the early 1990s, who said something to the effect that the twentieth century has proved that you cannot force people to remain citizens of a country at the point of a gun. This may well prove to be the requiem for Iraq in the coming months.

EPILOGUE

It is mid-November 2005 as I conclude this book. The insurgency seemed to be at a lower level of intensity in August and early September. Of course 'lower' is a relative term; 'bad things' continued to happen every day in Iraq during that period. The number of US troops killed in August 2005—seventy-six—was one of the highest on record. October proved worse, with more than ninety deaths among US military personnel. By comparison with the April to July period, however, there seemed to be a lull in some areas like Baghdad and the area immediately to its south. Of course, as I mentioned in Chapter 5, the insurgency is still going strong in the Euphrates area, where US forces are hard-pressed to maintain presence. Are the insurgents on the run? Insurgent leaders have indicated that the intensive US operations of the summer had resulted in disruption of cells, the killings and abductions of key leaders, and some funding squeezes.

The US military was relentless, as reflected in the launching in early November 2005 of an offensive along the Iraqi border with Syria. The United States claims that it will maintain a permanent presence in the small, hardscrabble towns along the Euphrates where insurgents and foreign terrorists have established sanctuaries. This would be a positive step, particularly if we were to undertake reconstruction projects and provide basic services and employment in conjunction with this military presence. The end result, one would hope, would be to deprive the insurgents of such refuges and of the 'ratlines' along the Euphrates River that allow them to move men to the main urban centers.

The tragedy of the stampede on the bridge between Adhamiya and Khadimiya in Baghdad in late August, in which more than 1,000 Shi'a died during a religious holiday, seemed to unite the country in its grief. But I am not sure that is enough for Iraqis to cement their unity. Indeed, Moqtada al-Sadr, a man whom some Sunnis could not help but view as an Iraqi Arab nationalist and an ally against the new draft constitution, vowed revenge against the Sunnis for the bridge disaster because he put the blame squarely on them. The Ba'thist insurgents poured scorn on him and his movement. Moreover, the tit-for-tat killings between Sunnis and Shi'a continue unabated during September 2005. Tragedy struck again in Khadimiya, for example, when a suicide bomber detonated his payload among Shi'a laborers there on 14 September.

Indeed, my pessimistic view of the situation in Iraq by early fall 2005 remains unchanged. I will address three issues here to support my contention that the country's predicament, as I described in the conclusion, is not improving, namely the controversy over the constitution, the counter-insurgency operation in Tal Afar, and my interactions with a wide variety of Iraqis. I have incorporated my conversations with the Iraqis into my discussions of the fractious constitutional debate and the counter-insurgency operation in the Tal Afar area, in which I was a participant on the Coalition side.

The insurgency and counter-insurgency in Tal Afar

I wrote much of this final section in early September 2005 outside the city of Tal Afar, where some of the best-trained and most professional US forces that I have had the pleasure of working with, namely the 3rd Armored Cavalry Regiment ('Brave Rifles') are conducting urban counter-insurgency operations against insurgents and terrorists. Tal Afar, in western Nineveh Province, has attained an importance beyond what would have been expected of an isolated city of 160,000 to 220,000 that had been ignored for decades by the Hussein regime and those before it. An insidious insurgency fueled by serious socioeconomic problems and threats to identity has been taking place there since 2004. It is an insurgency in an area that I had a chance to observe at close hand between July and September 2005.[1]

Tal Afar. The name sounds exotic. But there is nothing very exotic about this city. On my first day of deployment there I went into town in a military convoy and, as I looked out of a Bradley, it occurred to me that Tal Afar looked like one of those forlorn humanoid settlements on a distant and barren planet in the outer reaches of the solar system, which we often see portrayed in science-fiction movies. Women clad in black *abayas*—an irrational idea in this heat—scurried from house to house carrying sacks or heavy-duty plastic bags with, no doubt, what little food they could buy from a store here and there. The market place was desolate and shut down. Many buildings were crumbling, and twisted metal and steel rods shot straight into the sky from decades-old buildings that seemed to sag under the weight they were shouldering. Trash lay everywhere, particularly the ubiquitous plastic water bottles that everyone seems to be using these days in Iraq because of the contaminated water supply. In some places people had gathered the trash together and were burning it in the streets, producing a lingering, acrid smell. But the most consistent and appalling stench was that of sewage. The city does not have a sewerage system so the sewage flows down the streets and collects at the southern end of the city in a forest known to US troops as 'Shitwood Forest', for obvious reasons.

Although Tal Afar may be nothing to look at, it is strategically located. Alexander the Great marched past on his way to destroy the Persian Empire. The Ottoman army passed through on its way to defeat the Safavid dynasty that ruled Iran, and the Ottomans later established a fort in the city. In the 1920s the British built another fort outside Tal Afar to maintain a colonial presence in this remote northern region and to combat smugglers. Even the city's inhabitants, who are neither particularly well-educated nor cosmopolitan, recognize the importance of its location. Indeed, if one were to look at Tal Afar's importance from a modern perspective a number of key points stand out. First, it lies at the fault line of three distinct and historically feuding cultures and ethnicities: the Turkic, the Indo-European (Kurdish) and the Semitic (Arab). The Turkmen and Turkey have valid fears that the Kurds may seek to incorporate Tal Afar and Kirkuk into their autonomous region. Second, it lies athwart communications and smuggling routes. Insurgents have used it as a way station for foreign fighters coming from Syria on their way to Mosul and the northern-central areas of Iraq. Third, Tal Afar lies on a religious fault line, as do the cities immediately south of Baghdad (Yusufiyah, Mahmudiyah and Iskandariyah) and Diyala Province (which is 50 percent Sunni and 50 percent Shi'a).

Another important aspect of Tal Afar is that 95 percent of its inhabitants are Iraqi Turkmen, making it the second-largest Turkmen city in Iraq after Kirkuk. However, unlike Kirkuk it is a poor city. Its current infrastructure was first put into place during the regime of Abd al-Karim Qasim (1958–60). It was he who brought electricity and piped water into the city. Nothing has been done to improve the infrastructure since. Hussein neglected Tal Afar. It was said that when the city requested a zoo sometime in the 1970s, Hussein joked that a wall be put around the city itself. But Tal Afar has become the focus of attention for neighboring Turkey and, of course, Iraqi Turkmen political groups and the Iraqi Turkmen diaspora in Turkey and the West. It is also viewd as important by the Kurdish autonomous region, which the Kurds wish to enlarge and in my judgment include western Nineveh with Tal Afar. This will extend their boundaries to Syria and they will be able to incorporate the Yezidi Kurds, erroneously known to the rest of the Iraqis as 'devil worshippers'. Days after Hussein's regime fell the Kurdistan Democratic Party of Massoud Barzani sent a party official named 'Abdul Khaleq' to become mayor of a city that contained very few Kurds. He occupied the mayor's office and ran up the Kurdish flag. A crowd of angry Turkmen demonstrated outside his 'office' and ordered him to take down the flag and leave or die. He refused. The following day he was killed and his flag was burned. The Turkmen and the Kurds loathe each other. The entry of Kurdish *peshmerga* forces thinly disguised as Iraqi security units to put down the disturbances of September 2004 has not been forgotten, nor has the behavior of these forces. But Turkmen and Kurdish divisions proved to be the least of the city's problems.

Tal Afar is divided by sectarianism. If it were merely a Turkmen city without religious differences, our problems would have been somewhat simplified. But the city's Turkmen population is divided between Sunnis and Shi'a. Approximately 70 percent of the population are Sunni Turkmen and 25 percent are Shi'a Turkmen. The Shi'a were formerly adherents of the Bektashi Shi'a order, which was viewed as a relatively 'lax' sect. In the early years of independent monarchical Iraq Shi'a politicians in Baghdad became acquainted with the Shi'a Turkmen of Tal Afar; a deputation of Shi'a notables from the city were introduced to Shi'a *ulema*. In the 1950s Twelver Shi'a clerics came from the south and proselytized among the Shi'a Turkmen. Among them was a key figure known as Mullah Mahmoud. There was also a migration of young Shi'a Turkmen *tullab* (religious students) to study *fiqh* and *usul* al-Shi'a in Najaf. Many of these students were sponsored by Ayatollah Mohsen al-Hakim, the senior cleric in Iraq at the time.[2] The Shi'a Turkmen tribes (the Julagh/Chulagh, Beit Khoja and Saada, and part of the Halaybek) converted to Twelver Shi'ism.

But sectarianism between the two groups of Turkmen was not a prominently divisive factor for the three decades of the former regime, for several reasons. First, the Sunni and Shi'a Turkmen intermarried; some of the Turkmen tribes contained Sunnis and Shi'a. Second, the former regime suppressed sectarianism and maintained tight control over religious proselytizing—*al zahira al-diniyyah*—particularly by the Shi'a theological schools. The theological schools in Najaf saw a dramatic decline in the number of students as a result of political oppression, exile, executions and purges. Third, the barely suppressed differences between Sunni and Shi'a Arabs that existed in Saddam's Iraq because of the struggles over political power, ideology and resources did not exist among the Sunni and Shi'a Turkmen. The Turkmen's common ethnicity trumped sectarianism. With the downfall of Hussein, the situation began to change (see below).

Tal Afar is an insurgent bastion. While it is true that the insurgency has been largely Sunni Arab and has attracted few members of other ethno-sectarian groups, this has not been true, as Iraqi researchers have shown, of the Sunni Turkmen minority. The Turkmen from Tal Afar have played a significant role in the insurgency. By contrast the largely solid middle-class Sunni Turkmen population of Kirkuk has traditionally used political and legal means to advance its political agendas. This has not necessarily been successful, I might add that in a two-hour meeting in Kirkuk in August 2005 members of the Iraqi Turkmen Front—an umbrella organization of several Turkmen parties—tried to portray a can-do image.

The Sunni Turkmen grievances are an intricate and inter-twined mix of material and nonmaterial ones; in other words, anger and concern over loss of livelihood (material) and threats to identity (nonmaterial). To explain the material grievances one must refer to the basis of traditional socioeconomic activity in the city. Under the Ba'th regime Tal Afar's economy rested on four foundations.

The first was agriculture and pastoralism, which was the domain of the tribes around the city. Agricultural produce was brought and sold in the city's market. Some of the city's inhabitants with aspirations for better education went and studied agriculture and brought their skills back to the city.

The second was the trucking business. When Iraq's economy took off in the mid-1970s (after the oil price rise) a major trucking industry developed, carrying goods into the country via Jordan and Turkey. (Trucking through Syria was nonexistent due to the poor state of relations between the two Ba'th regimes.) The business surged during the Iran-Iraq war (1980–8), declined precipitously at the end of the war and slowed to a trickle after sanctions were imposed on Iraq from 1990 to 2003. A considerable number of men were thrown out of work. They are now part of the insurgency.

The third foundation was part of the underground or unofficial economy, smuggling, a traditional activity largely carried out by the Arab tribes to the north of the city, but in which the Turkmen actively participated. When sanctions hit Iraq, the incomes of the city's people, particularly those tied to the regime, were supple-mented by sanctions-busting smuggling. (These same smuggling routes are now used to bring foreign fighters and funds into Iraq.)

The fourth was state employment. While the Ba'th regime did not devote many resources to build up the decrepit infrastruc-ture of Tal Afar, the city was not ignored completely. Many of its able-bodied men from the Sunni and Shi'a tribes, but especially the former, joined the armed forces, security and intelligence services, and the Ba'th Party in significant numbers. A considerable number of Turkmen NCOs and senior officers returned to the city as either veterans or purged personnel after having served in Iraq's three ruinous wars. Others either joined the local bureaucratic and security infrastructure or became elementary-school and middle-school teachers. The teachers of Tal Afar left a lot to be desired. When Saddam began *al hamla al-imaniyah* (Enhancement of Islamic Faith) in the mid-1990s, little did he realize that he was opening the way for Salafist thought to seep into the school system. Salafists seek to return Islam to the pristine purity of the time of the Prophet Muhammad and his immediate successors. In the 1990s several summarized tracts of the writings of Muhammad Ibn Abdul Wahhab, the Saudi 'reformer' who sought to save Islam in the Arabian Peninsula, began to appear in Tal Afar, where they were propagated by the teachers. When Saddam fell in April 2003 and the CPA in its infinite wisdom destroyed all vestiges of the state institutions of the former regime, thousands found themselves out of work. They are part of the insurgency too.

The above analysis described the material sources of grievances as I ascertained them from discussions with numerous individuals from the city. The following will describe the nonmaterial sources, or the identity crisis being suffered by the Turkmen of Tal Afar. Under the former regime they, unlike their brethren in Kirkuk, did not develop a sense of themselves as Turkmen in opposition to the Ba'th. While they knew they were Turkmen, most had 'Arabized' or become fervent Iraqi nationalists through intermarriage with Arabs and instruction in the Ba'thist education system. Moreover, to enter lucrative state employment Turkmen were forced to put 'Arab' as their ethnic origin in their applications. I noticed how strong this was among the Farhats when I spoke with a number of them in July and August 2005. Some were confused as to whether their identity was Arab or Turkmen. One even ventured to tell me that they are Arabs who speak Turkmen. I tried to explain that no Arab tribe would ever give up Arabic as an element of its identity. He did not understand me. Another told me that they are historically tied to Turkey but that neither Turkey nor their Turkmen brethren in Kirkuk have done anything for them. By contrast with the Kirkuk Turkmen, very few in Tal Afar had been able to develop links with the Turkmen diaspora or with Turkey because they could not read the Latin script of the Turkish language. Their Turkmen dialect is spoken, and very few can read the archaic Ottoman Arabic script. This is in contrast to the Turkmen of Kirkuk and other places—that is, those who lived in the Kurdish autonomous zone—whose sense of 'Turkishness' was strong and reinforced by contact with Turkey, through the Turkmen middle-class diaspora, and by their ability to read and write modern Turkish.

Another factor has arisen to shake the identity of the Turkmen. External forces have highlighted and sharpened the sectarian divisions among them. Now that the Shi'a are ensconced in power in Baghdad, the Shi'a minority in Tal Afar have been allowed access to the formidable mobilization capacities of the national Shi'a political organizations, who have suddenly discovered the plight of this Shi'a enclave in the north. Shi'a Turkmen and Arabs have cooperated in Kirkuk against Kurdish irredentism under the auspices of Moqtada al-Sadr's Jaish al-Mahdi. This is unlikely to happen in Tal Afar because the enemy is not the Kurds but other Turkmen, whom the Sunnis now identify totally with Shi'a power in Baghdad and with the Islamic Republic of Iran. The result has been to heighten Sunni fears of marginalization and irrational fears of sinister attempts to 'Shi'ify' Tal Afar. An example of this supposedly nefarious plan is the takeover of the city's police force by the Shi'a who are ostensibly supported in this endeavor by the Badr Organization. The Sunni

Turkmen have begun to articulate the view that a Baghdad-directed and Iranian-supported conspiracy is planning to take over the city. They have been encouraged in this by Sunni Islamist extremists who abhor the Shi'a and by nationalist former regime elements. In fact, the fear of the Shi'a threat is the key element in an insurgency that has increasingly fused (Sunni) Islamist and nationalist motifs. Islamist and nationalist insurgents alike loathe the Shi'a and hate Iran. Many of the Turkmen military personnel fought against Iran in the 1980s, precisely to prevent Iraq—to which they are attached as a country—from falling prey to Iranian machinations, and they see the returning Shi'a as an Iranian fifth column. The Islamists who aligned themselves with the disgruntled nationalists have an even darker view of the Shi'a, who they regard not as Muslims but as polytheists. This sentiment extends even to the young, many of whom told me that the Shi'a must leave Tal Afar and go back to *ard al-fasad*, the land of corruption (i.e. the Shi'a south).[3]

The Sunni Turkmen of Tal Afar are bereft of the political representation that would have enabled them to articulate their material and nonmaterial grievances in a better and more sustained manner other than through raucous meetings. The Turkmen have never been politically mobilized before except as members of the Ba'th party during the former regime, and have no well-organized political parties to represent them. Neither the Iraqi Islamic Party (IIP), whose stronghold is Mosul, nor the umbrella organization of the Turkmen in Iraq, the Iraqi Turkmen Front (ITF), have been able to mobilize the city and provide forums for the populace to articulate their grievances.[4] In an extensive interview with the Egyptian newspaper *Al-Ahram* in December 2003 the then president of the ITF, Dr Farouq Abdullah Abdel Rahman, talked a great deal about the overall status of the Turkmen in Iraq and about the Kirkuk tinderbox. One of the key points he makes in the interview, as do many other Turkmen, is that his community is a significant one in the life of Iraq: 'Turkmen are the third ethnic group in Iraq after Arabs and Kurds. They number some 3 million persons. Their marginalized role roves [*sic*] beyond doubt the desire to exclude them from the policies of the new Iraq.'[5] All of this hand-wringing would be fine if it were followed by decisiveness and action. It has not been, and to be fair that was not always the fault of the ITF. Abdel Rahman mentions Kirkuk; this is to be expected, for it is central to the three-way ethnic struggle between its Arab, Turkmen and Kurdish residents. But he made no mention of Tal Afar. This is unsurprising, because the Sunni Turkmen there had no political visibility in Iraq and nobody cared about the city. It was only when violence erupted in September 2004 and then became a norm that people began to 'appreciate' Tal Afar.

As the operation to return stability and security to the city, Operation Restoring Rights, kicked off in earnest in early September 2005 the insurgents launched their own information countercampaign, which sought to expose the 'real reasons' behind the US offensive in the city. One Ba'thist wrote an article, 'Demographic Reasons behind the American Terrorism in Tall Afar', which mirrored and articulated the seemingly conspiratorial and deep-seated fears of the Sunnis I talked with. The article makes three claims. First, the operation was designed to encircle 'Arab, Turkmen, and mixed areas in Iraq with a Kurdish perimeter to prevent any communication with Arab and Turkmen groups in Syria and Turkey'.[6] In other words, it was supposed to extend the territorial extent of the Kurdish autonomous region into Nineveh, right up to the Syrian border. Second, the operation was aimed at 'distracting the Iraqis with nationalist and sectarian struggles'.[7] I am not quite sure what the verbose Ba'thist author means, but would guess that the United States is accused of promoting ethno-sectarian violence in the country. Finally, the operation is charged with 'changing the demographics of the al-Jazirah area (North West Iraq) which has not happened since the Mongolian [*sic*] invasion of Iraq'.[8] This over-blown statement refers, I think, to allowing the Kurds to move *en masse* to settle in Nineveh Province.

The operation in Tal Afar did not last long. There was some initial fierce resistance but the area in which the most dedicated and motivated insurgents were supposedly concentrated, the Sarai, a rabbit warren of alleyways and ancient houses, was largely empty of residents and of insurgents. I watched as one of the few old residents remaining in the city tried desperately to extricate himself from a wadi where he was cowering and move towards our soldiers, who sent him on his way. Many of the insurgents were killed or captured, or had fled into the outlying districts. Others chose to make a stand in the Hai al-Qadisiya neighborhood.

The real trick for the United States is how to restore order, basic services and security, and commence a program of long-term reconstruction to reduce material grievances. There is considerable willingness and motivation to engage in this Phase IV task, but I am unsure that the funds or the materials necessary will come from the current Iraqi government. We only have to look at the non-reconstruction of Fallujah to feel pessimistic. First, the Iraqi government is dysfunctional. I doubt whether any of the ministries that are meant to be playing a role will rise to the occasion. Second, there is simply very little available in the way of funds. Third, many Sunni Turkmen locals do not think this government is particularly concerned with the well-being of this largely Sunni city despite its declarations of commitment to equal treatment of all citizens.

Dealing with the nonmaterial or identity grievances is likely to be a more difficult task, but we can begin by ensuring that the Turkmen are not abused by the vaunted Iraqi security forces whom the Turkmen—as do the Sunni Arabs—view not as national security forces but as thinly disguised Kurdish and Shi'a militia. Ralph Peters, writing about the Iraqi security forces in the Tal Afar operations, stated that 'the Iraqis fighting beside us performed professionally, standing up in the line of fire for their new government'.[9] This is wishful thinking; Peters was not there and I was. I am also sure he is unaware that the inhabitants of Tal Afar are not Sunni Arabs but Sunni Turkmen. Furthermore, the city was not held hostage by fanatical foreign terrorists; rather it was a homegrown insurgency, as I pointed out above. Iraqi officials repeated this hoary cliché about significant numbers of foreign fighters infiltrating from Syria, a claim that coincided with the rise in the accusations leveled by Baghdad and Washington against Damascus for its lackadaisical attitude towards controlling the foreigners that *do make it through into Iraq*. The number of foreign fighters involved was minuscule, not more than 5 percent of the total captured.

For the most part the Iraqi security forces in Tal Afar were divided by an ethno-sectarian chasm. While most of the *peshmerga* units of Kurdish fighters incorporated into the Iraqi army performed with restraint and discipline, they could not resist painting 'KDP' (for Kurdistan Democratic Party) on houses they cleared. The enlisted men with whom I talked said they did not wish to be there and that they would prefer to return to Kurdistan. Others believed that the area should be incorporated into the Kurdish region and were willing to join the fight to rid the city of terrorists. Many of the Kurdish troops and their officers—including a senior Kurdish officer and his adjutant—were admirable men and I grew close to them. Indeed, I came to love the Kurds for their principles and equal commitment to Iraq if it should succeed, or to their own homeland of Kurdistan, to which, they declared roundly and repeatedly, they would decamp if Iraq were to unravel. I cannot say the same for the Shi'a Arab units or soldiers, most of whom I pitied. Many were unkempt and ill-disciplined, wearing mismatched uniforms and carrying dirty weapons. Others evoked nothing but alarm. Some of the Shi'a units from the south were insufferable; they were a militia pure and simple. One unit in particular would have been nothing more than a death squad had it been given the chance to rampage through Sunni areas. These are the 'nationalist Iraqis' to whom Ralph Peters refers.

The constitutional debates of 2005

The second event of late summer 2005 that leads me to doubt whether the country will attain stability and security anytime soon occurred as the three main communities tussled over the constitution. The latter will have an impact on whether the insurgency continues and on the future of the country, and for months Iraq's politicians and parties had haggled over the draft versions. The 15 August deadline was extended once, twice, three times as details were hammered out and refined. Finally, to great fanfare, a historic compromise between the main ethnic and sectarian groups was declared by beaming officials on state television. There was just one problem, which intruded like the proverbial gate-crasher into this 'joyous' occasion. The Sunnis, the restive minority everybody agreed had to be included to make the constitution a success, wasted no time in denouncing the draft constitution, which they said would only fan the flames of the insurgency. It was in this context, during the fractious and bitter debates, that Iraq's deep divisions over the role of Islam, the issue of federalism and resource-sharing, and the nature of Iraq's national identity, among other things, came dramatically to the fore. I will address the issues I mentioned because they are key to the future of the country and to whether it is able to surmount the insurgency. In late September 2005 the respected International Crisis Group issued a report that argues that the constitution may indeed fuel the insurgency if Sunni concerns are not assuaged.[10]

On the role of Islam the question was whether it should be *the* or *a* source of legislation for the country. The Shi'a political parties argue that a much bigger role for Islam is the answer to many of Iraq's ills. 'I don't see where the concern is—all rights are guaranteed under Islam,' says Saad Jawad Qindeel, SCIRI's head of political affairs. 'We are willing to meet all stipulations for protecting individual rights, but Islam is a big part of the character of the Iraqi people.'[11] He added that the Shi'a parties are willing to compromise—but in ways unlikely to satisfy the secular Kurds. He says they would prefer that Islam be the 'only source' of Iraqi legislation, but would be willing to live with a constitution that calls Islam 'a source' of legislation, if a further stipulation is added: 'That no legislation be enacted that violates the basic truths of Islam.'[12]

The position of the Sunnis on this issue is not at all clear to me or even to them. The Ba'thist indoctrination against the mixing of religion and politics still animates many of the insurgents. Many Sunnis are still secular, even among those who are fighting to protect Islam. Fighting for Islam does not, however, translate into a desire to create an Islamic system of government. The extremists Sunnis who are interested in implementing an Islamic system in Iraq are a minority and, furthermore, whether the constitution declares Islam to be a source or the source of legislation is irrelevant to them because they see the constitution as illegitimate. Many Sunni political groups are inclined to promote Islam and its values in the future Iraq. This is the view of the IIP, but it does not mean that there is a desire among Sunnis to impose a theocracy. Moreover, there is the issue of reconciling Sunni and Shi'a views of Islamic governance; I do not think that this is possible. Many Sunnis with whom I talked viewed the Shi'a notion of Islamic governance with unalloyed horror as the creation of a theocracy with loyalty to the Islamic Republic of Iran.

The Kurds adamantly made their preferences clear. In a speech to one of two Kurdish regional parliaments, KDP leader and Kurdish regional President Massoud Barzani signaled that the Kurds will not deviate from their view that Islam cannot be the basis of Iraq's identity: 'We will not accept that Iraq's identity is an Islamic one. There will be no bargaining over our basic rights.'[13] Many Kurds see the adoption of a secular constitution as the best guarantee of individual rights in the new Iraq. Politics is the art of the possible but religion is about moral absolutes, several Kurds in the Nineveh area told me in the summer and fall of 2005. It became rapidly apparent to me, on the basis of my discussions with Kurdish officers and even enlisted men, that the Kurds are truly the most progressive group of people in the country.

The issue of federalism and resource-sharing is another key question dividing the three largest communities. The Kurds expect the future Iraq to be a federal state with considerable devolution of power and wide-ranging latitude in decision-making for the autonomous regions. As long as the relationship between the Kurdish region and the rest of the country is federal, they will care little if nationwide federalism is not implemented. But a number of Kurdish officials believe that nationwide federalism would strengthen their region; unsurprisingly they approved of the desire of some Shi'a to create a set of federal provinces in the south.

The Sunni Arabs have proven to be the most ferocious critics of the idea of federalism. Again, even here the Sunni opposition to federalism seems confused. They do not oppose federalism for the Kurds but bitterly oppose it for the Shi'a south. More revealingly, very few Sunnis have even considered it a viable option for themselves. Why? The Sunnis are irrationally wedded to the notion of a centralized state. This is intricately tied to their Arab nationalist ideology, of which it is one of the central principles. They seem not to understand that such a state in the new Iraq is not necessarily to their benefit, because the Shi'a would control it. So the question becomes, why are they still wedded to that obsolescent notion of the state? The answer suddenly came to me after discussions with Sunnis in the summer and fall of 2005. *Many are convinced that they will seize control of the state again.* They are genuinely convinced that the only reason the Shi'a are able to rule is because of US support. Of course, not all of them think like that. Even those who are disinclined to view things in conspiratorial terms have a hard time accepting the notion of federalism because it is seen as damaging to Iraq's national identity. Finally, federalism has implications for the oil-poor Sunni center. If the north and the south were to create full-fledged federal provinces they would have the lion's share of the oil, leaving the center with little. Neither the Kurdish north nor the Shi'a south would be likely to want to share with the Sunnis what they see as rightfully theirs. Indeed, as an example of what could occur, Barzani at one point during the debates over the constitution initially demanded that 65 percent of the revenues from the Kirkuk oil fields go to the Kurdish autonomous region, which even the Shi'a-dominated government said was unacceptable.[14]

In this context, Sunni Arabs met US Ambassador Zalmay Khalilzad to demand that federalism be dropped from the charter. Saleh Mutlak said: 'We told them that the decision of adopting any kind of administrative system for new Iraq should be left to the next national assembly.'[15] Mutlak reiterated that the Sunnis would reject the draft if it adopted a federal structure for Iraq, adding: 'This is a red line for us as it concerns the unity of Iraq and we will not bargain on this.'[16] Another leading Sunni Arab politician, Adnan al-Dulaimi, was even more vociferous in his denunciation of federalism:

We reject establishing federalism in the center and south of Iraq because it constitutes a prelude to the dismemberment of Iraq and the consolidation of sectarianism. Large masses of our brothers the Arab Shiites share the same position with us in facing up to the anti-Arabists because they want to change the identity of Iraq … We call for dissolving the national assembly because it did not receive the draft constitution on time and for not drafting the constitution based on reaching consensus between the sects of the Iraqi people.[17]

Sunni opposition to the constitution was widespread, and not merely among the insurgents or the two nationalist individuals quoted above, who are part of the legitimate Sunni political scene in Iraq. Even a member of the government, Ghazi Yawer, who became one of Iraq's two vice presidents after the January 2005 elections, viewed the country's new constitution as a threat to national unity and said he was considering asking his supporters to reject it at the October 2005 referendum. Yawer said Sunni Arabs are living under a 'dictatorship of the majority',[18] referring to the dominance of Shi'a Muslims and Kurds in the government. 'The Iraqi national identity is diminishing more and more, and this constitution is not helping that,' argues Yawer.[19] He said he did not know if he should urge his constituents to vote against the draft constitution, or to accept it and focus on the elections for a new national assembly, to be held in December 2005. According to US journalist Hannah Allam, '[Yawer's] bitterness suggested that even moderate and US-friendly Sunnis are feeling increasingly alienated in their struggle for a place in the new Iraq'.[20] 'My mind says yes, because we have to move along, but my heart is saying no because I feel this is really not what we want for this country,' al-Yawer said of the constitution. 'I will go and vote "no," but I will keep in my mind that the biggest possibility is that it's going to pass, so I have to prepare from now.'[21] Yawer added that while Shi'a and Kurdish politicians celebrated the finalization of the proposed constitution on 28 August 2005, he was trying to calm concerned Sunni tribal leaders from the Sunni triangle. 'Most of them are against the constitution,' he said. 'They were very unhappy. They were worried. More than angry, they are worried about, "Where are we going? What is Iraq?"'[22] These fears emerged clearly during my brief discussion with a leading sheikh of the Shammar tribe in his sprawling villa near Rabiyah.

Sunni fears over national identity, described in detail in Chapter 2, have not abated. Instead they have increased, and the proposed constitution has helped enormously to intensify those fears. For the Sunnis the deliberate policy of 'de-Arabizing' Iraq's identity was evident in the reluctance to refer to Iraq as an Arab country, and merely to refer to its Arab and Arabized people, who constitute 78 percent of the population, as part of the Arab world.

In numerous discussions with Sunni Arabs and Sunni Turkmen, I asked them why they did not call for an autonomous (or even independent) Sunni Turco-Arab region in the center, one that would reach an agreement with either the Kurds or the Shi'a on the equitable sharing of oil resources in return for the acceptance of federalism (or partition). Such an entity in the center would continue to exercise its separate identity, and to look westwards to the Arab world and possibly also north to Turkey. Whenever I mentioned this as a possible future I would receive vacuous and uncomprehending looks. 'Iraq is one nation or an indivisible nation,' the Sunnis would repeat robotically while the country fell apart around them and three mutually exclusive identities were emerging. After such conversations it struck me that while the Sunnis have had to deal with a series of catastrophic events in the past three years, they have not had a paradigm shift in their thinking or strategy to adjust to this changed world. In many cases they continue to be wedded to the shibboleths of the past, without adjusting to fit the realities of the present. To put it another way, I argued with them that they can maintain their Arab nationalist credentials and deepen their links with the wider Arab world to the west (and with Turkey) by settling for a smaller region for themselves, instead of trying to go for broke (i.e. regain control of the entire country). If the Sunnis had any sophisticated negotiation sense they would enter into discussions with the Kurds over the future of, and sharing of resources from, the oil-producing area of Kirkuk. If they can crack the tactical Kurdish-Shi'a alliance against them, they will enlarge their political options and bargaining power. However, as things stand the Sunni insurgency may prevent or hinder the emergence of stability in a larger Shi'a-dominated Iraq for decades to come, as did the Kurdish rebellions to the consolidation of Sunni control. But the Sunni insurgency can never recover the past for those who constitute the *restorationist* element of the insurgency.

An almost paranoid fear exists among Sunnis of Iran's influence in the government of Ibrahim al-Jaafari. I also noticed this in my interactions with Sunni Arabs and Sunni Turkmen; even the Kurds mentioned it on several occasions. It is this baleful Iranian influence that is perceived as hindering the entry of Sunnis into the political process and preventing them from gaining positions in the government machinery. Many Sunnis say they feel the ruling Shi'a political parties are simply fronts for Iranian interests.

They also fear that the party militias, and even the government police and army, single Sunnis out for arrests or worse as revenge for the years that Hussein's Sunni-dominated government persecuted the Shi'a. As one Sunni said: 'The interior ministry threw out all the Sunnis and won't accept any more. Most of the assassinations these days are done by Badr.'[23] 'We feel like we don't exist or are put aside,' said another Sunni, whose husband was formerly a high-ranking official in Hussein's security forces. 'I feel like the Americans after the occupation they supported only the Shiites and they ignore us on purpose. We are part of the Iraqi people.'[24]

Another source of anger is the outlawing of the Ba'th Party, which many Sunnis view as yet another Coalition and Iraqi government effort to efface that community's identity. Moreover, many Sunnis have argued that they want a leadership that asserts Iraq's national identity, not an ethnic or sectarian one. Many have said that former Prime Minister Iyad Allawi—a secular Shi'a but a former member of the Ba'th Party—is the politician closest to their views. 'We don't look for a leader to be a Sunni to lead us. We want someone like Iyad Allawi. Their ethnicity is not important. [We want someone] who fulfills the dreams of Iraqis, it doesn't matter who he is. Someone to take care of security and electricity,' says Yasser Kaha Ibrahim, a Sunni administrative worker.[25]

There is a strange but aimless unanimity in Sunni opinion about national identity and the political situation in Iraq, but the Sunnis have neither managed to adopt a coherent and unified ideological stance, nor succeeded in producing a leader around whom they could rally. Sunni political parties are vociferous but have found little popular support; until they do the insurgency will remain a potent and destructive force that best articulates Sunni disgruntlement. One of the reasons why the Sunnis are confused is, as mentioned above, their irrational insistence that they and the Kurds are the majority of the population. I would sit stunned and perplexed as members of the IIP or Sunni Turkmen groups would spin out phantasmagorical statistics, arguing that the total Sunni element (Arabs, Kurds and Turkmen) made up 60 to 65 percent of the population. When I would interject and argue politely that they might be wrong, because the Shi'a birth rate is higher, they would roundly condemn my figures, asserting that there is a Coalition conspiracy to 'overinflate' the number of Shi'a for political reasons (i.e. because the Coalition are pro-Shi'a). Another interpretation is that the number of Shi'a has been vastly inflated by the allegedly massive influx of Iranians—and Iraqi exiles returning from Iran.

As I was working on this final section, the Sunnis were gearing to try to defeat the draft constitution in what promised to be a bitter referendum battle on 15 October 2005. There were two ways in which it could have been rejected. First, a simple majority of all

voters could have cast 'no' ballots, an extremely unlikely outcome
given that the Shi'a and the Kurds—who generally favored the
constitution—alone made up almost 80 percent of Iraq's population. Second, even if the draft constitution had been approved by a
simple majority, it could have been defeated if two-thirds of voters
in three or more provinces rejected it. The Sunni Arabs, who uniformly turned their backs on the document and are thought to be a
majority in four of Iraq's eighteen provinces, could have torpedoed
the 15 October referendum had they been able to muster a two-
thirds majority in three provinces. They were banking on it.

There was, however, concern among the Sunnis that the Kurds
and Shi'a would argue that there was only way one to defeat it, and
that was for a simple majority to vote no. They tried that ploy, but
backed down when both the United States and the Sunnis reacted
negatively. Nonetheless, Sunnis in their droves registered to vote
and, from what I could ascertain in meetings with numerous Sunnis in the Mosul and Tal Afar area between July and September
2005, they were determined to vote.

I spoke with many Sunnis about their participation in the referendum and they pointed out their key fears. First, they knew that
they were not as well-prepared as the Shi'a and the Kurds. There
was voter ignorance, particularly in the more remote areas. Second, Sunni political organizations lacked campaigning muscle and
funds, a point that came across poignantly in a three-hour meeting
with members of the IIP in Mosul on 30 July 2005. Third, the Sunnis pointed out that they were afraid not only of the insurgents,
but also that Shi'a militias and *peshmerga* masquerading as government forces would attempt to prevent them from voting. Finally,
they believed that there could well be 'irregularities' in the final
voting results.

In the end the Sunnis were, as I pointed out in Chapter 3, unable to defeat the draft constitution, much to the chagrin of the

insurgent leadership and of the majority of the community. Parliamentary elections will be held on 15 December 2005. The Sunni community is redoubling its efforts to vote in that election. Whether this will help in the efflorescence of an effective political wing of the insurgency and a slow but steady march towards the community's entry into the political process remains to be seen.

If, on the other hand, the situation worsens in 2006, the United States—already weary and taxed to the limit—may choose to leave the Iraqis to their own devices. Nor would I be surprised if the allegedly enlightened people it had brought along to rule the new Iraq chose to flee to the comfort of their homes in exile, where they would return to their previous careers as doctors, professors, investment bankers or analysts.

The words of a cynical Kurdish observer may well be prophetic, even if they are a throwback to Vietnam: 'They will all be fighting for the last seat on the American helicopter fleeing the green zone when the American leave. For us, the Kurds, we will just go up in the mountains.'[26] Those who remain behind to fight over the rotting carcass of the Iraqi state will be the survivors of a process of political Darwinism: ruthless, merciless, and not averse to engaging in ethnic cleansing of the Other.

NOTES

Preface

1. Judy Keen, 'Bush to Troops: Mission Accomplished,' *USA Today*, 5 June 2003, p. 1.

2. Clive Jones, 'A Reach Greater than the Grasp': Israeli Intelligence and the Conflict in South Lebanon 1990–2000,' *Intelligence and National Security* 16, 3 (2001), p. 2.

3. For studies that explore the complex definitional issues concerning the types of violence undertaken by groups against the state see Adria Lawrence, 'Defining Challenges to the State: Civil Wars, Uprisings, Protests and Riots in the context of Social Movements,' Draft Paper Presented at the Workshop on Organizations and State-Building, University of Chicago, 20 May 2002; Donald Hamilton, *The Art of Insurgency: American Military Policy and the Failure of Strategy in Southeast Asia*, Westport, CT: Praeger, 1998, pp. 13–38.

4. The literature on insurgency and counter-insurgency is huge and I read or skimmed a significant portion of it in the course of researching and writing this book. I have found the following books on insurgency and counter-insurgency to have been the most helpful in formulating my arguments and setting up my framework: Ted Robert Gurr, *Why Men Rebel*, Princeton University Press, 1970; Bard O'Neill, *Insurgency and Terrorism: Inside Modern Revolutionary Warfare*, Washington, DC: Brassey's, 1990; Robert Thompson, *Defeating Communist Insurgency: The Lessons of Malaya and Vietnam*, New York: Praeger, 1966; Otto Heilbrunn, *Partisan Warfare*, New York: Praeger, 1962; Michael Collins, *The Path to Freedom*, Boulder: Roberts Rinehart, 1996; David Galula, *Counterinsurgency Warfare: Theory and Practice*, New York: Praeger, 1964; Truong Chinh, *Primer for Revolt: The Communist Take-over in Vietnam*, New York:

Frederick Praeger, 1963; Lieutenant Colonel T.N. Greene (ed.), *The Guerilla and How to Fight Him*, New York: Praeger, 1962; *Small Wars Manual: United States Marine Corps 1940*, Manhattan, KS: Sunflower University Press, n.d.; Walter Laqueur, *Guerilla: A Historical and Critical Study*, Boulder: Westview Press, 1984; Douglas Blaufarb, *The Counterinsurgency Era: US Doctrine and Performance 1950 to the Present*, New York: Free Press, 1977; *Selected Military Writings of Mao-Tse-Tung*, Peking: Foreign Language Press, 1967.

5. The term 'small war' which has come back into vogue was defined by one of its practitioners, the British officer C.E. Caldwell, at the turn of the twentieth century as 'all campaigns other than those where both the opposing sides consisting of regular troops … it comprises campaigns undertaken to suppress rebellions and guerilla warfare in all parts of the world where organized armies are struggling against opponents *who will not meet them in the open field …*'. C.E. Caldwell, *Small Wars: Their Principles and Practice*, Lincoln: University of Nebraska Press, 1996, p. 21; emphasis added.

6. One can plausibly make the argument, as others have done, that guerrilla warfare can be used methodologically as a shorthand to describe the methods/means of insurgent movements; that is to say, assassinations, sabotage, bombings, hit-and-run raids, ambushes, and so on.

7. Headquarters, Department of the Army, *Counterinsurgency Operations*, FMI 3-07.22, Washington, DC: Department of the Army (<http://www.globalsecurity.org/military/library/policy/army/fm/3-07-22/ch1.htm>).

8. O'Neill, *Insurgency and Terrorism*, p. 13.

9. CIA, *Guide to the Analysis of Insurgency*, quoted in Daniel Byman, Peter Chalk, Bruce Hoffman, William Rosenau and David Brannan, *Trends in Outside Support for Insurgent Movements*, Santa Monica: RAND, 2001, p. 4.

10. Rex Hudson, *The Sociology and Psychology of Terrorism: Who Becomes a Terrorist and Why?* Report Prepared by the Federal Research Division, Library of Congress, Washington, DC: Library of Congress, 1999, <http://www.loc.gov/rr/frd/pdf-files/Soc_Psych_of_Terrorism.pdf>.

11. O'Neill, *Insurgency and Terrorism*, p. 24. This definition can, of course, be challenged by those who argue that acts of sabotage against economic or critical infrastructure where nobody dies are acts of terror.

12. The targeting of so-called native collaborators—whether civilian or military—with the foreign presence does not make the Iraqi insurgents any different from the Irish Republican Army during the Irish Rebellion in 1919–21, the Algerian Front de Liberation Nationale (FLN) during the war of independence, or the Vietcong during the Vietnam war. See Ariel Merari,

'Terrorism as a Strategy of Insurgency,' *Terrorism and Political Violence* 5, 4 (1993), 213–51.

13. Here I have benefited greatly from the discussions of revolutionary or insurgent terrorism in Martha Crenshaw Hutchison, *Revolutionary Terrorism: The FLN in Algeria, 1954–1962*, Stanford: Stanford University Press, 1978; Alistair Horne, *A Savage War of Peace: Algeria 1954–1962*, New York: Penguin Books, 1987, pp. 105–27.

14. In this sense the massacre of European civilians in the town of Philippeville by a unit of the Algerian FLN was not only or primarily in response to the harsh repressive measures of the French military, but was designed to elicit a merciless counterresponse on the part of the French and the European settlers (which it did) and close all avenues of compromise between the two sides (which it also did). As Jacques Soustelle, the liberal governor of Algeria, said: 'It was not only the sacked houses or the poor mutilated corpses that the *fellagha* [the Algerian Muslim insurgents] left in their passage, it was confidence, hope, peace. A somber harvest of hatred sprouted in the bloodshed. Terror dominated minds. Far from being brought together by the ordeal, human beings were going to divide themselves and tear themselves to pieces' (Horne, *Savage War of Peace*, pp. 122–3). The 'men of goodwill' of both races in the Algerian war receded into the background or were discredited and Soustelle himself became a believer in the use of harsh means to stamp out the native Algerian insurgency.

15. See the following new, outstanding studies: Caroline Elkins, *Imperial Reckoning: The Untold Story of Britain's Gulag in Kenya*, New York: Henry Holt, 2005; David Anderson, *Histories of the Hanged: The Dirty War in Kenya and the End of Empire*, New York: W.W. Norton, 2005.

16. In the 3rd Armored Cavalry Regiment based in Tal Afar we often joked about these acronyms. We even came up with a few of our own, including anti-regimental fighters (ARF) or anti-regimental Saddamist elements (ARSE).

17. Monica Prieto, 'Militant Group Ansar al-Sunnah Army Interviewed,' *El Mundo*, 5 October 2003, trans. in FBIS–EUP20031007000351 (<https://portal.rccb.osis.gov>; access password restricted).

18. Galula, *Counterinsurgency Warfare*, pp. 19–20; see also pp. 18–25 for an extended discussion of the nature and importance of the cause for an insurgent. See also Robert Tomes, 'Schlock and Blah: Counter-insurgency Realities in a Rapid Dominance Era,' *Small Wars and Insurgencies* 16, 1 (2005), 37–56.

19. The key general studies to date are Bruce Hoffman, *Insurgency and Counterinsurgency in Iraq*, Occasional Paper OP-127-IPC/CMEPP, Santa Monica, CA:

National Security Research Division, RAND, June 2004; Ian Beckett, *Insurgency in Iraq: An Historical Perspective*, Carlisle, PA: Strategic Studies Institute, US Army War College, 2005, <http://www.strategicstudiesinstitute.army. mil/pdffiles/PUB592.pdf>; Steven Metz, 'Insurgency and Counterinsurgency in Iraq,' *Washington Quarterly* 27, 1 (Winter 2003–4), 25–36; Anthony Cordesman, *Iraq's Evolving Insurgency*, Washington, DC: Centre for Strategic and International Studies, 2005 (19 May), <http://www.csis.org/features/050512.IraqInsurg.pdf> (working draft, since updated; <http://www.csis. org/media/csis/pubs/051209_iraqiinsurg.pdf>.) Cordesman has written several more updates on the insurgency at the CSIS website. Michael Eisenstadt, 'Assessing the Iraqi Insurgency (Part II): Devising Appropriate Measures,' *Policywatch* 979 (2005) (accessed online); Michael Eisenstadt, 'The Sunni Arab Insurgency: A Spent or Rising Force?' *Policywatch* 1028, 26 August 2005 (accessed online); Sergeant Christopher Alexander, Captain Charles Kyle and Major William McCallister, 'The Iraqi Insurgent Movement,' 14 November 2003 (paper in my possession); and Ahmed Hashim, 'Insurgency in Iraq,' *Small Wars and Insurgencies* 14, 3 (2003), 1–22.

Chapter 1 · Evolution of the Iraqi Insurgency

1. Riad Kahwaji, 'Iraq Prepares For Urban Combat As Tensions Mount,' *Defense News*, 3 February 2003 (<http://ebird.dtic.mil/Feb2003/s20030203150772.html>).

2. Vernon Loeb, 'Bracing for "Primordial Combat",' *Washington Post*, 31 October 2002, p. 1. According to accounts by journalists who relied on information relayed to the United States by unreliable defectors and opposition groups, Saddam Hussein told his officials to prepare Iraq to wage urban warfare. Brian Whitaker, 'Iraq Plans Urban Warfare to Thwart US,' *Guardian*, 9 August 2002 (accessed online). See also Greg Miller and John Hendren, 'Saddam Indicates Plans for Urban War,' *International Herald Tribune*, 9 August 2002 (accessed online).

3. Philip Sherwell, 'Iraqis Resigned to Defeat as Preparations for War Begin,' *Sunday Telegraph* (London), 22 September 2002, p. 30.

4. LBC Satellite Television, interview with Tariq Aziz, 1830 GMT in Arabic, 1 April 2003.

5. *ibid*.

6. For an extensive journalistic discussion of the weaknesses of the Iraqi forces

in 2003 see, *inter alia*, Robert Schlesinger, 'As US Masses, Weakened Iraqi Forces Sit Tight,' *Boston Globe*, 12 January 2003, p. 1.

7.   Quoted in Tom Bowman, 'Iraqi Forces Down, Not Out,' *Baltimore Sun*, 6 October 2002 (accessed online).

8.   Vernon Loeb, 'Hussein Defenders Seen as Hard Corps Loyalists,' *Washington Post*, 17 November 2002, p. 27.

9.   The weaknesses of the Iraqi army were many and have been extensively detailed in the following works: Mark Heller, 'Iraq's Army: Military Weakness, Political Utility' in Amatzia Baram and Barry Rubin (eds), *Iraq's Road to War*, New York: St Martin's Press, 1993, pp. 37–50; Mark Heller, 'Politics and the Military in Iraq and Jordan, 1920–1958: The British Influence,' *Armed Forces and Society* 4, 1 (1977), 75–99. For an analysis of the formation of the Iraqi army in the 1920s, see Paul Hemphill, 'The Formation of the Iraqi Army, 1921–1933,' in Abbas Kelidar (ed.), *The Integration of Modern Iraq*, London: Croom Helm, 1979, pp. 88–109. The most detailed studies of the weaknesses of the Iraq Army are Staff Colonel Ahmed al-Zaidi, *Al-bina' al ma'anawi lil-quwat al-musallaha al-iraqiyah* (The Building of Combat Cohesion in the Iraqi Armed Forces), Beirut: Dar al-Rawda, 1990; Kenneth Pollack, *Arabs at War: Military Effectiveness, 1948–1991*, Lincoln: University of Nebraska Press, 2002, pp. 148–266.

10.   Faleh Jabar, 'Iraq: The Military Response,' *Le Monde Diplomatique*, January 2003, <http://mondediplo.com/2003/01/03military>; James Zumwalt, 'The Iraqi Military's Achilles Heel is Saddam Hussein,' *Los Angeles Times*, 26 December 2001, Metro Part 2, p. 13.

11.   Ghassan Shirbil, interview with General Nizar al-Khazraji, *Al-Hayah*, 29 November 2002, p. 10 (FBIS-GMP20021129000114).

12.   *ibid*.

13.   *ibid*.

14.   *ibid*.

15.   *ibid*.

16.   In a report in the aftermath of the war, a number of anti-Saddam Iraqi officers engaged in a postmortem of their army's weaknesses and performance during Operation Iraqi Freedom. Muhammad Abdallah al-Sahwani: 'Our former large army was an oppressive one. It was divided into the Republican Guard, Special Forces, the Fedayeen, and other divisions. It was an unprofessional army that is made of policemen trusted by Saddam. This is why they were ineffective in the war.' Muhammad Kurayshan, interview with Iraqi officers, Al-Jazeera Satellite Television, 1605 GMT, 6 May 2003.

17. See Esther Schrader, 'In Baghdad, a Solid Offense Met the Shadow of a Defense,' *Los Angeles Times*, 10 April 2003 (<http://ebird.dtic.mil/Apr2003/s20030411174467.html>).

18. Thomas Ricks, 'What Counted: People, Plan, Inept Enemy,' *Washington Post*, 10 April 2003, p. 1.

19. Craig Smith, 'In Documents, Glimpses of Failed Plan For Defense,' *New York Times*, 10 April 2003 (accessed online).

20. Juan Tamayo, 'Iraqis Seem Unaware of Enemy Location,' *Miami Herald*, 9 April 2003 (accessed online).

21. Laurie Kassman, 'Iraqi Major on the Defeat of Iraqi Military,' *Iraqi Crisis Bulletin*, 17 April 2003, <http://www.iraqcrisisbulletin.com/archives/041703/html/iraqi_major_on_the_defeat_of_i.html>.

22. David Zucchino, 'Iraq's Swift Defeat Blamed on Husseins,' *Los Angeles Times*, 11 August 2003 (accessed online).

23. ibid.

24. On poor morale among Iraqi troops in the north facing anti-Hussein Kurdish *peshmerga* guerrillas, see David Filipov, 'Iraqi Deserters Describe Front-line Despair,' *Boston Globe*, 3 April 2003, <http://www.boston.com/dailyglobe2/093/nation/Iraqi_deserters_describe_front_line_despair+.shtml>.

25. ibid.

26. ibid.

27. ibid.

28. Scott Peterson and Peter Ford, 'From Iraqi Officers, Three Tales of Shock and Defeat,' *Christian Science Monitor*, 18 April 2003, p. 1.

29. John Burns, 'Fear of Hussein May Be Yielding to Doubt,' *New York Times*, 27 October 2002 (accessed online).

30. John Burns, 'In Iraq, Fear and Mumbling at the Top,' *New York Times*, 22 December 2002. On the remarkably surreal state of the country on the eve of war, see Johanna McGeary, 'Inside Saddam's World,' *Time*, 4 May 2002 (accessed online); Maggie O'Kane, 'Iraqi Rich Make Mockery of Sanctions,' *Guardian*, 21 November 1998 (accessed online); Robert Collier, 'Iraq's New Elite Living Large,' *San Francisco Chronicle*, 15 January 2003, p. 1; Susan Glaser, 'A Regime of Payoffs and Persecution,' *Washington Post*, 17 April 2003, p. 1. The best lengthy analyses of the last months of the Ba'th regime include the following outstanding studies: G.W.F. Vigeveno, *Irak en de erfenis van Saddam Hoessein* (Iraq in the Prison of Saddam Hussein), Research Essay, Gravenhage: Nederlands Instituut voor Internationale Betrekkingen, 2003, <http://www.

clingendael.nl/publications/2003/20030100_cli_ess_vigeveno.pdf>;   International Crisis Group, *Iraq Backgrounder:What Lies Beneath*, Middle East Report 6, Amman/Brussels: International Crisis Group, 2002, <http://www.
crisisgroup.org/library/documents/report_archive/A400786_01102002.
pdf>; International Crisis Group, 'Voices from the Iraqi Street,' *ICG Middle
East Briefing* 3, 4 December 2002, <http://www.crisisgroup.org/library/
documents/report_archive/A400837_04122002.pdf>.

31. See Colin Heaton, *German Anti-partisan Warfare in Europe 1939–1945,* Atglen,
    PA: Schiffer Military Publishing, 2001.

32. Zucchino, 'Iraq's Swift Defeat Blamed on Husseins.'

33. Eliot Blair Smith, 'Guerilla Attacks Put Unit on Edge,' *USA Today*, 27 March
    2003, p. 4; Vernon Loeb, 'Iraq's "Outside-In" Strategy More Effective than
    Anticipated,' *Washington Post*, 28 March 2003, p. 32; Mary Beth Sheridan,
    'Troops Find a Different Foe than Expected,' *Washington Post*, 7 April 2003,
    p. 19.

34. Michael Slackman, 'Fearing Revenge, Hussein's Militia Forces Lie Low and
    Deny Hurtful Role,' *Los Angeles Times*, 16 April 2003 (accessed online).

35. Peter Ford, 'War Views Meld Old Arab Nationalism, New Islamism,' *Chris-
    tian Science Monitor,* 7 April 2003.

36. E.A. Torriero, 'Tikrit: Hussein's Hometown Vows Guerilla Struggle,' *Chicago
    Tribune*, 18 March 2003, p. 1.

37. *ibid.*

38. Jonathan Finer, 'Marines Struggle to Discern Friend from Foe in South,'
    Washington Post, 28 March 2003, p. 30; Chris Ayres, 'Shepherds by Day Turn
    into Warriors by Night,' *The Times* (London), 28 March 2003 (<http://
    ebird.dtic.mil/Mar2003/s20030328168579.html>); Dexter Filkins, 'End-
    less Supply Convoy is Frustrated Endlessly,' *New York Times*, 28 March 2003
    (<http://ebird.dtic.mil/Mar2003/s20030328168697.html>).

39. Vivienne Walt, 'Thousands of Iraqis Head Home to Fight,' *USA Today*, 27 March
    2003, p. 6. On the nationalism factor, see also Joseph Galloway, 'Two Worries
    for US: Guerilla War, Iraqi Nationalism,' *Philadelphia Inquirer*, 27 March 2003
    (<http://ebird.dtic.mil/Mar2003/s20030327168195.html>).

40. *ibid.*

41. Rick Atkinson, 'Confused Start, Swift Finish,' *Washington Post*, 13 April 2003,
    p. 1. See also John Kifner, 'Constant Iraqi Attacks are Holding up the Allied
    Forces Trying to Reach Baghdad,' *New York Times*, 28 March 2003, in which
    Colonel Ben Saylor of the 1st Marine Division is quoted as saying: 'We've
    been contested every inch, every mile on the way up.' See also Ann Scott

Tyson, 'Inside the "Most Intense" Fight Yet,' *Christian Science Monitor*, 28 March 2003, p. 1.

42. Rick Atkinson, 'General: A Longer War Likely,' *Washington Post*, 28 March 2003, p. 1.

43. Robin Gedye, 'Oh My God, I'm Going to Die,' *Daily Telegraph* (London), 28 March 2003, <http://www.telegraph.co.uk/news/main.jhtml?xml=/news/2003/03/28/wtroop28.xml>.

44. Atkinson, 'General: A Longer War Likely'.

45. Bob Drogin and Greg Miller, 'Plan's Defect: No Defectors,' *Los Angeles Times*, 28 March 2003, p. 1.

46. In some places, though, US forces were unpleasantly surprised by Iraqi tactics and battlefield successes such as those against the M1A1 Abrams tanks and the Apache Longbow helicopter gunship; for details see Vernon Loeb, 'Tactics Show Iraqis Learned Lessons of War,' *Washington Post*, 27 March 2003, p. 27.

47. Tony Perry and Tyler Marshall, 'Hussein's Irregulars Slow US Advance,' *Washington Post*, 28 March 2003 (<http://ebird.dtic.mil/Mar2003/s20030328168869.html>).

48. David Zucchino, *Thunder Run: Three Days in the Battle for Baghdad*, London: Atlantic Books, 2004, p. 14.

49. Sean Boyne, 'Iraq Tactics Attempted to Employ Guerilla Forces,' *Jane's Intelligence Review*, July 2003, p. 19.

50. 'In the Triangle of Terror,' *Der Spiegel*, 25 August 2003.

51. Alissa Rubin, 'Resistance Simmers as Iraqis Await Government,' *Los Angeles Times*, 22 June 2003 (accessed online). See also Daniel Williams, 'Disheartened Iraqis Feel Assaulted from All Sides,' *Washington Post*, 9 August 2003, p. 1.

52. Among the most insightful discussions of the origins and workings of ORHA and the CPA are studies by Larry Diamond (*Squandered Victory: The American Occupation and the Bungled Effort to bring Democracy to Iraq*, New York: Times Books, 2005) and Toby Dodge (*Inventing Iraq: The Failure of Nation Building and a History Denied*, New York: Columbia University Press, 2003).

53. See 'Iraq's Sunnis Seethe over Loss of Prestige,' *Houston Chronicle*, 6 June 2003 (accessed online).

54. Mitchell Prothero, 'Interview with Anti-US Iraqi Cell,' UPI.com, 3 December 2003 (<http://ebird.afis.osd.mil/ebfiles/s20031205238775.html>).

55. *ibid*.

56. Edmund Lawrence, 'As Iraqis' Disaffection Grows, US Offers Them a

Greater Political Role,' *New York Times*, 7 June 2003 (<http://ebird.dtic.mil/Jun2003/s20030609190873.html>).

57. *ibid.*

58. *Dar al-Salam*, 14 August 2003, p. 1 (FBIS-GMP20030817000101, <http://imos.rccb.osis.gov>).

59. David Rohde, 'Free of Hussein's Rule, Sunnis in North Flaunt a Long-hidden Piety,' *New York Times*, 23 April 2003 (accessed online).

60. Meeting with Iraqi Islamic Party leaders, Mosul, 30 July 2005.

61. Rajiv Chandrasekaran, 'Sunnis in Iraq Protest US Occupation,' *Washington Post*, 19 April 2003, p. 1

62. *ibid.*

63. 'Iraq's Sunnis Seethe over Loss of Prestige,' *Houston Chronicle*.

64. Ian Fisher, 'US Force Said to Kill 15 Iraqis during Anti-American Rally,' *New York Times*, 30 April 2003, p. 1.

65. *ibid.*

66. Ali Abd al-Amir, 'Al-Fallujah's Clerics, Intellectuals Refuse Defeated Leader's Message, Emphasize they Confront the United States without Saddam, Ba'th Party,' *al-Hayat*, 20 July 2003, p. 3 (FBIS-GMP2003072000037, <https://imos.rccb.gov>).

67. Mohammad Bazzi, 'The Epicenter of Anti-US Hatred,' *Newsday*, 18 November 2003, p. 4.

68. Hazem al-Amin, 'The Resistance in the "Sunni Triangle",' *Dar al-Hayat*, 10 November 2003, <http://english.daralhayat.com>. The article is badly translated from Arabic into English, and I was unable to locate it in Arabic.

69. Bazzi, 'The Epicenter of Anti-US Hatred.'

70. al-Amin, 'The Resistance in the "Sunni Triangle".'

71. *ibid.*

72. Anthony Shadid, '2 US Soldiers Killed in Restive Iraqi City,' *Washington Post*, 28 May 2003, p. 1.

73. Joshua Hammer, 'Fallujah: In the Hands of Insurgents,' *Newsweek*, 24 May 2004 (accessed online).

74. Laura King, 'Insurgents and Islam Now Rulers of Fallouja,' *Los Angeles Times*, 13 June 2004, p. 1.

75. Ann Scott Tyson, 'A Search for patterns as Iraq Unrest Spreads,' *Christian Science Monitor*, 26 June 2003, <http://www.csmonitor.com/2003/0626/p01s01-woiq.html>; Donna Abu-Nasr and Pauline Jelinek, 'New Iraq Attacks Raising Questions,' *Guardian*, 29 June 2003, <http://www.guardian.co.uk/worldlatest/story/0,1280,-3960354,00.html>; David Teather,

'Forces in Iraq Face Mounting Attacks,' *Guardian*, 27 June 2003, <http://www.guardian.co.uk/Iraq/Story/0,2763,986107,00.html>.

76. Thomas Ricks, 'US Adopts Aggressive Tactics on Iraqi Fighters,' *Washington Post*, 28 July 2003, p. 1.

77. Rowan Scarborough, 'US Miscalculated Security for Iraq,' *Washington Times*, August 28, 2003, p. 1.

78. *ibid*.

79. *ibid*.

80. For extensive details of the policy failures, mistakes and lies made during the Vietnam War see David Kaiser, *American Tragedy: Kennedy, Johnson, and the Origins of the Vietnam War*, Cambridge, MA: Belknap Press, 2000; Robert Mann, *A Grand Delusion: America's Descent into Vietnam*, New York: Basic Books, 2000; H.R. McMaster, *Dereliction of Duty: Lyndon Johnson, Robert McNamara, the Joint Chiefs of Staff, and the Lies that Led to Vietnam*, New York: Harper Collins, 1997; A.J. Langguth, *Our Vietnam: The War, 1954–1975*, New York: Simon & Schuster, 2000. For the best analysis of the mistakes and failures relating to the Iraqi war, see James Fallows, 'Blind into Baghdad,' *Atlantic Monthly* 293, 1 (2004), 52–69.

81. The best and most detailed study that submits the Iraq as Vietnam analogy to careful scrutiny is Jeffrey Record and W. Andrew Terrill, *Iraq and Vietnam: Differences, Similarities and Insights*, Carlisle Barracks, PA: Strategic Studies Institute, US Army War College, 2004.

82. Gwynne Dyer, 'A Guerilla War Takes Root: Iraqis Opposed to US are Destroying Structures and Services on which the Population Depends,' *Toronto Star*, 20 August 2003 (accessed online).

83. LBC Satellite Television, 12 GMT, 23 August 2003 (FBIS-NES, 23 August 2003).

84. Susan Milligan and Stephen Glain, 'Violence Derails Iraq Rebuilding,' *Boston Globe*, 24 August 2003 (accessed online).

85. Alisa Rubin and Carol Williams, 'Postwar Saboteurs Target US Credibility,' *Los Angeles Times*, 20 August 2003, p. 1.

86. See William Booth and Daniel Williams, 'US Soldiers Face Persistent Resistance,' *Washington Post*, 10 June 2003, p. 1.

87. Interviews in Baghdad, Ramadi, Balad, Tikrit, and Mosul, November 2003.

88. See Brian Knowlton, 'US Surprised in Iraq by Insurgents' Fight,' *International Herald Tribune*, 27 October 2003, p. 1.

89. See Jonathan Landay, 'CIA has Bleak Analysis of Iraq,' *Philadelphia Inquirer*, 12 November 2003, p. 1.

90. Only April 2004 has been worse in terms of US casualties.

91. Jeffrey Gettleman, 'Mix of Pride and Shame follows Killings and Mutilation by Iraqis,' *New York Times*, 2 April 2004, p. 1.

92. *ibid.*

93. The scandal at Abu Ghraib did that, but was yet to come.

94. Thanassis Cambanis, 'Enemies Find Common Ground,' *Boston Globe*, 7 April 2004 (accessed online).

95. Thanassis Cambanis, 'Wide Fighting in Iraq,' *Boston Globe*, 7 April 2004, <http://www.boston.com/news/world/middleeast/articles/2004/04/07/wide_fighting_in_iraq?mode=PF>.

96. Jeffrey Gettleman and Douglas Jehl, 'Fierce Fighting with Sunnis and Shi-ites Spreads to 6 Iraqi Cities,' *New York Times*, 7 April 2004, p. 1. See also Mark Matthews and Tom Bowman, 'On Road to Peace: Violence,' *Baltimore Sun*, 7 April 2004 (<http://ebird.afis.osd.mil/ebfiles/s20040407273607.html>).

97. Alissa Rubin, 'US Losing Support of Key Iraqis,' *Los Angeles Times*, 10 April 2004, p. 1.

98. Anthony Cordesman, *The 'Post Conflict' Lessons of Iraq and Afghanistan: Testimony to the Senate Foreign Relations Committee*, Washington, DC: Center for Stra-tegic and International Studies, 2004, p. 13 (<http://foreign.senate.gov//testimony/2004/CordesmanTestimony040519.pdf>).

99. Timothy Phelps, 'Failure May Now be an Option,' *Newsday*, 23 May 2004 (<http://www.libertypost.org/cgi-bin/readart.cgi?ArtNum=50721>).

100. Daniel Williams, 'As Violence Deepens, So Does Pessimism,' *Washington Post*, 18 May 2004, p. 1.

101. *ibid.*

102. Rajiv Chandrasekaran, 'A Grand Mission Ends Quietly,' *Washington Post*, 29 June 2004, p. 1.

103. Luke Harding, 'I Already Feel I'm Dead,' *Salon.com*, 15 September 2004, <http://www.salon.com/news/feature/2004/09/15/insurgency/print.html>.

104. Stanley Reed, 'Iraq: Rising Radicalism, Falling Hopes,' *Business Week*, 7 April 2004, <http://www.businessweek.com:/print/bwdaily/dnflash/apr2004/nf2004048_7779_db039.htm>.

105. Howard LaFranchi, 'US Falling Deeper and Deeper into Iraq Quagmire,' *Christian Science Monitor*, 8 April 2004 (accessed online).

106. Jim Michaels and Charles Crain, 'Insurgents Showing No Sign of Letting Up,' *USA Today*, 22 August 2004 (accessed online).

107. Rajiv Chandrasekaran, 'Violence in Iraq Belies Claims of Calm, Data Show,' *Washington Post*, 26 September 2004, p. 1.

108. Alissa Rubin, 'Iraqi City on the Edge of Chaos,' *Los Angeles Times*, 28 September 2004, p 1.

109. Greg Jaffe, 'US, Iraqi Forces Strike Insurgents in City of Samarra,' *Wall Street Journal*, 1 October 2004, p. 3.

110. Lee Gordon, 'Iraqi Insurgents Turn against "Out of Control" Saudi al-Qaeda Fighters,' *Daily Telegraph* (London), 30 May 2004, <http://www.telegraph.co.uk/news/main.jhtml?xml=/news/2004/05/30/wirq30.xml>.

111. Soledad O'Brien, 'Time Reporter: Iraqi Resistance Finely Organized, Cut-throat,' *CNN.com International*, 8 December 2003, <http://edition.cnn.com/2003/WORLD/meast/12/08/cnna.ware/index.html>.

112. Sara Daniel, 'Irak: à Falouja, dans l'antre des "forces du Mal",' *Nouvel Observateur Hebdo* 2025, 28 August 2003, <http://archives.nouvelobs.com/recherche/article.cfm?id=122896&mot=irak%20falouja&mm=08&mm2=11&aa=2003&n_mag=0,8&num=2025&m2=8>.

113. *ibid.*

114. Ashraf Khalil and Edmund Sanders, 'Attack on Iraqi Brigade Shatters Fallouja Calm; Major Pipelines Hit,' *Los Angeles Times*, 10 June 2004 (accessed online); Edward Wong, 'Attackers Hit Oil Pipelines, Police and a US Convoy,' *New York Times*, 10 June 2004 (accessed online).

115. *Al Ansar* forum, FBIS-GMP20040617000234, 17 June 2004 (<https://portal.rccb.osis.gov>).

116. Matthew Stannard, 'The Challenge of Controlling Iraq as Rebel-Held Zones Proliferate; Pressure Mounts for Pentagon to Act before January Election,' *San Francisco Chronicle*, 24 September 2004 (accessed online).

117. For analyses of the combat in Fallujah see Patrick McDonnell, 'Reality of Combat Hits US Platoon,' *Los Angeles Times*, 10 November 2005, p. 1; Matthew McAllester, 'You Move. You Coil. You Move,' *Seattle Times*, 9 November 2004.

118. Edward Wong and Eric Schmitt, 'Rebel Fighters Who Fled Attack May Now Be Active Elsewhere,' *New York Times*, 10 November 2004 (accessed online).

119. Tony Perry, 'After Fallouja, Marines' Mission Shifts Northwest,' *Los Angeles Times*, 18 February 2005 (accessed online).

120. Edward Wong, 'Sunni Party Leaves Iraqi Government over Falluja Attack,' *New York Times*, 10 November 2004.

121. See Anthony Shadid, 'Iraqi Fighters Keep up Attacks,' *Washington Post*, 12 December 2004, p. 32; Scott Wilson, 'US Troops, Insurgents Battle across Iraq,' *Washington Post*, 13 December 2004, p. 17.

122. Wong and Schmitt, 'Rebel Fighters Who Fled Attack.' Insurgents attacked and seized parts of Ramadi; see Ali Hamdani and Richard Parry, 'Militants Unleash Wave of Attacks across Iraq,' *The Times* (London), 10 November 2004.

123. Colin McMahon, 'Troops Sweep into Mosul to Quell Pre-vote Violence,' *Chicago Tribune*, 17 January 2005 (<http://ebird.afis.osd.mil/ebfiles/e20050118346466.html>).

124. '15 Killed in Baghdad Shiite Mosque Blast after Zarqawi Vows Holy War,' Agence France Presse, 21 January 2005.

125. For example, in late January 2005 Sunni terrorists launched suicide-bombing attacks in Baghdad against a Shi'a mosque and a wedding party, killing a total of twenty-two people. See Liz Sly, 'Shiites Target of Attacks in Iraq,' *Baltimore Sun*, 22 January 2005, p. 1.

126. Statement posted by 'Mansur Billah' in *Baghdad al-Rashid Forum*, <http://www.baghdadalrashid.com>.

127. Rory McCarthy and Brian Whitaker, 'Iraq Violence Spreads to "Safe" Areas,' *Guardian,* 18 January 2005, <http://www.guardian.co.uk/Iraq/Story/0,2763,1392871,00.html>.

128. See, *inter alia*, 'Iraq's Holy City of Najaf Swarms with Voters,' Reuters, 30 January 2005; Dan Murphy, 'For Shiites, a Sense of Triumph,' *Christian Science Monitor*, 31 January 2005 (accessed online); Rory Caroll, 'Patient Shias File in to End Centuries of Exclusion,' *Guardian*, 31 January 2005; William Wallis, 'Basra's Shia Voters Flock to Polling Stations,' *Financial Times*, 30 January 2005 (accessed online).

129. Anthony Shadid, 'Iraqis Defy Threats as Millions Vote,' *Washington Post*, 31 January 2005, p. 1; Steve Komarow, 'On Election Day, Elation and Payback,' *USA Today*, 31 January 2005, p. 1.

130. 'In Samarra, Fear Keeps Voters Away,' Reuters, 30 January 2005; Tony Perry, 'Turnout is Low in Sunni-dominated Province,' *Los Angeles Times*, 30 January 2005 (accessed online); Tony Perry, 'Polls Stand Empty in Sunni Stronghold,' *Los Angeles Times*, 31 January 2005 (accessed online).

131. See Patrick McDonnell, 'Iraqi Insurgency Proves Tough Nut to Crack,' *Los Angeles Times*, 26 January 2005 (accessed online).

132. See Hamza Hendawi, 'Cautious Sense of Security Comes to Iraq,' Associated Press, 4 February 2005.

133. Thanassis Cambanis, 'Dozens Die in Iraq as Attacks Mar Shi'ite Holy Day,' *Boston Globe*, 20 February 2005, p. 1.

134. Dexter Filkins, 'Low Voting Rate Risks Isolation for Sunni Iraqis,' *New York Times*, 3 February 2005, p. 3.

135. Doug Struck, 'With Elections Past, Many Are Critical of US Presence,' *Washington Post*, 17 February 2005, p. 12.

136. *ibid.*

137. 'Iraqi Sunnis Demand a Voice in the New Government,' *International Herald Tribune*, 21 February 2005.

138. *ibid.* See also 'Iraqi Sunni Calls for Involvement in the Political Process,' *Arabicnews.com*, 21 February 2005, <http://www.arabicnews.com/ansub/Daily/Day/050221/2005022110.html>, in which the chairman of the Sunni Waqf Endowment, Adnan al-Duleimi, called upon the various Sunni Arab groups to present a united front and to participate in political life.

139. Ala'a Hasan, 'Unified Front for the Liberation of Iraq Refuses to Participate in the Political Process: It Stresses it Obtained Regional Support, Insists on Resisting the Occupation,' *Al-Watan,* 11 February 2005 (FBIS-NES, 11 February 2005); emphasis in original.

140. *ibid.*

141. Doug Struck, 'Sunnis Weigh the Risks of Running,' *Washington Post*, 26 January 2005, p. 1.

142. *ibid.*

143. Abd al-Azim Muhammad, 'The Iraqi Scene,' Al-Jazeera Satellite Television, Doha, 1715 GMT, 6 February 2005.

144. Doug Struck, 'Sunni Clerics Offer Their Cooperation,' *Washington Post*, 3 February 2005, p. 20. See also Luciano Gulli, 'Election or Not, We Want Sunni Ministers,' *Il Giornale*, 1 February 2005, p. 4 (FBIS-EUP20050201000166).

145. 'Diyar al-Umari Interview with Umar Raghib,' Al Arabiya Television, Dubai, 1212 GMT, 2 February 2005.

146. Al-Sharqiyah Television, Baghdad, 1928 GMT, 14 February 2005 (FBIS-NES, 14 February 2005).

147. *ibid.*

148. Hamza Hendawi, 'Iraq Reported Working to get Insurgent Factions to Disarm,' *Philadelphia Inquirer*, 2 June 2005 (<http://ebird.afis.osd.mil/ebfiles/e20050602371600.html>).

149. Solomon Moore, 'Leaders in Iraq Attempt to Engage Insurgents,' *Los Angeles Times*, 28 April 2005 (accessed online).

150. *ibid.*

151. Trudy Rubin, 'Democracy in Iraq,' *Detroit Free Press*, 4 May 2005 (accessed online).

152. Patrick McDonnell and Solomon Moore, 'Iraq to Purge Corrupt Officers,' *Los Angeles Times*, 1 January 2005 (<http://www.informationclearinghouse.

info/article8725.htm>).

153. Steve Chapman, 'The Sobering Reality of the Iraq War,' *Chicago Tribune*, 2 June 2005.

154. Tom Gordon, 'Iraq Still on Track, Says Jeffco's Vines,' *Birmingham News* (Alabama), 1 June 2005 (<http://ebird.afis.osd.mil/ebfiles/e20050602371551.html>).

Chapter 2   Origins and Motives of the Insurgency

1. Thomas Ricks, 'Experts Question Depth of Victory,' *Washington Post*, 27 June 2003, p. 20.

2. *ibid*.

3. According to Peter Sluglett (*Britain in Iraq 1914–1932*, London: Ithaca Press, 1976, p. 300) the 'rough' censuses of 1920 and 1931 revealed that the Shi'a comprised around 55 percent of the population, the Sunni Arabs 22 percent and the Kurds 14 percent.

4. There has been a steady rise in the number of studies on Iraqi state formation and nation-building over the years. For the overview I present here I have relied heavily on the following: Hanna Batatu; *The Old Social Classes and the Revolutionary Movements of Iraq*, Princeton: Princeton University Press, 1979; Majid Khadduri, *Socialist Iraq: A Study in Iraqi Politics since 1968*, Washington, DC: Middle East Institute, 1978; Phebe Marr, *The Modern History of Iraq*, 2nd edn, Boulder, CO: Westview Press, 2004; Marion Farouk-Sluglett and Peter Sluglett, *Iraq Since 1958: From Revolution to Dictatorship*, London: Kegan Paul International, 1987; Mohammad Tarbush, *The Role of the Military in Politics: A Case Study of Iraq to 1941*, London: KPI, 1982; Reeva Simon, *Iraq Between the Two World Wars: The Creation and Implementation of a Nationalist Ideology*, New York: Columbia University Press, 1986; Ala'a Tahir, *Irak aux origines du régime militaire*, Paris: L'Harmattan, 1989; Malik Mufti, *Sovereign Creations: Pan-Arabism and Political Order in Syria and Iraq*, Ithaca: Cornell University Press, 1996; Charles Tripp, *A History of Iraq*, Cambridge University Press, 2000; Liora Lukitz, *Iraq: The Search for National Identity*, London: Frank Cass, 1995; Hosham Dawod and Hamit Bozarslan (eds), *La société irakienne: communautés, pouvoirs et violences*, Paris: Karthala, 2003; Reeva Simon and Eleanor Tejirian (eds), *The Creation of Iraq 1914–1921*, New York: Columbia University Press, 2004; Pierre-Jean Luizard, *La question irakienne*, Paris: Fayard, 2002; Aqil al-Nasseri, *Al-jaish wa al-sulta fi al-iraq al-maliki, 1921–1958* (The Army and the Power Structure in Monarchical Iraq, 1921–1958), Damascus: Al-Hasad,

2000 (from a dissertation in Swedish: Militar och makten undar Irakiska monarkisk 1921–1958); Toby Dodge, *Inventing Iraq: The Failure of Nation Building and a History Denied,* New York: Columbia University Press, 2003; Eric Davis, *Memories of State: Politics, History and Collective Identity in Modern Iraq*, Berkeley: University of California, 2005; Eric Davis, 'State-Building in Iraq during the Iran-Iraq War and the Gulf Crisis,' in Manus Midlarksy (ed.), *The Internationalization of Communal Strife*, 1993, pp. 69–91; Eric Davis and N. Gavrielides (eds), 'Statecraft, Historical Memory and Popular Culture in Iraq and Kuwait' in E. Davis and N. Gavrielides (eds), *Statecraft in the Middle East: Oil, Historical Memory and Popular Culture*, Miami: Florida International University Press, 1991, pp. 116–48; Hazem Saghiyeh, *Ba'th al-Araq: Sultat Saddam Qiyaman wa Hataman* (The Iraqi Ba'th: Saddam's Power, Its Rise and Collapse), London: Dar al-Saqi, 2003; Ahmed Hashim, 'Military Power and State Formation in Modern Iraq,' *Middle East Policy* X, 4 (2003), 29–47.

5. Stephen Helmsley Longrigg, *Four Centuries of Modern Iraq*, Oxford: Clarendon Press, 1925, p. 28.

6. Sluglett, *Britain in Iraq*, p. 301.

7. Longrigg, *Four Centuries of Modern Iraq*, p. 28.

8. Batatu, *The Old Social Classes*, p. 17.

9. On the implementation of the Ottoman reforms that led to the rise of Sunni Arab ascendancy, see Reeva Simon, 'The Education of an Iraqi Ottoman Army Officer' in Rashid Khalidi, Lisa Anderson, Muhammad Muslih and Reeva Simon (eds), *The Origins of Arab Nationalism*, New York: Columbia University Press, 1991, pp. 151–66.

10. For more details, see the memoirs of Jafar al-Askari, *A Soldier's Story: From Ottoman Rule to Independent Iraq,* London: Arabian Publishing, 2003, pp. 15–37.

11. Tripp, *A History of Iraq*, pp. 20–9.

12. Jonathan Kandell, 'Iraq's Unruly Century,' *Smithsonian*, May 2003, p. 46.

13. For more details on the causes, see Robert Martin Campbell, 'The Iraqi Enigma: Ethno-Sectarianism, Tribalism, State Ideology and Class,' MA thesis, University of Arizona, 1998, pp. 31–3. On the British counter-insurgency campaign, see Mark Jacobsen, '"Only by the Sword": British Counter-Insurgency in Iraq, 1920,' *Small Wars and Insurgencies* 2, 2 (1991), 323–63.

14. Sir Arnold Wilson, quoted in Graeme Sligo, 'The British and the Making of Modern Iraq,' *Australian Army Journal* 2, 2 (2005), 280.

15. See David Fromkin, *A Peace to End All Peace: The Fall of the Ottoman Empire and the Creation of the Modern Middle East*, New York: Henry Holt, 1989, p. 453.

16. Tripp, *A History of Iraq*, pp. 30–65.

17. John Keay, *Sowing the Wind: The Mismanagement of the Middle East 1900–1960*, London: John Murray, 2003, p. 161.

18. Cited in part in Amatzia Baram, *Culture, History and Ideology in the Formation of Ba'thist Iraq, 1968–89*, New York: St Martin's Press, 1991, p. 129.

19. For a succinct summary of the social construction of the Arab nationalist identity of the new country, see Reeva Simon, 'The Imposition of Nationalism on a Non-Nation State: The Case of Iraq During the Interwar Period, 1921–1941' in James Jankowski and Israel Gershoni (eds), *Rethinking Nationalism in the Arab Middle East*, New York: Columbia University Press, 1997, pp. 87–104.

20. On British influence over the Iraqi army, see Mark Heller, 'Politics and the Military in Iraq and Jordan, 1920–1958,' *Armed Forces and Society* 4, 1 (1977), 75–86.

21. For excellent analyses of the political and socioeconomic foundations of the Ba'thist regime, see Faleh Jabar, 'State and Society in Iraq: A Totalitarian State in the Twilight of Totalitarianism,' *Jurist* 1, 6 (2001), 14–31; Faleh Jabar, 'Parti, clans et tribus, le fragile équilibre du régime irakien' (Party, Clans and Tribes: The Fragile Equilibrium of the Iraqi Regime), *Le Monde Diplomatique*, October 2002, pp. 4–5, <http://www.monde-diplomatique.fr/2002/10/JABAR/17020>.

22. See David Baran, 'L'adversaire irakien,' *Politique Étrangère* 1, 2 (2003), 60–2.

23. I have relied extensively on the excellent analyses of Faleh Jabar, 'The State, Society, Clan, Party and Army in Iraq: A Totalitarian State in the Twilight of Totalitarianism' in Faleh Jabar, Ahmed Shikara and Keiko Sakai (eds), *From Storm to Thunder: Unfinished Showdown between Iraq and US*, Tokyo: Institute of Developing Economies, 1998, pp. 1–27; Isam al-Khafaji, 'In Search of Legitimacy: The Post-Rentier Iraqi State,' *Social Science Research Council/Contemporary Conflicts*, n.d., <http://conconflicts.ssrc.org/iraq/khafaji/>; Eric Davis, 'The Uses of Historical Memory,' *Journal of Democracy* 16, 1 (2005), 57–8.

24. See Erik Ringmar, *Identity, Interest and Action: A Cultural Explanation of the Swedish Intervention in the Thirty Years War*, Cambridge University Press, 1996.

25. I realize that the whole notion of identity and identity crisis is a rich field in international relations. I do not wish to enter into esoteric debates here. Moreover, I began addressing this issue in the summer of 2005 in Tal Afar. I did not have the resources, time or energy to address theoretical and methodological issues. But I did have the ability, albeit limited by the 'unsettled' environment, to collect field data. I interviewed dozens of Sunni Arabs and Turkmen basically asking them: what do you think of the new Iraq? How do

you fit in the new Iraq? How do you think you would need to adapt to the new Iraq? And what do you think of the future of the country? Almost all of them gave answers that were pessimistic or negative, and none were able to conceive of a scenario in which the new Iraq was reflective of their collective identity. Nor were they able to conceive of how they could change any of their values or readjust their identities to fit in with the new Iraq. (Part of the problem stems from the pronounced tendency to see themselves as the majority in terms of sect.)

26. Daniel Williams, 'In Sunni Triangle, Loss of Privilege Breeds Bitterness,' *Washington Post*, 13 January 2004, p. 1.

27. Anthony Shadid, 'In New Iraq, Sunnis Fear a Grim Future: Once Dominant, Minority Feels Besieged,' *Washington Post*, 22 December 2003, p. 1 (<http://www.pulitzer.org/year/2004/international-reporting/works/shadid10.html>).

28. *ibid.*

29. *ibid.*

30. Williams, 'In Sunni Triangle.'

31. Nir Rosen, 'Iraq: Enemies and Neighbors,' *Asian Times*, 24 February 2004, <http://www.atimes.com/atimes/Middle_East/FB24Ak02.html>.

32. *ibid.*

33. *ibid.*

34. *ibid.*

35. Interviews in Baghdad, November 2003, February-March 2004; observations in Tal Afar, July-September 2005.

36. *ibid.*

37. Mitch Potter, 'In Iraq's Sunni Heartland, Rebels Have a New Cause,' *Toronto Star*, 13 December 2004 (accessed online).

38. Neil MacFarquhar, 'Iraq's Anxious Sunnis Seek Security in the New Order,' *New York Times*, 10 August 2003.

39. Hamid al-Humud, 'The Role of Sunni Arabs in building the new Iraq,' *Al-Hayah*, 14 December 2003, p. 9 (FBIS-GMP20031215000151, <https://portal.rccb.osis.gov>).

40. *ibid.*

41. Borzou Daraghi, 'The Puzzle of Sunnis' Leadership Vacuum,' *Los Angeles Times*, 5 July 2005, <http://www.latimes.com/news/nationwide/world/la-fg-sunnis5jul05,14943220.story>.

42. *ibid.*

43. *ibid.*

44. *Al Sa'ah*, 19 July 2003, p. 1 (FBIS-GMP20030722000023, < http://imos. rccb.osis.gov >).

45. *ibid.*

46. *ibid.*

47. I heard this view articulated many times in Iraq, including from among the least-educated Sunni Arabs and by the young. November 2003–April 2004; July-September 2005.

48. For more details see Alan Sipress, 'Feeling Besieged, Iraq's Sunnis Unite,' *Washington Post*, 6 January 2004, p. 11.

49. Shadid, 'In New Iraq, Sunnis Fear a Grim Future.'

50. Amir Ibrahim, 'Encounter,' (Interview with Dr Muthana Harith al-Dari), *Baghdad Al-Sharqiyah Television*, 15 March 2005 (FBIS, 15 March 2005, <https://www.portal.rccb.osis.gov>).

51. *ibid.*

52. Robert Worth, 'For Some in Iraq's Sunni Minority, a Growing Sense of Alienation,' *New York Times*, 8 May 2005 (<http://ebird.afis.osd.mil/ebfiles/e20050508367202.html>).

53. *ibid.*

54. Gerhard Sporl and Bernhard Zand, 'The Wrath of the Conquered,' *Der Spiegel*, 21 July 2003 (<http://www.spiegel.de/spiegel/english/0,1518,258027. html>).

55. Mark Danner, 'Taking Stock of the Forever War,' *New York Times Magazine*, 11 September 2003, p. 53.

56. Maureen Fan and Drew Brown, 'US Losing Trust around Baghdad,' *Miami Herald*, 13 November 2003 (<http://ebird.afis.osd.mil/ebfiles/e20031113233079.html>).

57. Gaith Abdul-Ahad, 'The US is Behaving as if Every Sunni is a Terrorist,' *Guardian*, 26 January 2005, <http://www.guardian.co.uk/Iraq/Story/0,2763,1398636,00.html>.

58. Daraghi, 'The Puzzle of Sunnis' Leadership Vacuum.'

59. Worth, 'For Some In Iraq's Sunni Minority, a Growing Sense of Alienation.'

60. *Al Basrah.net* website, 27 April 2005.

61. 'The Political and Strategic Program of the Iraqi Resistance Under the Leadership of the Arab Socialist Ba'th Party,' *Al-Majd* (Amman), 15 September 2003, p. 5 (FBIS-GMP20030917000049, 15 September 2003, <https://imos.rccb.osis.gov>).

62. *ibid.*

63. *Albasrah.net*, 21 January 2004; also in the Palestinian online weekly *Al-Dar*,

23 January 2004 (FBIS-GMP20040123000183, <https://portal.rccb.osis. gov>).

64. *ibid*.

65. Message from Saddam Hussein on the occasion of Ramadan, 16 November 2003 (<http://comitesirak.free.fr/freng/saddam15.htm>).

66. For more details, see 'Statement from the Arab Ba'ath Socialist Party,' 7 February 2005 (<http://comitesirak.free.fr/baath/baath-050207-en.htm>).

67. Ewen MacAskill, 'Home Town Defies Ban on Saddam Birthday Party,' *Guardian,* 29 April 2003 (accessed online).

68. 'Tikrit Mostly Calm, Quiet as Many Flee: But Some Residents Angry at Takeover', *Chicago Tribune*, 16 April 2003, <http://www.chicagotribune. com/news/nationworld/iraq/chi-0304160149apr16,1,1666030.story? ctrack=1&cset=true>.

69. Douglas Birch, 'In Hussein's Hometown, Many Want Him Back,' *Baltimore Sun,* 16 April 2003 (accessed online).

70. Brian Bennett, 'Inside the Hunt for Saddam,' *Time,* 28 July 2003 (accessed online).

71. Tod Robberson, 'Tikrit Residents Wary Of Troops,' *Dallas Morning News,* 16 April 2003 (accessed online).

72. Renato Caprile, 'We Are More Skilled than the Vietcong: This is How We Fight in Iraq,' *La Reppublica*, 3 June 2005 (FBIS-EUP20050603058006, <http://www.fbis.gov>).

73. *ibid*

74. *Albasrah.net*, 21 January 2004; *Al-Dar*, 23 January 2004.

75. *ibid*.

76. Al-Jazeera Satellite Television, FBIS-NES, 10 August 2003.

77. Christophe Ayad, 'Hide and Seek with Iraqi Resistance', *Liberation*, 8 October 2003 (FBIS-NES, 8 October 2003).

78. *ibid*.

79. *ibid*.

80. Michel Bole-Richard, 'Baasiste impénitent, Mohammed Ibrahim Oda juge "enrichissants" ses cent jours de prison,' *Le Monde*, 19 January 2004.

81. *ibid*.

82. Discussions with a well-placed journalist who has had extensive access to the insurgents, Tal Afar, September 2005.

83. Mark Fineman, Warren Veith and Robin Wright, 'Dissolving Iraqi Army Seen by Many as a Costly Move,' *Los Angeles Times*, 24 August 2003, p. 1.

84. *ibid*.

85. *ibid.*

86. *ibid.*

87. *ibid.*

88. Paul Martin, '"Antiterrorfront" to Take Over Some Security Tasks,' *Washington Times*, 25 November 2003, p. 1.

89. Michael Slackman, 'US Policies Lead To Dire Straits For Some In Iraq,' *Los Angeles Times*, 10 June 2003, p. 1.

90. Abbas abu al-Nur, 'Officers on the Verge of Suicide,' *Al Sa'ah,* 31 May, 2003, p. 12 (trans. FBIS-NES, 31 May 2003, accessed online); emphasis added.

91. Cited in Ahmed Hashim, 'Saddam Husayn and Civil-Military Relations in Iraq: The Quest for Legitimacy and Power,' *Middle East Journal* 57, 1 (2003), pp. 28–9; emphasis added.

92. See, for example, 'Iraqis Revolt in Northern Iraqi Town after Weapons Search,' *Iraq Report* 6, 24 (2003), <http://www.globalsecurity.org/wmd/library/news/iraq/2003/05/24-300503.htm>.

93. Marc Lacey, 'Jobs in Jeopardy, Iraqi Soldiers Vow to Fight if Allies Don't Pay,' *New York Times*, 25 May 2003, p. 1. See also 'Unpaid Iraqi Soldiers Rally at Baghdad Base,' Associated Press, 12 May 2003 (<http://www.chron.com/cs/CDA/ssistory.mpl/special/iraq/1905724>).

94. Ilene Prueher, 'Jobless Iraqis Issue Threats,' *Christian Science Monitor*, 5 June 2003 (accessed online).

95. 'Iraq: Former Officer Calls For Small, Professional Army,' *Al-Ta'akhi*, 7 July 2003 (trans. FBIS, 7 July 2003, <https://imos.rccb.osis.gov>).

96. Nicholas Riccardi, 'In Iraq, an Army Day for No Army,' *Los Angeles Times*, 7 January 2004.

97. Christian Parenti, 'Two Sides,' *Nation*, 23 February 2004, <http://www.thenation.com/doc.mhtml?i=20040223&s=parenti>.

98. *ibid.*

99. *ibid.*

100. *ibid.*

101. *ibid.*

102. Quoted in Pepe Escobar, 'Fallujah: A Multilayered Picture Emerges,' *Asia Times*, 27 September 2003.

103. Isaiah Berlin, 'The Bent Twig: A Note on Nationalism,' *Foreign Affairs* 1 (1972), 17; emphasis added.

104. David Hawkins, 'Iraqi Fighters: Yankees Go Home,' *CBSNEWS.com*, 21 July 2003, <http://www.cbsnews.com/stories/2003/07/21/eveningnews/main564357.shtml>.

105. Jean-Claude Renet, 'The Iraqi Resistance,' *Paris Oumma.com*, 18 January 2005 (trans. FBIS, 18 January 2005, <https://imos.rccb.osis.gov>).

106. Anthony Shadid, 'Father Seeks Vindication but Finds Death in Fallujah,' *Washington Post*, 15 February 2005, p. 1.

107. Zaki Chehab, 'Inside the Resistance,' *Guardian*, 13 October 2003.

108. For more on the US operational methods and their impact on the Iraqis, see Chapter 5.

109. Mike Donkin, 'US Tactics Fuel Iraqi Anger,' *BBC News*, 28 July 2003, <http://news.bbc.co.uk/2/hi/middle_east/3102823.stm>.

110. 'How GI Bullies are Making Enemies of Their Iraqi Friends,' *Sydney Morning Herald*, 12 April 2004.

111. Jeffrey Gettleman, 'Anti-US Outrage Unites a Growing Iraqi Resistance,' *New York Times*, 11 April 2004.

112. *ibid*.

113. Andrea Nicastro, 'Nel covo dei terroristi sunniti: "Cosi ammazziano gli infideli"' (In the Sunnite Terrorists' Lair: 'This Is How We Kill Infidels'), *Corriere della Sera*, 6 February 2005, p. 5 (FBIS-NES, 6 February 2005).

114. *ibid*.

115. Patrick Graham, 'Beyond Fallujah: A Year with the Iraqi Resistance,' *Harper's Magazine*, June 2004 (posted 17 November 2004, <http://www.harpers.org/BeyondFallujah.html>).

116. *ibid*.

117. Niko Price, 'Iraqi Fisherman Says He Caught Americans,' Associated Press, 27 August 2003.

118. Hannah Allam, 'Iraqi Fighters Reject Label of Terrorist,' *Knight Ridder*, 13 September 2003 (accessed online).

119. Videotape sent to Al-Jazeera Satellite Television, 1300 GMT, 17 August 2003 (FBIS-NES, 17 August 2003).

120. Scott Johnson, 'Inside an Enemy Cell,' *Newsweek*, 18 August 2003 (accessed online).

121. *ibid*.

122. *ibid*.

123. Hamza Hendawi, 'Fallujah Calm, but Anger Runs Deep,' *Army Times*, 30 July 2003 (<http://www.armytimes.com/story.php?f=1-292925-2067351.php>).

124. Vivienne Walt, 'Bitterness Grows in Iraq Over Deaths of Civilians,' *Boston Globe*, 4 August 2003, <http://www.boston.com/dailyglobe2/216/nation/Bitterness_grows_in_Iraq_over_deaths_of_civilians+.shtml>.

125. Patrick Graham, 'Americans Sow Seeds of Hatred,' *Guardian*, 9 November 2003, <http://observer.guardian.co.uk/international/story/0,,1080989,00.html>.

126. Interviews in Karrada, Baghdad, November 2003.

127. Anthony Shadid, 'In Searching Homes, US Troops Crossed the Threshold of Unrest,' *Washington Post*, 30 May 2003, p. 1.

128. *ibid*.

129. Charles Clover, 'Clash of Cultures Fuels Low-Level War of Increasing Animosity,' *Financial Times*, 2 June 2003, p. 10.

130. *ibid*. See also 'Iraq's Sunnis Seethe over Loss of Prestige,' *Houston Chronicle*, 6 June 2003, <http://www.chron.com/cs/CDA/printstory.mpl/special/iraq/1940702>.

131. Eric Davis, 'Iraq's Sunni Clergy Enter the Fray,' *Religion in the News* 7, 3 (2005), 9–11, 24.

132. For more details, see Jamal Sankari, *Fadlallah: The Making of a Radical Shi'ite Leader*, London: Saqi Books, 2005, pp. 67–9.

133. On the role of Islamism in Iraq under the regime of Saddam Hussein, see Michael Hudson, 'The Islamic Factor in Syrian and Iraqi Politics' in James Piscatori (ed.), *Islam in the Political Process,* Cambridge University Press, 1983, pp. 73–97; Hrair Dekmejian, *Islam in Revolution: Fundamentalism in the Arab World,* Syracuse University Press, 1985, pp. 127–36; Chibli Mellat, 'Iraq' in Shireen Hunter (ed.), *The Politics of Islamic Revivalism: Diversity and Unity,* Washington, DC: Center for Strategic and International Studies, 1988, pp. 71–87. The most detailed study of political Islam under Saddam is in Faleh Jabar (ed.), *Ayatollahs, Sufis and Ideologues: State, Religion and Social Movements in Iraq,* London: Saqi Books, 2002.

134. See Alexandre del Valle, 'Le renouveau islamiste en Irak: conséquence de la diplomatie' (Renewal of Islam in Iraq: The Outcome of Diplomacy), 5 March 2001, <http://www.alexandredelvalle.com/publications.php?id_art=39>.

135. Jason Burke, 'Saddam Wields Sword of Islam,' *Observer*, 19 December 1999 (<http://www.guardian.co.uk/Print/0,3858,3943263,00.html>).

136. Asifah Musa, 'Al-Shira Reveals the Facts behind What is Happening in Al-Fallujah: American Provocations and Bathist False Reports are behind the Recent Clashes …' *Al-Shira,* 7 June 2003, p. 2 (cited in *Tides Middle East Report* 104; accessed online).

137. *ibid*.

138. Moni Basu, 'Secular No More, Saddam Adopts Radicalized Islam,' *Atlanta Journal-Constitution,* 3 January 2003 (accessed online).

139. Michael Slackman, 'Hussein Putting His Mark on Islamic Faith,' *Los Angeles Times,* 4 November 2001 (accessed online).

140. Pepe Escobar, 'Iraq Diary, Part 2: The Vanishing Middle Class,' *Asia Times*, 30 March 2002, <http://www.atimes.com/front/DC30Aa02.html>.

141. *ibid.* See also Tom Heinen, 'Former Middle Class Now Cobbles Together Existence,' *Milwaukee Journal Sentinel*, 6 August 2000, <http://www.jsonline.com/news/insideiraq/aug00/life07080600.asp>.

142. For an extensive survey of the collapse of Iraq's socioeconomic infrastructure and steady impoverishment, see Larry Johnson, 'A Nation Sagging under the Weight of Sanctions: Caught in a Spiral of Poverty and Death,' *Seattle Post-Intelligencer,* 11 May 1999.

143. *ibid.*

144. Shadid, 'In New Iraq.'

145. *ibid.*

146. Patrick Bishop, 'Americans Are Objects of Hatred in Falluja's Mosques,' *Daily Telegraph* (London), 15 September 2003 (<http://ebird.dtic.mil/Sep2003/s20030915217165.html>).

147. *ibid.*

148. Remy Ourdan, 'Des oulémas sunnites accusent les chiites de "purification ethnique"' (Sunni ulema accuse the Shi'a of 'ethnic cleansing'), *Le Monde*, 7 September 2003, p. 1.

149. Dan Murphy, 'Radical Islam Grows among Iraq's Sunnis,' *Christian Science Monitor*, 28 July 2004 (accessed online). See also Nicholas Pelham, 'Iraq's Holy Warriors Draw Inspiration from Arab Puritan of Another Century,' *Financial Times*, 18 March 2004 (<http://ebird.afis.osd.mil/ebfiles/s20040318267913.html>).

150. Cecile Hennion and Remy Ourdan, 'Refuser l'occupation, par les mots et par la guerre,' *Le Monde*, 23 October 2004, Dossier, p. III.

151. Didier Francois, 'The Salafists Lie in Ambush in Baghdad,' *Liberation* (Paris), 13 January 2004 (FBIS-EUP20040113000014, 13 January 2004, <http://portal.rccb.osis.gov>).

152. See, *inter alia,* Edward Wong, 'Uprising Has Increased the Influence of Sunni Clerics,' *New York Times,* 31 May 2004 (accessed online); Hannah Allam, 'Extremism Sweeping Iraq among Sunni, Shiite Muslims Alike,' *Knight Ridder Newspapers,* 14 June 2004 (accessed online); Pierre Barbancey, 'Irak: Parmi les imams sunnites de la résistance,' *L'Humanite*, 11 November 2003 (accessed online).

153. On the emergence of the Islamists in Mosul after the ouster of the regime,

see David Rohde, 'Free of Hussein's Rule, Sunnis in North Flaunt A Long-hidden Piety,' *New York Times*, 23 April 2003, p. 13.

154. Rory McCarthy, 'All We Are Asking is for Them to Pull Out,' *Salon.com*, 16 December 2004, <http://www.salon.com/news/feature/2004/12/16/iraqi_insurgents/print.html>.

155. *ibid.*

156. Didier Francois, 'Mossoul sous la férule des imams sunnites,' *Liberation*, 24 April 2003, <http://www.liberation.fr/imprimer.php?Article=105859>.

157. *ibid.*

158. *Al Sharq al-Awsat,* 22 June 2003 (FBIS-NES, 22 June 2003, accessed online).

159. Sophie Shihab, 'La résurgence du courant salafiste dans le creuset sunnite témoigne d'une radicalisation contre les Américains ,' *Le Monde*, 15 November 2003.

160. Romesh Ratnesar with Phil Zabriskie, 'The Rise of the Jihadists,' *Time*, 26 January 2004.

161. Mariam Fam, 'Iraqi Resistance Takes Many Shapes, Forms,' *Guardian*, 7 November 2003.

162. *ibid.*

163. 'Inside the Resistance,' *Sydney Morning Herald*, 16 August 2003, <http://www.smh.com.au/articles/2003/08/15/1060936052309.html>.

164. Rory McCarthy, 'For Faith and Country: Insurgents Fight On,' *Guardian*, 16 December 2004, <http://www.guardian.co.uk/international/story/0,3604,1374581,00.html>.

165. François, 'The Salafists Lie in Ambush in Baghdad.'

166. *ibid.*

167. Anthony Shadid, 'Iraq's Once Privileged Sunnis Increasingly See US as Enemy,' *Washington Post*, 1 June 2003, p. 1 (<http://ebird.dtic.mil/Jun2003/s20030602189210.html>).

168. Discussions, Iraq, November 2003 to March 2004, July to September 2005.

169. 'Introduction to the Political and Strategic Program,' *Al-Majd*, 15 September 2003, p. 1 (FBIS, GMP200030917000045).

170. Caprile, 'We Are More Skilled than the Vietcong.'

171. Ahmed Hashim, 'Terrorism and Complex Warfare in Iraq,' *Jamestown Foundation*, 18 June 2004, <http://www.jamestown.org/news_details.php?news_id=51>; emphasis added.

172. Ghaith Abdul-Ahad, 'The US is Behaving as if Every Sunni is a Terrorist,' *Guardian*, 26 January 2005 <http://www.guardian.co.uk/print/0,3858,5111992–103680,00.html>.

173. Lisa Clifford, 'Defusing Sunni Anger,' *Iraqi Crisis Report* 101, Institute for War and Peace Reporting, 26 January 2005, <http://www.iwpr.net.index.pl? archive/irq/irq_101_1_eng.txt>.

174. Alix de la Grange, 'The Liberation of Baghdad is Not Far Away,' *Asian Times*, 25 June 2004, <http://www.atimes.com/atimes/Middle_East/FF25Ak07. html>.

175. Renet, 'The Iraqi Resistance.'

176. 'Al-Zarqawi's Group Says US Acknowledges Defeat; Salafi Leader on Foreign Fighters, Establishing of Caliphate,' *Jihadist Websites—FBIS Report*, 25 March 2005 (<http://www.portal.rccb.osis.gov>).

Chapter 3 The Insurgents' Way of Warfare

1. Daniel Williams, 'Violence in Iraq Overtakes an Oasis of Relative Calm,' *Washington Post*, 16 November 2003, p. 24, <http://www.washingtonpost.com/ ac2/wp-dyn/A46620-2003Nov15?language=printer>.

2. Mariam Fam, 'In Northern City of Mosul, Rising Tensions Endanger US Soldiers,' *Miami Herald*, 31 December 2003; 'In Mossul herrscht die Angst' (Fear reigns in Mosul), *Neue Zürcher Zeitung*, 16 December 2004 (<http://www. nzz.ch/dossiers/2002/irak/2004.12.16-al-articleA2AWB.html>).

3. This section on Samarra relies on the excellent analysis by Hazem al-Amin, 'Samarra and its Sister Towns and the Signs of a Fundamentalist Advance on Iraq's Pan-Arab Cities,' *Al-Hayat*, 14 July 2003, p. 9 (FBIS-GMP20030715000073, <http://portal.rccb.osis.gov>).

4. Jim Krane, 'Saboteurs Knock out Oil Pipelines, Power,' *Philadelphia Inquirer*, 15 September 2004 (<http://ebird.afis.osd.mil/ebfiles/e20040915320800. html>).

5. See Patrick Cockburn, 'The British Army's Authority has Never Looked More Fragile,' *Independent*, 20 September 2005, <http://news.independent.co.uk/ world/middle_east/article313846.ece>; Terri Judd and Colin Brown, 'Under Fire: British Soldiers Attacked in Basra,' *Independent*, 20 September 2005 (<http://news.independent.co.uk/world/middle_east/article313847.ece>).

6. 'Nouveaux Messages de Saddam Hussein aux chiites irakiens,' 13 August 2003, *Comites Irak/Iraq Committees* <http://comitesirak.free.fr/freng/saddam 11.htm>.

7. Alix de la Grange, 'The Liberation of Baghdad is Not Far Away,' *Asian Times*, 25 June 2004, <http://www.atimes.com/atimes/Middle_East/FF25Ak07. html>; emphasis added.

8. On this period see, for example, Jeffrey Gettleman, 'Anti-US Outrage Unites a Growing Iraqi Resistance,' *New York Times*, 11 April 2004 (accessed online); Karl Vick, 'Shiites Rally to Sunni "Brothers",' *Washington Post*, 9 April 2004, p. 1.

9. Ferry Biedermann, 'Portrait of an Iraqi Rebel,' *Salon*, 16 August 2003, <http://www.salon.com/news/feature/2003/08/16/sunni/index_np.html>.

10. Farnaz Fassihi and Yochi Dreazen, 'In Hussein Hometown, Tension and Defiance,' *Wall Street Journal*, 16 December 2003 (<http://ebird.afis.osd.mil/ebfiles/s20031216242304.html>).

11. Michael Eisenstadt, 'The Sunni Arab Insurgency: A Spent or Rising Force?' *Policywatch* 1028, 26 August 2005, <http://www.washingtoninstitute.org/templateC05.php?CID=2362>.

12. de la Grange, 'Liberation of Baghdad.'

13. Ellen Barry, 'US Support in Iraq Fades after Raids,' *Boston Globe*, 15 June 2003, p. 1.

14. Quoted in Charles Glover, Mark Huband and Roula Khalaf, 'Smiles and Shrugs Speak Volumes about Nature of Attacks on American Troops,' *Financial Times*, 25 September 2003 (accessed on-line).

15. Damien McElroy, 'This is Jabir: Policeman by Day, Terrorist by Night,' *Sunday Telegraph* (London), 19 October 2003, <http://www.telegraph.co.uk/news/main.jhtml?xml=/news/2003/10/19/wirq219.xml&sSheet=/news/2003/10/19/ixnewstop.html>.

16. de la Grange, 'Liberation of Baghdad.'

17. 'Iraqi Resistance Cannot be Defeated: Prepared for Ten Year War,' *Arab Monitor*, 30 July 2005 (accessed on-line).

18. For an extensive discussion that asserts that the former regime planned much of the insurgency, see Joe Klein, 'Saddam's Revenge,' *Time*, 18 September 2005 (accessed online).

19. 'Iraqi Resistance Cannot be Defeated,' *Arab Monitor*.

20. 'Introduction to the Political and Strategic Program,' *Al-Majd*, 15 September 2003, p. 1 (FBIS-GMP20030917000045).

21. Observations in Rabiah border post, July 2005; notes from author's diary.

22. *ibid.*

23. Alexis Debat, '"Foreign Fighters," Terrorism and the Iraqi Handover,' *In the National Interest* 3, 25 (2004), <http://www.inthenationalinterest.com/Articles/Vol3Issue25/Vol3Issue25Debat.html>.

24. Darren Foster, 'Crossing the Line,' *San Francisco Chronicle*, 21 March 2004, p. 8, <http://www.sfgate.com/cgi-bin/article.cgi?file=/chronicle/archive/

2004/03/21/CMGQI5DIKR10.DTL>.

25. Pers. comm. (interview with author).

26. Foster, 'Crossing the Line.'

27. Debat, '"Foreign Fighters".'

28. Mireille Duteil and Olivier Weber, 'La spirale de la guérilla' (The Guer-rilla Spiral), *Le Point*, 19 December 2003, <http://www.lepoint.fr/monde/document.html?did=139885> (trans. in FBIS, 19 December 2003, <https://portal.rccb.osis.gov>).

29. Richard Beeston and James Hider, 'Following the Trail of Death: How For-eigners Flock to Join Holy War,' *The Times* (London), 25 June 2005.

30. Soledad O'Brien, 'Time Reporter: Iraqi Resistance Finely Organized, Cut-throat,' 8 December 2003, *CNN.com International*, <http://edition.cnn.com/2003/WORLD/meast/12/08/cnna.ware/index.html>.

31. Ghaith Abdul-Ahad, 'Outside Iraq but Deep in the Fight: A Smuggler of In-surgents Reveals Syria's Influential, Changing Role,' *Washington Post*, 8 June 2005, p. 1, < http://www.washingtonpost.com/wp-dyn/content/article/2005/06/07/AR2005060702026.html >.

32. *ibid.*

33. Yaroslav Trofimov, 'Iraqi Resistance Strikes a Chord with Locals on Mideast Street,' *Wall Street Journal*, 26 March 2003, p. 1.

34. 'Text of Al-Battar Articles Praising Al-Zarqawi Group's Allegiance to Bin Ladin,' *Jihadist Websites*, *FBIS Report*, 28 October 2004 (FBIS-GMP20041028000299, <http://portal.rccb.osis.gov>).

35. *ibid.*

36. *ibid.*

37. Jeffrey Gettleman, 'Zarqawi's Journey: From Dropout to Prisoner to Insur-gent Leader,' *New York Times*, 13 July 2004, p. 8.

38. Al-Jazeera Satellite Television, Doha, 1813 GMT, 27 December 2004.

39. Interviews with Muhammad al-Ta'i, Al-Fayha Television, Dubai, 0915 GMT, 1 February 2005.

40. *ibid.*

41. *ibid.*

42. 'Background of Jihad Recruits in the Netherlands,' Ministerie van Binnen-landse Zaken en Koninrijksrelaties (Ministry of the Interior and Kingdom Rela-tions, Netherlands), 10 March 2004, <http://www.minbzk.nl/wwwaivdnl/actueel_publicaties/parlementaire/background_of_jihad>.

43. *ibid.*

44. The saga of 'Abu Anas al-Shami' is in Edmund Sanders, 'War Blazed Imam's

Path to Extremism,' *Los Angeles Times*, 27 September 2004 (<http://ebird. afis.osd.mil/ebfiles/s20040927323860.html>).

45. Patrick McDonnell, 'Coalition Gains Insight into Iraq's Foreign Insurgents,' *Los Angeles Times*, 9 February 2004, p. 1.

46. *ibid.*

47. *ibid.*

48. Mohamad Bazzi, 'A New Jihad vs America? Iraq Fight Draws Arab Men,' *Long Island Newsday*, 20 July 2003, p. 6 (<http://ebird.dtic.mil/Jul2003/s200307213.html>).

49. *ibid.*

50. *ibid.*

51. On Iraqi Salafists, including *imams* who participate in violence, see Scott Peterson, 'How Wahhabis Fan Iraqi Insurgency,' *Christian Science Monitor*, 17 September 2003, <http://www.csmonitor.com/2003/0917/p01s04-woiq.html>.

52. Bazzi, 'A New Jihad vs America?'.

53. Feurat Alani, 'The Three Frenchmen's Network,' *Le Point,* 10 February 2005 (FBIS-NES, 10 February 2005). European intelligence uncovered surprisingly well-established networks of Muslim militants with affiliations that stretch across Europe to operatives in North America, North Africa, the Middle East and Central Asia. Elaine Sciolino and Desmond Butler, 'Europeans Fear That the Threat from Radical Islamists is Increasing,' *New York Times,* 8 December 2002 (accessed on-line). Militant networks have had considerable experience in training recruits to have working knowledge of bomb-making and weapons and in sending fighters with false documents into Chechnya and Afghanistan in pursuit of the *jihad*. See Peter Finn and Sarah Delaney, 'Al Qaeda's Tracks Deepen in Europe,' *Washington Post,* 22 October 2002, p. 1; Tom Hundley, 'Islamic Radicalism Festers in Europe,' *Chicago Tribune,* 25 February 2002 (accessed on-line). The experience would come in handy when smuggling foreign fighters into Iraq.

54. 'European Network for Smuggling Jihadists: Wanted Majati Appears in Tangier,' *Al-Hayah,* 11 February 2005, p. 5 (FBIS-NES, 11 February 2005).

55. Bryan Bender, 'Study Cites Seeds of Terror in Iraq: War Radicalized Most, Study Finds,' *Boston Globe*, 17 July 2005, <http://www.boston.com/news/world/middleeast/articles/2005/07/17/study_cites_seeds_of_terror_in_iraq>.

56. Reuven Paz, 'Arab Volunteers Killed in Iraq: An Analysis,' *Project for the Research of Islamist Movements (PRISM) Occasional Papers* 3, 1 (2005), <http://www.e-prism.org/images/PRISM_no_1_vol_3_-_Arabs_killed_in_Iraq.pdf>.

57. *ibid*.

58. Bender, 'Study Cites Seeds of Terror in Iraq.'

59. Alissa Rubin, 'US Finds War in Iraq is Far from Finished,' *Los Angeles Times*, 29 June 2003, <http://www.latimes.com/news/nationworld/iraq/complete/la-fg-iraqmil29jun29,1,2789659.story>.

60. Mohammad Bazzi, 'A Promise to Fight On,' *Newsday*, 10 July 2003 (accessed online).

61. US Army Training and Doctrine Command, *A Military Guide to Terrorism in the Twenty-First Century*, TRADOC DCSINT Handbook Version 3.0, Fort Leavenworth, KS: US Army Training and Doctrine Command, 2005, pp. 3-5–3-6.

62. Observations in Iraq, November 2003 to March 2004, July to September 2005.

63. Sophie Shihab, 'La résistance irakienne a l'occupation est de plus en plus organisée,' *Le Monde*, 12 June 2003.

64. *ibid*.

65. Larry Kaplow, 'Community Shields Iraqi Insurgents,' *Atlanta Journal-Constitution*, 19 July 2003 (<http://ebird.dtic.mil/Jul2003/s20030721201828.html>).

66. Observations in Baghdad, Sadr City, Mosul and Tal Afar, November 2003 to March 2004, July to September 2005.

67. James Janega, 'In Ramadi, GIs Fight an Elusive, Expert Foe,' *Chicago Tribune*, 1 November 2004 (<http://ebird.afis.osd.mil/ebfiles/e20041102333914.html>).

68. *ibid*.

69. Greg Grant, 'Anatomy of an IED,' *Army Times*, 15 August 2005, p. 14.

70. *ibid*.

71. Colonel Mark Klingelhoefer, *Captured Enemy Ammunition in Operation Iraqi Freedom and Its Strategic Importance in Post-Conflict Operations*, US Army War College Strategy Research Project, Carlisle Barracks, PA: US Army War College, 2005, p. 2, <http://www.strategicstudiesinstitute.army.mil/pdffiles/ksil72.pdf>.

72. 'Commander of Group from Saddam's Fedayeen Says: We Are Reorganizing Our Ranks and Getting Inspiration from the Belief that Our President is Still Alive and Will Return to Power,' *Al-Aswar*, 15 July 2003, p. 2 (FBIS-GMP20030716000024, <http://imos.rccb.osis.gov>).

73. 'Hostile Arabic Website Continues Militant Training Encyclopedia,' *Global Issues Report*, 22 March 2005.

74. 'Hostile Website Provides Instructions to Make IEDs and Car Bombs,' *Global Issues Report*, 20 May 2005.

75. *ibid.*

76. 'Iraqi Resistance Cannot be Defeated,' *Arab Monitor*.

77. *Information Clearinghouse*, 10 December 2004 (<http://www.occupationwatch.org>).

78. 'Website Offers Instructions for Crossing Syrian-Iraqi Border: "This is the Road to Iraq",' *Global Issues Report*, 9 June 2005.

79. Jonathan Steele and Michael Howard, 'US Confused by Iraq's Quiet War,' *Guardian,* 17 July 2003, <http://www.guardian.co.uk/Iraq/Story/0,2763,1000482,00.html>.

80. For is a brilliant and insightful article on the nexus between crime and resistance in Iraq, see Anthony Shadid, 'They Deal in Danger: Iraqi Militiaman's Fatal Error Offers Look into Anti-Occupation Campaign,' *Washington Post,* 4 September 2003, p. 1.

81. Yochi Dreazen, 'For Many Iraqis, A New Daily Fear: Wave of Kidnappings,' *Wall Street Journal*, 22 July 2004, p. 1.

82. This section is based on extensive monitoring of the English, French, German and Arabic media outlets, and statements and propaganda of the insurgent groups posted on various websites monitored over the course of the past three years.

83. Hannah Allam, 'Fleeting Militant Cells Further Cloud Insurgency,' *San Diego Union-Tribune*, 8 November 2004 (<http://ebird.afis.osd.mil/ebfiles/s20041109336043.html>).

84. Quoted in Ahmad al-Masri, 'Ansar al-Sunnah Army Views in Videotape for the First Time Its Operations Against Occupation Forces in Iraq,' *Al Quds al-Arabi*, 21 February 2004, p. 4 (FBIS-GMP20040221000064, <https://portal.rccb.osis.gov>).

85. LBC Satellite Television, 1928 GMT, 31 August 2003.

86. Jody Biehl, 'Abducted in Iraq: Four Months on Planet Bin Laden,' *Spiegel Online*, 21 January 2005, <http://service.spiegel.de/cache/international/0,1518,337867,00.html>.

87. *ibid.*

88. *ibid.*

89. Michel al-Kik, interview with Georges Malbrunot, Al-Jazeera Satellite Television, Doha, 1730 GMT, 3 January 2005.

90 . 'The Confrontation in the Field is Governed by the Iraqi Resistance's Conditions, Not by the US President's Plans and Objectives,' *Al-Majd*, 23 November

2003 (FBIS-GMP20031125000030, <http://portal.rccb.osis.gov>).

91. *ibid.*

92. 'Iraqi Resistance Cannot be Defeated,' *Arab Monitor*.

93. 'Introduction to the Political and Strategic Program,' *Al-Majd*.

94. 'The Confrontation in the Field,' *Al-Majd*.

95. *ibid.*

96. 'Introduction to the Political and Strategic Program,' *Al-Majd*.

97. Dan Eggen and Scott Wilson, 'Suicide Bombs Potent Tools of Terrorists,' *Washington Post*, 17 July 2005, p. 1, <http://www.washingtonpost.com/wp-dyn/content/article/2005/07/16/AR2005071601363.html>.

98. *ibid.*

99. *ibid.*

100. 'Iraqi Resistance Cannot be Defeated,' *Arab Monitor*.

101. 'The Confrontation in the Field,' *Al-Majd*.

102. 'Al-Zarqawi Announces Anti-Shia "Umar Corps", Vows to Continue Fighting,' *Jihadist Websites—FBIS Report*, 9 July 2005 (FBIS-GMP20050709564001, <http://www.fbis.portal.gov>).

103. 'Anti-Shia Theme Central to Al-Zarqawi Rhetoric,' FBIS-FEA20050922009410, 26 September 2005, <http://www.fbis.gov>.

104. 'Introduction to the Political and Strategic Program,' *Al-Majd*.

105. *El Mundo*, 5 October 2003 (FBIS-EUP20031007000351, <https://portal.rccb.osis.gov>).

106. *ibid.*

107. *ibid.*

108. Philip Sherwell, 'Saddam Terror Chief Steps up Resistance,' *Sunday Telegraph* (London), 21 September 2003 (<http://ebird.dtic.mil/Sep2003/e20030922218770.html>).

109. 'Diario de la resistencia iraquí,' *CSCAweb*, October 2004, <http://www.nodo50.org/csca/agenda2004/resistencia/diario_octubre-04.html>.

110. Salah al-Mukhtar, 'The Iraqi Resistance is Geared to Keep on Fighting for a Decade to Come,' *Albasrah.net*, 24 July 2005, <http://www.albasrah.net/en_articles_2005/0705/salah_0705.htm>. Spelling, punctuation, grammar as per original.

111. 'Baath Party Holds a Conference in Jordan Featuring Iraqi Speakers,' *Global Issues Report*, 19 August 2005.

112. *ibid.*

113. *ibid.*

114. *Al-Hayah*, 31 December 2004, p. 4 (FBIS-GMP20041231000024, <https://

www.fbis.gov>).

115. Pers. comm. (conversations with a journalist who has met with key insurgent groups and leaders), Tal Afar, September 2005. For a similar assessment, see also Thanassis Cambanis, 'Iraq's Ba'athists Rebound on 2 Fronts,' *Boston Globe*, 15 May 2005, <http://www.boston.com/news/world/middleeast/articles/2005/05/15/in_iraq_outlawed_baathists_rebound/>.

116. *Al- Basrah.net*, 27 April 2005. Spelling, punctuation, grammar as per original.

117. In the survey below I do not give a detailed chronology of every attack among the various target types since April 2003. This would be an unwieldy endeavor of little analytical worth in the context of this study. I am trying to show is the tight link between the insurgents' operational goal—to collapse the occupation—and the tactics employed to bring about this collapse.

118. Gregg Zoroya, 'If Ramadi Falls, "Province Goes to Hell",' *USA Today*, 12 July 2004, p. 4.

119. Patrick McDonnell, 'No Shortage of Fighters in Iraq's Wild West,' *Los Angeles Times*, 25 July 2004, p. 1.

120. Richard Oppel, '25 insurgents Are Killed Trying to Overrun US Outpost in Mosul,' *New York Times*, 30 December 2004, p. 8.

121. Sabrina Tavernise and Kirk Semple, 'Deadliest Suicide Bombing against GI's in Months Kills 4 in Iraq,' *New York Times*, 8 November 2005 (<http://ebird.afis.mil/ebfiles/e20051108400701.html>).

122. Mark Washburn, 'In Iraq, Uphill Fight vs Bombs,' *Philadelphia Inquirer*, 12 June 2005, <http://www.philly.com/mld/philly/news/11872781.htm>.

123. *ibid*.

124. Scott Johnson and Melinda Liu, 'The Enemy Spies,' *Newsweek*, 27 June 2005 <http://www.msnbc.msn.com/id/8272786/site/newsweek/>; Rowan Scarborough, 'Rebels Improve Bomb Schemes in Iraq,' *Washington Times*, 25 April 2005, p. 1.

125. 'Iraqi Groups Warn All Truck Drivers,' *Aljazeera.net*, 4 August 2004, <http://english.aljazeera.net/NR/exeres/4D1C99B6-9C9C-4D24-B360-18562998D310.htm>.

126. Colin Freeman, 'Officials Targeted by Iraqi Killers,' *Scotsman*, 17 July 2003, <http://news.scotsman.com/archive.cfm?id=774812003>.

127. See Daniel Williams, 'Working with US Proves to Be Deadly,' *Washington Post,* 7 September 2003, p. 21.

128. Vivienne Walt, 'For Iraqis Aiding US, The Dangers Are Growing,' *Boston Globe*, 14 September 2003 (<http://ebird.dtic.mil/Sep2003/s20030915217229.html>).

129. de la Grange, 'Liberation of Baghdad.'

130. Michael Ware, 'The Enemy with Many Faces,' *Time*, 27 September 2004 (<http://ebird.afis.osd.mil/ebfiles/s20040920322336.html>).

131. *ibid*.

132. Mariam Fam, 'Attacks on Police in Iraq Kill Four,' Associated Press, 6 July 2005.

133. FBIS-GMP20050104000044, 1 January 2005, <https://www.fbis.gov>.

134. Dave Moniz, 'Car Bombing Increase Prompts Changes in US Forces' Tactics,' *USA Today*, 9 June 2005, p. 13.

135. Sara Daniel, 'The Hostage Killers Speak,' *Nouvel Observateur*, 5 August 2005 (<http://occupationwatch.org/article.php?id=6180&printsafe=1>)

136. Dan Murphy, 'Abductions Surge in Iraq,' *Christian Science Monitor*, 27 July 2004, p. 1; Hannah Allam, 'Baghdad Becomes Captive of Extremists,' *Philadelphia Inquirer*, 27 July 2004.

137. Warren Vieth and Alissa Rubin, 'Iraq Pipelines Easy Targets for a Saboteur,' *Los Angeles Times*, 25 June 2003 (<http://www.commondreams.org/headlines03/0625-06.htm>).

138. See Ron Synovitz, 'Iraq: Sabotage of Civilian Infrastructure Seen as Resistance Strategy,' Radio Free Europe/Radio Liberty,< http://www.rferl.org/nca/features/2003/08/18082003155415.asp>; Dan Murphy, 'Sabotage Still Clogs Iraq's Oil,' *Christian Science Monitor*, 4 November 2003, <http://www.csmonitor.com/2003/1104/p01s04-woiq.htm>.

139. Alissa Rubin, 'Attack Is a Media Coup for Iraq Resistance, Experts Say,' *Los Angeles Times*, 27 October 2003, p. 1.

140. Nayif Kurayyim, 'The Era of Resistance Enters a New Phase,' *Al-Safir*, 12 July 2003 (FBIS-GMP20030713000226, 12 July 2003).

141. Another weakness has already been addressed briefly: the weak and ambiguous external state support for the insurgency.

142. Ware, 'Enemy with Many Faces.'

143. *ibid*.

144. Tawfiq Taha, telephone interview with Dr Ibrahim Yusuf al-Shammari, Al-Jazeera Satellite Television, Doha, 0900 GMT, 4 July 2005.

145. Caroline Alexander, 'Iraqi Insurgent Groups Want Official Dialogue with the US,' *Bloomberg.com*, 4 July 2005, <http://www.bloomberg.com/apps/news?pid=71000001&refer=us&sid=aPTEecfR9VPo>.

146. *ibid*.

147. Stephen Ulph, 'Islamist Insurgents Seek to Contain PR Disaster: Notes of Defeatism,' *Terrorism Focus* 2, 13 (2005), <http://jamestown.org/terrorism/

news/article.php?articleid=2369741&printthis=1>.

148. Nicholas Pelham, 'Political Arm of Falluja Militants Claims Key Role,' *Financial Times*, 26 April 2004.

149. *ibid.*

150. *ibid.*

151. Hamza Hendawi, 'Iraq's Sunni Arabs Have Choices to Make,' Associated Press, 16 October 2005 (<http://www.msnbc.msn.com/id/9720875/>).

152. Gareth Porter, 'The Game's Still on for Sunnis,' *Asia Times*, 2 November 2005, <http://www.atimes.com/atimes/Middle_East/GK02Ak01.html>.

153. *ibid.*

154. Pers. comm., Mosul, July 2005.

155. 'Iraqi Front Demands US Withdrawal,' *Aljazeera.com*, 29 June 2005, <http://english.aljazeera.net/NR/exeres/72AD9B13-2788-4FB8-8C0B-64BAE3C25749.htm>.

156. Patrick Quinn, 'Sunni Announces A Political Group For Iraqi Insurgents,' *Philadelphia Inquirer*, 30 June 2005 (<http://ebird.afis.osd.mil/ebfiles/e20050630376939.html>).

157. Abd al-Latif al-Musawi, 'Al-Samarrai: Iraqi National Bloc Will Harvest Votes in the Upcoming Elections; 11 Resistance Groups Negotiate to Form Political Leadership,' *Al-Zaman*, 31 October 2005, p. 3 (FBIS -GMP20051101521004 (<http://www.fbis.gov>).

158. Pers. comm. with Sunnis, northern Iraq, July-August 2005.

159. Borzou Daraghi, 'The Puzzle of Sunnis' Leadership Vacuum,' *Los Angeles Times*, 5 July 2005 (<http://ebird.afis.osd.mil/ebfiles/e20050705377682.html>).

160. See, for example, 'Major Parties and Contenders for December Parliamentary Elections,' *RFE/RL Reports* 8, 40 (2005), <http://www.rferl.org/reports/iraq-report/2005/11/40-231105.asp>.

161. Cecile Hennion, 'Hostages, Attacks, Fighting: Iraq Descends into Chaos,' *Le Monde*, 9 September 2004 (FBIS-EUP2004090900043, <https://www.fbis.gov>).

162. Lee Gordon, 'Foreign Fighters Gain Fallujah Foothold,' *Age*, 1 June 2004, <http://www.theage.com.au/articles/2004/05/31/1085855497136.html?from=storyrhs>.

163. Karl Vick, 'Insurgent Alliance is Fraying in Fallujah,' *Washington Post*, 13 October 2004, p. 1.

164. *ibid.* See also 'Who Are the Insurgents—and Can They Be Defeated?' *The Economist*, 10–16 July 2004 (<http://ebird.afis.osd.mil/efiles/

s20040709301808.html>); Nicholas Blanford, 'Iraqi Resistance Tiring of Foreign Fighters,' *Daily Star* (Lebanon), 16 July 2004, <http://www.dailystar. com.lb/article.asp?edition_id=10&categ_id=2&article_id=6314>.

165. *ibid.*

166. Anthony Shadid, 'Father Seeks Vindication but Finds Death in Fallujah,' *Washington Post*, 15 February 2005, p. 1, <http://www.washingtonpost. com/wp-dyn/articles/A24571-2005Feb14.html>.

167. Ian Fisher and Edward Wong, 'Iraq's Rebellion Develops Signs of Internal Rift,' *New York Times*, 11 July 2004, <http://occupationwatch.org/article. php?id=5870>.

168. Al Arabiya Television, Doha, 1400 GMT, 26 August 2003. The ideological background of these groups is unclear.

169. Jihadist Websites, *FBIS Report in Arabic*, 25 May 2005 (FBIS-GMP20050525325002, <https://www.fbis.gov>).

170. *ibid.*

171. Ashraf Khalil, 'Sunnis, Shiites Divided in Response to Attack on Fallouja,' *Los Angeles Times*, 11 November 2004 (<http://ebird.afis.osd.mil/ebfiles/ e20041111336632.html>).

172. Thanassis Cambanis, 'Fractured Iraq Sees a Sunni Call to Arms,' *Boston Globe*, 27 March 2005, <http://www.boston.com/news/world/middleeast/ articles/2005/03/27/fractured_iraq_sees_a_sunni_call_to_arms/>.

Chapter 4 Contending National Identities

1. See, for example, David McDowall, *A Modern History of the Kurds*, 3rd edn, London: I.B. Tauris, 2005, pp. 151–83, 287–368; Gareth R.V. Stansfield, *Iraqi Kurdistan: Political Development and Emergent Democracy*, London: RoutledgeCurzon, 2003; Edmond Ghareeb, *The Kurdish Question in Iraq*, Syracuse University Press, 1981; Sa'ad Jawad, *Iraq and the Kurdish Question, 1958– 1970*, London: Ithaca Press, 1981; Brendan O'Leary, John McGarry and Khaled Salih (eds), *The Future of Kurdistan in Iraq*, Philadelphia: University of Pennsylvania Press, 2005.

2. Carol Williams, 'Iraqi Kurds Seem Willing to Put Dream on Hold,' *Los Angeles Times*, 26 May 2003, p. 1.

3. Neela Banerjee, 'Kurds Await Iraq's Embrace, and Hope Its Not Too Tight,' *New York Times*, 26 January 2004, p. 10.

4. Karl Vick and Daniel Williams, 'Kurds in a New Iraq Must Find an Identity,' *Washington Post*, 22 April 2003, p. 12.

5.   ibid.

6.   ibid.

7.   ibid.

8.   Bannerjee, 'Kurds Await Iraq's Embrace.'

9.   Susan Taylor Martin, 'Iraqi Kurds Optimistic in Face of Uncertainty,' *St Petersburg Times* (Florida), 23 May 2004 (accessed online).

10. Daniel Williams, 'As Kurds Mourn, Resolve Hardens,' *Washington Post*, 3 February 2004, p. 14. See also Jeffrey Gettleman and Edward Wong, 'Grief and Anger Overwhelm the Kurds of Northern Iraq,' *New York Times*, 3 February 2004 (accessed online).

11. Catherine Philp, 'Bombs Fire Kurdish Desire for Independence,' *The Times* (London), 3 February 2004 (accessed online).

12. See Chris Kutschera, 'Kurdistan Irak: Un îlot de prospérité et de tranquillité' (Iraqi Kurdistan: An Island of Prosperity and Calm), 28 October 2003, <http://www.chris-kutschera.com/prosperite_paradoxale.htm>; Stanley Reed, 'Forging One Nation from Three Agendas,' *Businessweek*, 18 December 2003 (accessed online).

13. Toby Dodge, *Iraq's Future: The Aftermath of Regime Change*, Adelphi Paper 372, International Institute for Strategic Studies, London: Oxford University Press, pp. 50–1.

14. For more details on the politics and political economy of elite control in Iraqi Kurdistan, see the works of Michael Leezenberg, such as 'Humanitarian Aid in Iraqi Kurdistan,' *Cahiers d'études sur la Méditeranée orientale et le monde Turco-Iranien* 29, January-June 2000.

15. I observed this phenomenon in Ninevah Province in summer and fall 2005.

16. Quoted in Rajiv Chandrasekaran, 'Postwar Tremors Deepen Fissures in Iraqi Society,' *Washington Post*, 29 September 2003, p. 1.

17. Deborah Horan, 'Kurds Who Helped US Fight Rebels Lose Fight for Respect,' *Chicago Tribune*, 1 June 2004 (accessed online).

18. See, for example, Luke Harding, 'Kurdish Fighters Take Kirkuk,' *Guardian*, 11 April 2003, <http://www.guardian.co.uk/The_Kurds/Story/0,2763,934373,00.html>.

19. Atef Saqr, 'Le nouvel Iraq doit être fondé sur un fédéralisme géographique' (The new Iraq must be founded on geographic federalism), *Al-Ahram Hebdo*, 7 May 2003 <http://hebdo.ahram.org.eg/arab/ahram/2003/5/7/Doss0.htm>. For an account of fighting between Arabs and Kurds over farmland, see also Moni Basu, 'Iraqi Kurds, Arabs Reap a Bitter Harvest,' *Atlanta Journal-Constitution*, 29 May 2003 (accessed online). For an analysis of the

growing Kurdish control over Kirkuk, see Scott Wilson, 'Kurds' Influence in Kirkuk Rises along with Discord,' *Washington Post*, 19 May 2003, p. 10.

20. Dan Murphy, 'Kurds' Struggle Intensifies Ethnic Conflict in Kirkuk,' *Christian Science Monitor*, 9 January 2004.

21. Stephen Franklin, 'Iraq's Boiling Melting Pot,' *Chicago Tribune*, 4 January 2004 (accessed online).

22. Marwan Anie and Jackie Spinner, 'Regional Kurdish Victory Could Lead to Conflict,' *Washington Post*, 14 February 2005, p. 8.

23. Paul McGeough, 'The Kurds Are Back, and They Mean Business,' *Sydney Morning Herald*, 12 February 2005 (accessed online).

24. Michael Howard, 'Insurgents Stir up Strife in Kirkuk,' *Washington Times*, 17 May 2004, p. 1.

25. *ibid*.

26. Phil Smucker, 'Iraq: A Land of Splintered Loyalties,' *Scotland on Sunday*, 14 March 2004 (http://scotlandonsunday.scotsman.com/international.cfm?id=294242004).

27. Quoted in Stanley Reed, 'Forging One Nation from Three Agendas,' *Businessweek*, 18 December 2003 (accessed online).

28. Feisal Istrabadi, an Iraqi lawyer and now ambassador to the UN. Steven Weisman, 'Kurdish Region in Northern Iraq will get to Keep Special Status,' *New York Times*, 5 January 2004, p. 1.

29. Kurdistan is essentially run by two tribal mafias. Tom Hundley, 'Island of Stability in Volatile Iraq,' *Chicago Tribune*, 25 January 2004, p. 1.

30. Pers. comm. (conversations with Kurdish officers), Nineveh Province, July-August 2005.

31. *ibid*.

32. John Daniszewski, 'Kurds Wonder Where They Fit in the New Iraq,' *Los Angeles Times*, 27 July 2004.

33. Pers. comm. (with a European journalist who interviewed senior members of the Iraqi government in summer 2005), June 2005.

34. Juan Cole, 'Informed Comment: Thoughts on the Middle East, History, and Religion,' August 2005, <http://www.juancole.com/2005_08_01_juancole_archive.html>.

35. Jeffrey Fleishman, 'A US Ally Caught between Two Goals,' *Los Angeles Times*, 27 May 2004 (accessed online).

36. *ibid*.

37. Fleishman, 'A US Ally Caught.'

38. Charles Radin, 'Kurds' Aims Threaten Iraq Stability Efforts,' *Boston Globe*,

26 May 2003, p. 1.

39. *Arbil Khabat*, KDP paper, Irbil, 1 February 2005 (FBIS-GMP20050202000209, <https://www.fbis.gov>).

40. Peter Ford, 'Multitude of Militias Pose Threat to Democracy in Iraq,' *Christian Science Monitor*, 25 April 2003 (<http://ebird.dtic.mil/Apr2003/s20030425179907.html>).

41. On the origins of Shi'ism, see: Yann Richard, *L'islam chi'ite: croyances et idéologies,* Paris: Fayard, 1991; Mohammad-Ali Amir-Moezzi and Christian Jambet, *Qu'est ce que le shi'isme?* Paris: Fayard, 2004. For the following summary on the emergence of the Shi'a in Iraqi history I relied on: Pierre-Jean Luizard, *La Formation de l'Irak Contemporain: Le role politique des ulemas chiites à la fin de la domination Ottomane et au moment de la creation de l'Etat irakien*, Paris: CNRS Editions, 2002; Yitzhak Nakash, *The Shiis of Iraq*, Princeton University Press, 2003; Faleh Jabar, *The Shi'ite Movement in Iraq*, London: Saqi Books, 2003; Hasan al-Allawi, *The Shi'is and the National State in Iraq, 1914–1990*, Qom: Dar al-Thaqafah lil-Tiba'a wa al-Nashr, n.d.; Joyce Wiley, *The Islamic Movement of Iraqi Shi'as*, Boulder: Lynne Rienner Publishers, 1992.

42. See, for example, Nakash, *The Shiis of Iraq*; Luizard, *La Formation de l'Irak Contemporain*.

43. Pierre-Jean Luizard, *La question irakienne*, Paris: Fayard, 2002, p. 10.

44. Pierre Martin, 'Le clergé chiite en Irak hier et aujourd'hui,' *Maghreb-Machrek*, January-February 1987, pp. 31–3. See also Frederic Wehry, 'The Insurgent State: Politics and Communal Dissent in Iraq, 1919–1936,' MA thesis, Princeton University, 2002.

45. For an excellent analysis of the Shi'i clerical establishment see Falah Abdul Jabbar, 'Clerics, Tribes, and Urban Dwellers in South of Iraq: The Potential for Rebellion' in Toby Dodge and Steven Simon (eds.), *Iraq at the Crossroads: State and Society in the Shadow of Regime Change*, International Institute for Strategic Studies, Adelphi Paper 354, Oxford: Oxford University Press, 2003, pp. 161–77.

46. Guilain Denoeux, *Urban Unrest in the Middle East: A Comparative Study of Informal Networks in Egypt, Iraq and Lebanon*, Albany: SUNY Press, 1993, pp. 56–70, 127–48.

47. See Hanna Batatu, 'Iraq's Shi'a, their Political Role, and the Process of their Integration into Society' in Barbara Freyer Stowasser (ed.), *The Islamic Impulse*, London: Croom Helm, 1987, p. 207.

48. Arnold Hottinger, 'Wehe den Besiegten: die irakischen Schitten,' *Neue Zürcher Zeitung*, 3 March 2003 (accessed online).

49. Batatu, 'Iraq's Shi'a,' pp. 210–11.

50. *Seda-ye-Edalat*, 1 August 2002, p. 6 (FBIS-IAP20020808000066, 1 August 2002, <http://imos.rccb.osis.gov>).

51. Adeed Dawisha, 'Identity and Political Survival in Saddam's Iraq,' *Middle East Journal* 53, 4 (1999), 553–67.

52. Joyce Wiley, *The Islamic Movement of Iraqi Shi'as*, Boulder: Lynne Rienner, 1992, pp. 45–71.

53. Saddam Hussein, 'A View of Religion and Heritage' in Naji al-Hadithi (ed.), *On History, Heritage, and Religion*, Baghdad, 1981, p. 24.

54. Ofra Bengio, 'Shi'is and Politics in Ba'thi Iraq,' *Middle Eastern Studies* 21, 1 (1985), 1–14.

55. Babak Rahimi, 'Ayatollah Ali al-Sistani and the Democratization of Post-Saddam Iraq,' *MERIA—Middle East Review of International Affairs* 8, 4 (2004) (accessed online).

56. *ibid.*; emphasis added.

57. See Dan Murphy, 'Iraq's Critical Sistani Factor,' *Christian Science Monitor*, 20 January 2005 (<http://www.csmonitor.com/2005/0120/p01s04-woiq.html>).

58. *ibid.*

59. *ibid.*

60. Observations in Tal Afar and Mosul, July-September 2005.

61. On SCIRI, see Jabar, *Shi'ite Movement in Iraq*, pp. 235–63.

62. Pers. comm., summer 2005.

63. Largely derived from Mahan Abedin, 'Iraq's SCIRI, Caught between Tehran and Washington,' *Daily Star*, 19 August 2003 (accessed online).

64. On the origins of the Moqtada phenomenon, see 'Moqtada Al-Sadr, la voix radicale des chiites irakiens,' *Le Monde*, 4 April 2004; Patrice Claude, 'Moqtada Al-Sadr, l'imam rebelle,' *Le Monde*, 13 May 2004.

65. Christophe Ayad, 'Moqtada al-Sadr, le radical impulsive,' *Liberation*, 6 April 2004 (accessed online). See also 'Looking at the activities of the Sadr Dynasty in Iraq,' *Jumhuri-ye Eslami*, 4 July 2004 (FBIS, <https://portal.rccb.osis.gov>).

66. Al Arabiya Satellite Television, Dubai, 0625 GMT, 26 July 2003.

67. Fadil Rashad, 'Shaykh Ali Sumaysim, 'We Do Not Seek to Establish an Islamic State, However, We Want Islam to be a Primary Source for Legislation,' *Al-Hayah*, 9 February 2005 (FBIS-NES, 9 February 2005).

68. *ibid.*

69. *ibid.*

70. I visited Kut in early March 2004. It is located in one of the poorest of Iraq's provinces, and a long conversation with an Iraqi there revealed the extent of the unemployment problem and growing support among the young for the movement of Moqtada al-Sadr.

71. See, for example, Scott Calvert, 'In Najaf, Regime's Symbols Tumble,' *Baltimore Sun*, 4 April 2003 (accessed online).

72. Ahmed Hashim, 'Understanding the Roots of the Shi'a Insurgency in Iraq,' *Terrorism Monitor* 2, 13 (2004), 3–5, <http://www.Jamestown.org/publications_details.php?volume_id=400&issue_id=3004&article_id=2368183>.

73. *ibid.*

74. Tom Hundley, 'Iraq's Destiny Tied to Mosque Politics,' *Chicago Tribune*, 18 May 2003, p. 1.

75. Hamza Hendawi, 'Young Cleric from Southern City Showcases Shiite Power in Post-Saddam Iraq,' Associated Press, 13 January 2004 (accessed online).

76. Kim Ghattas, 'Young Cleric Finds Focus for Anger of Baghdad's Poor,' *Financial Times*, 30 July 2003, <http://ebird.dtic.mil/Jul2003/s20030731205186.html>.

77. *ibid.*

78. Pamela Constable, 'Shortages Ignite Violence in Iraq,' *Washington Post*, 11 August 2003, p. 1. See also Richard Oppel and Robert Worth, 'Riots Continue over Fuel Crisis in Iraq's South,' *New York Times*, 11 August 2003 (accessed online); Gary Marx, 'Faith Withering in Wake of Riots,' *Chicago Tribune*, 21 August 2003 (accessed online).

79. Pamela Constable, 'Clashes Rise in Southern Iraq,' *Washington Post*, 14 January 2004, p. 14.

80. Nicholas Blanford, 'Iraqis Battle Gangs in Basra,' *Christian Science Monitor*, 24 March 2004 (<http://ebird.afis.osd.mil/ebfiles/s20040324269554.html>).

81. Vernon Loeb, 'In Shiite Slum, Army's New Caution,' *Washington Post*, 22 October 2003, p. 1.

82. Alex Berenson, 'Anti-US Harangues, but Iraq's Shiites Heed Four Ayatollahs,' *New York Times*, 22 October 2003 (accessed online); Howard LaFranchi, 'Key Shiites Soften Tone toward US,' *Christian Science Monitor*, 19 November 2003, p. 1.

83. Al-Manar Televison, Beirut, 0843 GMT, 28 October 2003.

84. *ibid.*

85. Haydar al-Allaq, 'I Absolutely Do Not Want to Participate in Power Nor Do

I Seek a Political or Administrative Post ...' *Al-Da'wah*, 10 December 2003, p. 2 (trans. in FBIS, 10 December 2003, <https://portal.rccb.osis.gov>).

86. For an extensive and authoritative analysis of CPA missteps *vis-à-vis* Moqtada, see Rajiv Chandrasekaran and Anthony Shadid, 'US Targeted Fiery Cleric in Risky Move,' *Washington Post*, 11 April 2004, p. 1.

87. Ahmed S. Hashim, 'Baghdad Blues: Experiences, Interviews and Observations,' *Diary,* October 2003 to March 2004, entry for mid-March 2004.

88. See Laura King, 'Resentment among Shias Alarms Washington,' *Dawn*, 11 October 2003, <http://www.dawn.com/2003/10/11/int17.htm>. Several journalistic accounts have also pointed to the growing despair and anger of the inhabitants of Medinat Sadr. See, for example, Inga Rogg, 'Stadt der Wut, stadt der angst: Eindrücke aus der Hochburg des radikalen Schiitenführers Muktada as-Sadr,' *Neue Zürcher Zeitung am Sonntag*, 11 April 2004.

89. Text of Moqtada al-Sadr's Friday sermon in Kufa, 30 July 2004. 'Dealing with Religious Observances, Domestic and International Politics,' *Ansar al-Mahdi*, 6 August 2004, p. 3.

90. *ibid.*

91. Jeffrey Gettleman, 'Signs that Shiites and Sunnis are Joining to Battle Americans,' *New York Times*, 9 April 2004 (accessed online); Jeffrey Gettleman, 'Anti-US Outrage Unites a Growing Iraqi Resistance,' *New York Times*, 11 April 2004 (accessed online); Anthony Loyd, 'Traditional Foes Unite to Fight their Common Enemy: The Americans,' *The Times* (London), 17 May 2004 (accessed online).

92. Quoted in Michael Schwartz, 'Tomgram: Schwartz, What Triggered the Shia Insurrection?", *TomDispatch.com*, 12 April 2004, <http://www.tomdispatch.com/index.mhtml?pid=1371>.

93. Dan Murphy, 'No Wide Shiite Rally to Sadr's Forces,' *Christian Science Monitor*, 7 April 2004, p. 1.

94. Interviews in Al Hillah, November 2003, March 2004. By way of contrast, Moqtada's movement had more influence in impoverished cities such as Kut, which has no redeeming features to recommend it, and which I visited in early March 2004. In that city a group of energetic young clerics either sympathetic to or with direct links to Moqtada had built an effective and efficient network of social and security services.

95. Hannah Allam, 'Iraqi Shiites fighting war "of the soul",' Knight Ridder Newspapers, 5 August 2004 (<http://www.iranexpert.com/2003/iraqishiites5august.htm>).

96. *ibid.*

97. Raheem Salman and T. Christian Miller, 'Fed-up Residents of Najaf Turn against Rebel Cleric,' *Los Angeles Times*, 24 August 2004.

98. Paul Quinn-Judge, 'Heeding the Call of the Cleric,' *Time*, 31 May 2004.

99. Tom Lasseter, 'Cleric's Army Quietly Takes Control,' Knight Ridder News Service, 14 July 2004 (accessed online). See also Tom Lasseter, 'Al-Sadr Militia: Warriors and Traffic Cops,' *Detroit Free Press*, 14 July 2004 (<https://ebird.afis.osd.mil/ebfiles/s20040715303476.html>), in which one resident was quoted as saying: 'Who runs Sadr City? Only the Mahdi's Army.'

100. Michel Bole-Richard, 'A Nadjaf, où le calme est revenu, l'Armée du Mahdi veille et guette les initiatives du gouvernement irakien,' *Le Monde*, 15 July 2004 (accessed online).

101. Paul Wiseman and David Enders, 'Al-Sadr's Intentions, Ambitions Unclear,' *USA Today*, 16 July 2004, p. 7.

102. *ibid.*

103. Alissa Rubin, 'Shiites' Struggle Turns Inward,' *Los Angeles Times*, 16 July 2004 (<http://ebird.afis.osd.mil/ebfiles/e20040716303936.html>).

104. Mitch Potter, 'Iraqi Cleric's Army Girds for Uprising,' *Toronto Star*, 6 July 2004.

105. Scott Wilson, 'In Place of Gunfire, a Rain of Rocks,' *Washington Post*, 9 July 2004, p. 1.

106. Anthony Shadid, 'For Rebuilders of Sadr City, Gratitude Tainted by Mistrust,' *Washington Post*, 17 December 2004, p. 1.

107. Anthony Shadid, 'Sadr's Disciples Rise Again to Play Pivotal Role in Iraq,' *Washington Post*, 29 August 2005 (<http://www.washingtonpost.com/wp-dyn/content/article/2005/08/29/AR2005082901795.html>).

108. *ibid.*

109. Rahimi, 'Ayatollah Ali al-Sistani.'

110. Anthony Shadid, 'A Struggle for Iraqi Clergy's Soul,' *Washington Post*, 30 June 2003, p. 1.

111. Moqtada alternates between statements that show respect or disdain for the senior Iranian-born Ayatollah Sistani. On occasions Moqtada's contempt shows clearly. When Sistani suggested that Moqtada take his fight against the US outside of the holy city of Najaf, Moqtada retorted: 'If there is one man who needs to leave, that is precisely al-Sistani. *He is an Iranian. I am a child of this country.* I was here when he was safe and sound in Tehran. I, my family, and my people have paid a very high price in blood under Saddam.' Renato Caprile, 'The United States Can Kill Me, but Iraq Will Turn into an

Inferno,' *La Repubblica*, 26 April 2004, p. 5 (FBIS-EUP20040426000085, 26 April 2004, <https://portal.rccb.osis.gov/>). See also n. 64, p. 429, this vol., for references regarding the origins of the Moqtada phenomenon.

112. For more detailed discussions of the dynamics of internal Shi'a factionalism and strife in the post-Saddam era see Faleh Jabar, 'The Worldly Roots of Religiosity in Post-Saddam Iraq,' *Middle East Report* 227 (2003), 12–18.

113. Borzou Daraghi, 'Shiites Struggle for Power,' *Pittsburgh Post-Gazette*, 5 September 2003, <http://www.post-gazette.com/pg/pp/03248219294.stm>.

114. *ibid.*

115. Ewen MacAskill, 'Army of the Dispossessed Rallies to Mahdi,' *Guardian*, 8 April 2004, <http://www.guardian.co.uk/Iraq/Story/0,2763,1188061,00. html>.

116. Anthony Shadid, 'Political Violence Surges in Iraq,' *Washington Post*, 26 August 2005, p. 1, <http://www.washingtonpost.com/wp-dyn/content/article/2005/08/25/AR2005082500294.html>.

117. See James Meeks, 'Sunni or Shia, Fault Line Runs between Haves and Have Nots,' *Guardian*, 11 April 2003 (accessed online).

118. James Sherwell, 'Baghdad's Cinemas and Shops Attacked by Islamic Enforcers,' *Sunday Telegraph* (London), 1 June 2003 (accessed online); Mark Mueller, 'Many in Baghdad Shudder at the Swift Rise in Clerics,' *Newhouse News Service*, <http://www.Newhousenews.com/archive/Mueller050603.html>.

119. Conversations with Shi'a Iraqi army personnel who are supporters of Moqtada, summer 2005, and with middle class Shi'a officers of the new Iraqi army who had also served in the former army, Mosul, 2005.

120. Observations in Tal Afar, and conversations with Sunnis there and in Mosul, July-September 2005.

Chapter 5   Ideology, Politics and Failure to Execute

1.   Larry Cable, 'Reinventing the Round Wheel: Insurgency, Counter-Insurgency, and Peacekeeping Post Cold War,' *Small Wars and Insurgencies* 4, 2 (1993), 228.

2.   A US academic and counter-insurgency officer has developed the notion of 'best practices' as applied to counter-insurgency. See Kalev 'Gunner' Sepp, 'Best Practices in Counterinsurgency,' paper in possession of A. Hashim.

3.   The French effort is the subject of a vast literature in French and English. For recent assessments that I read for this study, see Lieutenant Commander James Rogers, *Tactical Success is Not Enough: The French in Algeria 1954–1962*,

Newport, RI: Department of Joint Military Operations, Naval War College, 2004; Major Gregory Peterson, *The French Experience in Algeria, 1954–1962: Blueprint for US Operations in Iraq*, Fort Leavenworth, KS: School for Advanced Military Studies, Army Command and General Staff College, 2003.

4. George Packer, *The Assassins' Gate: America in Iraq*, New York: Farrar, Straus and Giroux, 2005, p. 13.

5. Toby Dodge, 'Iraqi Transitions: From Regime Change to State Collapse,' *Third World Quarterly* 26, 4–5 (2005), 705–21; David Hendrickson and Robert Tucker, 'Revisions in Need of Revising: What Went Wrong in the Iraq War,' *Survival* 47, 2 (2005), 7–32.

6. See Robert Cassidy, 'Winning the War of the Flea,' *Military Review*, September-October 2004, p. 41; the seminal study is John Nagl, *Learning to Eat Soup with a Knife: Counterinsurgency Lessons from Malaya and Vietnam*, Westport, CT: Praeger Publishers, 2002.

7. On the alleged plan to democratize the Middle East, see, *inter alia*, Rachel Bronson, 'Reconstructing the Middle East,' *Brown Journal of World Affairs* X, 1 (2003), 271–80. For a good journalistic account, see Barbara Slavin, 'Some See Victory Extending beyond Baghdad,' *USA Today*, 11 April 2003, p. 6.

8. Quoted in Dana Milbank and Peter Slevin, 'Bush Cites Hope for Iraq's Future,' *Washington Post*, 27 February 2003, p. 1

9. See Maggie O'Kane, 'Iraqi Rich Make Mockery of Sanctions,' *Guardian*, 21 November 1998 (http://www.guardian.co.uk/World_Report/Story/0,2867,324842,00.html); Robert Collier, 'Iraq's New Elite Living Large,' *San Francisco Chronicle*, 15 January 2003, p. 1; Susan Glaser, 'A Regime of Payoffs and Persecution,' *Washington Post*, 17 April 2003, p. 1. The best lengthy analyses of the last months of the Ba'th regime include the following outstanding studies: G.W.F. Vigeveno, *Irak en de erfenis van Saddam Hoessein* (Iraq in the Prison of Saddam Hussein), Research Essay, Gravenhage: Nederlands Instituut voor Internationale Betrekkingen, 2003, <http://www.clingendael.nl/publications/2003/20030100_cli_ess_-vigeveno.pdf>; International Crisis Group, *Iraq Backgrounder:What Lies Beneath*, Middle East Report 6, Amman/Brussels: International Crisis Group, 2002, <http://www.crisisgroup.org/library/documents/report_archive/A400786_01102002.pdf>; International Crisis Group, 'Voices from the Iraqi Street,' *ICG Middle East Briefing* 3, 4 December 2002, <http://www.crisisgroup.org/library/documents/report_archive/A400837_04122002.pdf>.

10. John Hendren, 'An Architect of War Draws Blueprint for Peace,' *Los Angeles Times*, 13 April 2003, p. 1.

11. *ibid*.

12. *ibid*.

13. A possible indicator of what the neoconservatives might really have had in mind is contained in Robert Kaplan, 'A Post-Saddam Scenario,' *Atlantic Monthly*, November 2002 (accessed online).

14. Robert Blecher, 'Free People Will Set the Course of History: Intellectuals, Democracy and the American Empire,' *Middle East Report*, March 2003, <http://www.merip.org/mero/interventions/blecher_interv.html>.

15. Ashraf Fahim, 'Building a Better Arab,' *Middle East International*, 27 June 2003, pp. 26–8.

16. I do not recall the conference title, but it took place in Georgetown, Washington, DC, in 1998.

17. Neil Clark, 'The Return of Arabophobia,' *Guardian*, 20 October 2003, <http://www.guardian.co.uk/comment/story/0,3604,1066569,00.html>.

18. Rory McCarthy, 'False Dawn of Peace Lost in Violent Storm,' *Guardian*, 8 April 2004, <http://www.guardian.co.uk/international/story/0,,1188020,00.html>.

19. Alex Rodriguez, '"Gurgling Gasp" Now a War Cry,' *Chicago Tribune*, 19 July 2004, p. 1, <http://www.chicagotribune.com/news/nationworld/chi-0407190193jul19,1,4538048.story?coll=chi-newsnationworld-hed>.

20. Robin Wright, 'Series of US Fumbles Blamed for Turmoil in Postwar Iraq,' *Washington Post*, 11 April 2004, p. 15.

21. Rodriguez, '"Gurgling Gasp" Now a War Cry.'

22. Interviews in Karrada, Baghdad, November 2003.

23. Tony Karon, 'The Shiites the US Thinks it Knows,' *Time*, 11 March 2004, <http://www.time.com/time/columnist/karon/article/0,9565,599934,00.html>.

24. *ibid*.

25. Susan Sachs, 'Shiite Clerics' Ambitions Collide in an Iraqi Slum,' *New York Times*, 25 May 2003 (<http://ebird.dtic.mil/May2003/s20030527188030.html>).

26. *ibid*.

27. Mohamad Bazzi, 'A Challenge from Shiites,' *Long Island Newsday*, 31 March 2003, <http://www.newsday.com/news/nationworld/iraq/ny-woshia313199553mar31,0,228860.story>.

28. *ibid*.

29. *ibid*.

30. *ibid.*

31. Neil Sheehan, *A Bright Shining Lie: John Paul Vann and America in Vietnam*, London: Pimlico, 1998.

32. Quoted in Christopher Dickey, 'The Long Goodbye,' *Newsweek*, 26 May 2004, <http://www.msnbc.com/id/5060790/site/newsweek/site/newsweek/>.

33. *ibid.*

34. Patrick Tyler, 'In Reversal, Plan for Iraq Self-Rule Has Been Put Off,' *New York Times*, 17 May 2003 (accessed online).

35. *ibid.*

36. Rajiv Chandrasekaran, 'US Sidelines Exiles Who Were to Govern Iraq,' *Washington Post*, 8 June 2003, p. 22.

37. *ibid.*

38. Rajiv Chandrasekaran, 'How Cleric Trumped US Plan for Iraq: Ayatollah's Call for Vote Forced Occupation Leader to Rewrite Transition Strategy,' *Washington Post*, 26 November 2003, p. 1.

39. I relied heavily on the following for this section: Larry Diamond, *Squandered Victory: The American Occupation and the Bungled Effort to Bring Democracy to Iraq*, New York: Henry Holt, 2005; Chandrasekaran, 'How Cleric Trumped US Plan for Iraq.'

40. Robin Wright, 'Series of US Fumbles Blamed for Turmoil in Postwar Iraq,' *Washington Post*, 11 April 2004, p. 15.

41. The best analyses of the state of Iraq after the end of the war and of the failures of ORHA are International Crisis Group, 'Baghdad: A Race against the Clock,' *ICG Middle East Briefing* 6, 11 June 2003, <http://www.crisisgroup.org/library/documents/report_archive/A401000_11062003.pdf>; Diamond, *Squandered Victory*.

42. Thomas Hobbes, *Of Man: Being the First Part of Leviathan*, New York: Bartleby, 2001, <http://www.bartleby.com/34/5/13.html>.

43. Ray Salvatore Jennings, *The Road Ahead: Lessons in Nation-Building from Japan, Germany, and Afghanistan for Postwar Iraq*, Peaceworks 49, Washington, DC: United States Institute of Peace, 2003 (<http://ics.leeds.ac.uk/papers/pmt/exhibits/2165/pwks49.pdf>).

44. An insightful analysis of the general level of policy expertise on Iraq in Washington, DC, is found in David Baran (pseud.), 'Iraq: Misreading the Vital Signs,' *Le Monde Diplomatique*, April 2003, <http://mondediplo.com/2003/04/06>.

45. Rajiv Chandrasekaran, 'Iraq's Ragged Reconstruction,' *Washington Post*, 9 May 2003, p. 1.

46. Daniel Eisenberg, 'Can Anyone Govern This Place?' *Time*, 26 May 2003, p. 32.

47. *ibid*.

48. *ibid*.

49. Hannah Allam, 'Violence Plagues Rebuilding of Iraq,' *Philadelphia Inquirer*, 25 May 2004, p. 1.

50. See Richard Oppel and Robert Worth, 'Riots Continue over Fuel Crisis in Iraq's South,' *New York Times*, 11 August 2003 (accessed online); Pamela Constable, 'Shortages Ignite Violence in Iraq,' *Washington Post*, 11 August 2003, p. 1.

51. Peter Foster, 'America's Rebuilding of Iraq is in Chaos, Say British,' *Daily Telegraph* (London), 17 June 2003, p. 1, <http://www.telegraph.co.uk/news/main.jhtml?xml=/news/2003/06/17/wirq17.xml&sSheet=/news/2003/06/17/ixnewstop.html>.

52. *ibid*.

53. Joshua Hammer, 'Uncivil Military,' *New Republic*, 1 March 2004, p. 16, <http://www.tnr.com/doc.mhtml?i=20040301&s=hammer030104>.

54. T. Christian Miller, 'Violence Trumps Rebuilding in Iraq,' *Los Angeles Times*, 21 February 2005, p. 1.

55. *ibid*.

56. *ibid*.

57. UNDP and Iraqi Central Organization for Statistics and Information Technology, *Iraq Living Conditions Survey 2004*, Baghdad: United Nations Development Program and Iraqi Central Organization for Statistics and Information Technology, Ministry of Planning and Development Cooperation, 2005, <http://www.iq.undp.org/ILCS/overview.htm> (Vol. 1, *Tabulation Report*; Vol. 2, *Analytical Report*; Vol. 3, *Socio-economic Atlas*).

58. David Cortright, 'Progress in Iraqi Freedom Stained by Growing Hardship,' *Christian Science Monitor*, 7 June 2005, <http://www.csmonitor.com/2005/0607/p09s01-coop.html>; Neil MacDonald, 'New Survey of Iraqis Warns on Jobs and Nutrition,' *Financial Times*, 12 May 2005.

59. Cameron Barr, 'Leader Stifled by War's Reality,' *Washington Post,* 20 February 2005, p. C1, <http://www.washingtonpost.com/ac2/wp-dyn/A38396-2005Feb19>.

60. T. Christian Miller, 'Some Iraq Projects Running out of Money, US Says,' *Los Angeles Times*, 8 September 2005, <http://www.latimes.com/news/nationworld/world/la-fg-rebuild8sep08,1,2576935.story?coll=la-headlines-world&ctrack=1&cset=true>.

61. Rory Carroll and Julian Borger, 'Iraq Rebuilding under Threat as the US Runs out of Money,' *Guardian*, 9 September 2005, <http://www.guardian.co.uk/Iraq/Story/0,2763,1566176,00.html>.

62. Jonathan Morgenstein, 'A Reality Check from Iraq,' *Center for American Progress*, 13 July 2005, <http://www.americanprogress.org/site/pp.asp?c=biJRJ8OVF&b=883467>.

63. Max Weber, 'Politics as a Vocation,' lecture, Munich University, 1918. Published in H.H. Gerth and C. Wright Mills (trans. and eds), *From Max Weber: Essays in Sociology*, New York: Oxford University Press, 1946, pp. 77–128; emphasis in original.

64. Faye Bowers, 'Delicate Challenge of Taming Iraq's Militias,' *Christian Science Monitor*, 13 April 2004, <http://www.csmonitor.com/2004/0413/p02s01-usmi.html>.

65. Charles Clover and Gareth Smyth, 'Decision by Kurds to Keep Militia Deals Blow to Coalition,' *Financial Times*, 29 July 2003, p. 10.

66. Rajiv Chandrasekaran and Robin Wright, 'Iraqi Militias near Accord to Disband,' *Washington Post*, 22 March 2004, p. 1.

67. *ibid.*

68. Kim Murphy, 'Militia May Disarm, but it Won't Dissolve,' *Los Angeles Times*, 5 April 2004 (<http://ebird.afis.osd.mil/ebfiles/e2004045272917.html>).

69. *ibid.*

70. *ibid.*

71. Anne Ciezadlo, 'Though Battle-Hardened, Iraq's Kurdish Militia Struggles for Role,' *Christian Science Monitor*, 2 March 2005, <http://www.csmonitor.com/2005/0302/p05s01-woiq.html>.

72. Yochi Dreazen, 'Disarming Iraq's Many Militias Poses Major Challenges for US,' *Wall Street Journal*, 28 April 2003 (<http://ebird.dtic.mil/April 2003/e20030428180559.html>).

73. Mina al-Oraibi, 'American Major General Warns that the Presence of Militias Stands in the Way of "Ultimate Peace" in Iraq,' *Asharq Alawsat* (London), 25 August 2005, <http://aawsat.com/english/news.asp?section=1&id=1392>.

74. *ibid.*

75. *ibid.*

76. Dexter Filkins, 'Failing to Disband Militias, US Moves to Accept Them,' *New York Times*, 25 May 2004, p. 1; Orly Halpern, 'US Closes In On Deal With Iraqi Cleric,' *Christian Science Monitor*, 25 May 2004, p. 1.

77. See, for example, Charles Recknagel, 'Iraq: Prime Minister Says Most Militias Agree to Disband,' Radio Free Europe/Radio Liberty, 8 June 2004,

<http://www.rferl.org/featuresarticle/2004/06/b6bfe71e-f57a-4c89-9f30-04fcd4e60aee.html>.

78. Thomas Ricks and Rajiv Chandrasekaran, 'US Plans to Enlist Iraqis in Operations,' *Washington Post*, 20 July 2003, p. 1; Dexter Filkins, 'US and the Iraqis Discuss Creating Big Militia Force,' *New York Times*, 31 August 2003; Eric Schmitt, 'US is Creating an Iraqi Militia to Relieve GI's,' *New York Times*, 21 July 2003, p. 1.

79. Ann Scott Tyson, 'US Assembles New Iraqi Army,' *Christian Science Monitor*, 22 July 2003, p. 1. See also Carol Williams, 'Iraqi Officials Fault US on Handoff,' *Los Angeles Times*, 22 August 2003; Robert Burns, 'US Ready to Begin Rebuilding Iraq Army,' *Newsday.com*, 12 June 2003.

80. Daniel Williams, 'Loyalties in New Iraqi Police Forces Scrutinized,' *Washington Post*, 4 September 2003, p. 10.

81. John Daniszewski, 'Hundreds Line Up To Join New Iraqi Army,' *Los Angeles Times*, 22 July 2003 (<http://ebird.dtic.mil/Jul2003/e20030722202501.html>).

82. Ian Simpson, 'Leaks Plague Battle against Iraqi Insurgents,' *Boston Globe*, 12 May 2005, <http://www.boston.com/news/world/middleeast/articles/2005/05/12/leaks_plague_battle_against_iraqi_insurgents>.

83. *ibid*.

84. Rod Nordland, 'Tribe versus Tribe,' *Newsweek*, 24 January 2005 at <http://www/msnbc.msn.com/id/6831675/site/newsweek/>.

85. Sharon Behn, 'Iraqi Police Defy Danger,' *Washington Times,* 23 February 2005, p. 1, <http://www.washtimes.com/world/20050222-115008-1137r.htm>.

86. Scheherezade Faramarzi. 'Some Police Resent US, Are Sympathetic toward Guerillas,' *Oakland Tribune*, 29 November 2003.

87. 'Religious Fervor behind Iraqi Fighting,' Associated Press, 5 November 2003 (<http://www.msnbc.com/news/989521.asp?0cv=CA01&cp1=1>).

88. Faramarzi. 'Some Police Resent US.'

89. Tish Durkin, 'The Buffness Deficit,' *Atlantic*, 1 April 2004 (<http://www.keepmedia.com:/jsp/article_detail_print.jsp>).

90. *ibid*.

91. Patrick Tyler, 'Police Chief under Hussein Sees No Reason to Say Sorry,' *New York Times*, 19 May 2003 (<http://ebird.dtic.mil/May2003/s20030519186491.html>).

92. Durkin, 'The Buffness Deficit.' For more on the problems of the police in Sunni areas, see Paul Wiseman, 'Beleaguered Police Keep Faces Hidden in Fallujah:

Attackers Outgun, Outnumber Officers,' *USA Today*, 16 February 2004, <http://www.usatoday.com/news/world/iraq/2004-02-15-fallujah-usat_x.htm>.

93. Andrea Stone, 'Thousands of Iraqis Enlist in Army,' *USA Today*, 21 July 2003, p. 5.

94. *ibid*.

95. Tom Lasseter, 'Iraqi Security Forces Lack Training, Equipment, Support,' *Guardian Online* (Dayton, OH), 14 January 2004, <http://www.theguardianonline.com/media/paper373/news/2004/01/14/News/Iraqi.Security.Forces.Lack.Training.Equipment.Support-580945.shtml?norewrite&sourcedomain=www.theguardianonline.com>.

96. *ibid*.

97. Anthony Shadid, 'Iraqi Security Forces Torn between Loyalties,' *Washington Post,* 25 November 2003, p. 1.

98. *ibid*.

99. *ibid*.

100. Edward Wong, 'US Military Arrests an Iraqi Commander,' *New York Times*, 27 September 2004 (accessed online).

101. *ibid*.

102. Antony Loyd, 'I'm More Scared of Going out with These Guys than Fighting Insurgents,' *The Times* (London), 11 February 2005, <http://www.timesonline.co.uk/article/0,,7374-1479363,00.html>.

103. *ibid*.

104. See, for example, Mike Dorning, 'Trainer "Leads from the Front": US Officer Sees the Problems and the Promise of Iraqi Troops,' *Chicago Tribune*, 16 February 2005.

105. Loyd, 'I'm More Scared of Going out with These Guys.'

106. For an early and perceptive analysis of the failings of the newly constituted Iraqi security forces, see John Daniszewski, 'Iraqi Security Forces Far From Ready,' *Los Angeles Times,* 16 November 2003 (accessed online); Bradley Graham, 'Iraqi Security Forces Fall Short, Generals Say,' *Washington Post,* 13 April 2004, p. 1. For detailed open-source analyses of the weaknesses of Iraqi Security Sector Reform until May 2004, see Ahmed S. Hashim, 'Military Power and State Formation in Modern Iraq,' *Middle East Policy* X, 4 (2004), 29–47; Riad Kahwaji, 'Slow Rebuilding of Army Could Threaten Iraq's Future,' *Defense News,* 26 January 2004 (accessed online); Ahmed S. Hashim, 'Security Sector Reform in Post-Saddam Iraq,' unpublished paper, February 2005; Thom Shanker and Eric Schmitt, 'Delivery Delays Hurt US Efforts to

Equip Iraqis,' *New York Times,* 22 March 2004, p. 1.

107. Dean Calbreath, 'Iraqi Army, Police Force Fall Short on Training,' *San Diego Union-Tribune*, 4 July 2004 (<http://ebird.afis.osd.mil/ebfiles/s20040707301322.html>).

108. *ibid.*

109. Ed Blanche, 'Iraqi Allies Cannot be Trusted,' Special Report, *Jane's Information Group*, 1 May 2004, <http://www4.janes.com> (restricted access).

110. *ibid.*

111. *ibid.*

112. Betsy Pisik, 'Iraqi Police under Siege,' *Washington Times*, 28 June 2004, p. 1.

113. *ibid.*

114. *ibid.*

115. *ibid.*

116. Tony Karon, 'Why Iraq's Not Getting Better,' *Time*, 15 September 2004 (accessed online).

117. Aamer Madhani, 'In Race to Train Iraqi Security Force, GIs Find Trust is Biggest Obstacle,' *Chicago Tribune*, 14 July 2004 (<http://ebird.afis.osd.mil/ebfiles/e20040715303359.html>).

118. *ibid.*

119. *ibid.*

120. Ann Barnard, 'New Iraqi Forces Face Security Test at Polls,' *Boston Globe*, 28 January 2005, <http://www.boston.com/news/world/middleeast/articles/2005/01/28/new_iraqi_forces_face_security_test_at_polls/>.

121. *ibid.*

122. *ibid.*

123. Rory McCarthy, 'US Marines Put on Alert as More Die and Polling Stations Bombed,' *Guardian*, 28 January 2005, <http://www.guardian.co.uk/Iraq/Story/0,2763,1400496,00.html>.

124. Bassem Mroue, 'Iraqi General: Troops Need Time,' *Chicago Tribune*, 28 January 2005 (<http://ebird.afis.osd.mil/ebfiles/e20050129348629.html>).

125. Bryan Bender, 'Report Paints Bleak Picture of Iraqi Forces,' *Boston Globe*, 8 January 2005, p. 1, <http://www.boston.com/news/world/middleeast/articles/2005/01/08/report_paints_bleak_picture_of_iraqi_forces?pg=full>.

126. *ibid.*

127. Robin Wright and Josh White, 'US Plans New Tack after Iraq Elections,' *Washington Post*, 23 January 2005, p. 20, <http://www.wpni.com/wp-dyn/articles/A29420-2005Jan22.html>.

128. *ibid.*

129. Eric Schmitt, 'General Seeking Faster Training of Iraq Soldiers,' *New York Times*, 23 January 2005, p. 1, <http://www.nytimes.com/2005/01/23/international/middleeast/23military.tml?ex=1264136400&en=8e99ad1e46e3289d&ei=5090&partner=rssuserland>.

130. *ibid.* for an excellent analysis of the relationship between US military advisers and their Iraqi 'students', see the long article by Steve Fainaru, 'US Attempts to Build Trust, Leaders In Iraq,' *Washington Post*, 23 January 2005, p. 1. This article specifically explores the relationship between Lieutenant Colonel Adel Abbas, commander of the 23rd Battalion, 6th Brigade of the Iraqi Intervention Force, and his US adviser, Major Frank Shelton of the 3rd Marine Division, 3rd Marine Expeditionary Force.

131. Aamer Madhani, 'Iraqi Forces Mark Holiday in Cross Hairs,' *Chicago Tribune*, 7 January 2005.

132. Ghaith Abdul-Ahad, 'New Blood,' *Guardian*, 19 July 2005, <http://www.guardian.co.uk/Iraq/Story/0,2763,1531519,00.html>.

133. *ibid.*

134. *ibid.*

135. *ibid.*

136. Ferry Biedermann, 'They are Arabs and You Can't Trust Them,' *Salon.com*, 17 February 2005, <http://www.salon.com/news/feature/2005/02/17/mosul/index_np.html>.

137. *ibid.*

138. *ibid.*

139. *ibid.*

140. *ibid.*

141. Observations in summer 2005, Tal Afar.

142. Patrick Cockburn, 'Corruption Threatens to Leave Iraq with a "Ghost Army",' *Independent*, 15 July 2005.

143. *ibid.*

144. Hannah Allam, 'Iraq Arms Scandal Unfolds,' *Philadelphia Inquirer*, 15 July 2005, p. 1.

145. Craig Smith, 'Big Guns for Iraq? Not So Fast,' *New York Times*, 28 August 2005, s. 4, p. 1.

146. Hannah Allam, 'Overhauling Iraqi Security Forces Could Cause Collapse, Analysts Say,' *Knight Ridder Washington Bureau*, 13 March 2005, <http://www.realcities.com/mld/krwashington/11127663.htm>.

147. *ibid.*

148. *ibid.*

149. Michael Smith, 'Hoon Admits Resistance Came as a Shock to Allies,' *Daily Telegraph* (London), 19 March 2004 (<http://ebird.afis.osd.mil/ebfiles/s20040319268302.html>).

150. Stephen Hedges, 'Former General Says US Military Didn't Expect Iraqi Insurgency,' *Chicago Tribune*, 15 July 2004.

151. The exception, I think, is to be found in the original US Marine Corps *Small Wars Manual*, written in the 1930s. It is dated, of course, except for the first thirty pages or so. These contain among the most brilliant words on the essential nature of 'small wars', or irregular wars and insurgencies.

152. Rodriguez, '"Gurgling Gasp" Now a War Cry.'

153. 'Saddam Aide Linked to Al-Qaida, Claims US,' *Guardian*, 30 October 2003, <http://www.guardian.co.uk/alqaida/story/0,12469,1074141,00.html>.

154. Tini Tran, 'US Commander: American Troops Averaging 3–6 Deaths, per Week,' *San Francisco Chronicle*, 2 October 2003, <http://www.sfgate.com/cgi-bin/article.cgi?f=/news/archive/2003/10/02/international1037EDT0547.DTL>.

155. Robert Reed, 'Who's Behind Iraq Attacks Up for Debate,' Associated Press, 31 October 2003 (accessed online).

156. Elaine Grossman, 'Officers in Iraq: War Tactics Offer Little Prospect of Success,' *Inside the Pentagon*, 30 September 2004, <http://www.d-n-i.net/grossman/officers_in%20_iraq.htm>.

157. Vernon Loeb, 'Instead of Force, Friendly Persuasion,' *Washington Post*, 5 November 2003, p. 24.

158. Thomas Ricks, 'Intelligence Problems in Iraq are Detailed,' *Washington Post*, 25 October 2003, p. 1.

159. *ibid.*

160. Daniel Barnard, 'The 1920 Iraqi Revolt Against British Occupation: Strategic Misperceptions, Military Suppression and Collective Punishment,' paper in possession of A. Hashim, p. 3.

161. Sir Percy Cox wrote to London: 'As in 1918, so now, the military situation in Mesopotamia is conditioned by external rather than by internal situation. The principal external factors are Bolsheviks, Turks, and Syrians, in order names.' Barnard, 'The 1920 Iraqi Revolt,' p. 2. See also David Fromkin, *A Peace to End All Peace: The Fall of the Ottoman Empire and the Creation of the Modern Middle East*, New York: Henry Holt, 1989, p. 453.

162. Sir Aylmer Haldane, *The Insurrection in Mesopotamia, 1920*, London: W. Blackwood and Sons, 1922, p. 312.

163. Daniel Barnard, 'The 1920 Iraqi Revolt,' p. 4.

164. Once again I am indebted to Daniel Barnard ('The 1920 Iraqi Revolt,' p. 12).

165. Frederick Kagan, 'Blueprint for Victory,' *Weekly Standard* 11, 7 (2005), <http://www.weeklystandard.com/Content/Public/Articles/000/000/006/249zzgbd.asp>.

166. For the US military operations in central Iraq in June 2003 and the reactions of the local populace, see Sophie Shihab, 'En Irak, les Américains engagent des combats meurtriers,' *Le Monde*, 13 June 2003; 'Les Etats Unis face a une "resistance organisée" en Irak,' *Le Monde*, 13 June 2003; Michael Slackman, 'US Operation Yields Fury in Central Iraq,' *Los Angeles Times*, 13 June 2003 (accessed online); Ilene Prusher, 'US Anti-guerilla Campaign Draws Iraqi Ire,' *Christian Science Monitor,* June 16, 2003, <http://www.csmonitor.com/2003/0616/p10s01-woiq.html>; Ellen Barry and Bryan Bender, 'US Support in Iraq Fades after Raids,' *Boston Globe*, 15 June 2003, p. 1.

167. Douglas McGregor, 'War Strategy: Dramatic Failures Require Drastic Changes,' *Saint Louis Post-Dispatch,* 19 December 2004 (accessed online).

168. Scott Wallace, '"God, I Hate These People," says the Sergeant. Some Utter the V-word: Vietnam,' *Independent*, 20 July 2003 (accessed online).

169. Rajiv Chandrasekaran and Scott Wilson, 'Iraqi City Simmers with New Attack,' *Washington Post*, 2 May 2003, p. 21.

170. Mark MacKinnon, 'How to Make Friends and Occupy People,' *Globe and Mail* (Toronto), 26 July 2003.

171. Mark Mazetti, 'Good Marines Make Good Neighbors,' *Slate*, 25 February 2004, <http://slate.msn.com/id/2096027/>.

172. Grossman, 'Officers in Iraq.'

173. *ibid.*

174. Edward Wong, 'The Reach of War: Rebellion; In Anger, Ordinary Iraqis are Joining the Insurgency,' *New York Times*, 28 June 2004, p. 9.

175. *ibid.*

176. Nicholas Blandford, 'Attacks Turning to US Allies in Iraq,' *Christian Science Monitor*, 1 December 2003, p. 1.

177. Bradley Graham and Walter Pincus, 'US Hopes to Divide Insurgency,' *Washington Post*, 31 October 2004, p. 1.

178. *ibid.*

179. Sir Robert Thompson, cited in Anthony James Joes, *The History and Politics of Counterinsurgency: Resisting Rebellion*, Lexington: University of Kentucky Press, 2004, p. 156.

180. Jill Caroll, 'Old Brutality among New Iraqi Forces,' *Christian Science Monitor*, 4 May 2005, <http://www.csmonitor.com/2005/0504/p01s04-woiq.htm>.

181. *ibid.*

182. Hussein Ali al-Yasiri and Imad al-Shara, 'National Guard Abuses Anger Public,' *Iraq Crisis Report* 92, 29 November 2004, <http://www.iwpr.net/?p=icr&s=f&o=167162&apc_state=heniicr7ef9c7335d052c21dc30a65edb5bb7d4>.

183. *ibid.*

184. Edward Wong, '8 Months after US-Led Siege, Insurgents Rise Again in Falluja,' *New York Times*, p. 1.

185. *ibid.*

186. Steve Negus and Awadh al-Ta'i, 'Sunnis Feel Full Force of Lightning Strike,' *Financial Times*, 29 June 2005 (<http://ebird.afis.osd.mil/ebfiles/e20050629376716.html>).

187. Morgenstein, 'A Reality Check from Iraq.'

188. McCarthy, 'False Dawn of Peace.'

189. Tom Lasseter, 'Insurgency Concentrated in Areas along Euphrates River,' *Knight Ridder Washington Bureau*, 25 August 2005, <http://www.realcities.com/mld/krwashington/12476637.htm>.

190. *ibid.*

191. *ibid.*

192. *ibid.*

193. *ibid.*

194. *ibid.*

195. *ibid.*

196. *ibid.*

197. *ibid.*

198. Omer Mahdi and Rory Carroll, 'Under US Noses, Brutal Insurgents Rule Sunni Citadel,' *Guardian*, 22 August 2005, <http://www.guardian.co.uk/Iraq/Story/0,2763,1553969,00.html>.

199. *ibid.*

200. *ibid.*

201. *ibid.*

202. *ibid.*

203. *ibid.*

204. *ibid.*

205. *ibid.*

206. David Galula, *Counterinsurgency Warfare; Theory and Practice*, New York: Praeger, 1964, p. 82.

207. *ibid.,* p. 77.

208. Lasseter, 'Insurgency Concentrated in Areas along Euphrates River.'

209. Tom Lasseter, 'US Army Officers Cite Lack of Troops in Key Region,' *Knight Ridder Washington Bureau*, 31 May 2005, <http://www.realcities.com/mld/krwashington/11781484.htm>.

210. Ronald Haycock, *Regular Armies and Insurgency*, London: Croom Helm, 1979, p. 59.

211. 'Present at the Creation,' *The Economist*, 29 June 2002, pp. 3–34.

Conclusions

1. See Erik Ringmar, *Identity, Interest and Action: A Cultural Explanation of Sweden's Intervention in the Thirty Years War*, Cambridge University Press, 1996, p. 3. This is a detailed theoretical and case study of the intangible and nonmaterial reasons why nations/states or peoples choose to fight.

2. Observations in Baghdad, November 2003 to March 2004; discussions with Sunni Arabs during the same period.

3. See, for example, Ahmed S. Hashim, 'Iraq's Chaos: Why the Insurgency Won't Go Away,' *Boston Review*, October-November 2004, <http://www.bostonreview.net/BR29.5/hashim.html>.

4. Nils Butenschøn, *Politics of Ethnocracies: Strategies and Dilemmas of Ethnic Domination*, University of Oslo, 2001, <http://www.statsvitenskap.uio.no/ansatte/serie/notat/fulltekst/0193/Ethnocr-2.html>; emphasis in original.

5. Deborah Pasmantier, 'Communal Tensions High in Iraq Six Months after Baghdad fell,' Agence France Presse, 7 October 2003.

6. LBC Satellite Television, 19 February 2004; quoted in 'Inside Iraq', Radio Free Europe/Radio Liberty, 27 February 2004, <http://rfe.rferl.org/reports/iraq-report/2004/02/7-270204.asp>.

7. Patrick McDonnell, 'Iraqis See the Enemy Next Door,' *Los Angeles Times*, 10 December 2003, p. 1.

8. *ibid.*

9. James Hider, 'A Civil War in All but Name as Sunni and Shia Fight to the Death,' *The Times* (London), 30 April 2005 (<http://ebird.afis.osd.mil/ebfiles/e20050430365884.html>).

10. Emad Hasan al-Shara'a, 'Shia Militia Takes on the Insurgents,' *Iraqi Crisis Report* 126, 24 May 2005.

11. 'Iraq: Sunni-Shiite Acrimony Intensifies,' *FBIS Analysis*, 20 May 2005, <http://www.fbis.gov>.

12. James Hider, 'The Sunni-Shia Hate Boils Over,' *Australian*, 16 July 2005.

13. Tom Lasseter, 'Some Fear Shiite Political Ascendancy May Give Way to Civil War,' *Philadelphia Inquirer*, 12 December 2004 (<http://ebird.afis.osd.mil/ebfiles/e20041212341329.html>)

14. Neil MacDonald, 'After Iraq Attacks, Calls for Militias Grow,' *Christian Science Monitor*, 18 July 2005 (<http://ebird.afis.mil/ebfiles/e20050718380104.html>). On increased fears of civil war, see James Hider, 'Weekend of Slaughter Propels Iraq towards All-out Civil War,' *The Times* (London), 18 July 2005.

15. Alex Berenson, 'A Baghdad Neighborhood, Once Hopeful, Now Reels as Iraq's Turmoil Persists,' *New York Times*, 14 December 2003 (accessed online).

16. Interviews in Al-Hillah, 29 November 2003.

17. Interviews with Sunni Arabs, Baghdad, November 2003.

18. Nicolas Pelham, 'Sectarian Tensions Rise in Iraq as US Attack Looms,' *Christian Science Monitor*, 18 March 2003, <http://www.csmonitor.com/2003/0318/p07s02-wome.html>.

19. *ibid*.

20. Valentinas Mite, 'Iraq: Sunni, Shi'a Parties Have Conflicting Visions of Future,' Radio Free Europe/Radio Liberty, 3 November 2003, <http://www.rferl.org/features/2003/11/03112003163526.asp>.

21. *ibid*.

22. *ibid*.

23. Edward Wong, 'Iraqi Kurds Detail Demands for a Degree of Autonomy,' *New York Times*, 18 February 2005 (http://www.nytimes.com/2005/02/18/international/middleeast/18kurds.html?ex=1266469200&en=d87bdb2c06e471ce&ei=5090&partner=rssuserland).

24. As far as I can ascertain the first serious detailed discussion of 'managed partition' is in Liam Anderson and Gareth Stansfield, The Future of Iraq: Dictatorship, Democracy or Division? London: Palgrave, 2004.

25. The strongest promoters of the three-state solution are Leslie Gelb ('The Three-State Solution,' *New York Times*, 25 November 2003) and Peter Galbraith ('Iraq: Bush's Islamic Republic,' *New York Review of Books* 52, 13 (2005), <http://www.nybooks.com/articles/18150>). Both make a compelling case.

26. Sara Daniel, 'Irak: le défi kurde,' *Nouvel Observateur Hebdo* 2109, 7 April 2005, <http://archives.nouvelobs.com/recherche/article.cfm?id=137246>.

27. *ibid*.
28. Wong, 'Iraqi Kurds Detail Demands.'
29. *ibid*.
30. Roula Khalaf, 'Iraq's Main Oil-Producer Provinces Consider Forming Break-away Region,' *Financial Times*, 30 September 2004 (accessed online).
31. Borzou Daragahi, 'Sunni Ire Appears to Have Been Stoked, Not Calmed,' *Los Angeles Times*, 27 August 2005 (<http://www.myantiwar.org/view/57575.html>).
32. Trudy Rubin, 'Iraqis Far from Ready to Defend Themselves,' *Baltimore Sun*, 15 July 2005, <http://www.baltimoresun.com/news/opinion/oped/bal-op.rubin15jul>.
33. *ibid*.
34. *ibid*.

Epilogue

1. Very little is available on Tal Afar in English. I found a very old book on the city's history in Arabic in the *qaimaqam*, or mayor's office, in the Qalaa—the old Ottoman castle that stands on a hill and dominates the city. Unfortunately the book is in bad shape; it is falling apart and has no cover. I have incorporated some details from it into my discussion. However, most of the analysis here relies on my own observations and on interviews and discussions with locals, Sunni and Shi'a. I talked to ordinary townsfolk, sheikhs, clerics, municipal workers and young adults.
2. Pers. comm. (conversation with a Shi'a cleric in Tal Afar), September 2005.
3. Pers. comm. (conversations in the streets of Tal Afar), August 2005.
4. Pers. comm. (side conversations during meetings with the Sheikhs of the Sunni al-Farhat tribe), August 2005.
5. Abd al-Halim Ghazali, 'Interview with the New President of the Turkmen Front in Iraq,' *Al-Ahram*, 20 December 2003, p. 7 (FBIS-GMP20031220000161).
6. 'Al-Basrah Net Writer Discusses Attack on Tall Afar,' FBIS-GMP20050913371016, 13 September 2005 (accessed online).
7. *ibid*.
8. *ibid*.
9. Ralph Peters, 'Count on the Cavalry,' *New York Post*, 13 September 2005 (accessed online).
10. International Crisis Group, 'Unmaking Iraq: A Constitutional Process Gone

Awry,' *ICG Middle East Briefing* 19, 26 September 2005, <http://www.crisisgroup.org/home/index.cfm?l=1&id=3703>.

11. Dan Murphy and Jill Carroll, 'Why Iraq's Sunnis Fear Constitution,' *Christian Science Monitor*, 24 August 2005, <http://www.csmonitor.com/2005/0824/p01s01-woiq.html?s=hns>.

12. *ibid*.

13. Dan Murphy, 'Iraqis Far Apart over Role of Islam,' *Christian Science Monitor*, 9 August 2005, <http://www.csmonitor.com/2005/0809/p01s04-woiq.html>.

14. *ibid*.

15. Quoted in Seb Walker, 'Last Ditch Constitution Bid,' *News.com.au*, 15 August 2005, <http://www.news.com.au/story/0,10117,16264543-38201,00.html>.

16. *ibid*.

17. Al Arabiya Television, Dubai, 1204 GMT, 4 September 2005 (FBIS-GMP20050904544002).

18. Hannah Allam, 'Iraq's Highest-ranking Sunni Muslim Arab Criticizes Constitution,' *Knight Ridder Washington Bureau*, 29 August 2005, <http://www.realcities.com/mld/krwashington/12508042.htm>.

19. *ibid*.

20. *ibid*.

21. *ibid*.

22. *ibid*.

23. Murphy and Carroll, 'Why Iraq's Sunnis Fear Constitution.'

24. *ibid*.

25. *ibid*.

26. Ghaith Abdul-Ahad, 'Fiddling while Baghdad Burns,' *Observer*, 28 August 2005, <http://observer.guardian.co.uk/comment/story/0,6903,1558020,00.html>.

BIBLIOGRAPHY

PRIMARY SOURCES

Albasrah.net, <http://www.albasrah.net/index1.html> (insurgent website).

Baghdad al-Rashid Forum, insurgent website, <http://www.baghdadal-rashid.com>.

Foreign Broadcast Information Service, various years, but particularly 2003–5, <http://www.fbis.gov>.

Free Arab Voice, <http://www.freearabvoice.org/index.htm> (insurgent statements, descriptions of operations).

Hashim, Ahmed S., 'Baghdad Blues: Experiences, Interviews and Observations,' diary, October 2003 to March 2004.

Interviews and conversations with various journalists, 2003–5.

Interviews with Iraqis in Baghdad and other Iraqi cities; November 2003 to March 2004.

Interviews with Iraqis in Mosul, Kirkuk and Tal Afar, July to September 2005.

Iraqi Resistance Report, various reports, accessed 2003–5, <http://www.albasrah.net/moqawama/english/iraqi_resistance.htm>.

Jihadist websites, accessed regularly between mid-summer 2003 and spring 2005.

SECONDARY SOURCES

Books, book chapters, theses, essays and reports

Abdul-Jabar, Faleh (ed.), *Ayatollahs, Sufis and Ideologues: State, Religion and Social Movements in Iraq*, London: Saqi Books, 2002.

———, *The Shi'ite Movement in Iraq*, London: Saqi, 2003.

Akehurst, John, *We Won a War: The Campaign in Oman 1965–1975*, Wilton, England: Michael Russell, 1984.

Alawi, Hasan al-, *Al-Shia wa al-dawla fi al-Irak 1914–1990* (The Shi'is and the State In Iraq 1914–1990), Qom: Dar al-thaqafa lil-tiba'a wa al-nashr, 1990.

Amir-Moezzi, Mohammad-Ali and Christian Jambet, *Qu'est-ce que le shi'isme?* (What is Shi'ism?), Paris: Fayard, 2004.

Anderson, David, *Histories of the Hanged: The Dirty War in Kenya and the End of Empire*, New York: W.W. Norton, 2005.

Anderson, John Lee, *The Fall of Baghdad*, New York: Penguin, 2004.

Askari, Jafar al-, *A Soldier's Story: From Ottoman Rule to Independent Iraq*, London: Arabian Publishing, 2003.

Ballentine, Karen, and Jake Sherman, *The Political Economy of Armed Conflict: Beyond Greed and Grievance*, Boulder, CO: Lynne Rienner, 2003.

Baram, Amatzia, *Culture, History and Ideology in the Formation of Ba'thist Iraq, 1968–89*, New York: St Martin's Press, 1991.

———, and Barry Rubin (eds), *Iraq's Road to War*, New York: St Martin's Press, 1993.

Baran, David (pseudo.), *Vivre la tyrannie et lui survivre: L'Irak en transition*, Paris: Arthème Fayard, 2004.

Batatu, Hanna, *The Old Social Classes and the Revolutionary Movements of Iraq: A Study of Iraq's Old Landed and Commercial Classes and of its Communists, Ba'thists, and Free Officers*, Princeton University Press, 1979.

———, 'Iraq's Shi'a, Their Political Role, and the Process of Their Integration into Society' in Barbara Freyer Stowasser (ed.), *The Islamic Impulse*, London: Croom Helm in association with Center for Contemporary Arab Studies, Georgetown University, 1987, pp. 204–13.

Beckett, Ian, *Modern Insurgencies and Counter-Insurgencies: Guerillas and their Opponents since 1750*, London: Routledge, 2001.

————, *Insurgency in Iraq: An Historical Perspective*, Carlisle, PA: Strategic Studies Institute, US Army War College, 2005, <http://www.strategicstudiesinstitute.army.mil/pdffiles/PUB592.pdf>.

————, and John Pimlott (eds), *Armed Forces and Modern Counter-insurgency*, New York: St Martin's Press, 1985.

Bengio, Ofra, *Saddam's Word: Political Discourse in Iraq*, Oxford University Press, 1998.

Blaufarb, Douglas, *The Counterinsurgency Era: US Doctrine and Performance, 1950 to the Present,* New York: The Free Press, 1977.

Bonney, Richard, *Jihad: From Qur'an to Bin Laden*, London: Palgrave, 2005.

Bozarslan, Hamit, *Violence in the Middle East: From Political Struggle to Self-Sacrifice,* Princeton, NJ: Markus Wiener, 2004.

Buckley, John, 'A Model Of Insurgency: Reflections of Clausewitz's Paradoxical Trinity And Lessons for Operational Planners considering Conventional Forces in Unconventional Conflicts,' School of Advanced Military Studies, US Army Command and General Staff College, Fort Leavenworth, Kansas, May 1995.

Bunker, Robert, and John Sullivan, *Suicide Bombings in Operation Iraqi Freedom*, Land Warfare Paper 46W, Arlington, VA: Institute of Land Warfare, Association of the United States Army, 2004.

Byman, Daniel, Peter Chalk, Bruce Hoffman, William Rosenau and David Brannan, *Trends in Outside Support for Insurgent Movements*, Santa Monica, CA: RAND, 2001.

Caldwell, C.E., *Small Wars: Their Principles and Practice*, Lincoln: University of Nebraska, 1996.

Campbell, Robert Martin, 'The Iraqi Enigma: Ethno-Sectarianism, Tribalism, State Ideology and Class,' MA thesis, University of Arizona, 1998.

Catherwood, Christopher, *Churchill's Folly: How Winston Churchill Created Modern Iraq,* New York: Carroll and Graf, 2004.

Clutterbuck, Richard, *The Long Long War: Counterinsurgency in Malaya and Vietnam*, New York: Praeger, 1966.

Collins, Michael, *The Path to Freedom*, Boulder, CO: Roberts Rinehart, 1996.

Cordesman, Anthony, *The 'Post Conflict' Lessons of Iraq and Afghanistan:*

Testimony to the Senate Foreign Relations Committee, Washington, DC: Center for Strategic and International Studies, 2004.

———, *Iraq's Evolving Insurgency*, Washington, DC: Centre for Strategic and International Studies, 2005 (19 May), <http://www.csis.org/features/050512.IraqInsurg.pdf> (working draft, since updated; <http://www.csis.org/media/csis/pubs/051209_iraqiinsurg.pdf>.)

———, and Nawaf Obaid, *Saudi Militants in Iraq: Assessment and Kingdom's Response*, Washington, DC: Center for Strategic and International Studies, 2005.

Crenshaw, Martha, *Revolutionary Terrorism: The FLN in Algeria, 1954–1962*, Stanford University Press, 1978.

Dawod, Hosham, and Hamit Bozarslan (eds), *La société irakienne: Communautés, pouvoirs et violences*, Paris: Karthala, 2003.

Davis, Eric, 'State-building in Iraq during the Iran-Iraq War and the Gulf Crisis' in Manus Midlarsky (ed.), *The Internationalization of Communal Strife*, London: Routledge, 1993, pp. 69–91.

———, *Memories of State: Politics, History, and Collective Identity in Modern Iraq*, Berkeley: University of California Press, 2005.

——— and N. Gavrielides, 'Statecraft, Historical Memory and Popular Culture in Iraq and Kuwait' in E. Davis and N. Gavrielides (eds), *Statecraft in the Middle East: Oil, Historical Memory and Popular Culture*, Miami: Florida International University Press, 1991, pp. 116–48.

Dekmejian, R. Hrair, *Islam in Revolution: Fundamentalism in the Arab World*, Syracuse University Press, 1985.

Denoeux, Guilain, *Urban Unrest in the Middle East: A Comparative Study of Informal Networks in Egypt, Iraq and Lebanon*, Albany: SUNY Press, 1993.

Diamond, Larry, *Squandered Victory: The American Occupation and the Bungled Effort to Bring Democracy to Iraq*, New York: Times Books, 2005.

Dodge, Toby, *Inventing Iraq: The Failure of Nation Building and a History Denied*, London: Hurst/New York: Columbia University Press, 2003.

———, *Iraq's Future: The Aftermath of Regime Change*, Adelphi Paper 372, IISS, London: Oxford University Press, 2005.

Dodge, Toby, and Steven Simon (eds.), *Iraq at the Crossroads: State and Society in the Shadow of Regime Change*, Adelphi Paper 354, International Institute for Strategic Studies, Oxford University Press, 2003.

Drew, Dennis, *Insurgency and Counterinsurgency: American Military Dilemmas and Doctrinal Proposals*, Report AU-ARI-CP-88–1, Maxwell Air Force Base, AL: Air University Press, 1988.

Elkins, Caroline, *Imperial Reckoning: The Untold Story of Britain's Gulag in Kenya*, New York: Henry Holt, 2005.

Etherington, Mark, *Revolt on the Tigris: The Al-Sadr Uprising and the Governing of Iraq*, London: Hurst, 2005.

Fall, Bernard, *The Two Vietnams: A Political and Military Analysis*, New York: Praeger, 1963.

Farouk-Sluglett, Marion, and Peter Sluglett, *Iraq Since 1958: From Revolution to Dictatorship*, London: Kegan Paul International, 1987.

Fromkin, David, *A Peace to End All Peace: The Fall of the Ottoman Empire and the Creation of the Modern Middle East*, New York: Henry Holt, 1989.

Galula, David, *Counterinsurgency Warfare: Theory and Practice*, New York: Praeger, 1964.

Gates, John Morgan, *Schoolbooks and Krags: The United States Army in the Philippines 1898–1902*, Westport, CT: Greenwood Press, 1973.

Gerolymatos, Andre, *The Balkan Wars: Conquest, Revolution and Retribution from the Ottoman Era to the Twentieth Century and Beyond*, New York: Basic Books, 2002.

Ghareeb, Edmond, *The Kurdish Question in Iraq*, Syracuse University Press, 1981.

Grau, Lester, and Michael Gress, *The Soviet-Afghan War: How a Superpower Fought and Lost*, Lawrence: University Press of Kansas, 2002.

Greenberg, Robert, 'The US Response to Philippine Insurgency,' PhD diss., Fletcher School of Law and Diplomacy, Tufts University, 1994.

Greene, T.N. (ed.), *The Guerilla and How to Fight Him*, New York: Praeger, 1962.

Gunaratna, Rohan, and Peter Chalk, *Jane's Counter Terrorism,* 2nd edn, Coulsdon, England: Jane's Information Group, 2002.

Gurr, Ted Robert, *Why Men Rebel*, Princeton University Press, 1970.

Gwynn, Sir Charles, *Imperial Policing*, London: Macmillan, 1934.

Hadithi, Naji al- (ed.), *On History, Heritage, and Religion*, Baghdad, 1981.

Haj, Samira, *The Making of Iraq 1900–1963: Capital, Power and Ideology*, Albany: State University of New York, 1997.

Halberstam, David, *The Making of a Quagmire: America and Vietnam during the Kennedy Era,* New York: Alfred Knopf, 1988.

Hamdi, Walid, *Rashid Ali al-Gailani: The Nationalist Movement in Iraq 1939–1941,* London: Darf, 1987.

Hamilton, Donald, *The Art of Insurgency: American Military Policy and the Failure of Strategy in Southeast Asia,* Westport, CT: Praeger, 1998.

Hammes, Thomas X., *The Sling and the Stone: On War in the 21st Century,* St Paul, MN: Zenith Press, 2004.

Heaton, Colin, *German Anti-partisan Warfare in Europe 1939–1945,* Atglen, PA: Schiffer Military, 2001.

Heilbrunn, Otto, *Partisan Warfare,* New York: Praeger, 1962.

Heller, Mark, 'Iraq's Army: Military Weakness, Political Utility' in Amatzia Baram and Barry Rubin (eds), *Iraq's Road to War,* New York: St Martin's Press, 1993, pp. 37–50.

Helms, Christine Moss, *Iraq: Eastern Flank of the Arab World,* Washington, DC: Brookings Institution Press, 1984.

Hemphill, Paul, 'The Formation of the Iraqi Army, 1921–1933' in Abbas Kelidar (ed.), *The Integration of Modern Iraq,* London: Croom Helm, 1979, pp. 88–109.

Herd, Graeme, *Weak Authoritarianism and Iraqi State Building,* Middle East Series 05/57, Swindon: Conflict Studies Research Centre, Defence Academy of the United Kingdom, 2005.

Hernon, Ian, *Britain's Forgotten Wars: Colonial Campaigns of the 19th century,* Phoenix Mill, England: Sutton Publishing, 2004.

Hoffman, Bruce, *Insurgency and Counterinsurgency in Iraq,* Occasional Paper OP-127-IPC/CMEPP, Santa Monica, CA: RAND National Security Research Division, 2004, <http://www.rand.org/pubs/occasional_papers/2005/RAND_OP127.pdf>.

Hoffman, Bruce, and Jennifer Taw, *Defense Policy and Low-Intensity Conflict: The Development of Britain's 'Small Wars' Doctrine during the 1950s,* Santa Monica, CA: Rand, 1991.

Horne, Alistair, *A Savage War of Peace: Algeria 1954–1962,* New York: Penguin Books, 1987.

Hosmer, Stephen, *The Army's Role in Counterinsurgency and Insurgency,* Santa Monica, CA: Rand, 1990.

Hudson, Michael, 'The Islamic Factor in Syrian and Iraqi Politics' in James Piscatori (ed.), *Islam in the Political Process*, Cambridge University Press, 1983, pp. 73–97.

Hunter, Shireen (ed.), *The Politics of Islamic Revivalism: Diversity and Unity*, Washington, DC: Center for Strategic and International Studies, 1988.

Hussein, Saddam, 'A View of Religion and Heritage' in Naji al-Hadithi (ed.), *On History, Heritage, and Religion*, Baghdad, 1981.

International Crisis Group, *Iraq Backgrounder: What Lies Beneath*, Middle East Report 6, Amman/Brussels: International Crisis Group, 2002, <http://www.crisisgroup.org/library/documents/report_archive/A400786_01102002.pdf>.

Ishow, Habib, *L'Irak paysanneries politiques agraires et industrielles au XXe Siècle*, Paris: Publisud, 1996.

Jabar, Faleh A., 'The State, Society, Clan, Party and Army in Iraq: A Totalitarian State in the Twilight of Totalitarianism' in Faleh A. Jabar, Ahmed Shikara, and Keiko Sakai (eds), *From Storm to Thunder: Unfinished Showdown between Iraq and US*, Tokyo: Institute of Developing Economies, 1998, pp. 1–27.

—— (ed.), *Ayatollahs, Sufis and Ideologues: State, Religion and Social Movements in Iraq*, London: Saqi Books, 2002.

——, 'Clerics, Tribes, and Urban Dwellers in South of Iraq: The Potential for Rebellion' in Toby Dodge and Steven Simon (eds), *Iraq at the Crossroads: State and Society in the Shadow of Regime Change*, International Institute for Strategic Studies, Adelphi Paper 354, Oxford University Press, 2003, pp. 161–77.

——, *The Shi'ite Movement in Iraq*, London: Saqi Books, 2003.

——, *Postconflict Iraq: A Race for Stability, Reconstruction, and Legitimacy*, Special Report 120, Washington, DC: US Institute of Peace, 2004.

——, Ahmed Shikara, and Keiko Sakai (eds), *From Storm to Thunder: Unfinished Showdown between Iraq and US*, Tokyo: Institute of Developing Economies, 1998.

James Jankowski and Israel Gershoni (eds), *Rethinking Nationalism in the Arab Middle East*, New York: Columbia University Press, 1997.

Jawad, Sa'ad, *Iraq and the Kurdish Question, 1958–1970*, London: Ithaca Press, 1981.

Jennings, Ray Salvatore, *The Road Ahead: Lessons in Nation-Building from Japan, Germany, and Afghanistan for Postwar Iraq*, Peaceworks 49, Washington, DC: US Institute of Peace, 2003.

Joes, Anthony James, *The History and Politics of Counterinsurgency: Resisting Rebellion*, Lexington: University of Kentucky Press, 2004.

Johnson, Chalmers, *Autopsy on People's War*, Berkeley: University of California Press, 1973.

Johnson, Dominic, *Overconfidence and War: The Havoc and Glory and Positive Illusions*, Cambridge, MA: Harvard University Press, 2004.

Kaiser, David, *American Tragedy: Kennedy, Johnson, and the Origins of the Vietnam War*, Cambridge, MA: Belknap Press, 2000.

Keay, John, *Sowing the Wind: The Mismanagement of the Middle East 1900–1960*, London: John Murray, 2003.

Kelidar, Abbas (ed.), *The Integration of Modern Iraq*, London: Croom Helm, 1979.

Kerkvliet, Benedict, *The Huk Rebellion: A Study of Peasant Revolt in the Philippines*, Berkeley: University of California Press, 1977.

Khadduri, Majid, *Socialist Iraq: A Study in Iraqi Politics Since 1968*, Washington, DC: Middle East Institute, 1978.

Khafaji, Isam al-, 'War as a Vehicle in the Rise and Demise of a State-Controlled Society: The Case of Ba'thist Iraq' in Steven Heydeman (ed.), *War, Institutions, and Social Change in the Middle East*, Berkeley: University of California Press, 2000.

Khalidi, Rashid, *et al. The Origins of Arab Nationalism*, New York: Columbia University Press, 1991.

Langguth, A.J. *Our Vietnam: The War, 1954–1975*, New York: Simon & Schuster, 2000.

Laqueur, Walter, *Guerilla: A Historical and Critical Study*, Boulder. CO: Westview Press, 1984.

Lawrence, T.E., *Seven Pillars of Wisdom: A Triumph*, New York: Anchor Books, 1991.

Lomperis, Timothy, *From People's War to People's Rule: Insurgency, Intervention and the Lessons of Vietnam*, Chapel Hill: University of North Carolina Press, 1996.

Long, Jerry, *Saddam's War of Words: Politics, Religion, and the Iraqi Invasion of*

Kuwait, Austin: University of Texas, 2004.

Longrigg, Stephen Helmsley, *Four Centuries of Modern Iraq*, Oxford: Clarendon Press, 1925.

Luizard, Pierre-Jean, *La Formation de l'Irak Contemporain. Le rôle politique des ulemas Chiites a la fin de la domination ottomane et au moment de la création de l'Etat Irakien*, Paris: CNRS Editions, 1991.

——, *La Question irakienne*, Paris: Fayard, 2002.

Lukitz, Liora, *Iraq: The Search for National Identity*, London: Frank Cass, 1995.

McCuen, John, *The Art of Counter-revolutionary War: The Strategy of Counter-insurgency,* London: Faber and Faber, 1966.

McDowall, David, *A Modern History of the Kurds*, London: I.B. Tauris, 2005.

McMaster, H.R., *Dereliction of Duty: Lyndon Johnson, Robert McNamara, the Joint Chiefs of Staff, and the Lies that Led to Vietnam*, New York: Harper-Collins, 1997.

Mann, Robert, *A Grand Delusion: America's Descent into Vietnam*, New York: Basic Books, 2000.

Manwaring, Max, *Shadows of Things Past and Images of the Future*: *Lessons for the Insurgencies in Our Midst*, Carlisle, PA: Strategic Studies Institute, US Army War College, 2004, <http://www.strategicstudiesinstitute.army.mil/pdffiles/PUB587.pdf>.

Mao Zedong, *Selected Military Writings of Mao Tse-tung*, Peking: Foreign Languages Press, 1967.

——, *On Guerilla Warfare*, trans. by Samuel Griffith II, Urbana: University of Illinois Press, 2000.

Marques, Patrick, 'Guerilla Warfare Tactics in Urban Environments,' Master of Military Art and Science (MMAS) thesis, US Army Command and General Staff College, Fort Leavenworth, 2003.

Marr, Phebe, *The Modern History of Iraq*, 2nd edn, Boulder, CO: Westview Press, 2004.

Mellat, Chibli, 'Iraq' in Shireen Hunter (ed.), *The Politics of Islamic Revivalism: Diversity and Unity,* Washington, DC: Center for Strategic and International Studies, 1988, pp.71–87.

Midlarsky, Manus (ed.), *The Internationalization of Communal Strife*, London: Routledge, 1993

Mockaitis, Thomas, *British Counterinsurgency, 1919–60*, New York: St Martin's Press, 1990.

Mohamedou, Mohammed-Mahmoud, 'State-building and Regime Security: A Study of Iraq's Foreign Policy Making During the Second Gulf War,' PhD diss., City University of New York, 1996.

Mufti, Malik, *Sovereign Creations: Pan-Arabism and Political Order in Syria and Iraq*, Ithaca, NY: Cornell University Press, 1996.

Nagl, John, *Learning to Eat Soup with a Knife: Counterinsurgency Lessons From Malaya and Vietnam*, Westport, CT: Praeger, 2002.

Nafziger, George, and Mark Walton, *Islam at War: A History*, Westport, CT: Praeger, 2003.

Nakash, Yitzhak, *The Shi'is of Iraq*, Princeton University Press, 2003.

Nasseri, Aqil al-, *Al-jaish wa al-sulta fi al-irak al-malikiyah, 1921–1958* (The Army and the State in Monarchical Iraq, 1921–1958), Damascus: Alhassad for Publishing and Distribution, 2000.

Newsinger, John, *British Counterinsurgency: From Palestine to Northern Ireland*, London: Palgrave, 2002.

O'Leary, Brendan, John McGarry and Khaled Salih, *The Future of Kurdistan in Iraq*, Philadelphia: University of Pennslyvania Press, 2005.

O'Neill, Bard, *Insurgency and Terrorism: Inside Modern Revolutionary Warfare*, Washington, DC: Brassey's, 1990.

Paget, Sir Julian, *Counter-insurgency Operations: Techniques of Guerilla Warfare*, New York: Walker, 1967.

Paret, Peter, *French Revolutionary Warfare from Indochina to Algeria: The Analysis of a Political and Military Doctrine*, New York: Praeger, 1964.

Peterson, Gregory, *The French Experience in Algeria, 1954–1962: Blueprint for US Operations in Iraq*, School of Advanced Military Studies, Fort Leavenworth, KS: School for Advanced Military Studies, Army Command and General Staff College, 2003.

Piscatori, James (ed.), *Islam in the Political Process*, Cambridge University Press, 1983.

Pollack, Kenneth, *Arabs at War: Military Effectiveness, 1948–1991*, Lincoln: University of Nebraska Press, 2002.

Porch, Douglas, *Wars of Empire*, London: Cassell Military, 2001.

Ramakrishna, Kumar, *Enemy Propaganda: The Winning of the Malayan Hearts and Minds 1948–1958*, Richmond, England: Curzon Press, 2002.

Record, Jeffrey, and W. Andrew Terrill, *Iraq and Vietnam: Differences, Similarities and Insights*, Carlisle Barracks, PA: Strategic Studies Institute, US Army War College, 2004.

Richard, Yann, *L'Islam chi'ite,* Paris: Fayard, 1991.

Ringmar, Erik, *Identity, Interest and Action: A Cultural Explanation of Sweden's Intervention in the Thirty Years War*, Cambridge University Press, 1996.

Rogers, James, *Tactical Success is Not Enough: The French in Algeria 1954–1962*, Newport, RI: Department of Joint Military Operations, Naval War College, 2004.

Rooney, David, *Guerilla: Insurgents, Patriots, and Terrorists from Sun Tzu to Bin Laden*, London: Brassey's, 2004.

Saghiyah, Hazem, *Ba'th al-Iraq: Sultat Saddam Qiyamahu wa hatamuhu* (Iraq's Ba'th: Saddam's Power, its Rise and Collapse), London: Dar al-Saqi, 2004.

Sankari, Jamal, *Fadlallah: The Making of a Radical Shi'ite Leader*, London: Saqi Books, 2005.

Schafer, Michael, *Deadly Paradigms: The Failure of US Counterinsurgency Policy*, Princeton University Press, 1988.

Sheehan, Neil, *A Bright Shining Lie: John Paul Vann and America in Vietnam*, New York: Random House, 1988.

Shikara, Ahmed, *Iraqi Politics 1921–41: The Interaction between Domestic Politics and Foreign policy*, London: LAAM, 1987.

Silber, Laura, and Allan Little, *Yugoslavia: Death of a Nation*, London: Penguin Books, 2002.

Simon, Reeva S., *Iraq between the Two World Wars: The Creation and Implementation of a Nationalist Ideology*, New York: Columbia University Press, 1986.

——, 'The Education of an Iraqi Ottoman Army Officer' in Rashid Khalidi et al. *The Origins of Arab Nationalism*, New York: Columbia University Press, 1991, pp. 151–61.

——, 'The Imposition of Nationalism on a Non-Nation State: The Case of Iraq During the Interwar Period, 1921–1941' in James Jankowski and Israel Gershoni (eds), *Rethinking Nationalism in the Arab Middle East*, New York: Columbia University Press, 1997, pp. 87–104.

—— and Eleanor Tejirian (eds), *The Creation of Iraq 1914–1921*, New York: Columbia University Press, 2004.

Sluglett, Peter, *Britain in Iraq, 1914–1932*, London: Ithaca Press, 1976.

Small Wars Manual: United States Marine Corps 1940, Manhattan, KS: Sunflower University Press, n.d.

Smith, Anthony, *National Identity*, London: Penguin Books, 1991.

Spector, Reeva, and Eleanor Tejirian (eds), *The Creation of Iraq 1914–1921*, New York: Columbia University Press, 2004.

Stansfield, Gareth R.V., *Iraqi Kurdistan: Political Development and Emergent Democracy*, London: RoutledgeCurzon, 2003.

Stowasser, Barbara Freyer (ed.), *The Islamic Impulse*, London: Croom Helm in association with Center for Contemporary Arab Studies, Georgetown University, 1987

Taber, Robert, *War of the Flea*, Washington, DC: Brassey's, 2002.

Tahir, Ala'a, *Irak. Aux origines du régime militaire*, Paris: L'Harmattan, 1989.

Tarbush, Mohammad, *The Role of the Military in Politics: A Case Study of Iraq to 1941*, London: Kegan Paul International, 1982.

Thompson, Robert, *Defeating Communist Insurgency: The Lessons of Malaya and Vietnam*, New York: Praeger, 1966.

——, *No Exit from Vietnam*, London: Chatto and Windus, 1969.

Trinquier, Roger, *Modern Warfare*, New York: Frederick Praeger, 1964.

Tripp, Charles, *A History of Iraq*, Cambridge University Press, 2000.

Truong Chinh, *Primer for Revolt: The Communist Takeover in Vietnam*, New York: Praeger, 1963.

UNDP and Iraqi Central Organization for Statistics and Information Technology, *Iraq Living Conditions Survey 2004*, Baghdad: United Nations Development Program and Iraqi Central Organization for Statistics and Information Technology, Ministry of Planning and Development Cooperation, 2005 (Vol. 1, *Tabulation Report*; Vol. 2, *Analytical Report*; Vol. 3, *Socio-economic Atlas*).

Valeriano, Napoleon, and Charles T.R. Bohannon, *Counter-guerilla Operations: The Philippine Experience*, New York: Frederick Praeger, 1962.

Vigeveno, G.W.F. *Irak en de erfenis van Saddam Hoessein* (Iraq in the Prison of Saddam Hussein), Research Essay, The Hague: Nederlands Instituut voor Internationale Betrekkingen, 2003, <http://www.clingendael. nl/publications/2003/20030100_cli_ess_vigeveno.pdf>.

Waldron, Arthur, and Edward O'Dowd, *Mao Tse-Tung on Guerilla Warfare*, Baltimore, MD: Nautical and Aviation Publishing Co. of America, 1992.

Warner, Denis, *Certain Victory: How Hanoi Won the War*, Kansas City: Sheed Andrews and McMeel, 1977.

Wiley, Joyce, *The Islamic Movement of Iraqi Shi'as*, Boulder, CO: Lynne Rienner, 1992.

Wilson, Arnold, *Mesopotamia 1917–1920: A Clash of Loyalties—A Personal and Historical Record*, London: Oxford University Press, 1931.versaire irakien,' Politique étrangère 1, 2 (2003).

Zaidi, Ahmed al-, *Al-bina' al-ma'anawi lil-quwat al-musallaha al-irakiyah* (The Building of Combat Cohesion in the Iraqi Armed Forces), Beirut: Dar al-Rawdha 1990.

Zucchino, David, *Thunder Run: Three Days in the Battle for Baghdad*, London: Atlantic Books, 2004.

Journal articles

Baran, David (pseud.), 'L'adversaire irakien,' *Politique étrangère* 1, 2 (2003).

Bengio, Ofra, 'Shi'is and Politics in Ba'thi Iraq,' *Middle Eastern Studies* 21, 1 (1985), 1–14.

Berlin, Isaiah, 'The Bent Twig: A Note on Nationalism,' *Foreign Affairs* 1 (1972).

Boyne, Sean, 'Iraq Tactics Attempted to Employ Guerilla Forces,' *Jane's Intelligence Review*, July (2003), 19.

Bronson, Rachel, 'Reconstructing the Middle East,' *Brown Journal of World Affairs* X, 1 (2003), 271–80.

Bunker, Robert, and John Sullivan, 'Suicide Bombings in Operation Iraqi Freedom,' *Military Review*, January-February (2005), 69–79.

Cable, Larry, 'Reinventing the Round Wheel: Insurgency, Counterinsurgency, and Peacekeeping Post Cold War,' *Small Wars and Insurgencies* 4, 2 (1993), 228–62.

Cassidy, Robert, 'Feeding Bread to the Luddites: The Radical Fundamentalist Islamic Revolution in Guerilla Warfare,' *Small Wars and Insurgencies* 16, 3 (2005), 334–59.

———, 'The British Army and Counterinsurgency: The Salience of Military Culture,' *Military Review*, May-June (2005), pp. 53–9.

———, 'Why Great Powers Fight Small Wars Badly,' *Military Review*, September-October (2000), 41–53.

Davis, Eric, 'The Uses of Historical Memory,' *Journal of Democracy* 16,1 (2005).

Cole, Juan, 'Chiites et Sunnites unis par le nationalisme,' *Le Monde Diplomatique*, May (2004), 11–12.

Dawisha, Adeed, 'Identity and Political Survival in Saddam's Iraq,' *Middle East Journal* 53, 4 (1999), 553–67.

———, 'The Prospects for Democracy in Iraq: Challenges and Opportunities,' *Third World Quarterly* 26, 4–5 (2005), 723–37.

Deady, Timothy, 'Lessons from a Successful Counterinsurgency: The Philippines, 1899–1902,' *Parameters*, Spring 2005, pp. 53–67.

Debat, Alexis, '"Foreign Fighters," Terrorism and the Iraqi Handover,' *In the National Interest* 3, 25 (2004), <http://www.inthenationalinterest. com/Articles/Vol3Issue25/Vol3Issue25Debat.html>.

Dilegge, David, and Matthew van Konynenburg, 'View from the Wolves' Den: The Chechens and Urban Operations,' *Small Wars and Insurgencies* 13, 2 (2002), 171–84.

Dodge, Toby, 'Iraqi Transitions: From Regime Change to State Collapse,' *Third World Quarterly* 26, 4–5 (2005), 705–21.

Eisenstadt, Michael, 'Assessing the Iraqi Insurgency (Part II): Devising Appropriate Measures,' *Policywatch* 979 (2005), <http://www. washingtoninstitute.org/templateC05.php?CID=2284>.

———, 'The Sunni Arab Insurgency: A Spent or Rising Force,' *Policywatch* 1028 (2005), <http://www.washingtoninstitute.org/templateC05. php?CID=2362>.

Emery, Norman, 'Information Operations in Iraq,' *Military Review*, May–June (2004), 11–14.

Eppel, Michael, 'The Elite, the *Effendiyya*, and the Growth of Nationalism and Pan-Arabism in Hashemite Iraq, 1921–1958,' *International Journal of Middle East Studies* 30 (1998), 227–50.

Fallows, James, 'Blind into Baghdad,' *Atlantic Monthly* 293, 1 (2004), 52–69.

Gates, Scott, 'Recruitment and Allegiance: The Microfoundations of Rebellion,' *Journal of Conflict Resolution* 46, 1 (2002), 111–30.

Grant, Thomas, 'The Protraction of Internal Wars,' *Small Wars and Insurgencies* 3, 3 (1992), 241–56.

Hack, Karl, 'Corpses, Prisoners of War and Captured Documents: British and Communist Narratives of the Malayan Emergency, and the Dynamics of Intelligence Transformation,' *Intelligence and National Security* 14, 4 (1999), 211–41.

Hain, Raymond, 'The Use and Abuse of Technology in Insurgent Warfare,' *Air and Space Power Chronicles*, <http://www.airpower.maxwell.af.mil/airchronicles/cc/hain.html>.

Hashim, Ahmed S., 'Insurgency in Iraq,' *Small Wars and Insurgencies* 14, 3 (2003), 1–22.

——, 'Saddam Husayn and Civil-Military Relations in Iraq: The Quest for Legitimacy and Power', *Middle East Journal* 57, 1 (2003), 28–9.

——, 'Foreign Involvement in the Iraqi Insurgency,' *Terrorism Monitor* 2, 16 (2004).

——, 'Military Power and State Formation in Modern Iraq,' *Middle East Policy* X, 4 (2004), 29–47.

——, 'Understanding the Roots of the Shi'a Insurgency in Iraq,' *Terrorism Monitor* 2, 13 (2004), 3–5, <http://www.jamestown.org/publications_details.php?volume_id=400&issue_id=3004&article_id=2368183>.

Heller, Mark, 'Politics and the Military in Iraq and Jordan, 1920–1958,' *Armed Forces and Society* 4, 1 (1977), 75–86.

Hendrickson, David, and Robert Tucker, 'Revisions in Need of Revising: What Went Wrong in the Iraq War,' *Survival* 47, 2 (2005), 7–32.

International Crisis Group, 'Voices from the Iraqi Street,' *ICG Middle East Briefing* 3 (2002), <http://www.crisisgroup.org/library/documents/report_archive/A400837_04122002.pdf>.

——, 'Baghdad: A Race against the Clock,' *ICG Middle East Briefing* 6 (2003), <http://www.crisisgroup.org/library/documents/report_archive/A401000_11062003.pdf>.

——, 'Unmaking Iraq: A Constitutional Process Gone Awry,' *ICG Middle East Briefing* 19 (2005), <http://www.crisisgroup.org/home/index.cfm?l=1&id=3703>.

'Iraqis Revolt in Northern Iraqi Town after Weapons Search,' *Iraq Report* 6, 24 (2003), <http://www.globalsecurity.org/wmd/library/news/iraq/2003/05/24-300503.htm>.

Heller, Mark, 'Politics and the Military in Iraq and Jordan, 1920–1958: The British Influence,' *Armed Forces and Society* 4, 1 (1977), 75–99.

Hills, Alice, 'Hearts and Minds or Search and Destroy? Controlling Civilians in Urban Operations,' *Small Wars and Insurgencies* 13, 1 (2002), 1–24.

Hills, Alice, 'Security Sector Reform and Some Comparative Issues in the Police-Military Interface,' *Contemporary Security Policy* 21, 3 (2000), 1–26.

Hurley, Matthew, 'Saddam Hussein and Iraqi Air Power,' *Airpower Journal*, Winter 1992, pp. 4–16.

Jabar, Faleh A., 'A Totalitarian State in the Twilight of Totalitarianism,' *Jurist* 1, 6 (2001), 14–31.

——, 'Parti, clans et tribus: le fragile équilibre du régime irakien' (Parties, Clans and Tribes: The Fragile Equilibrium of the Iraqi Regime), *Le Monde Diplomatique*, October (2002), 4–5.

——, 'The Worldly Roots of Religiosity in Post-Saddam Iraq,' *Middle East Report* 227 (2003), 12–18.

Jacobsen, Mark, 'Only by the Sword: British Counter-Insurgency in Iraq, 1920,' *Small Wars and Insurgencies* 2, 2 (1991), 323–63.

Jones, Clive, '"A Reach Greater than the Grasp": Israeli Intelligence and the Conflict in South Lebanon 1990-2000,' *Intelligence and National Security* 16, 3 (2001), 2.

Jones, Tim, 'The British Army, and Counter-Guerilla Warfare in Transition, 1944–1952,' *Small Wars and Insurgencies* 7, 3 (1996), 265–307.

Kandell, Jonathan, 'Iraq's Unruly Century,' *Smithsonian*, May (2003).

Khafaji, Isam al-, 'In Search of Legitimacy: The Post-Rentier Iraqi State,' *Social Science Research Council/Contemporary Conflicts* 2002, <http://conconflicts.ssrc.org/iraq/khafaji/pf/>.

Knights, Michael, 'US Responds to Iraq IED Threat,' *Jane's Intelligence Review*, November (2005), 12–17.

Leezenberg, Michael, 'Humanitarian Aid in Iraqi Kurdistan,' *Cahiers d'études sur la méditerranée orientale et le monde turco-iranien* 29 (2000).

McFate, Montgomery, 'Anthropology and Counterinsurgency: The Strange Story of their Curious Relationship,' *Military Review*, March-April (2005), 24–38.

——, and Andrea Jackson, 'An Organizational Solution for DoD's Cultural Knowledge Needs,' *Military Review*, July-August (2005), 18–21.

Merari, Ariel, 'Terrorism as a Strategy of Insurgency,' *Terrorism and Political Violence* 5, 4 (1993), 213–51.

Merom, Gil, 'The Social Origins of the French Capitulation in Algeria,' *Armed Forces Society* 30, 4 (2004), 601–28.

Metz, Steven, 'Insurgency and Counterinsurgency in Iraq,' *Washington Quarterly* 27, 1 (2003–4), 25–36.

——, and Raymond Millen, 'Insurgency and Counterinsurgency in the 21st Century: Reconceptualizing Threat and Response,' *Special Warfare*, February (2005), 6–21.

Mockaitis, Thomas, 'The Origins of British Counter-Insurgency,' *Small Wars and Insurgencies* 1, 3 (1990), 209–25.

Nagl, John, 'Learning to Eat Soup with a Knife,' *World Affairs* 161, 4 (1999), 193–9.

Nolan, David, 'From FOCO to Insurrection: Sandinista Strategies of Revolution,' *Air University Review*, July-August (1986), <http://www.airpower.maxwell.af.mil/airchronicles/aureview/1986/jul-aug/nolan.html>.

Olsen, John Andreas, 'Saddam's Power Base,' *Den norske Atlanterhavskomite, Det Sikkerhetspolitiske bibliotek* 4 (2003) <http://www.atlanterhavskomiteen.no/publikasjoner/sp/2003/4_utskrift.htm>.

Paz, Reuven, 'Arab Volunteers Killed in Iraq: An Analysis,' *Project for the Research of Islamist Movements (PRISM) Occasional Papers* 3, 1 (2005), <http://www.e-prism.org/images/PRISM_no_1_vol_3_-_Arabs_killed_in_Iraq.pdf>.

Popplewell, Richard, '"Lacking Intelligence": Some Reflections on Recent Approaches to British Counter-Insurgency, 1900–1960,' *Intelligence and National Security* 10, 2 (1995), 336–52.

Rahimi, Babak, 'Ayatollah Ali al-Sistani and the Democratization of Post-

Saddam Iraq,' *MERIA—Middle East Review of International Affairs* 8, 4 (2004).

Ramakrishna, Kumar, 'Content, Credibility, and Context: Propaganda Government Surrender Policy and the Malayan Communist Terrorist Mass Surrenders of 1958,' *Intelligence and National Security* 14, 4 (1999), 242–83.

Sarkesian, Sam, 'Low Intensity Conflict: Concepts, Principles, and Policy Guidelines,' *Air University Review*, January-February (1985), <http://www.airpower.maxwell.af.mil/airchronicles/aureview/1985/jan-feb/sarkesian.html>.

Sligo, Graeme, 'The British and the Making of Modern Iraq,' *Australian Army Journal* II, 2 (2005), 275–86.

Smith, Simon, 'General Templar and Counter-insurgency in Malaya: Hearts and Minds, Intelligence and Propaganda,' *Intelligence and National Security* 16, 3 (2001), 60–78.

Tomes, Robert, 'Schlock and Blah: Counter-insurgency Realities in a Rapid Dominance Era,' *Small Wars and Insurgencies* 16, 1 (2005), 37–56.

Ulph, Stephen, 'Islamist Insurgents Seek to Contain PR Disaster: Notes of Defeatism,' *Terrorism Focus* 2, 13 (2005), <http://jamestown.org/terrorism/news/article.php?articleid=2369741&printthis=1>.

Westenhoff, Charles, 'Airpower and Political Culture,' *Airpower Journal*, Winter 1997, <http://www.airpower.maxwell.af.mil/airchronicles/apj/apj97/win97/westy.html>.

Yasiri, Hussein Ali al-, and Imad al-Shara, 'National Guard Abuses Anger Public,' *Iraq Crisis Report* 92 (2004), <http://www.iwpr.net/index.pl?archive/irq/irq_92_1_eng.txt>.

US government publications

Baumann, Robert F., 'Compound War Case Study: The Soviets in Afghanistan' in Thomas M. Huber (ed.), *Compound Warfare: That Fatal Knot*, Fort Leavenworth, KS: US Army Command and General Staff College Press, 2002, <http://cgsc.leavenworth.army.mil/carl/download/csipubs/compound_warfare.pdf>.

Beckett, Ian, *Insurgency in Iraq: An Historical Perspective*, Carlisle, PA:

Strategic Studies Institute, US Army War College, 2005, <http://www.strategicstudiesinstitute.army.mil/pdffiles/PUB592.pdf>.

Department of the Army, *Counterinsurgency Operations*, Field Manual Interim 3–07.22, Washington, DC: Department of the Army, 2004.

Colonel Mark Klingelhoefer, *Captured Enemy Ammunition in Operation Iraqi Freedom and Its Strategic Importance in Post-Conflict Operations*, US Army War College Strategy Research Project, Carlisle Barracks, PA: US Army War College, 2005, <http://www.strategicstudiesinstitute.army.mil/pdffiles/ksil72.pdf>.

Linn, Brian McAllister, 'The US Army and Nation Building and Pacification in the Philippines,' Combat Studies Institute, US Army Command and General Staff College, Fort Leavenworth, KS, 2004, <http://www-cgsc.army.mil/csi/research/Conference/LinnPaper.asp>.

Special Operations Research Office, *Case Studies in Insurgency and Revolutionary Warfare: Algeria 1954–1962*, Vol. 2, Washington, DC: American University, 1963.

US Army Training and Doctrine Command, *A Military Guide to Terrorism in the Twenty-First Century*, TRADOC DCSINT Handbook 1, Version 3.0, Fort Leavenworth, KS: US Army Training and Doctrine Command, 2005

Unpublished papers in author's possession

Baran, David (pseud.), 'L'aAlexander, Christopher, Charles Kyle and William McCallister, 'The Iraqi Insurgent Movement,' 14 November 2003.

Beckett, Ian, 'Reflections on Insurgency,' n.d.

Hashim, Ahmed S., 'Security Sector Reform in Post-Saddam Iraq,' February 2005.

Hoffman, Frank, 'Principles for the Savage Wars of Peace,' June 2005.

Lawrence, Adria, 'Defining Challenges to the State: Civil Wars, Uprisings, Protests and Riots in the Context of Social Movements,' draft paper presented at the Workshop on Organizations and State-Building, University of Chicago, 20 May 2002.

Marston, Daniel, 'Force Structure for High- and Low-intensity Warfare:

The Anglo-American Experience and Lessons for the Future,' mimeograph.

Metz, Steven, 'Small Wars: From Low Intensity Conflict to Irregular Challenges,' draft, 3 June 2005.

Sepp, Kalev, 'Best Practices in Counterinsurgency,' June 2005.

Newspapers, newsmagazines and other media

Al Arabiya Television (Dubai)
Al-Hayat
Al-Jazeera Satellite Television (Doha)
Al-Majalla
Al-Sharq al-Awsat
Al Sharqiyah Television (Baghdad)
Al-Zaman (Baghdad)
Agence France Presse
Asian Times
Associated Press
Atlantic Monthly
Baltimore Sun
Boston Globe
Christian Science Monitor
Daily Star (Lebanon)
Dallas Morning News
The Economist
Harper's
Knight Ridder Newspapers
LBC (Lebanese Broadcasting Corporation) Satellite Television
Le Monde
Le Monde Diplomatique
Miami Herald
New York Times
Philadelphia Inquirer
Radio Free Europe/Radio Liberty
Der Spiegel

Sydney Morning Herald
Time
The Times (London)
USA Today
Washington Post
Zaman (Ankara)

INDEX